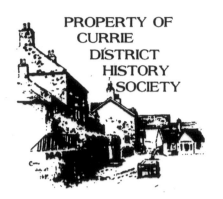

D1179066

VIRGINS AND VIRAGOS

by the same author

THE DAYS OF DUCHESS ANNE
MARY OF GUISE

VIRGINS
AND VIRAGOS

A History of Women in Scotland
from 1080 to 1980

Rosalind K. Marshall

COLLINS
8 Grafton Street, London W1
1983

William Collins Sons & Co. Ltd
London · Glasgow · Sydney · Auckland
Toronto · Johannesburg

*The publisher acknowledges the financial assistance
of the Scottish Arts Council
in the publication of this volume.*

British Library Cataloguing in Publication Data

Marshall, Rosalind K.
Virgins and viragos, a history of women in
Scotland from 1080 to 1980.
1. Women – Scotland – History
I. Title
305'.4'09411 (expanded)   HQ1599.S/

ISBN 0-00-216039-0

First published 1983
© Rosalind K. Marshall 1983

Photoset in Baskerville
Made and printed in
the United States of America

For Professor Emeritus Gordon Donaldson
H.M. Historiographer in Scotland

CONTENTS

List of Illustrations   8
Acknowledgements   9
Introduction   11

PART 1: TO 1560: THE PASSIVE WOMAN?
1 For Better or Worse   17
2 Women's Work   41

PART 2: 1560–1707: WIVES AND MOTHERS
3 Courtship and Marriage   63
4 Harmony and Discord   87
5 Motherhood   105
6 Education and Leisure   123
7 Activities   142

PART 3: 1707–1830: WOMEN IN SOCIETY
8 The Woman of the World   167
9 The Marital Bond   189
10 The Learned Lady   205
11 The Home and Beyond   223

PART 4: 1830–1980: THE ACTIVE WOMAN
12 The March of the Intellect   247
13 The Emancipation of Women   268
14 The Fruits of Freedom   293

Notes   317
Index   341

ILLUSTRATIONS

Between pages 160–161

  1 Janet Scott
 2a Mrs Esther Kello
 2b Juliana Ker, Countess of Haddington
  3 Rachel Chiesly, Lady Grange
  4 The Henwife of Castle Grant
 5a A Glasgow Shopkeeper of the 1790s
 5b A Highland Wedding
  6 Jane Welsh, Mrs Thomas Carlyle
  7 Mary Fairfax, Mrs William Somerville
  8 Flora Drummond

ACKNOWLEDGEMENTS

In writing this book I have had the benefit of most helpful advice and information from a large number of friends, colleagues and correspondents. Mr Andrew McPherson, Director of the Centre for Educational Sociology in the University of Edinburgh, brought to my notice a wealth of useful sources for the study of modern Scottish education, while Mr David Sellar of the Department of Scots Law in the University of Edinburgh gave me most valuable guidance on the subject of the matrimonial law of property in medieval and twentieth-century Scotland. Mr A. E. Anton suggested further legal sources for the medieval period, and Professor T. C. Smout of the University of St Andrews kindly permitted me to read his article on Scottish marriage in advance of its publication. Dr Emily B. Lyle drew my attention to a number of interesting lines of research and Dr Margaret H. B. Sanderson generously put at my disposal her references to the signatures of medieval women.

Dr Walter Makey, Dr Michael Lynch, Mr James Brown and Mr James Arthur allowed me to discuss with them problems of women burgesses and shared with me their own findings. Dr Helen Bennett drew my attention to female bonnet-makers and Miss Elspeth King of Glasgow Museums and Art Galleries pointed out the existence of the charming portrait of the Glasgow shopkeeper. Dr John Imrie, Dr Iain Brown, Mr Christopher Hartley, Mrs Pauline Maclean, Miss Joan Ferguson, Miss Myrtle Baird, Dr I. F. Grant, Dr Frances Shaw, Mrs Flora Isserlis, Mrs Nan Marshall, Mrs Winifred Coutts, Miss Karin Harrington and the late Miss Maureen Richardson referred me to various interesting items of information, and to them all I am most grateful.

In my pursuit of details of the activities of twentieth-century Scotswomen, I have received valuable assistance from a number of individuals and institutions, notably Mr W. Wallace Mair, Secretary of the Faculty of Actuaries, Mr Nigel Morrison, Clerk of the Faculty of Advocates, Mr J. M. Ritchie, Secretary of the Scottish Branch of the Royal Institution of Chartered Surveyors, Mr J. G. C. Barr, Deputy Secretary of the Law Society of Scotland, Mr Charles McKean, Secretary and Treasurer of the Royal Incorporation of Architects in Scotland, Mr B. McKenna, Secretary of the Institute of Bankers in Scotland, Mrs G. Thomson, Administrative Assistant of the Institute of Chartered Accountants in Scotland, Mr B. K. Pearce of the Institute of Civil Engineers, Mr Ken Symon, Press Officer of the Church of Scotland, and Dr Anne M. Shepherd of the Royal Medical Society.

[9]

Various private owners and institutions have kindly permitted me to quote from their archives, and I am grateful to the Duke of Atholl, the Duke of Hamilton and Captain the Honourable G. E. I. Maitland-Carew for allowing me to do this. References and quotations from legal records appear with the approval of the Keeper of the Records of Scotland, and from Crown-copyright material, both printed and manuscript, by kind permission of the Controller of HM Stationery Office. I would also wish to express my appreciation to those owners who have made their family archives available for research by placing them in the Scottish Record Office, and I am especially grateful to the Marquis of Lothian, the Earl of Airlie, the Earl of Dalhousie, the Earl of Leven and Melville, the Earl of Mar and Kellie and Sir John Clerk of Penicuik Bt. for allowing me to quote so extensively from their collections. My thanks also go to the Trustees of the National Library of Scotland, Edinburgh City Libraries and all those owners of portraits who have consented to their use as illustrations: their names are to be found in the captions.

Mrs Ann Munro produced an excellent typescript of the complete book, with great care and enthusiasm, ably assisted in its checking by Mrs Betty Lowson. I would also thank Miss Rona Shiach and Dr May G. Williamson for their meticulous proof-reading, and Miss Shona Angus for her invaluable help with the making of the index. The finished text is far from being the last word on the history of Scottish women, but if it encourages further investigation of a fascinating subject, then it will have fulfilled one of its principal purposes.

EDINBURGH
September 1981

INTRODUCTION

'Scottish women of any historical interest are curiously rare', said the celebrated twentieth-century poet Hugh MacDiarmid, and at first sight this observation might seem perfectly correct.[1] We can call to mind readily enough a few women like Mary, Queen of Scots, and Flora MacDonald, whose romantic exploits have assured them a place in folk tradition as well as in the pages of history books. Yet they would appear to form an exceptional minority endowed with unusual spirit at a time when their female contemporaries apparently existed in uneventful obscurity.

This impression is reinforced by the belief that women in past centuries lived out their lives in humble subservience to men. Most of us are familiar with the stereotype of the Victorian wife as a poor, downtrodden creature who addressed her husband respectfully by his formal title and surname, endured his physical attentions with fortitude rather than pleasure, bore his numerous children to the ruination of her own health and meekly submerged her personality in his. If that was how women lived a hundred years ago, it seems all too probable that in previous centuries the situation must have been even worse. After all, we know that until recent times a girl's husband was chosen for her, and the legal textbooks make it clear that a woman's position at law corresponded with that of a minor: she was the responsibility of her father until she married, whereupon she became the responsibility of her husband.

Even so, anyone reading historical documents will soon encounter tantalising references to women possessed of undeniably forceful personalities, determinedly pursuing their own ambitions and vigorously playing a part in the world beyond the home. This being so, were the well-known Scottish heroines so exceptional? Did their mothers and sisters and friends really live in such subordination to the opposite sex, or has our view of the past been distorted by our lack of knowledge?

Any attempt to examine the activities of women in Scotland at a given period is strictly limited by the amount of written evidence available and, naturally enough, the further back in time the researcher goes, the fewer are the documents which have survived. There is nothing in Scotland to compare with, say, the famous Paston letters of medieval England. Very few Scottish letters from before 1550 are extant, and the number written by Scotswomen before 1650 is disappointingly small. Women do feature in medieval chronicles, but these narratives often have a strong fanciful element, and, although women's names and doings are to be found in the more mundane burgh records, land transactions and ecclesiastical papers, there is no means by which we can find direct evidence of their thoughts and emotions at this early period. Even in the seventeenth century, information is largely confined to the upper sections of society, and if the present book appears at times to be preoccupied with the lives of the aristocracy, this is from necessity, not choice.

In the later period, the problems of the historian are of a different kind. There is an abundance of material, both printed and in manuscript, for the last hundred and fifty years. Government records, business archives, census reports, newspapers, the minute books of societies and organizations all add to the new range of evidence available, and in the last decade researchers into these sources have begun to turn their attention to the history of women. Many interesting and valuable studies of women's education, economic position and political activities are now in progress, but a vast amount of research remains to be done before a comprehensive picture can emerge. Paradoxically, it is much more difficult to examine family letters for the modern period: while the owner of private archives may be happy for the scholar to read through the intimate correspondence of his long-dead ancestors, he will naturally have reservations about bringing before the public gaze the personal confidences of his more immediate relatives. In consequence, many archive collections dwindle away in the mid-nineteenth century, the more recent documents remaining with the present owner's private papers.

Given these limitations, there is nevertheless a wealth of scattered information available about the lives of past women, and by searching out what they themselves have written and what other people have said about them, we can discover a fascinating new dimension to the history of Scotland. How were women treated by fathers and husbands, by society and the law? What did they feel about their own role? What were their ambitions, frustrations and satisfactions? Were they so different from their modern counterparts? This book is not a catalogue of the deeds of outstanding women, but, rather, an attempt to examine what it has meant to be a woman in Scotland in past centuries.

PART ONE

To 1560:
THE
PASSIVE WOMAN?

CHAPTER ONE

For Better or Worse

'THE NAME OF HIS WIFE remains unknown', 'His bride's name is lost to history', 'He married about 1290, but no details have come down to us'. Sentences such as these occur time and time again in the earlier chapters of family history books, underlining for the modern reader the difficulties of studying the role of women in the medieval period. Chronicles concern themselves with the deeds of kings and men of war, charters record essentially masculine land transactions, and no personal correspondence survives to bring to life those women whose names occur fleetingly in lists of tenants, court records and the like. Indeed, not until the time of Gruoch, wife of Macbeth, in the mid-eleventh century do we know the name even of a Scottish queen. For this reason alone, we tend to think that medieval Scotswomen played a largely passive part, an impression which is enhanced by the undeniably restrictive legal provisions of the time. Yet here and there a sudden phrase, a passing reference, a brief aside can suggest with vividness that women were far from being merely the submissive servants of fathers, husbands and sons. Their circumstances were very different from those of their twentieth-century descendants, but their emotions were as strong and their personalities as developed as ours are today.

To begin at the beginning, the female child born in medieval Scotland came into the world with the help of an older woman: a relative, a neighbour or an experienced person who was to all intents and purposes a professional midwife. In an age long before antiseptics and anaesthesia were known, childbirth was an extremely dangerous business and all too often mother or baby perished. Many of those infants who were born alive would die in the first weeks or the first years of life, for the rate of child mortality was distressingly high. These tragedies apart, the new baby was

[17]

rubbed down with salt, wrapped in swaddling bands and placed in a wooden cradle made for her by her father or by a local craftsman, depending upon the resources of her family. Breast-fed by mother or wet-nurse, she was in due course unwrapped from her cocoon of swaddling, weaned and put down to walk. It was then not long before she was toddling around in the wake of her mother, learning to fetch and carry, helping with the chores of the house and attending to the needs of the younger brothers and sisters who swiftly followed, often at yearly intervals.

A daughter's role in the family was clearly understood. Feudal society was carefully structured, but regardless of the stratum to which a girl belonged, she knew from her earliest years that her destiny in life was marriage and childbearing. Some women rebelled against this expectation, some delighted in it, but many simply accepted it without question. In a dangerous world where life was frequently disrupted by warfare, plague and famine, the husband was still quite literally the protector and provider while his wife managed his house and brought up his family. It followed that a daughter should be taught to sew, spin, cook, clean, nurse the sick and rear children. For many centuries, female education was to be strictly vocational and in the Middle Ages there was no question of a woman being given what we would term an academic education: learning for learning's sake would have been an unnecessary distraction and one for which there would scarcely have been time.

Childhood passed quickly. There was no transitional period of adolescence before adult life was reached, for a female was legally permitted to marry at the age of twelve and quite a few did so. Certainly by the time a girl approached her middle teens, her parents were discussing her future in serious manner, as the choice of her husband lay with them. This situation was in no way peculiar to medieval Scotland, for it is the norm in any pre-industrial society. When daughters live at home and are not economically self-supporting it is customary to find that the selection of their marriage partners lies with their father.[1] Often enough parental choice can coincide with a girl's own preference, but there were certain groups of women who had absolutely no say in the ordering of their own future. Where there were overriding political or territorial considerations, a father would treat his daughter with what modern generations would regard as callous indifference. Royal princesses are the extreme example of this phenomenon. They were used as pawns in the diplomatic game, and in this Scottish kings were no different from other medieval European monarchs.

To take but one example, James I of Scotland decided in 1428 to marry his eldest daughter to the heir to the French throne, in furtherance of his policy of strengthening his country's traditional alliance with France. Princess Margaret was only eleven when the negotiations were completed, but she was informed that she must leave for her new home as soon as the necessary arrangements could be made. James was not without affection for his children. When he accompanied her to the port of Dumbarton to bid her farewell they exchanged tearful embraces, and indeed the King was so overcome with emotion that he cut short the leave-taking ceremony and retired abruptly from the scene. Sentiment could not, however, be allowed to interfere with affairs of state. The Princess duly set sail with a fleet of Scottish ships and a retinue of a hundred and forty young people as her personal attendants. She made a stately progress through the north of France to Tours, and there she was married to the thirteen-year-old Dauphin. A fortnight later, almost all her Scots were sent home and as the weeks went by the Princess found her unprepossessing husband to be not only neglectful but openly hostile. Medieval male heirs were as much the victims of enforced marriages as females were, and he did not take to his Scottish bride. The Princess sought solace in reading literature and writing poetry, thereby arousing her husband's jealous suspicion. She was to spend nine unrewarding years in France before her early death at the age of twenty.[2]

Undeterred by this unhappy experience, James I proceeded to make similarly ambitious marriages for his other daughters. Isabella became Duchess of Brittany, Eleanor married the Duke of Austria, Mary became the wife of Wolfort, Lord of Campvere, and Annabella's first husband was Louis, Count of Geneva. Only Joan, who was deaf and dumb, was omitted from these carefully-arranged unions: she was married off to a Scottish earl. Significantly, it was those kings who were independent, powerful and anxious to make their mark on the international scene who were particularly active in marrying their daughters to influential foreigners. William the Lion, by way of contrast, had been compelled to accept the husbands chosen for his daughters by King John of England, and indeed his own marriage had been dictated by his powerful neighbour. Again, the Stewart kings before James I had not enjoyed his measure of prestige and had been content to bestow their daughters upon members of the Scottish nobility.[3]

Even more vulnerable than princesses were orphaned heiresses. By feudal law a superior had to give his consent before the daughter of one of his tenants-in-chief could marry, and if a father died the superior could dispose of the girl much as he wished. He was not supposed to marry her to a man of lesser rank than she, for by so doing he would reduce her status, but if he did not want her for one of his own relatives, he could actually sell her hand in marriage to the highest bidder. The result was that a girl could be given in marriage to an unscrupulous stranger interested only in her fortune.

Worse than that, some heiresses were actually seized and carried off by men anxious to gain control of their wealth. This was what happened in 1404 to Isabella, Countess of Mar in her own right. Her first husband's death had left her unprotected. Seizing his opportunity, Sir Alexander Stewart, grandson of Robert II, captured both the Countess and her castle of Kildrummy. In August of that year Isabella handed over to him her titles and her lands. The charter by which she did so was presumably made under duress and remained invalid because the King did not confirm it. However, a month later she again made over to Sir Alexander her earldom and her estates, and in December she married him.

Almost as unpleasant must have been the position of those young women whose marriages were arranged in an attempt to pacify feuds. This was a common practice in fourteenth and fifteenth-century Scotland. In 1393 Mor, the daughter of Colin Campbell in Argyll, was married to Hector MacLean 'in order to establish peace and harmony among their family and friends, whereas until now there have only been wars, dissensions, murders and other grave scandals'. Elizabeth Douglas in Orkney became the wife of William St Clair 'for consolidating peace among their parents and friends', and after Sir Robert Erskine wounded and imprisoned two of Christian Menteith's cousins, she married him in an attempt to heal the resulting feud. How these women fared at the hands of their in-laws goes unrecorded, but foregoing events hardly made a promising basis for marital harmony.[4]

Of course not all weddings took place in such spectacular circumstances, but it remains true that the landed families as well as royalty usually had powerful reasons for using their daughters to

[20]

secure or further their own position. Constantly striving with each other, engaging in long-term feuds and relying for support upon those tied to them by the bonds of kinship, they saw marriage as a valuable means of strengthening existing links and cementing new friendships. This was particularly so in a country like Scotland, where a woman retained her maiden name throughout her life and never did sever her connections with her own family. In spite of marriage, she continued to be identified with her own kin and so could provide a valuable connection between the two groups.[5]

The eagerness of an ambitious father to form a political alliance or enlarge his territorial possessions could have bizarre results. Child marriages, for example, were not uncommon. Because of the danger that death might frustrate their plans, parents were willing to arrange marriages for children only a few years old. As the years went by, more and more people disapproved of this practice but even as late as 1550 William, 5th Lord Crichton, was exerting himself to obtain Alan, Lord Cathcart, and Andrew, son of the Master of Semple, as husbands for his daughters. Alan he planned to marry to Elizabeth as soon as she was fourteen, while Margaret would become young Semple's bride when she was twelve.[6]

Equally strange to our eyes was the habit of offering substitutes should death carry off the prospective bride or groom. This practice is well illustrated in the agreement made between King William the Lion of Scotland and King John of England in 1209. Sealing the Treaty of Norham in the hope of bringing peace to their respective countries, William agreed that on 16 August he would deliver to the English at Carlisle not only hostages for the keeping of the peace but his two eldest daughters, Margaret and Isabella. Margaret was to marry King John's heir, Prince Henry, then aged two, while Isabella would become the bride of either Prince Richard, at that time an infant of seven months, or of a leading English nobleman. It was further stipulated that, if either prince should die before his wedding could take place, the survivor would marry Margaret. Similarly, if either princess died prematurely the other would marry Prince Henry. The young princesses accordingly went south with their retinues and spent the next few years travelling from one royal residence to the next in the household of the Queen of England. The accounts of the time provide brief glimpses of their lives; they were fitted with dark green robes trimmed with rabbits' fur in Nottingham one winter, then in Winchester were provided with deerskin hoods and fur mantles. The marriages envisaged by the treaty never did take place, however, and it was not until both King William and King John were dead that they became the wives of mere English noblemen, much to the resentment of the Scots.[7]

The type of double arrangement incorporated in the Treaty of Norham was not the prerogative of the royal family. Other parents too were anxious to ensure that their carefully arranged alliances took place, come what might. In 1420, Dame Mary Murray handed over her daughter Alison to Sir William Hay on the understanding that she would become the wife of his heir, David. Should David die, Alison was to be given to one of the younger sons. Even as late as 1584 Lord Ruthven was so anxious for a connection with Alexander, 6th Lord Home, that he gave him the choice of his daughters Beatrix and Lilias, an offer Lord Home ungallantly refused.[8]

Ambitious as landed fathers might be, even they were limited in their choice by certain ecclesiastical rules. Canon Law followed the prohibitions laid down in the Book of Leviticus and, from the time of the Fourth Lateran Council in 1215, said that no-one might marry a person within the fourth degree of consanguinity. Consanguinity is the relationship created by descent from a common parentage, so a daughter was related to her father in the first degree. Cousins shared a grandfather and were therefore related in the second degree, son to father being one degree and father to grandfather the second. To say that persons within the fourth degree might not marry meant that the great great grandchildren of a common ancestor were forbidden to do so. Complicated this might seem, but there were further prohibitions, since each degree of consanguinity had its corresponding degree of affinity. A widow could not marry anyone related to her former husband, up to the fourth degree of consanguinity. The thinking behind this was that by physical union a man and woman became one flesh, so the woman was related to each member of the man's family as though they were her own blood relatives. Moreover, affinity resulted from illicit intercourse as well as from marriage, so if a woman had been a man's mistress she was not allowed to marry his brother, cousin, second cousin or third cousin.

On a rather more elevated note, the prospective bride had to remember about spiritual consanguinity. A godmother could not marry her godchild, nor could her daughter do so. The godmother was also prevented from marrying her godchild's father. Similar impediments affected anyone who had acted as sponsor at a child's confirmation, and there was spiritual affinity as well as spiritual consanguinity . This maze of relationships made it very difficult in a small country to avoid marrying someone within the forbidden degrees. When the Earl of Fife's son Murdach planned to marry the Earl of Lennox's daughter Isabella, it was discovered that Isabella was in the fourth degree of consanguinity to Murdach's first wife, and that, before her own birth, Isabella's father had been Murdach's godfather. Fortunately, the complications could be sorted out easily enough. For the payment of a sum of money to the Holy See, a papal dispensation could be obtained permitting the wedding to take place or regularizing it if it had already done so. On other occasions, when partners wished their marriage to be annulled, it was simple enough to claim that some fairly tenuous but illegal relationship existed but that the couple had not realized that they were not technically free to marry.[9]

Consanguinity and affinity apart, the choice of a groom was also restricted by the financial resources of the bride's parents. By English standards, Scotland was not a wealthy country and very few Scottish peers formed matrimonial alliances outside Scotland. In part this may have been due to lack of opportunity, reluctance to send a daughter to a distant part and so forth, but it was also because Scottish fathers could not afford to give the dowries expected by wealthier noblemen elsewhere. The consequence was that, in a sample of 150 daughters of Scottish peers who married before 1600, only four became the wives of foreigners and the surprisingly low figure of a further three married Englishmen. The others were given to husbands from the Scottish peerage and landed Scottish families.[10]

In practice, this meant that most Scottish girls married men from approximately the same social class and from the same locality as themselves. Their husbands were rarely complete strangers. More often than not the young couple would have known each other from childhood, particularly if the families involved were already allies. Familiarity is no guarantee of liking, of course, but at least it did away with the fear experienced by a bride sent to people she had never before met.

Moreover, there were those girls who had the spirit and determination to stand out against a match which was not to their taste. A notarial instrument records that in 1494 Margaret, the daughter of William, Lord Ruthven, absolutely refused to marry

John Oliphant, the bridegroom chosen for her by her parents. This put Lord and Lady Ruthven in an embarrassing position, for the Oliphants pointed out that a firm agreement had been made and that bride and groom were now old enough to fulfil their obligations. The exasperated couple therefore took Margaret along to the notary public and, in front of him, 'earnestly required and implored Margaret Ruthven their daughter to contract and complete marriage in face of the Church with John Oliphant'. Margaret refused yet again. Lord Ruthven formally asked her the reason for her behaviour whereupon she replied 'and said because she had no carnal affection nor favour for him', and, moreover, had told them so a year before. The notary carefully recorded their words, and Lord and Lady Ruthven held themselves to be absolved of any blame in the unhappy affair. It was obviously John himself who aroused Margaret's antipathy rather than the institution of matrimony, for she later married four times.

Janet Stewart, who came from an ordinary enough background, also had the courage to resist parental pressure, although she found it difficult. 'Compelled by force and fear of death . . . and coerced by her parents', she 'unwillingly, mournfully, objecting and with grief' was contracted to marry Robert Lindsay. The wedding ceremony actually took place, but Janet ignored the pleas and threats of husband and family alike and refused to consummate the marriage, which was eventually annulled. Possibly she and Margaret were already in love with someone else. One girl who would not give up the man of her choice was Christian Penicuik. Her suitor Edmund Rutherford asked her hand in marriage over and over again, but each time her father refused. Christian therefore arranged a time and place so that Edmund could come and take her away. This he did, and they were married at once, whereupon her irate parents tried to accuse Edmund of having abducted and raped her.[11]

The fact that Janet's parents, who were not particularly wealthy, were so determined demonstrates that all but the poorest families had a vested interest in a daughter's marriage. If property was involved at all, they wished and indeed had to be party to the marriage settlement and this was so even if the property consisted not of vast estates but of a small shop or a modest piece of land. Personal prejudices, long-standing feuds or friendships and considerations of status were in the minds of almost all parents when the future of their daughters was being discussed. Again, parental

[24]

authority was very important and was upheld by the Church, so the extent to which a girl's wishes were considered depended very much upon the individuals concerned: the tolerance and affection of a father for his daughter, the amount of influence exerted over both of them by the mother and the determination or submissiveness of the daughter herself all played their part.

This is not to say that love and passion did not exist in medieval Scotland: quite the contrary. Apart from anything else, the number of men and women who had illicit relationships, not to mention illegitimate children, before marriage demonstrates that mutual attraction between the sexes was just as strong six hundred years ago as it is today. Even if romantic love was not regarded as being a necessary ingredient of marriage, its power was still recognized. It formed, for example, a perfectly acceptable facet of the story of the famous Scottish patriot William Wallace as it was told in a long poem some hundred and fifty years after his death. Wallace is known to history as the determined leader who struggled against Edward I of England during the Wars of Independence. The poem is therefore primarily concerned with his martial exploits, but it also tells of how he fell in love with an eighteen-year-old girl when he saw her in church in Lanark. She was living under the protection of the English, but apart from the danger that this meant for Wallace she was suitable in every way. Her reputation was impeccable and she had a comfortable inheritance. According to the poet, Wallace hesitated to propose marriage to her for fear that love would distract him from his avowed intent of driving out the English. Since she valued chastity she refused to become his mistress and so he resolved to forget her. That did not prove easy, however. To his chagrin he discovered that 'great desire remained into his mind', and try as he might he could not stop thinking about her. Impelled to go back and see her, he promised to marry her once the wars were over. Her eventual death at the hands of the enemy gave his struggle against the English a greater urgency. Whether or not one accepts the poet's version as being grounded in fact, his assumption that his readers would sympathize with Wallace's dilemma illuminates something of medieval attitudes. Love as a potent force was quite familiar to them.[12]

Wallace's romantic adventures – the Lanark maiden was not his first female friend – in no way detracted from his reputation, but the maiden's chastity was entirely proper and enhanced hers.

The double standard which permits men sexual licence while demanding chastity from women is commonly found when arranged marriages are the norm. Men entering into loveless partnerships were able to reassure themselves with the thought that they could find consolation elsewhere, but not so women. Aristocratic ladies of the sixteenth century might enjoy the dalliance of courtly love, flirting with gallant young men, but adultery should not be countenanced. Unwilling brides were more likely to be persuaded into matrimony by the thought that a single woman's position was an unenviable one. In a Roman Catholic country like Scotland chastity was a valued ideal and there was no particular prejudice against spinsters, but legally their position was weak and economically most of them relied upon the support of male members of their family. Even if she were married to a less than sympathetic husband, a woman could at least run her own household and find comfort in her children. Some women did prefer to remain single, but few did so by choice and others were ready enough to accept a husband who did not accord with the highest romantic standards.[13]

The only women who were completely free to marry whom they pleased were widows, and even they had to seek the consent of the king if they were heiresses. A widow's father had no say in her choice of a second husband. Some were obviously eager to take advantage of this freedom. Marjorie, Countess of Carrick in her own right, was married at a very early age to Adam de Kilconquhar. He set off for the Crusades not long afterwards and died on his journey. One day, when Marjorie was out riding, she encountered Robert Bruce, a strikingly handsome young man. Some versions of the story say that he was bringing her news of her husband's death, others report that he was simply out hunting on her estates, but whatever the circumstances Marjorie was instantly attracted to him. Somewhat impetuous by nature, she had her retainers seize him and carry him off to her castle, where she kept him until he agreed to marry her. The king was furious when he heard, for she had not sought his consent. He seized her estates as punishment but she made amends by paying a heavy fine and Robert was reconciled to his fate when he was made Earl of Carrick. Their five sons and five daughters were to include Robert Bruce, later King of Scots.[14]

Most widows found husbands without having to go to such lengths, for they brought with them wealth and possessions from their previous marriage. It was not uncommon to find women remarrying three and four times. Agnes Stewart, the illegitimate daughter of James, Earl of Buchan, had an exciting matrimonial career. Before she was married at all she became the mistress of King James IV and bore him a daughter. She was then married off respectably to Adam, 2nd Earl of Bothwell. Two years later he perished at the Battle of Flodden and within twelve months she was the bride of Alexander, 3rd Lord Home. Their union was of equally short duration for in 1516 he was executed for treason. A brief interval elapsed and then she became the wife of Robert, 4th Lord Maxwell. They were together for more than twenty years but when he died it was not long before she took her fourth and final husband, Cuthbert Ramsay.[15]

Whatever the background of family argument, disappointment and even despair, once a marriage had been agreed in principle, the procedure was clear enough. Before the Reformation, marriage was a sacrament as well as a civil contract, and the Church concerned itself in matters of marriage settlements, divorce and the like. In the early twelfth century Pope Paschal II had found it necessary to remind the Scottish clergy and laity that they must observe the Christian laws of marriage, and by the end of the century bishops' courts had been established. All matrimonial causes came within their jurisdiction.[16] It is not, therefore, surprising to find that when a couple became formally engaged their 'spousals' or 'handfasting' often took the form of a religious ceremony. A legal document of 1532 records how, on 13 February at eight o'clock in the evening, David Boswell and Lady Janet Hamilton went with their friends to the lodgings of one of Lady Janet's relatives in the small burgh of Linlithgow. Henry Louk, a local curate, asked David if he would marry Lady Janet and he agreed. She gave her consent, whereupon the curate joined the hands of the young couple and betrothed them. They then 'took the oath, as is the custom of the church'. The witnesses included not only Lady Janet's influential relatives but a local sheriff clerk, and the whole proceedings were given more weight by being recorded by a notary. A record of another handfasting gives us the actual words used. On 24 July 1556, the vicar of Aberdour officiated at the spousals of Robert Lauder, younger, of the Bass and the Earl of Bothwell's daughter, Lady Jane Hepburn. The future bridegroom said, 'I, Robert Lauder, take thou Jane Hepburn to my spoused wife, as the law of the Holy Kirk shows, and thereto I plight thou my troth.' Jane made a similar promise, and so the couple were engaged.[17]

Not all spousals were as formal as this, but even if they simply took the form of a verbal promise, they were much more binding than a modern engagement. In 1555, one young woman had to go to a notary and get him to draw up a document describing how she had been 'handfast' to a certain man, but now, of her own free will, wished to release him. She therefore renounced the 'bond of handfasting' and set him at liberty to marry whom he pleased.[18] The reason why the spousals were so important was that, if a couple followed up the betrothal by having intercourse, they were then legally married. The marriage was imperfect and incomplete, because it lacked the wedding service, but the man and woman were henceforth as permanently husband and wife as if they had gone on and been married at the church. This form of irregular marriage was technically described as being *per verba de futuro*. It was often misunderstood by later historians in the nineteenth century, who believed that a handfasting was a trial marriage which could be dissolved at will, but this was not so.[19]

Whether or not the spousals were to be completed by a marriage service, the two families would soon be involved in lengthy discussions about the marriage settlement. It is not possible to find precise details of the law of matrimonial property in the Middle Ages, but various sources do provide information. There is *Regiam Majestatem*, the most influential treatise in medieval Scots law. Much argument has taken place as to the date of its compilation, but it seems to have been drawn up at least as early as the beginning of the fourteenth century. Much of it is concerned with general laws of property, and with criminal causes, but there are sections on financial matters and on the restrictions which affected a married woman. Again, sixteenth-century treatises like *The Practicks of Sir James Balfour of Pittendreich* obviously record many regulations which had been in force since the middle ages and, finally, there are the marriage contracts themselves. Once the two families had agreed the terms of the settlement, these were often written down and thus the marriage contract came into being. It has often been imagined that only the great families had marriage contracts drawn up, but this was not so. Contracts of burgesses, tradesmen and even servants survive, following much the same scheme as those of earls, knights and lairds.

Most contracts began with the promise to marry before a given date, which was usually that of a church festival a few weeks ahead. Some simply said 'as soon as is convenient' and in quite a few the date was left blank, but it was usually envisaged that a fairly short interval would elapse between the betrothal and the wedding.

The promise itself made, the contract then passed on to financial matters. Its most basic provision was a statement of the dowry which the bride would bring with her. In Scotland this was called the tocher. It might be a very large sum indeed like the 60,000 crowns which Mary of Gueldres brought when she married King James II of Scotland, or it might be the mere £20 Scots given by John Fullarton, a burgess of Ayr, when his daughter Mariota married John Pettigrew in 1521. No comprehensive study of sixteenth-century marriage contracts has yet been made but it would seem that tochers were steadily rising. The daughter of an earl would have a tocher of around 5000 merks Scots at the beginning of the century, but nearer 10,000 merks by the end, while the figure for a lord's daughter rose from around 2000 merks to 8000 or 9000 and a burgess's from £20 to 150 merks.[20]

There is also evidence that in the earlier period tochers were paid not only in money but in goods or even in services. In the early fourteenth century Angus Og, Lord of the Isles, married Agnes, the daughter of Guy O'Cathan of Ulster, and is said to have received with her a tocher of 140 men of every surname in O'Cathan's territory. Even by the mid-sixteenth century lesser men did not always have enough ready money to be able to give cash. Marion Marshall married William Dewar in 1554 and took with her in tocher £20 Scots, a bed, several cupboards, a pot worth 20/- Scots, a spinning wheel, a piece of wool, some oatmeal and malt and all the clothes she needed.[21]

If the bride died childless within a year and a day of the marriage, the tocher reverted immediately to her family, but if she had borne children, her husband had the right to retain the tocher for the rest of his life. This was so even if only one child had been born and had survived for no more than a few hours. As long as the husband could produce two neighbours who could testify that they had heard the baby cry, then he was allowed to retain the tocher.

In return for what he received with his bride, the husband had to make provision for her future. This he did originally by making her a gift of lands or goods at the church door on their wedding day. In England the gift was known as the dower and in Scotland it was called the terce. If the husband failed to make any such gift, then a third of his heritage was understood to belong to his wife, hence the term 'terce'. Various rules affected the terce. The husband was not permitted to give more than a third of his lands in terce, though he could give less if he so desired. He could not give as terce any lands he had received as tocher with a previous wife, nor could he include the principal dwelling place in the terce. For her part, once the bride had accepted the offer she could ask for no more, regardless of how wealthy her husband might become in later years. Should the husband have no lands to make the endowment, he could give his bride goods instead. The idea was not so much that the terce would sustain her throughout her years of widowhood should her husband die first, but, as one sixteenth-century authority put it, so that 'if it happen her husband to decease before her, she may the more easily be married with another man.'[22]

At this comparatively early stage, not all contracts took a set form, but the variations are often illuminating in themselves. Some settlements were no more than a mutual promise that if one partner died the other would inherit all the property. Other contracts stipulated the tocher and nothing else. Sometimes the terce was provided not by the groom's family, as it should have been, but by the bride's own relatives. Gavin Hamilton, Commendator of Kilwinning, seems to have been so pleased to marry off his aunt Elizabeth Hamilton that he both provided the tocher of 400 merks Scots and gave the couple lands to support them. Even so, he did not seem particularly optimistic about the outcome, for he made the bridegroom promise that if he repudiated Elizabeth he would hand back the tocher within forty days and would allow her to occupy the lands unmolested.[23]

This was an unusual provision and suggests that it may have been a case of a younger man marrying an older woman for her money. On such occasions the parents were willing to give more towards the marriage than would normally have been expected. To take one instance, which occurred a few years after the Reformation, Isabel Tennant married John Winning, a young merchant, in 1566. Her mother not only gave with her a tocher of 140 merks Scots but provided her with a house, a shop in Edinburgh and a share of a small-holding left by her late father. In return, John merely promised that when he returned from a voyage to Danzig he would add 60 merks to the tocher to buy a piece of land where he and Isabel could live.[24]

The place of residence was a point quite frequently covered in the contract, for it was customary for a young couple to begin their life together in the home of one set of parents. This was a sensible enough arrangement since it allowed them time to gather together some possessions of their own before they set up house. Indeed, it was often the only accommodation available for them. It might not always work out harmoniously, of course, and some people took precautions against future difficulties. When Mary Borthwick from Greenlaw married and moved in with her mother-in-law it was stated that, if the two women could not agree together, the old lady would provide some alternative accommodation for the couple elsewhere.[25]

Occasionally, arrangements safeguarding the children of any previous marriage were also incorporated, for if the surviving parent died, the lot of a stepchild might not be an enviable one. James Fawcup in Kincavil was therefore required to promise that he would pay his stepdaughter a tocher of 47 merks when she married, and Alexander Auld in Linlithgow gave an undertaking that if his wife died before him he would not set his stepchildren to work on their small piece of land while they were still under age.[26]

All in all, however, it seems that it was the medieval bridegroom who gained financially from the marriage settlement. To revert to the example of the royal family, the tocher of Mary of Gueldres might be 60,000 crowns, but James II provided her with lands to the value of only 10,000 crowns. Similarly the brides of James III and James IV received mere fractions of the sums they brought with them.[27] The evidence is often defective and the value of lands unless stated is impossible to calculate, but it would seem that this balance was true of the rest of society. The tocher was, after all, the great inducement to a man to marry a particular woman, and in return the bride was not looking for immediate financial gain but rather for future security and enhanced status.

Once the settlement had been agreed orally or a contract had been signed, preparations for the actual marriage ceremony could go ahead. A necessary preliminary was the calling of banns. This was not simply a formality. Objections could be and sometimes were raised. Seeing one of her male friends about to slip through her fingers, a widow named Janet Muir leaped to her feet and publicly declared that the bridegroom had contracted spousals with her and that they were married 'by *verba de futuro*'. She later admitted that there was no truth in the allegation, which she had made up out of malice, but there must have been other occasions when an incomplete marriage did indeed lie in the past of one of the couple about to marry.[28]

In more usual circumstances, the preliminaries passed off without incident. On the wedding day, the bride and groom with their relatives and guests met at the door of the parish church and there the ceremony took place. It began with the future husband and wife swearing on the Gospels that there was no let or hindrance to the marriage and that neither of them had previously entered into a contract with a different partner. The father of the bride gave her away or, if he was dead, a friend would do it. The priest placed the bride's right hand in the right hand of the groom. If she was a widow, she would wear gloves, but if she was single her hands would be bare. The groom then said, 'I take thee to my wedded wife' and the bride replied 'I take thee to my wedded husband.' Both followed these words with, 'In the name of the Father and the Son and the Holy Spirit.' After that they kissed each other. There was a pause, then the priest would enquire what terce was being provided for the bride. This satisfactorily answered, the priest said a prayer and gave the benediction. Only after that did the company pass into the church for nuptial mass.

It is important to notice that the plighting of the troth was what actually constituted the marriage ceremony. It might be done in public or in private, with or without mass, and the presence of the priest was not strictly necessary. Obviously the Church was anxious that weddings should be held in the priest's presence at the parish church and marriage was certainly a sacrament, but strictly speaking the husband and wife were themselves ministers of that sacrament. Again, it should be noted that the vital factor was the consent of bride and groom, not the consent of the parents or the family or of anyone else. No doubt few brides would have been willing to turn back at that point, but the possibility was always there.[29]

The celebrations which followed would last for several days. It is difficult to find any descriptions from the pre-Reformation period, although the festivities described by seventeenth and eighteenth-century observers obviously had their roots in the distant past.[30] A royal wedding, of course, was an occasion for rejoicings on a grand scale and from as early as 1280 there survives a Latin song composed to mark the marriage of King Eric of Norway and Princess Margaret of Scotland. Certainly the wedding itself took place in Bergen but the song's author seems to have been a Scottish friar and it is reasonable to suppose that it was the sort of tribute usually composed upon such occasions. It is interesting to note that, as well as praising the Princess and giving thanks for her safe arrival, the song hopes:

'Like Rachel, may she ever keep her husband's love,
Like Esther, with the King most high in favour prove,
Like Leah, may she be with numerous offspring blest,
And like Susanna, steadfast aye in virtue rest.'[31]

The records kept in the Royal Exchequer show something of the preparations made when David, heir to King Robert I of Scotland, married the English Princess Joanna at Berwick on Sunday, 17 July 1328. New garments trimmed with squirrel and miniver were provided for knights, squires and others. Over three hundred ells of napery were purchased, and twice as much towelling. As for food, the royal kitchens required 4360 pounds of almonds, 600 pounds of rice, 40 loaves of sugar, 180 pounds of pepper, 55 pounds of mace, 74 pounds of cinnamon and various other spices including 5 pounds of the exotically named 'grain of paradise'. Large quantities of sweets were bought, a pipe of honey, 2 pipes of olive oil, 7 barrels of eels, and, of course, wine – 20 casks of it. So many people crowded round to see the celebrations that the wall of Holy Trinity churchyard was broken down, and later had to be repaired at a cost of thirteen shillings and fourpence.[32] The bride on that occasion was seven years old, the bridegroom four.

Once the celebrations were over, the bride was installed in her new home, which was often in the household of her parents-in-law. In effect, she had passed from being the daughter of one man to being the wife of another. This may seem perfectly obvious, but it does make clear her legal position. In law a woman was virtually a minor, first of all subordinate to her father and then to her husband. Only if she were eventually widowed did she gain a measure of freedom. A wife could not, for example, give away or sell any part of her moveable goods over the value of fourpence without her husband's consent, unless she were making a moderate charitable gift or giving as a present her own clothing. Even then she was supposed to have her husband's consent, as many of the legal documents of the period show. In 1284 Mary Johnstone decided to donate a smallish annuity to the canons of Innerpeffray. After she had done so, her husband ratified the gift, in order to prevent it from being called in question, 'because Mary was at the time when it was made subject to her husband in law of matrimony'. If any such gift were made without a husband's consent, it could be declared null and void.[33]

Similarly, a wife would not give away any of the terce settled on her at marriage. This was firmly stated to be the law because, 'as the woman is in the power of her husband, it is not to be wondered at that her terce as well as everything else belonging to her should be at her husband's disposal.' Moreover, a man could actually give away or sell his wife's terce if he felt so inclined, 'and in this, as in all other matters not contrary to the law of God, she must willingly acquiesce.' If the husband did sell the terce against the wife's wishes, she was unable to claim it back when he died, but she would, of course, be entitled to a third of what he left in the usual way. His powers over her heritable property were much more limited, but he did administer it on her behalf.

Strangely enough, any gifts of property between husband and wife after the marriage settlement was agreed were theoretically forbidden. It was felt that such presents might somehow lead to 'mutual impoverishment'. There was, however, an easily available loophole, for if such a gift was made and was never revoked, it became irrevocable on the death of the partner who had made it.

For his part, the husband could not do entirely as he pleased. No man was allowed to dispose of his wife's lands without her consent and, if he did so, she could reclaim them after his death although not before it, for 'so long as the husband is living, the wife is under his power and he was lord of all that pertained to his wife, but only during his lifetime.' Property apart, no married woman was allowed to act as surety for a debt, nor could she institute any legal action against her husband without his consent. Even when she came near the end of her days, she could not make a will without his agreement. An unmarried heiress could do so, as could a widow, but because a wife's property belonged legally to her husband she was not allowed to dispose of it. An interesting comment by the author of *Regiam Majestatem* makes it clear, however, that the strict legal position did not always hold good. Having explained that because she was 'under the authority of a husband' a wife needed his consent, the author goes on to say, 'Nevertheless, it would be a dutiful act and very creditable to the husband if he conceded a reasonable part of his estate to his wife' which she might bequeath as she pleased. This 'reasonable part' was to be the terce which she would enjoy as a widow, and 'this is what most husbands usually do, much to their credit.'[34]

That little comment serves as a reminder that legal provisions should not always be read too literally. A woman's position at law was indeed equivalent to that of a minor, but we must see this in the context of a dangerous society in which physical force played a significant part, men conducted the public business of life, and the weak were too easily oppressed. Time and time again there are examples of widows having their goods taken from them and being threatened, bullied and even assaulted simply because they were known to be in a vulnerable position. They enjoyed greater freedom at law, they could dispose of their property as they wished, they could act as sureties for debt and they could draw up testaments, but they were at the mercy of predatory neighbours. If a woman's property belonged to her husband he would protect it and even in his absence an unscrupulous enemy might hesitate if he knew that he would have the male owner to reckon with afterwards, not merely a woman encumbered with children and unable to defend herself satisfactorily against physical assault. Undoubtedly a wife's status was inferior, but there were advantages in the system too, which are perhaps not immediately apparent to the modern observer.

Again, the personal element should not be discounted. There must have been husbands affectionate enough to modify what read as harsh legal provisions. With no personal correspondence surviving to illustrate human relationships it is difficult to tell how husbands and wives regarded each other, but there are at least some indications of their feelings. On the whole, it would seem that marriages arranged for a daughter by her parents were successful enough, mutual affection or simply a community of interest growing with increased maturity, the birth of children and the day to day business of living together. Unions which were agreed entirely by the families concerned with no natural affection between the young couple inevitably went through a difficult period of adjustment at the start. After Princess Margaret of England married Alexander III of Scotland in 1251 she spent months of misery in her new home. She and her husband were still children, and they were given separate apartments in Edinburgh Castle, not the most comfortable of royal residences. Margaret found her chambers cramped and the Scottish weather hard to bear. So distressing were reports from her household that her father eventually sent ambassadors north to see for themselves. They reached the conclusion that one of the English King's own representatives already in Scotland was to blame for much of the young Queen's unhappiness. At any Court there were always troublemakers ready to cause difficulties and stir up jealousy. Matters improved after the ambassadors' visit and in later years Margaret was cheered by occasional journeys to London.[35]

Obviously a child queen in a foreign land was confronted by special difficulties, but any bride who came as a stranger to her husband's household was bound to experience problems of adjustment, particularly if she was living in the home of her parents-in-law and had to play a subsidiary role to her husband's mother. Yet in spite of these initial trials, it would seem that most women settled down happily enough. Traditional stories tell of the love and attachment felt by wives for their husbands. There was Devorgilla, the daughter of the Lord of Galloway, who married John Baliol in 1233. She bore him four sons and three daughters, and when he died she displayed a somewhat macabre wifely devotion. She had his body embalmed and his heart placed in an ivory coffer bound with silver. At every mealtime this relic was placed solemnly on the table and when she entered the great hall she curtseyed to it. Silver dishes of each course served were placed before the coffer, and at the end of the meal they were taken out so that the food could be distributed amongst the poor in Baliol's memory. This Devorgilla did for the rest of her life, and when she died the ivory box was buried with her, 'between her paps'.[36]

This somewhat gruesome example apart, many husbands and wives must have enjoyed peaceful domestic felicity. Spectacular marital disputes come to our notice because they were unusual, but the daily doings of those who lived in quiet harmony leave little trace. When women's lives were touched by dramatic circumstances there is ample evidence that they acted as loving helpmates to their husbands, offering consolation, encouragement and practical assistance. Lady Seton was able to provide strength and support for her husband in tragic circumstances in 1333. Sir Alexander was Captain of Berwick, and when the town was besieged two of his sons perished: Thomas, the eldest, was captured and hanged by the enemy, while William was drowned. Shocked as she was, Lady Seton was the stronger of the two in this extremity. Seeing her husband's distress, she summoned all her courage and offered comfort. Their sons had died for the honour of their family and their cause, she said, and their deaths would not be wasted if the besiegers were repulsed. They had other living children, she reminded him, and she was still young enough to bear more sons. Hearing these words, Sir Alexander's courage revived.[37]

In less tragic circumstances, other wives came to the rescue and interceded for husbands who were in difficulties, often travelling long distances to act on their behalf. The Countess of Strathearn set out for Rochester in the south of England in 1307 when she heard that her husband was being kept prisoner there and Christiana, Countess of Dunbar, was but one of those who went to London on their husbands' concerns.[38] When Catherine Bellenden's third husband failed to convince the Queen Regent, Mary of Guise, that he did not owe her large sums of money, it was his wife who took up the pen and wrote explaining the situation, and the Earl of Huntly of the 1540s relied on his Countess not only to help him in his estate business but to advise him in his political manoeuvrings. Indeed, it was largely thanks to her efforts that he escaped from the English after they took him prisoner.[39]

Wives were far from being mere ciphers. Isabel Hoppar, a rich widow who married Archibald Douglas of Kilspindie in about 1515, is said to have 'totally ordered' her husband,[40] but perhaps the best known example of wifely influence is that of St Margaret. Margaret was an English princess, the sister of Edgar Atheling, and when he fled to Scotland after the Norman Conquest she and another sister went too. Landing on the shores of Fife, the little group were taken to Dunfermline, where the Scottish King, Malcolm III, had one of his residences. He accorded the visitors a suitable welcome and not long afterwards he married Margaret.

Her own chaplain wrote an account of her life and since then much has been made of her influence at the Scottish Court, where she introduced new ways and is said to have reformed both manners and ecclesiastical affairs. Historians today tend to place less emphasis on her effect on politics and the Church, but even those who do not wholeheartedly subscribe to her chaplain's adulatory view of her life still admit that she was a strong partner in a successful marriage. She had energy and determination, and like other women of decided character she was not content to play a subsidiary role. It is significant that four of her sons were called after her own English ancestors and none was given the name of any of her husband's forebears, as would have been expected.[41]

[37]

Not all unions were as harmonious, of course. It was inevitable that a number of arranged marriages would founder because of personal incompatibility, differences of outlook, prior attachments or longstanding hostility. Sometimes the difficulties were apparent from the start. In the late fourteenth century Robert II's son, Sir Alexander Stewart, was married to Euphemia, Countess of Ross, so that he would gain possession of her estates. He already had a relationship with a woman named Mariota, who had borne his children, and he was determined that he would not give her up. Such loyalty might have been admirable had it not been allied to other qualities which earned him the name 'the Wolf of Badenoch'. During their brief time together he ill-treated the Countess and it was not long before he deserted her altogether. She complained to the Church about his behaviour and in November 1398 he was excommunicated. The Bishops of Moray and Ross who pronounced the sentence told him that he must go back to his lawful wife. So furious was he at this, that in revenge he burned Elgin Cathedral and the towns of Elgin and Forres. Two years later the quarrel was still raging and the ecclesiastical authorities noted that 'the marriage has been the cause of wars, plundering, arson, murders and many other damages and scandals, and it is likely that more will happen if they remain united in this union.' They were divorced shortly afterwards.[42]

Occasionally, a wife was put away because she had borne no children. Anatomical knowledge was still in a rudimentary state and the wife was always held responsible for a childless marriage. Thomas, Earl of Mar, discarded his Countess for this reason and must have been sadly disappointed when his second marriage likewise failed to provide him with any offspring. Politics could also lead to the ending of a marriage. James I's daughter Annabella, who was the wife of the Count of Geneva, found herself in this situation. The French King disapproved of the match and by his intrigues finally persuaded the Count to repudiate his wife. Annabella was sent home to Scotland, where she promptly married the Earl of Huntly.[43]

Nor was it only men who were motivated by considerations of politics. In 1297, the Earl of Fife's daughter Isabella was married to John Comyn, Earl of Buchan. Comyn supported Edward I of England in his claims to be rightful King of Scots while Isabella was committed to the cause of his great enemy Robert Bruce. Her predicament became more and more awkward until in 1306 Bruce murdered her husband's cousin, and shortly afterwards made himself King of Scots. Isabella thereupon seized her husband's best horses and set off to ride to Scone, where she knew that Bruce would be crowned. The validity of the ceremony was liable to be called into question because her brother was staying away and it was his hereditary right to place the King upon the Stone of Destiny. Isabella was determined to remedy this and, although she arrived too late for the coronation, a second ceremony was performed at which she participated. The Stone of Destiny had already been removed by the English, but Isabella presumably placed Bruce on a throne instead. She was only twenty or so, but she knew her own mind and she never did return to her husband. Indeed, she was captured by the English not long afterwards and spent four years imprisoned in a cage of timber and iron at Berwick Castle.[44]

When husbands and wives did quarrel dramatically, it was possible for them to end the marriage provided they had at least modest financial resources. The Church, however, recognized only one ground for divorce and that was adultery. Either husband or wife could sue in the ecclesiastical courts, but even when they were successful they were permitted only divorce *a mensa et thoro* [*i.e.* of bed and board]. This meant that the legal ties of marriage were not dissolved although the couple were freed from their matrimonial duties and could thereafter live apart. If the wife were the guilty party she forfeited the terce and if it was the husband who had erred he lost the tocher.

This method of ending an unbearable relationship was effective enough if adultery were proven, although of course it did not permit the divorced man and woman to marry again. A more usual course was to seek a decree of nullity, which cancelled the marriage altogether. This could be obtained on the grounds of consanguinity, and since so many people were distantly related to one another it was easy enough to argue that husband and wife were within the forbidden degrees but had only recently discovered it. Another pretext was that a previous valid marriage had taken place in the past, presumably an incomplete one, and there were also cases where either husband or wife had been legally too young to marry at all.[45]

In a society which lacked a strong central government, there were those who did not seek a legal end to a marriage but took matters into their own hands. Isabella, Countess of Mar, was

[39]

widely suspected of having murdered her first husband in 1259 and as a result was forced to resign her earldom and leave Scotland with the man she had married instead. Likewise the four-times-married Lady Janet Gordon was generally believed to have smothered her first husband, and Lady Glamis was in 1528 accused of having murdered Lord Glamis. Finally, the wife's relatives might come to her rescue and when Maclean of Duart ill-treated his wife, Lady Catherine Campbell, her brother murdered him.[46]

Discord and violence there undoubtedly were, but medieval Scottish society obviously provided a whole spectrum of relationships between husband and wife. At one extreme were women like the Countess of Carrick who kidnapped her future husband and the Countess of Buchan who cheerfully deserted hers: at the other were girls forced into repugnant marriages when still mere children, and women abused by their husbands but unable to escape from the relationship which their parents had decreed for them. Most women's experience of marriage probably lay somewhere between these two extremes. Marital love and affection and mutual respect there undoubtedly were. The law might give a husband far more power over his wife than we would tolerate today, but women's expectations in the Middle Ages were different from ours and despite their legal disabilities many of them exercised considerable influence within the family, expressed forceful opinions, and generally engaged in a far wider range of activities than is often realized.

CHAPTER TWO

Women's Work

WHEN A GIRL MARRIED, she became mistress of her own household and so assumed a completely new set of responsibilities. Her first years as a wife might be spent in her husband's family home, in subservience to her mother-in-law, but sooner or later she would have her own establishment, be it a spacious castle or a one-roomed house. Strictly speaking, she was subject to her husband in all things, but to her he delegated the running of his household and the raising of his children. Although she was eventually answerable to him for the management of his possessions and the spending of his money, the domestic sphere was her particular province and there she had complete control.

In an age when most commodities were home-produced, this meant a good deal of hard, physical work. The preparation and cooking of food alone was a time-consuming task. A minority of families who lived in towns could purchase foodstuffs, but most housewives baked their own bread, churned butter and made cheese. Ale was the normal beverage and they brewed it themselves. Before the introduction of sugar, honey was the only available sweetener, and so it had to be collected from the hives. In the autumn, when the cattle were slaughtered, there was beef to be salted and hams had to be cured. The housewife was usually the person who looked after the poultry, collected the eggs, milked the cows and grew and dried herbs for both culinary and medicinal purposes.

Cooking apart, the domestic tasks of the household were many and varied. Spinning was a constant occupation, for wool had to be made into thread for the weaver, then clothes had to be sewn up. All the family's undergarments and most of the outer clothing were made at home: a tailor was only called in for special occasions. To the housewife fell the chores of filling mattresses and pillows, hemming tablecloths and sheets, making up soap and candles from animal fat and generally cleaning the home. In addition to all this, women were expected to take part in the seasonal work of the land, helping in the fields, especially at harvest time.[1]

Many women, whether or not they were wealthy, had maid-servants. These were usually young female relatives willing to learn the domestic skills of the home by sharing in the work. However, even the great lady in her castle and the prosperous burgess's wife in her town house were expected to have a practical knowledge of all the household tasks. Not only did they supervise in detail but they joined in the unrelenting work of keeping the family fed, clothed and reasonably comfortable. Nor could a wife escape the burden of bearing and rearing children, whatever her social position. We do not always appreciate the fact that, in the past, married women were likely to spend most of their childbearing years in a state of pregnancy, with all its attendant inconveniences and ills. Certainly, methods of contraception and abortion had been known since earliest times. The Egyptians knew of ways 'in order to cause that a woman should cease to conceive for one year, two years or three years' as early as 1550 BC and this type of knowledge was available in Western Europe in the Middle Ages. Some methods relied upon herbal concoctions, some upon superstitious spells or charms. These were obviously of varying efficacy and whether they were ever used in Scotland is impossible to say. If they were, they had no significant effect upon the birth rate, to judge by the numbers of women who did produce large families. The medieval Church emphasized that procreation was the true purpose of marriage and in an age of high mortality it was as well to have as many children as possible. After all, perhaps only a third of them would survive to adult life.[2]

There is more emphasis in the written records on attempts by barren women to conceive than on efforts by fertile women to avoid pregnancy. The shrine of St Adrian on the Isle of May at the mouth of the Forth was thought to have good effects in such cases and women went there hoping for a miracle which would allow them to bear a living child. Religious assistance was also sought when childbirth itself approached. Midwives and older women were skilled enough when a confinement was straightforward, but when the baby was lying in the wrong position or there were other complications there was little that could be done medically. A visit to the shrine of Our Lady of Loretto in Musselburgh, just outside

Edinburgh, was believed to ensure a trouble-free labour, and so pregnant women would go there to make gifts of money and to have their childbed linen blessed. Queen Mary of Guise walked the seven miles or so from the capital to the shrine, 'heavy with bairn' in the troubled weeks before her daughter Mary, Queen of Scots, was born. For those who could not undertake such a pilgrimage themselves, there were prayers which could be said to ease the pains of labour, and some of these are included in a handbook compiled by a Scottish merchant about 1400.[3]

While she awaited the birth of her child, a woman's activities were curtailed. Many women were strong and healthy, pregnancy causing them no difficulty, but others had their health undermined by perpetual childbearing and were never really well. Even the sturdiest found it wise to limit their activities as their confinement approached. Travel, for instance, was difficult enough at the best of times but if a woman was carrying a child it was positively dangerous. People could remember the sad example of Robert I's daughter, Marjorie Bruce. She was out riding near Paisley when she was expecting her first child. Her horse stumbled, she fell, and although her premature son was born alive and survived, she herself died.[4]

When the delivery was safely accomplished, the child was baptised soon afterwards in case he should die. The mother remained in bed, receiving visits from her women friends once she was strong enough. Indeed, it seems that when she was able to sit up in bed for the first time, the occasion was celebrated with a party. We know some of the details for the expenses incurred on behalf of one of James IV's mistresses in 1501. After the birth of her son, the master cook of the royal household was paid eight shillings for four dozen loaves or rolls of a very light, white bread. These he supplied for 'the lady's upsitting feast'. Forty days after the birth, the religious ceremony of purification took place and the mother was ready to resume normal life again. However, in poorer households this welcome interlude after the confinement was probably all too brief: a few days at most would elapse before the housewife was back at work once more.[5]

Leisure was a rare commodity in the Middle Ages. Of course, there were idle hours when girls and young women could romp about outside, enjoying simple games and generally finding an outlet for high spirits. In the winter they sat over the fire and gossiped as they sewed, discussing the latest doings of the locality, reminiscing about days gone by and telling stories handed down in the family. The festivals of the church year provided a welcome opportunity for gaiety and feasting, as did the family celebrations of baptism and marriage and the more solemn gatherings for funerals. In burghs there were plays and processions to be watched from time to time but, on the whole, recreation was mainly of a straightforward and homemade variety.

In the really great houses of the wealthiest of the peerage, ladies did have some idle hours when they could pass their time chatting to each other over a piece of needlework. Sewing was always a popular occupation and women sewed not only clothes but decorative furnishings for the home. Because of the perishable nature of fabrics, almost all the pieces worked by pre-Reformation ladies have long since vanished, but a little evidence does remain. Family inventories show that Sir Colin Campbell of Glenorchy's second wife, Katherine Ruthven, was an enthusiastic needle-woman. When she married him in 1550 she set about working a whole series of hangings, cushions and coverings. One of the sets of bed hangings which she sewed still survives. Worked in coloured wools and silks, it depicts the temptation and the expulsion of Adam and Eve from the Garden of Eden. It seems that Katherine copied the design from a popular woodcut of the period, but she added a personal touch of her own. Incorporated in the decorative work are her initials and those of her husband, linked by a true-lovers'-knot.[6]

As they stitched, ladies enjoyed that favourite medieval pastime, the asking of riddles, and they listened to music. Many of the large houses employed a regular group of professional musicians to entertain guests and some even had that most traditional figure of all, the harper, who sang lengthy ballads of past events. The more musically inclined ladies themselves sang, accompanying themselves on lute or harp. There was dancing, too, and when James IV made royal progresses through the north-east of Scotland he was entertained on more than one occasion by maidens who sang and danced.[7]

Indoor games provided a further diversion. Chess was popular with women as well as with men, so often the mistress of the household and her daughters could play. Dice and tables, a kind of backgammon, were favourites and on one winter day in 1496 Lady Lundy had no less illustrious an opponent than the King himself when she played at the tables. From the thirteenth century onwards card games were known. James V's queen, Mary of Guise, was an inveterate gambler, regularly losing at cards to the leading Scottish statesmen of the day.[8]

Outside, the more energetic women engaged in falconry and hunting. It was well known that Elizabeth Hepburn, the Prioress of Haddington in the early sixteenth century, was more enthusiastic about an invitation to join a royal hunting party than about her ecclesiastical duties, and Margaret Tudor was but one of those ladies at Court who enjoyed archery.[9] Gardens provided a further source of pleasure and ladies helped to plan them as well as walking and sitting in them. Mary of Guise had not long arrived in Scotland from France when she was writing home for cuttings of fruit trees. Apples, pears and plums already grew in her husband's kingdom but she wished to embellish his gardens further by introducing new varieties.[10]

Meagre though the evidence may be, there are distinct indications of intelligence and creativity in women's employment of their leisure hours. The devising and working of intricate needlework patterns required an artistic eye as well as deft fingers, while chess is hardly an entertainment for the unintelligent. There were gifted women storytellers and women poets too, as James IV's payment of fourteen shillings to the 'bard wife' [i.e. singing woman] in the Canongate of Edinburgh suggests.[11] Even the guessing of riddles could provide a measure of mental stimulation. Some were at the level of children's games but others took the form of quite elaborate puzzles and would seem to indicate that women were anxious to use their minds for something other than the planning of the next meal or the preparation of the family's winter wardrobe.

This is amply borne out by the energy and enthusiasm with which women undertook a number of activities beyond the entirely domestic. Most notable of all, of course, were those widowed queens who had the opportunity of exercising political power openly. Scotland suffered a long series of royal minorities and the successive foreign widows expected to and usually did have some part in the government. Once in that position, they were far from being mere figure-heads. Marie de Coucy managed to obtain a share in the government of Scotland when her husband died even though she remarried shortly afterwards, and when James II was killed, his wife Mary of Gueldres dominated the government. Similarly, Mary of Guise did not rest until she obtained the regency some years after the death of James V, and when she did succeed in grasping power, she played an extremely active part.[12]

Mary did not do so without opposition, and in his criticisms of female government her opponent, John Knox, made the first explicit statements of masculine prejudice against women to be found in Scottish history. He was not, however, speaking as a woman-hater. His object was to criticize the Roman Catholic Church and so he levelled his most vehement criticisms against two of the Catholic rulers of the time, Mary Tudor and Mary of Guise. Because he wished to see them replaced by Protestant princes, he found it convenient to argue that no woman should exercise political power. 'To promote a woman to bear rule, superiority, dominion or empire above any realm, nation or city is repugnant to nature', he declared in his *First Blast of the Trumpet against the Monstrous Regiment* of Women,* and he went on to elaborate his theme with relish. Nature had made women 'weak, frail, impatient, feeble and foolish . . . inconstant, variable, cruel and lacking in spirit of counsel and regiment'. Individual examples of able women made no difference. 'Woman in her greatest perfection was made to serve and obey man, not to rule and command him.' Women unjustly placed at the head of affairs would suffer a horrible fate and should be deposed from authority.[13]

These were strong words, designed to raise rebellion against the Catholic queens, yet even Knox in his private life sought the company of women and entered into long correspondences with them. The very vehemence of his invective suggests that he, along with the other men of his time, recognized the power of female influence. Ambitious women normally had to exercise this power indirectly, and it would seem that wives and mistresses were rarely afraid to offer their advice. They might not be able to sit in Parliament or Privy Council, but in the privacy of the bedchamber at night they could talk things over with their husbands and bring them round to a different way of thinking. Royal brides were frequently used by their own families in this way. After Henry III's daughter Margaret was married to the King of Scots, Henry expected her to send back regular reports of what was happening at Court, and when he sought Alexander III's aid against his own barons he gave instructions that Margaret was to use her influence in his cause. Henry VIII, on the other hand, was equally anxious to counteract the power of his sister

**i.e.* rule

[46]

Margaret Tudor over James IV. He wanted James to visit him in London and told his representatives that the meeting should be arranged 'without the ifs or ands of his wife, which might engender a great uncertainty and minister much matter of cavillation'. Margaret was pregnant, and Henry feared she would delay James by insisting on his presence when her time came.[14]

Women really came into their own when their husbands were ill or absent. Husbands often had to go away with the army, and the nobility were required to be in attendance at Court. They usually left their wives at home on such occasions to deal with tenants, supervise chamberlains and pacify local disputes. Before she rode off to join Robert Bruce's cause, the Countess of Buchan was managing her husband's estate in England for him. In 1389, the Countess of March was busy arranging a safe conduct with the English king so that a thousand of her sheep could safely graze in the Cockburnspath area under the watchful eye of her two shepherds, and when Lady Seton's husband was killed at the battle of Flodden in 1513, she ran her small son's estates for him until he came of age, whereupon she retired to the nunnery she had helped to found.[15]

Some ladies became positively pugnacious in defence of their rights, as Robert Dalzell of that Ilk found to his cost in 1456. In order to take possession of some lands in the barony of Morton, he had to obtain legal ownership of them from the holder of the barony, the widowed Janet Borthwick, Lady Dalkeith. Armed with the necessary document obtained from chancery, he arrived at the gates of Morton Castle and asked to see Janet's son. She herself appeared. Dalzell handed over his document and she scrutinized it closely. Finding that it was addressed not to herself but to her son, she gave it back indignantly. She was the holder of the barony, she informed him, and the request must come to her. Somewhat disconcerted, Dalzell retired. A month later he reappeared, bearing a new communication. This time it was addressed to 'the lord of the barony or to Janet, commonly called Lady Morton'. Needless to say, this form of wording pleased the recipient no better and she refused to have anything to do with the transaction. Dalzell was so annoyed that he attacked and despoiled some of her property, whereupon Janet took him to court and obtained £400 Scots in compensation. Dalzell had to wait for another ten years before her son gave him possession of his lands.[16]

A determined nature could be particularly useful in time of

war. All too often women were the innocent victims of military action, losing husbands, sons, homes, possessions and sometimes their own lives in the long years of conflict between England and Scotland. A number of valiant ladies found themselves defending family castles against the enemy. Robert I's sister, Christian Bruce, had suffered all manner of vicissitudes during the Wars of Independence, and towards the end of her life she found herself in charge of Kildrummy Castle when it was besieged by David of Strathbogie in the English interest. She held out resolutely and managed to keep the enemy at bay until her husband marched to her rescue. Strathbogie was killed soon afterwards, whereupon, curiously enough, it fell to his widow in turn to defend the island fortress of Lochindorb against the Scots. This particular siege lasted for seven months, until Edward III himself came to relieve her. By that time, she complained, she had lost not only all her money but her entire wardrobe.[17]

Women like Christian took an active part in supervising the defence of their castles, as the famous story of another resolute countess shows. In 1338 the Earl of March left the defence of his fortress of Dunbar to his wife, Black Agnes. The English promptly laid siege to the castle, bringing in an unusual number of engineers and some highly elaborate equipment. According to the chronicler's account, Agnes personally presided over the resistance with such devotion that the English commander was moved to complain that, came he early or came he late, Black Agnes was always at her gate. The better to show her defiance, whenever a missile struck her castle walls she sent her maidens out to the battlements with handkerchiefs to dust away the marks.[18]

In more peaceful times, the lady of the local castle would turn her mind to the welfare of the tenants on her estates, extending to them the type of maternal authority and solicitude which she exercised over the members of her own household. John Baliol's wife Devorgilla is traditionally believed to have ordered the building of a bridge over the River Nith at Dumfries. At the end of the thirteenth century, Isabella de Beaumont, Lady de Vescy, successfully asked royal permission for a weekly market to be held at Crail, in Fife, and the Duke of Albany's daughter is credited with having set up a hospital for lepers in Govan about 1350.[19]

Religious establishments were of particular interest to ladies, several of whom were responsible for major foundations. William the Lion's wife, Queen Ermengarde, was in the habit of visiting

[48]

Balmerino, on the south bank of the River Tay, for the sake of her health. She decided to found an abbey there and she went to considerable trouble to endow it. In 1229 the first monks arrived from Melrose and over the years the Queen made further gifts of property to them. When she died she was buried before the high altar of the abbey church.

Almost fifty years later, Devorgilla founded the Cistercian Abbey of Sweetheart in memory of her husband. Ysende, Countess of Strathearn, a generation after that, bequeathed lands to the Abbey of Inchaffray and in the sixteenth century it was Lady Seton who paid for erecting the nunnery of St Katherine of Siena in Edinburgh.[20]

Aristocratic ladies were obviously in a very special position, with opportunities available to them or even thrust upon them which did not accrue to everyone else. At a quite different level of society, however, women were also active beyond the domestic sphere and we are now realizing that a significant number of those who lived in burghs were engaging in commercial occupations. Probably because the written sources are meagre it was at one time believed that women did not actually work outside the home for money, unless as servants and nurses. Now, however, there have come to light various references which make it clear that some women did run shops and businesses.

An early example of female enterprise is to be found in an appeal made by Evota of Stirling to Edward I of England in 1304. In her message, Evota explained that when the English in Stirling Castle were besieged by the Scots, she had found the means of supplying the garrison with provisions. Her own fellow country-men took none too kindly to this when they found out what she was doing, and as a result they seized her property in Stirling, put her in prison for ten weeks, then banished her from the town. Edward's laconic response was to tell her to sue before his Lieutenant.[21]

More conventional were the activities of those women who kept stalls and shops in Edinburgh. Even they were not without fault, however, and in the 1520s a series of cases came up before the Town Council involving women who had illegally bought goods to sell them at inflated prices. Helen Bayne, often in trouble before for similar offences, was caught buying eggs and was banished from the town as a result. Margaret Clephane was trading illegally in oysters. Five women were banished for buying oats and Bessie Penne appeared personally to promise that never again would she

[49]

sell butter and cheese for extortionate sums. (Incidentally, sentences of banishment for life were rarely put into effect and were usually revoked after a week or two.) Twenty years later it was the female fruit sellers who were in trouble for quarrelling noisily in the High Street of Edinburgh with other traders and with the burgh officials.[22]

Rather more circumspect were those traders who numbered the Royal Court amongst their customers. In 1507, David Balfour's wife Elizabeth found herself very favourably placed. Not only was she given a special licence to brew ale for the Queen and her ladies, but she was to be allowed to ask whatever price she pleased. Ale apart, cloth was frequently supplied to the royal household by women. In the 1470s, James III sent his officials of the Wardrobe to Thomas Williamson's wife Isabel. She sold them linen for the royal shirts, black cloth for the King's hose and a variety of velvets, satins and rich silk stuffs to make into gowns and doublets. She could likewise provide velvet and damask for the Queen's cloaks and kirtles and could even produce forty squirrel skins to trim a gown. When the Queen gave birth to a prince it was Mrs Williamson who supplied the velvet for his coat, the cloth for his shirts and sheets and the brown material to cover his cradle. At the same time Marion Coupland sold the miniver with which his coat was lined and the wives of David Whitehead and John of Fawside supplied cloth of varying kinds to the Court. Twenty years later taffeta and broadcloth were purchased for the King from Henry Atkinson's wife and on another occasion, when he passed through Cupar in Fife, James IV purchased from Ellen of Dunino some English blue cloth for a jacket to wear under his armour.[23]

Female merchants and shopkeepers were not only to be found in Edinburgh. In the small burgh of Lanark, booths were let out by the town authorities to traders for a rent of half a merk or several shillings a year. Amongst those who paid the necessary rent in 1488 were Bessie Clarkson, Bessie Lockhart and Bessie Kerr.[24] Burghs were by this time privileged communities which had been granted special rights in order to encourage trade. Only those which had been set up by the King on royal lands could engage in overseas trade or sell foreign goods, and within the burgh's area it was only the burgesses who were allowed to carry on any form of retail trade, even in home-produced goods. The burgh was very much a community and so new members had to be admitted by the existing burgesses. They had to take an oath of loyalty not only to the King but to the burgh itself, and they had to undertake various responsibilities. It is therefore of particular interest to discover that certain women were admitted to their ranks.[25]

In the small Border town of Peebles, for instance, a woman named Meg Woodhall was made a burgess on 29 October 1459. Another eleven years passed before a second woman, Bessie Woodman, was admitted. In 1492, Margaret of Linton paid a silver merk in Peebles Tolbooth to become a burgess and five years after that Kate Walwood's fee was a hundred loads of stones to help to repair the bridge over the River Tweed.[26] Early evidence also comes from the Edinburgh records. Before anyone could become a member of Edinburgh's merchant guild he or she had first to be a burgess, and in 1407 Alison de Duscoull was made guild sister as heir to her brother Robert. We can safely infer from this that Alison was now carrying on her late brother's business and that she was possibly trading as a wool merchant. Moreover, the regulations laid down in 1508 about the privileges enjoyed by the children of burgesses explicitly include women. An eldest son was to pay 6s. 8d. to become a burgess, a second son 13s. 4d. and a burgess's daughter the same as a second son. To become a member of the guild, the daughter had to give an additional 20/-. Women were certainly taking the opportunity of becoming both burgesses and guild sisters by the early 1560s when, out of a total of fifty-one taverners deprived of their burgess and guild rights for keeping up prices, seventeen were women.[27]

Apart from supplying goods, a number of women provided services. They always performed their traditional role as nurses: not so much nurses of the sick, for people were looked after by their own families, but rather as wet-nurses and foster-mothers of children. Those who undertook this duty for the royal children appear from time to time in the accounts of the Lord High Treasurer as the recipients of gifts and pensions as well as of annual fees: 'to Janet Darroch of Stirling that fostered my lady, the King's sister' in 1474, alms of forty shillings; to Katherine Fyne, ten shillings a year 'for her good and thankful service done in the nursing, fostering and keeping' of Prince Alexander and to the three women who 'rocked and kept the bairns' in 1503, the sum of £3.[28]

Large numbers of unmarried girls acted as domestic servants, not just in the great houses but in the establishments of prosperous burgesses, lesser farmers and thriving tradesmen. They were not inevitably poor, exploited creatures. Often they were related to the family in which they worked and sometimes they were even willing to take their employers to court in a dispute. In 1517 Margaret Wightman went to the burgh court of Selkirk to complain that when her master Mr James Hog, burgess of the town, paid her a fee of seven shillings she gave it back into his safekeeping, along with a cap and two collars to the value of four shillings. To her indignation Mr Hog and his wife were now refusing to hand these over, so Margaret sought legal redress.[29]

Rather more specialized than the domestic servants were women who undertook skilled work, mainly in connection with sewing. When James IV wanted a new belt in the winter of 1494, three ounces of silk were delivered to Katherine Turing so that she could make it. Later she was sent thirty-two reels of gold thread to make tassels and fringes for the King's saddle. An unnamed woman in Stirling in 1502 was making tassels for religious vestments and at about the same time women were employed to sew up sheets, kerchiefs and pillowcases for the royal household. A further intriguing entry in the accounts records the payment of six shillings 'at the making of the hangings of scarlet and damask for sewing of the linen cloth of them, sewed by women' and in 1503 occurs a mention of two embroiderers, one of whom was a woman, Bessie Hogg.[30]

Women likewise feature as bonnetmakers in the records of various incorporations. Regulations drawn up by the bonnet-makers of Dundee in 1496 state that no woman 'shall occupy as for master of the craft foresaid but if she have been a freeman's wife and has substance of her own to labour with'. The Edinburgh records of the 1520s and 30s also mention women bonnet-makers and the 1530 document specifically states that the fee for admission of 'freeman or freewoman' is 30/- Scots, going on to add that 'neither master nor mistress of the craft' is to employ another's apprentice without his consent. These examples demonstrate that it was clearly possible at this period for women to be bonnet-makers in their own right.[31]

Of other female activities there are but brief glimpses. Margaret Atkinson was illegally manufacturing and selling wax in Leith in the 1520s, and in 1499 the Town Council of Edinburgh had forbidden any persons, 'men or women', to hold schools in the town. This move was designed to safeguard the rights of the existing grammar school. All in all, there seems to have been no identifiable prejudice against women earning their living. Indeed, in 1529 Janet Heriot, in trouble with the authorities for begging, was sternly told by Edinburgh Town Council that she must work for her living.[32] Widows who did not work were liable to be a burden on the local funds for the poor, and it is obvious from the records that wives regularly helped their husbands in their businesses. Again, there were always those women who turned to prostitution as a means of supporting themselves. One intriguing example of this activity occurs in the history of the monastery of Inchcolm, set on a small island in the Firth of Forth. In 1430 'a certain maiden named Mariota' persuaded the monks that she could be of service to them. She accordingly moved in, making a contract to the effect that they would supply her with food and clothing, in return for which she would make certain goods over to the abbey. This 'sinister and dishonourable arrangement' lasted happily for thirteen years, until the church authorities discovered it. Questions were asked, for it did not seem honourable 'that women should dwell among religious, and especially a single women, and it is feared that the religious dwelling there may yield to sins of the flesh and scandals thereby arise'. The Pope therefore gave orders that 'some good man was to expel and remove the maiden from the monastery', giving her compensation for the goods she had handed over, but deducting her expenses.[33]

As for women's own expectations, few could have set out in life with the intention of having a career as we today would understand it. Many must have accepted that they would begin as domestic servants for a year or two, putting in the time until they married. Those in the burghs particularly may have expected to help in their husbands' businesses just as their counterparts in the country helped in the fields. Again, they probably realized that if their husbands died young they would have to earn their living somehow or other. Work was not a means of social advancement for women, but an economic necessity. Possibly the only women who sought advancement through their own employment were nuns and mistresses. Convents were far from being havens for the contemplative life and a well-born, able woman could see in a career as an abbess a means of satisfying her ambition. Some indeed were willing to go to surprising lengths in pursuit of their desires. In 1429, the convent of South Berwick had long been dilapidated and the last prioress was dead. Agnes Brown, nun of St Bothans, saw this as a promising opportunity and, 'with greatest perils of roads and dangers of seas', took herself to Rome to ask the Pope to make her Prioress, offering to repair the buildings if he would agree. Her request was granted.[34]

A journey from Scotland to Rome at the beginning of the fifteenth century showed no small measure of determination, and it would have been interesting to have Agnes's own description of her adventures. It is sad indeed that the lack of written evidence leaves us with no direct indication of how women saw themselves, but at this period of history few Scotswomen could read or write. Before the invention of the printing press in the fifteenth century, the only documents were those kept by people involved in ecclesiastical, civil or judicial administration. The written word simply did not impinge upon the daily lives of most people although, as a means of religious enlightenment, the ability to read was a desirable skill and there were from the beginning certain women who acquired it.

One of the favourite stories told about St Margaret of Scotland centres upon the fact that she could read and her husband, King Malcolm III, could not. Educated on the continent in the eleventh century, Margaret possessed various devotional works when she was in Scotland. Malcolm admired her piety and so he used to abstract these books from her chamber in secret, then surprise her by producing them bound in fine leather studded with jewels. Wealthy ladies possessed books of hours and gospels and by the early sixteenth century the Scottish poet William Dunbar could allude to a prosperous widow sitting in church with her 'bright book' on her knee, 'with many lusty letters illuminate with gold'. Perhaps the widow's service book was more of a status symbol than anything else, but it would be reasonable to assume that throughout the Middle Ages a number of aristocratic and wealthy middle-class ladies could read.[35]

Writing was a different matter. Before the fifteenth century, it was a distinctly vocational accomplishment, the prerogative of a small group of professional men consisting of churchmen, lawyers and government officials. Women did not learn to write, and this applied throughout society. When Princess Margaret of Scotland wished to send a letter to her uncle the English King in 1280, she could not pick up a pen and write it herself. The modern observer would find it strange that she was nineteen years old and soon to be married but could not even sign her name, nor did she possess her own seal to close the letter. Instead, she had to rely on the services of a clerk. A hundred years later the situation was no different. When Queen Annabella of Scotland sent a message to Richard II of England giving news of her recent confinement, it was a scribe who penned the letter for her.[36]

This might appear a sorry state of affairs, but in fact few people could actually write, simply because they never needed to do so. In a world very different from our own, life was frequently disrupted by invasion, warfare, plague and famine. There was often no time to write down messages and it was all too easy for letters to fall into the wrong hands: to confide the import by word of mouth to a trusted messenger was by far the safest way. There was a much greater reliance generally upon the spoken word. Instructions by landowner to tenant, tenant to farm labourer, customer to tradesman and lawyer to client were passed on orally and that was that.

In the twelfth and thirteenth centuries there was therefore little practical disadvantage attached to feminine lack of literacy. Those women involved in public affairs would either send messages orally, as their husbands did, or they would use the services of a scribe. The spoken word could convey much to them and there was nothing to prevent them from joining in discussions and debates. Ladies who were at Court were in a particularly favourable situation. They could sit and listen to poems being declaimed, they could enjoy sophisticated music and dancing and they could attend plays and pageants. Robert Henryson, the fifteenth-century poet, wrote his famous 'Testament of Cresseid' with a female audience in mind: at one point the narrator specifically tells 'worthy women' that his ballad is made for their instruction.[37]

As time went on, literacy increased throughout the population and it is interesting to observe that women were not long behind men in learning to write. At first, most Scottish documents were in Latin but by 1400 the Scottish vernacular was being written down and this in itself made possible a widening of the group who could read and write. Fifty years after that, Scotsmen adopted the foreign custom of signing documents as well as sealing them, a practice which reflected a growing literacy and at the same time gave an added incentive to those who could not yet write. The earliest known Scottish land transaction to be signed by the grantor of the lands is dated 1443. Four years later comes an example of a burgess's signature and in 1458 there is that of a laird. Most interesting of all for our purposes, the earliest known signature of a woman is dated 1454, a mere eleven years after the first signed charter mentioned above.[38]

The present location of the document in question is unfortunately unknown, but its existence was recorded early last century by the Society of Antiquaries of Scotland, whose members inspected a facsimile. It bore the signature of Janet Dunbar, Countess of Moray, and there is no reason to doubt that it was genuine. Why Janet in particular was able to write remains a mystery. She held her title in her own right, for she and her younger sister were the only children of James, 4th Earl of Moray, and his wife Katherine Seton. The Earl spent three years in England as a hostage when Janet was a child and one might speculate that what he saw in the south encouraged his own interest in learning. However, he died in 1430, not long after his return to Scotland, so his parental influence was not of long duration. Thirteen or fourteen years after his death, Janet married her first husband, Lord Crichton. He died around the time when she signed the charter but she herself lived on until about 1500, marrying for a second time.[39]

Was Janet taught to write because her father had no sons and she was his heiress? Had he met Englishwomen who were literate and thought that his daughter should be so too? Did Janet herself choose to acquire these unusual skills because her family was left without a man at its head? Who, in any event, taught her? These questions will probably never be answered, for the documents which could tell us simply do not exist. One fact is reasonably certain, though. Wherever Janet did learn, it was unlikely to have been a Scottish nunnery.

At one time it was imagined that convents in Scotland formed centres of culture where the daughters of good families would achieve a fine education. This was far from being so. It was perfectly true, of course, that the unmarried daughters of the aristocracy were sometimes sent to spend several years in a nunnery even when there was no intention that they should eventually take the veil. In the past, historians made much of the fact that one of King James II's daughters spent several years in the Cistercian priory at Haddington. From this they inferred that she had been sent there to be educated, but that is an unwarrantable assumption. The Princess stayed in the priory for thirteen years, then later in life she stayed at another Cistercian house, Elcho, for a further thirteen years. During her time at Haddington the expenses paid for her were for board and lodging, nothing more. For one reason or another she was unsuitable for marriage and the convents provided an appropriate home for her.[40]

The sorry truth was that very few Scottish nuns were literate. Their numbers were in any event small: in the first half of the sixteenth century there were only eleven convents in Scotland and some of them had as few as half a dozen nuns. Moreover, the documents dealing with their various transactions show time and time again that the sisters could not write. When they wished to give their agreement to a document they had to ask a notary to guide their hands in order to make a signature. The famous exception to this is the convent of St Katherine of Siena in Edinburgh. Not only were the sisters more virtuous than their unsatisfactory counterparts elsewhere, but their competent and sometimes accomplished signatures, written in their own hand, without assistance, are to be found on the documents of their house, while a printed psalter belonging to one of them has numerous marginal notes in her own neat writing.[41]

Elsewhere, the nunneries could only have looked upon their wealthy lodgers as a welcome source of income. They continued for a lengthy period to take in girls from good families and when the English raided the convent at Elcho in 1547, it was reported that they carried off not only the small number of resident nuns but 'many gentlemen's daughters'. At best these girls may have been sent to Elcho to learn needlework and a little reading, but that would be the extent of their education.[42]

Girls who did learn to write were usually taught at home, perhaps by a member of their own family or by their brothers' tutor. The indications are that by 1500 Scottish noblemen were beginning to show an interest in reading and writing. It has been calculated that by that year no fewer than sixty per cent of them could at least sign their names and in the same period the signatures of lairds are fairly common. Anything written by a burgess before 1500 is difficult to find, but this may be because so few commercial records of the period have survived. The study of female literacy is similarly handicapped, for while families throughout the centuries would go to great trouble to preserve the records of property, sooner or later they usually threw away as being of no importance the personal letters of women. This was so even in the nineteenth century, when scholars sorting through family papers were apt to concentrate upon documents relating to political activities but discarded the written records of domestic and private life.

If Janet Dunbar could write competently in 1454, some of her female contemporaries must surely have been able to do so too. At any rate, from the time of Janet's own life we have further evidence. On 8 May 1472, a legal document was drawn up for Sir Robert Crichton of Sauchie. It was signed not only by his son but by his daughter-in-law, Dame Christian Erskine. This document still exists, with the somewhat sprawling signature, 'Cristian, Lady off Kynnoull' at the foot. Indeed, Christian wrote only slightly less well than her husband and she was obviously quite used to handling a pen. After 1500, more ladies' signatures appear. Katherine Stirling, Countess of Angus, signed a receipt in 1507 in a small neat hand. Thomas Kennedy of Bargany's wife Katherine added the customary 'with my hand' to her beautifully inscribed name in 1509. Seven years later Margaret, Countess of Cassillis, did less well: writing was obviously still something of an effort for her. Elizabeth Affleck's signature improved visibly between 1518 and 1520 and although in 1518 Margaret Lyon, Lady of Guthrie, had a rather laboured hand, she added in Latin the fact that her writing is her own.[43]

Signatures can tell us a little. More helpful are actual letters, but few have survived from before the mid-sixteenth century. Fortunately a group of letters written to James V's wife in the 1540s is still extant. Most of Mary of Guise's correspondents were men, but a few of them were the ladies of her Court. Elizabeth Keith, Countess of Huntly, often seems to have acted as her husband's secretary as well as advising him, writing letters on his behalf in her small, distinct hand. Again, Lady Home and Lady Gray were perfectly able to compose and write letters when family emergencies demanded. These ladies wrote in Scots. Their spelling was inconsistent and often phonetic, but this was only to be expected. Their husbands could do no better.[44]

Well-born ladies apart, we have the earliest signature of a middle-class Scotswoman in 1530. On February 24 that year Isobel Winzet signed a receipt with flowing, accomplished writing: 'Isobell, the spouse of John Fishar, with my hand'. As with Janet Dunbar's signature, it would be surprising if this particular example were the only one and it seems possible that some non-aristocratic girls were now going to school. Before the Reformation, there were two types of school in the towns. The grammar schools taught Latin and in theory were for boys only. The song schools trained boys in music for church services. It does seem, however, that a number of girls were allowed to attend the grammar schools and that in the country districts one or two went to the parish schools and there learned to write.[45]

On the continent, controversy was already raging about feminine education. Women who had learned to read and write were demanding that all girls should be taught to do so. Christine de Pisan, daughter of an Italian physician and astrologer at the French Court, felt particularly strongly about this issue. Herself widely recognized as one of the most learned women of the time, she believed that girls should be sent to school and taught the same subjects as boys, commenting that if women seemed to understand less it was because they did not go out into the world as men did. She owed her own education to her father, who had encouraged her interest, while her mother, on the contrary, 'held the usual feminine ideas on the matter' and thought that she should spend her time spinning.

This difference of opinion over the desirability of educating women was a favourite topic for dispute in medieval and Renaissance Europe. Clerics were particularly anxious to restrict a woman to her traditional role of wife and mother, and as a result, a furious literary debate raged for centuries. It was neatly summed up in one of the dialogues written by the great scholar Erasmus. This took the form of an imagined discussion between an abbot and an educated lady. The abbot declared roundly that it 'isn't feminine to be intellectual; women are made for pleasure . . . a spinning-wheel is a woman's weapon'. His adversary replied that she derived as much pleasure from reading as he did from hunting, drinking or gambling. 'Books destroy women's brains,' the abbot retorted briskly, causing the lady to bring forth the popular argument that in order to be an effective mother, a woman must have an education.[46]

These self-same arguments of medieval France and Renaissance Holland were to be heard in Scotland, but not until two centuries later. As far as it is possible to tell, the sixteenth-century Scotswoman did not question her role in life. That she would marry and bear children was an accepted fact, not a matter for controversy, and so it was only to be expected that she would be trained in the domestic arts rather than in logic and philosophy. As reading and writing became the necessary skills of her society, so would she learn to read and write. If she had an intelligent, questing mind, she would probably join in her brothers' arguments and read her father's books, but these activities have left no trace. However, although her education may have been sadly lacking by modern standards, it was no worse than that of many of the men she met and it certainly did not preclude her from engaging in activities which went beyond the strictly domestic.

Moreover, in her relationships with men, a woman was far from being a submissive, subservient creature forever at her husband's bidding. For their part, most men seem to have been willing enough to accept women as partners, albeit unequal ones, in the day-to-day business of life. One modern historian has detected a changed attitude towards the relationship between the sexes as early as the twelfth century.[47] That was the period when the cult of the Virgin saw its greatest popularity and along with the veneration of Christ's mother went a recognition that tenderness, compassion and the other gentler feminine qualities held a valued place in the world. A similar feeling was reflected in chivalry and the code of knightly warfare. Women who feature in the chronicles are usually described in a stylized way which emphasizes their virtue, sweetness and pleasant appearance. Knights defend the chastity of maidens and treat women with respect. Indeed, on one occasion Robert Bruce actually halted his army on the march to allow one of the women following his camp to give birth to a child.

Of course, women were no more idealized figures personifying the feminine virtues than they were downtrodden slaves of the men of their family. The flesh and blood females who married, bore children, defended castles, went to law, argued with neighbours and confronted their husbands, were real human beings with the idiosyncrasies and faults found at any period of history. Set in a society whose conventions were very different from our own, they nevertheless experienced the full range of human emotions and in their reactions and responses revealed themselves as being far removed from the passive, intimidated creatures some historians would have us believe that our female forebears were.

PART TWO

1560-1707:
WIVES
AND MOTHERS

CHAPTER THREE

Courtship
and Marriage

'LASSES MUST HAVE their own wills,' Patrick Smythe of
Braco commented wryly in the spring of 1657, when his sister
announced that she was utterly determined to marry the man of
her choice.[1] His remark would have startled anyone living in
medieval Scotland, where it was an accepted fact that parents
selected their children's marriage partners for them. The system
then had been relatively simple. Motivated by political or
territorial considerations, parents had met together and discussed
a settlement. The prospective bride and groom had usually known
each other from childhood and accepted the arrangements made
for them. If either felt a violent antipathy towards the other and
had sufficient resolution, he or she would hold out until the match
was abandoned. In most instances, however, parental authority
was not seriously challenged, and so child marriages or marriages
arranged on entirely practical grounds were considered as being in
no way untoward.

Now, however, the situation was much more complex, for
young men of the propertied classes were in general enjoying more
freedom. Sent off to university, then allowed to travel on the
continent, they spent their formative years outwith the immediate
sphere of family influence. It was inhibiting to live at home with a
dominating father overseeing every action: to travel around
abroad with an indulgent governor was altogether a different
matter. Moreover, the young man would probably spend some
time at Court on his return and there he would naturally join in the
flirtations and dalliance expected by the fashionable London ladies
he met. London had, by the seventeenth century, become the great
marriage market for the English peerage: there they competed for

heiresses, enjoying all manner of rivalry and romantic intrigue. The day when parents could hope to arrange their children's marriages quietly, with no reference to the young people themselves, had long since passed.[2]

Nevertheless, for most Scots there was no question of marrying in London. Only a very small proportion of the Scottish aristocracy took English brides, and the reason for this was not far to seek. An English girl of suitable background had a large dowry and her family would expect her husband to settle upon her much greater lands and revenues than most Scotsmen could afford. When the time came to marry, Scots therefore had to return home to seek a suitable wife. Often they were reluctant to do so, unwilling to relinquish their bachelor freedom, but sooner or later the prospect of a handsome dowry became too tempting to resist. Indeed, if there was an overlong delay, some older friend or relative would come along, urge the young man to marry and declare that he knew the very girl to make a suitable bride.[3]

Once set upon the search for a wife, the prospective bridegroom had definite criteria in mind. These were, to a large extent, strictly practical. The old considerations of political and territorial alliance were slow to die out, because in Scotland kinship remained an important factor until at least the beginning of the eighteenth century. A man looked to his relatives for support in Parliament, in his legal battles and in ordinary, day-to-day business. A connection with an influential family was still worth having and the matrimonial groupings of the aristocracy could, at times, appear positively menacing. In the 1620s, there was widespread alarm when it seemed as though the important house of Argyll would be linked through marriage to the even more powerful house of Hamilton. On a more modest scale, the Laird of Freuchie's friends felt they had to warn him that if he did not go through with his promised wedding to Lady Jane Fleming, he would alienate all her close relatives and make deadly enemies of the connected families of Roxburghe and Johnstone.[4]

Again, status remained an important consideration. 'It goes to my heart to see anything that has good blood misally themselves for a little money,' the Earl of Arran declared in 1696, when his uncle married a non-aristocratic girl, but the fact was that for most bridegrooms money was now what really mattered. Indeed, whenever a wedding was mentioned, it was not long before the bride's financial position entered the conversation. Soon after the

Earl of Eglinton's brother began showing an interest in the heiress of Lord Herries, a mutual friend was ready enough to admit, 'she is a very comely lady and a modest, about twenty-one years of age', but he then spent paragraphs assessing her tocher and the amount of lands her husband would have to settle on her. A few years later, Dame Juliana Ker bluntly condemned her son's choice of bride on the grounds that 'the tocher is very mean'. A similarly mercenary outlook was displayed by those husbands who were ready to overlook a woman's physical imperfections if she brought enough money: the young Earl of Cassillis married a forty-three-year-old widow much his senior but very rich.[5]

Not all were so insensitive, though, and there were signs that more humane considerations were gradually being taken into account. Some men, at least, were paying attention not only to the tochers but to the personal qualities of their brides. Probably with their own future happiness in mind, they would seek out a young woman of impeccable reputation. As Archibald, 8th Earl of Argyll, said in 1661, 'In the contracting of marriage, virtue is more to be considered than money,' though he did rather spoil the effect by adding that 'money is the sinew of love as well as war.'[6]

Modesty, a quiet manner and religious devotion all seemed to augur well for future domestic felicity. In a time of religious turmoil, piety was particularly valued by those of all shades of opinion, and so Lord Yester was in 1621 much encouraged to hear that a young lady of his acquaintance 'is turned a direct Puritan' and was 'so generally well spoken of for her carriage in everything' that he decided she was definitely worth pursuing. Feelings ran particularly high if any mixed marriage were contemplated and when the Earl of Airlie's mother heard in 1668 that he intended marrying a Catholic widow, she did everything she could, albeit unsuccessfully, to oppose the match.[7]

It was useful to have a wife who was a careful housekeeper. John Maxwell of Pollok's young sister was praised for her sensible education which would enable her to undertake 'the virtuous and frugal management of things'. Better still, she had many 'desirable accomplishments'. After all, a man wanted the mistress of his household to be presentable and, once introduced to a young lady, he could not but notice her appearance. Sometimes, this could be quite off-putting. Lord Lorne apparently neglected the 2nd Marquis of Hamilton's daughter because she was very dark and he preferred blondes, while Lord Archibald Hamilton was distinctly unimpressed by Lady Nairn's daughter. 'Her person is well enough,' he told his mother tepidly, 'considering the disadvantages of dress and want of seeing the world which she appears with.' Not surprisingly, he took the matter no further. Of course, not everyone was so particular and the 2nd Marquis of Tweeddale went stolidly ahead with his wedding to the powerful Duke of Lauderdale's only daughter in spite of the fact that, as one French wedding guest cruelly put it, 'she is very homely and like a monkey clothed with gold and silver.'[8]

So much for the negative aspect of appearance. Some men, on the other hand, threw caution to the winds when attracted by an unsuitable woman. There was Lord Balfour of Burleigh's son John, who insisted on marrying the daughter of Sir William Balfour of Pitcullo when he met and fell in love with her in spite of his father's wrath. Equally headstrong was Lord Broomhall's son Robert who, as a student at St Andrews University in 1663, eloped with Agnes Allan who worked in a tavern. George, 4th Earl of Winton, was similarly motivated by passion rather than good sense when he made an honest woman of Christian Hepburne, his mistress of four years' standing.[9]

Wealth, status, reputation and personal attraction: all were in a man's mind when he began a serious search for a wife, but how would his advances be received? Girls did not sit passively at home, waiting to be chosen by a suitor. Certainly, the day when an admirer arrived on the doorstep must have been an exciting one, but even the most sheltered young lady had definite ideas about the qualities her future husband should possess. Wealth and position were very important to her too, although few girls would have overlooked all other qualities as Lord Ogilvy's daughter Marion did when, at twenty-five, she married a man of eighty. Such was her power over Lord Coupar, her unfortunate partner, that she persuaded him to draw up a document leaving all his honours and estates to her and whoever she chose to marry once he was gone. When he did die soon afterwards, his family had the deed set aside but within three months the enterprising Marion was the wife of Lord Lindores.[10]

Her behaviour was exceptional, but to a lesser degree most girls did have in mind long-term security rather than romantic attraction or immediate financial reward. Ideally, they wished to marry a man of equal, if not superior, social standing and with money enough to give them what one father termed 'an easy life'.

The problem was that there were simply not enough well-placed young men available. Obviously in any generation there would be far more daughters of peers than there were heirs of peers for them to marry. The 11th Earl of Angus was doing exceptionally well when his first daughter became Lady Alexander, his second Lady Bargany, his fifth Countess of Annandale, his seventh Duchess of Queensberry, his eighth Duchess of Perth and his ninth Countess of Nithsdale. This was unusual, and many aristocratic girls had to content themselves with younger sons, baronets, soldiers, merchants and professional men.[11]

As a result, there was considerable social mobility and this in itself may have enhanced the already status-conscious attitude of the seventeenth-century peerage. There was always much criticism of the lady who married beneath herself, even though so many widows did this. The Dowager Countess of Mar, for example, deeply offended her mother by marrying a relative by marriage, Colonel Erskine. Her friend the Countess of Argyll had to come to the rescue, trying to persuade the old lady of the Colonel's worth. He was, she declared, 'one of the best-born gentlemen in Scotland, and one I lived long nearby, who never heard anything to his disadvantage'. On the contrary, the Colonel was 'well-beloved and well spoke of by all that was virtuous, and the which he really deserved, for he lived most unblameably and is a man frugal and civil, equal to his great birth, so I do not see it any disparagement to any lady to have married him'.[12]

Just as virtue was important for a man, so too did a woman look for an honourable husband. Mr John Carstares judged it wise to praise the Laird of Glanderston as being 'blameless in his visible deportment' when the latter went courting John Maxwell's sister, adding for good measure, 'I hope [he is] also religiously disposed, which is very valuable, especially at such a time when not many are so.' Religious persuasion probably weighed even more strongly with women than with men. Gabriela Stewart, the 2nd Duke of Lennox's sister, entered a nunnery rather than marry a non-Catholic and in 1661 Lady Elizabeth Kerr felt that the greatest merit of her own suitor, Colonel Nathaniel Rich, was his piety. Remarking that he was 'an alliance of my Lord Warwick's family', she went on to explain that 'what is more considerable to me is his nearer relation to the Lord.'[13]

Widows like the Countess of Mar often had other factors in mind. When Lady Mary Erskine, who had been the wife of the 6th

Earl Marischal, decided to marry Patrick, 1st Earl of Panmure, in 1638, she explained in the marriage contract, which she herself wrote out, that their design was 'without worldly ends and merely from a religious affection, whereby that they may live together to enjoy the company and conversation of each other'. Less fortunate in her choice was Lady Innermeath who, in the 1570s, cast discretion aside to marry as her second husband James, the son of Lord Gray. He was 'a young gentleman unlanded or provided of living' but she hoped 'that he should have maintained and defended and done the duty of a faithful husband to her in her age'. She was doomed to disappointment though, for she had to divorce him for adultery within a few years.[14]

Whatever the reasons underlying the choice of partner, the progress of the courtship was governed by certain conventions which had to be observed. There must be no premature commitment on either side and so no matter how eager the young woman or how ardent the suitor, they had to abide by the rules of etiquette. If the man had not met the girl before but had merely been told about her, he had to be particularly careful about how he proceeded. It would be embarrassing all round if it was generally known that he was thinking of wooing her so he would, if he were wise, proceed with caution. He might well decide to send an emissary to spy out the land for him and send back reports on the girl's appearance, manner and, of course, wealth. Sooner or later, though, he would want to see her for himself. When the young Laird of Bonnytoun heard about a promising heiress, her relatives arranged for him to have 'a short glance (but incognito)' at her. In a similar manner Anne, Duchess of Hamilton, urged her daughter Katherine to contrive a meeting between Katherine's brother Archibald and a likely young lady, but urged that they must see each other without anyone knowing why they did so. In that way, no-one's honour would be compromised.[15]

If the first meetings were a success, then the suitor proceeded further, paying calls and plying the lady with letters. When he did visit, he had to be careful to make a good impression. Isabel Gray pointed this out to her brother-in-law, John Clerk, in the mid-seventeenth century. Her nephew John should marry, she declared, and urged his father to send him to call on the Inglis of Cramond family who had an attractive daughter. 'If you think it convenient that he should go see that person,' she wrote, 'it is necessary that he have new clothes, for his clothes is very old and unhandsome to make visits to strangers upon such account.' This was all the more necessary where the Inglis family were concerned, for although 'grave in their apparel' they nevertheless 'love to see persons in good and honest clothes'.[16]

Men could go out visiting, but girls were not permitted to take the initiative. As the Earl of Morton explained in 1593 to his daughter's favoured suitor, he would make her play that part in the marriage arrangements 'which womanly modesty will permit', but he felt he must add, 'Ye know that it is a great disgrace for a gentlewoman to woo and then be disappointed.' In a similar vein, the Marchioness of Argyll in 1660 refused to allow her daughter to visit her fiancé who was ill and could not come to her, for that would have been 'such an imputation upon both her and all her interests'. A girl would be permitted to correspond with an admirer but must not give him too much encouragement while he, for his part, must not compromise her by being too ardent.[17]

Something of the delicate balance between enthusiasm and etiquette demanded by society can be seen in the Earl of Airlie's courtship of the widowed Mary, Marchioness of Huntly, in 1668. She was pursued by the Earl for several months in spite of his mother's disapproval, for this was the match made difficult by her Catholicism, a factor which did nothing to dampen her suitor's ardour. At first his addresses were well-received, but then he found himself under a cloud. Rumours had reached the Marchioness to the effect that he had been drinking in a tavern one day when a hair bracelet with a little ring on it had slipped from his arm. His companions were immediately full of curiosity and, so it was said, he boasted that both ring and bracelet had been presented to him by the Marchioness.

When she heard this, the lady was furious. The ring had certainly been hers, but, she reminded him sharply, he had snatched it from her maid. As for the hair, 'I disown it, for you was never so unreasonable as to desire such a thing and I swear, though you had, I would not have wronged modesty so far as to have granted it.' The Earl was dismayed and wrote back hastily to deny that he had ever uttered her name in public. His protestations were convincing, so she relented, but still forbade him to visit her. He could come as far north as Banff if he liked, but he was not to call on her in Elgin, for that would stir up all manner of unsavoury gossip.

The Earl was much cast down by this prohibition. She should not worry about rumours, he told her, for 'truly, my dearest, if ye

[69]

trouble with noises or reports that may pass, ye will never be at quiet and they will never give over talking until ye admit my visits with less ceremony.' The Marchioness saw the sense of this and allowed him to come, thus rendering him 'the happiest man alive'. He was by now signing his letters, 'My dearest dear, my dear Lady Marquis, Your Ladyship's most humble servant' while she had melted sufficiently to end hers, 'My dear lord, your lordship's most obedient, obliged, affectionate, faithful and most humble servant.' He plied her with letters, sent her honey and positively alarmed her by declaring that 'inevitable ruin' would attend him unless she altered the course of his stars by agreeing to marry him. This extravagant language earned him another rebuke, but his persistence was eventually rewarded for she married him the following year.[18]

A widow could do as she pleased, of course, but a young girl economically dependent on her family was not in such a favoured position, and when a courtship progressed to the point where an engagement seemed imminent, then the parents stepped in and took charge. In many instances, they had probably been influencing events already. Mothers, in particular, could apply all manner of pressure, subtle and otherwise. There was advice, cajolery and rebuke: a favoured candidate might be invited frequently to the house and his rivals discouraged. When Lord Montgomerie showed an interest in one of her daughters, Margaret, Countess of Wemyss, sang his praises on every possible occasion, having decided that he was 'not only a very witty man but one that has been all his life free from debauchery'. In the end her persuasions had no effect and her daughter married someone else, but that did not prevent the Countess from declaring at a later date that all another suitor's protestations of love would 'signify nothing except he gain my consent'.[19]

Parents no doubt believed that in directing events they were acting for the best. They had a healthy respect for the practical aspects of married life and they felt that if two suitable young people were brought together, love would surely follow. The Earl of Lothian certainly thought so, and when his Countess told him with satisfaction that their daughter seemed very happy with her new husband, he replied testily, 'It could hardly have been otherwise amongst honest, rational, discreet folk.' Try as they might to 'make the lass love the lad' as one mother put it, parents did not necessarily succeed. Even as opinionated a lady as the

Countess of Wemyss had to give way to the wishes of her daughters. Lord Montgomerie had been dismissed in spite of her efforts and although she declared roundly when Lord Northesk came to woo her daughter Margaret, 'I will not consent to let her marry anybody that appears to be an enemy both to the government of church and state,' it was not long before she was signing their marriage contract.[20]

The truth of the matter was that most parents were now prepared to take their children's wishes into account from the outset, and would have subscribed to the Duchess of Hamilton's view that unless 'parties themselves were satisfied, there ought to be no procedure by friends'.[21] By the mid-seventeenth century child marriages had become a thing of the past, finally abandoned by even the most mercenary in the face of public disapproval, and the selling of the marriage of heiresses was also extremely rare.

Of course, the reason why most negotiations did go smoothly was that the expectations of parents and children often coincided. The eligible young man and the available young woman were often as anxious as the parents were about long-term security, wealth and status. Girls from reasonably wealthy families still led sheltered lives and had simply no opportunity to meet unsuitable men with whom to fall romantically in love. Dependent upon their parents as they were they believed that they must submit to their families' wishes and were pleased to do so if an appropriate enough suitor presented himself. After all, everyone knew that unless parents were willing to be involved, there could be no marriage contract so no tocher, and few suitors were willing to persevere under those circumstances.

Even so, towards the end of the seventeenth century there were distinct signs that girls were thinking of the romantic rather than the practical aspects of marriage and that, if their parents would not give them freedom of choice, they would take it for themselves. Some, like Lilias Colquhoun, did so within the accepted conventions of courtship. When she was twenty-one Lilias was wooed by two widowers. One, the Laird of Buchanan, was positively venerable although he made up in enthusiasm for what he lacked in youth. The other, Sir John Stirling of Keir, was a handsome man in the prime of life. Lilias's family permitted both to call on her but from the start she declared her 'positive aversion' to the Laird and eventually sent him about his business so that she could marry Sir John.[22]

Equally set on having her own way was the Earl of Moray's only daughter in the 1640s. She fell in love with the 7th Laird of Freuchie, James Grant, only to meet with her father's determined opposition. When the old man died, her brother was equally adamant. However, Mary was prepared to wait for her opportunity. Having assured her brother that she had given up all thoughts of the Laird, she saw him off on a trip to England and promptly arranged her wedding. Her story ended happily for she was eventually reconciled with her brother, who agreed to hand over her tocher to the Laird.[23]

Some secret weddings were obviously at the instigation of adventurers. Ingenuous heiresses were an easy prey for unscrupulous men, and in 1671 James Somerville of Drum was prosecuted for contracting a marriage with Elizabeth Grahame, the only child of a wealthy Edinburgh merchant. She was just twelve years old but she had been allowed to go to the dancing school, and there James 'did insinuate himself in her favour' and eventually proposed to her. An illegal marriage was conducted by a notary and Elizabeth's irate father arrived to find the couple in bed together. He brought a legal action against them, as a result of which they were sentenced to imprisonment in the Edinburgh tolbooth and a fine of five hundred pounds.[24]

Other elopements were simply the outcome of mutual attraction. Sophia Clerk, for instance, ran off with Gabriel Rankin, a merchant, in 1702. Her father had opposed the match on the grounds that Rankin was poor and quite unsuitable for his daughter. Possibly in the hope of extracting the tocher from Sir John, Gabriel later wrote him an apologetic letter confessing that he was 'far inferior to what your daughter might have expected' and suggesting that he should call on him. Not in the least mollified, Sophia's father sent back word that he was not at home. Sophia then tried to add her persuasions, and in her deplorable writing with many a blot, composed a letter declaring, 'I can never expect you will be reconciled to me, only I beg that at any time you reflect on my neglect of duty to you, that you would forgive me.' Her pleas brought forth a stern reply in which Sir John told her that 'for the good of your sisters and brethren and for the advantage of all other men's bairns' she must be punished for 'such a complicated wickedness as you committed by your lewdness and disobedience, by your inordinate love to sensuality and implacable hatred of God and his ways, by your contempt of your father and your breach of promises and oaths'. In spite of these strong words he did relent in the end and it was to him that Sophia turned when she had her many spectacular quarrels with Gabriel in the years which followed.[25]

Finally, it was not only young, unmarried women who eloped. Occasionally a widow of mature years would arrange a secret marriage to avoid the public disapproval of her unsympathetic family and friends. The Countess of Wemyss did not elope when, in middle-age, she took as her second husband Viscount Tarbat, but she did have a very quiet wedding. Her daughter Margaret, Countess of Northesk, explained that 'there was nobody to see her married but her servants, to be witnesses, for she would desire none of her children, because she knew none of us was very well pleased with her marriage.' In similar manner, the twice-married Mary, Countess of Callandar, in 1703 planned a very quiet wedding to the Earl of Findlater. At first she had resisted his advances, explaining to him, 'I am fitter for my grave than to be a bride,' but in the end she succumbed and wrote to tell him that he must hire a hackney coach 'as if you were going to take the air', with his local minister accompanying him. She would meet him at Morton, outside Edinburgh, 'and I would presently take with you that same night in the hackney, so that you would not be much missed out of town.' He must tell no one of all this, she added, 'no, not your darling son'.[26]

By the end of the seventeenth century, elopements were still unusual, but the general aspect of marriage negotiations had changed irrevocably. The old political and territorial consider-ations had been superseded by the purely mercenary, and although the final settlement was as practical and as important as it had always been, it followed upon a period of courtship which had all the elements of a fashionable game. Men of the world joked about their wooing as though it were a military campaign. The Master of Yester 'still lays close siege' to the Countess of Dundonald, a friend reported in 1699, and a year later the Earl of Ruglen took lodgings close by those of the lady he was pursuing and announced that he had made himself 'master of all the advantageous posts in order to advance the siege'. Elusive bachelors were well aware of the manoeuvrings of ambitious mothers, and in 1704 the Duke of Hamilton felt it needful to warn his less experienced nephew against 'the craft of the persons concerned and the general assistance that's given to catch a young man like you'. By 1708 it could even be said of the same nephew that 'all the young women in this country are in town and courting him', a very different state of affairs from the day when young ladies did not do the wooing.[27]

All this was indeed a far cry from the carefully controlled arrangements of former times. Of course, the new ritual of selection was applied in only a small section of society at first. Poorer people who had no property to worry about had always been much more at liberty to marry whom they pleased, and they continued to do so. Again, some wealthy parents clung to old ways and tried to insist on determining the future of their children. For the most part, though, the aristocracy were adopting the new mode of behaviour and where they led, the middle class with their lively social aspirations would soon follow. Gradually, more and more people took to the latest ways and the attitude towards choice underwent a transformation.

It is difficult to assess what caused this shift in outlook in the seventeenth century. It has been argued that the Reformation brought about a new concern for the individual and a recognition of personal preference which had not hitherto existed.[28] However, it may be that the Reformation was not a great watershed in this respect but that it drew attention to alterations already under way. The motives of seventeenth-century people are revealed to us in their correspondence, but for the Middle Ages we have no such source. It may well be that young men and women always did try to influence their own futures; that those who succeeded in doing so have gone unrecorded and that we are left only with mentions of those who reacted violently to the plans of those around them. The recognition of individual preference might have been the result of continued pressure on parents over a long period of time, rather than a sudden shift of outlook which accompanied the changes in ecclesiastical affairs. Undoubtedly the formalities of courtship were new, and derived from the adoption of English fashions, but this was a relatively superficial alteration to manners rather than a radical revolution in attitudes and outlook.

Whatever the difference in the preliminaries of marriage, the practical arrangements altered but little. Although the Reformers were anxious to place less emphasis on the betrothal and successfully put an end to marriages *per verba de futuro*, they had no quarrel with the marriage contract, which by now had assumed a settled form. Most contracts began with the promise that the couple would marry, and for a time this clause continued to specify the date by which the ceremony should take place. In 1562, for instance, Margaret Borthwick in Greenlaw was promising to marry John Thomson by midsummer; four years later John Winning the merchant agreed to take Isabel Tennant as his wife within fifteen days, while in the following decade William Edgar, burgess in Dumfries, and Katherine Clerk, an Edinburgh burgess's daughter, were to marry before Michaelmas.[29] The date was legally supposed to be part of the contract, and if the day came and went without the ceremony taking place, one party could complain before a judge that the other was refusing to fulfil the agreement. The judge would then order the marriage to be solemnised within a certain period of time, imposing a fine for the delay.[30] Even so, as time went on it became customary to leave blank the date by which the wedding must be accomplished and relatively few seventeenth-century marriage contracts do stipulate it.

After the promise to marry came the provisions to be made by the husband and his parents for the wife. Usually the bride and groom were put in joint possession of a piece of land which in Scotland was termed the conjunct fee. The English term was jointure lands, the revenue being known as the jointure and this more manageable term will be used in the forthcoming discussion. During her husband's lifetime, the wife did not directly enjoy any revenues from the jointure lands, but the husband used the income to support her and their children. Upon his death, the wife drew a fixed annuity, the jointure, from the lands for her maintenance. This was a version of the terce of former times, a more modern arrangement than the old gift at the church door.[31]

The relationship between the size of the jointure and the tocher was the principal point at issue when any marriage contract was being negotiated. By law, if the jointure was agreed before the tocher was paid, it could exceed it. If it was not arranged until after the payment, the jointure had to be less. In fact, no-one would have considered making the jointure larger than the tocher. A large jointure meant that the bride's parents had been anxious about her welfare and had managed to negotiate favourable terms. A small jointure indicated that the groom's parents were dictating the terms. In sixteenth and seventeenth-century England, there was a distinct movement in favour of the groom. An average English jointure of the 1560s was a fifth of the bride's dowry but by 1700 it had fallen to between an eighth and a tenth. In Scotland, the change seems to have been more gradual. Few actual figures are available, because although the jointure lands are usually listed in contracts, their value is not. However, as late as 1686 the Earl of Panmure promised his bride, Lady Margaret Hamilton, a jointure which was a third of her tocher. Lady Helen Arbuthnott in 1698 was to receive a jointure to the value of a fifth of her tocher if her husband, John Macfarlane of that Ilk, died before her, while the Countess of Wemyss in 1696 declared that she would think a jointure which was a sixth of her daughter's tocher was perfectly acceptable.[32]

Of course, this should not be taken to mean that all contracts in Scotland favoured wives more than English settlements did. In the examples cited, the brides were all of greater social standing than their grooms. However, it can be safely inferred that, whatever the general trend, it was still possible for influential fathers to demand that generous provision be made for their daughters. Indeed, some unfortunate men felt sorely burdened by the necessity to provide for the widows of the family. William Baillie of Lamington considered himself to be particularly unlucky in 1670. Not only did his widowed mother draw a jointure of 5000 merks a year from his estates, but his grandmother's jointure was twice that amount. As a result, he was left with a mere 4000 merks a year for himself and in desperation went to the Privy Council to beg for some new arrangement to be made. The Council proved sympathetic, and his grandmother was ordered to pay him a quantity of victual each year and make over to him one of her coal mines.[33]

Incidentally, it is interesting to note that payment of jointures in victual rather than in money persisted for a long time in Scotland, where payments of rent in kind also lingered on. The jointure provided for Elizabeth, daughter of Sir James Dundas, should her husband Sir Patrick Murray of Langshaw die, was to be thirty-nine bolls of oats, thirteen bolls of bere (barley), a good and sufficient ox, the carriage of twelve consignments of goods over a long distance and thirty-six loads over a short distance, four dozen kain fowl and an annuity from the lands of Langshaw. Even as late as 1696, the Countess of Wemyss was prepared to have either an annuity of six thousand merks or seventy chalders of victual written into her daughter's marriage contract. Payment in kind, of course, had the obvious advantage that it would be unaffected by inflation, and that was an important consideration in the seventeenth century when money was falling in value.[34]

Any family really concerned for a daughter's welfare would likewise ensure that she would have accommodation if she were widowed or, as Janet Ryle's contract in 1578 rather charmingly put it, 'an house to sit in'. Throughout the period, there occur such references. In 1648, the Earl of Haddington undertook to build for his bride a 'commodious hall and chambers' with kitchen and outhouses, all suitably slated, since there was no dower house for her. Robert Hamilton of Silvertonhill in 1650 bound himself to repair a house for his wife and in 1686 the Earl of Panmure promised his bride his castle of Brechin should he die. Not everyone could afford to settle a specific jointure on his wife, however, and if none were set aside, then a widow would have the usual third of her husband's property when he died.[35]

Even if a jointure was not allocated in a marriage contract, a tocher always was. With the wider competition among young men for wealthy brides, it was in a girl's best interests to have as high a tocher as her family could afford to give her. The sums provided were steadily increasing. Usually, they were expressed in Scottish merks, a merk being two thirds of a pound Scots. By the seventeenth century, a pound Scots was worth a twelfth of a pound sterling, but in any event Scottish tochers were always smaller than English dowries. The disparity between the two countries was not so very great before 1600 but in the seventeenth century English dowries rose rapidly with the growth of London as a marriage market. Eligible young men flocked to the city in pursuit of heiresses and dowries rose accordingly. In Scotland there was not yet a centralised marriage market and there was, in any case, less money available.

The highest tochers of all were paid with great heiresses like Lady Elizabeth Maxwell, daughter of the Earl of Dirleton. In 1639 her tocher was an astonishing 288,000 merks.[36] This was because her father was an extremely wealthy man, recently elevated and eager to attract a member of the old, established aristocracy as a husband for her. Very occasionally, a large tocher was compensation for a physical defect, but more often a handsome sum could be taken as an indication of a father's affection for his daughter. Until the early seventeenth century they were not always paid in cash. Unusual arrangements lingered on in the late sixteenth century and when Margaret Johnson married John Thomson of

Bathgate in 1571, it was agreed that her father, a weaver, would not only give with her half his goods, but would instruct John in all the points of his craft. Two years later Janet Penny, an Edinburgh girl, took with her on marriage twenty merks, 'a sufficient garment of honest clothing' and as much of the furniture of her parents' house as they could spare. Even as late as 1593, Charles McAllaster of Tarbet gave with his daughter a tocher of 150,000 merks and forty 'great kye' [*i.e.* cows]. By the early seventeenth century, though, such variations had died out and the tocher was almost invariably expressed in money. It was normally payable in two instalments, with a monetary penalty for any delay.[37]

Once paid, the tocher might be put to various uses. Quite often the husband added it to his own resources and bought the lands which would form the jointure. This was the arrangement made by those in poorer circumstances. John Winning in 1566 promised to put his bride's tocher to this use, as did Valentine Beldam, a servant in Hamilton Palace in 1655, and John Norris, a baker in Perth in 1699. Some fathers, on the other hand, notably in the peerage, regarded the tocher as their own property and refused to let their sons have it. The 3rd Duke of Hamilton left no-one in any doubt about his intentions. He had three daughters to marry off and he fully expected to pay their tochers from the money brought in by his sons' wives. Upbraiding his heir for failing to marry, he told him, 'Before long your sister Susan will be married, which brings payments of tochers fast upon me and which should be your part by bringing in a good portion rather than being a charge to me.'[38]

If a large tocher may be interpreted as a sign of parental concern for a daughter, so too could an entirely new set of provisions. These appeared in a clause which made special arrangements for any daughters born of the marriage, should there be no sons. The reason for this was that if a man had only girls, he was liable to marry again and have a son by this second union. If that happened, all his property would pass to the boy and the daughters of the first marriage would be left without provision. Some fathers avoided this by making special bonds of provision, entitling their daughters to a certain sum of money when they reached a specific age, and now provisions like this were being written into the actual marriage contract. The custom was well-established in England by the 1640s. In Scotland the earliest example noted so far is contained in the contract of Archibald, Earl of Angus, and Lady Anna Stewart, sister of the influential James, Duke of Lennox. The arrangements were made at Whitehall in the summer of 1628 under the personal supervision of Charles I and it was agreed that 'suitable provision' was to be made should only daughters be born to Lady Anne. No sums were specified, but when the time came they would be agreed by Lennox, Angus and three other Scottish earls.[39]

This was obviously in direct imitation of the English model and, within ten years, Scottish contracts were making detailed arrangements of the kind usual in the south.[40]

If the bride's family was influential they often insisted that the tocher provided for an only daughter should be more than that given with the bride herself. When the Earl of Haddington married in 1648, the sum of 40,000 merks was promised for an only daughter of the union and that was double his own bride's tocher.[41] Larger provisions were obviously a wise step during a period of inflation, yet many families held to the belief that the only daughter's tocher ought to equal but not exceed that of her mother: the marriage contract of Lady Marion Cunningham in 1652 reveals that her tocher and that of an only daughter were each £10,000 Scots. Indeed when Margaret, Countess of Wemyss, was arranging her daughter's marriage she commented, 'And for children's portions, the ordinary rule is the mother's portion if but one daughter, and if there be two or more, so much more money as shall be agreed upon by friends.'[42]

The promise to marry, the jointure, the tocher and the provision for daughters: these were the principal features of any marriage contract. Occasionally there were one or two additional clauses designed to deal with special circumstances. If an heiress to an old family were marrying, arrangements for her son to carry on her family name and arms were sometimes included, as in the contracts of Anne, Duchess of Hamilton, in 1656 and Lady Henrietta Lindsay in 1691. Lady Henrietta's also contained an unusual clause stating that even if either party should die childless within a year and a day of the marriage, the widow should retain the terce or the widower the tocher, contrary to the legal provisions of the time. Some contracts safeguarded a bride's right to her own jewels and it was quite often agreed that the widow should receive half of the husband's belongings instead of the customary third, whether or not there were children of the marriage.[43]

The basic provisions of the marriage contract were found in

agreements made at all levels of society where property was involved. Farmers, weavers, bakers, dyers, millers and servants all made marriage contracts which, on a reduced scale, followed the pattern set by the peerage, and although their resources might be smaller, just as much careful thought went into their settlements. In 1677, for example, Margaret Muir, daughter of a Lanarkshire weaver, was engaged to Adam Muir at Corsfoordbait and her father provided as her tocher not money, but four rigs of farmland, reserving an annuity from the lands for himself. More elaborate was the settlement of William Low, a dyer in the small Perthshire burgh of Dunkeld in 1686. He was marrying Janet Morgan, daughter of a notary who by then had died. Janet brought with her a tocher of 1000 merks and in return William promised to buy lands worth 2000 merks a year for them to live on. This would provide the jointure, and if Janet were widowed, she would have the 2000 merks annually as well as her third of the household plenishing. Provision was also made for any daughters of the marriage. An only girl would have 1000 merks and, if more than one were born, the sum of 12,000 merks would be divided amongst them. Further, there was the unusual stipulation that if Janet were to die childless within three years, the tocher would revert to her sister Agnes.[44]

Marriage contracts were therefore far from being the prerogative of the aristocracy, but when two propertied families were embarking on a marriage alliance the term 'negotiations' aptly described the complicated financial discussions which followed. Lawyers were called in, calculations made and lengthy debates took place between leading members of both parties. 'I doubt not Your Lordship will make the best bargain you can for your niece,' said the Countess of Wemyss to her brother-in-law in 1696, when her daughter Margaret was about to marry the Earl of Northesk, and that was exactly how a settlement was regarded. Just as courtship had become 'a siege' in polite society conversation, so had the marriage negotiations become a battleground of financial bargaining. Sometimes discussion broke down entirely and the marriage foundered: on other occasions, friendly intervention saved the day and the match was accomplished. The Earl of Panmure actually ended negotiations with the Hamilton family and sent back the marriage token, but he and Lady Margaret Hamilton were genuinely in love and their wedding did take place after further talks.[45]

When the terms were agreed, marriage articles were drawn up and these were later extended into a contract. This could be a mere one-page sheet signed by both parties and witnessed or, in the case of the aristocracy, it could be a scroll fifteen feet long, made of pages fastened together at top and bottom, with signatures along the side as well as at the foot. The actual signing of this document continued to be something of an occasion, with family and friends gathering to see the couple put their names to the agreement. At one house a whole hogshead of wine was drunk at the signing but on another occasion the atmosphere was romantic rather than alcoholic. When the widowed Countess of Wemyss succumbed to the persuasions of the elderly widower, Viscount Tarbat, in spite of her family's disapproval, her son-in-law the Earl of Leven attended the signing of the contract and later told his Countess, 'Tarbat signed first, as is usual, and when he gave her the pen he kissed it, and after she had done, he kissed her hands and her mouth.' It is possible that so many evidences of affection were not the normal accompaniment to the signing, for Tarbat's letters show him to have been besotted with the Countess.[46]

Once the contract had been signed, the wedding itself followed soon afterwards. The Reformation had, of course, brought about various changes of procedure. There was no longer any question of seeking a papal dispensation if the couple were within the forbidden degrees, and the prohibitions upon relatives marrying had been greatly relaxed. Assuming that the couple were not first cousins or similarly close to each other and that the groom was at least fourteen and the bride twelve, the couple could go ahead and have their banns called, still a vital preliminary step. The minister made the proclamation during the normal service on three consecutive Sundays. He charged a small fee for doing so, and the marriage could take place the day after the third proclamation had been made, if so desired. Meanwhile, preparations for the rejoicings went ahead. In a wealthy family, these could occupy several weeks, as cattle on the estate were slaughtered, bread was baked in huge quantities and special supplies of wine, tobacco and sweetmeats were brought out from the nearest large town. Additional servants were often hired for the occasion, as well as extra wine glasses and cutlery being brought in.[47]

While the food was being gathered, there was also the bride's trousseau to worry about. Details of wedding dresses and other garments are not easy to find, but the bride's wardrobe was a matter of much concern and she would expect to take with her at least enough clothes to see her through the rest of the year. When the chamberlain of Kinneil married off his daughter in 1604, he saw that she had two new gowns, one of taffeta and one of silk, a hood, a velvet nightbonnet decorated with gold lace, a riding skirt and a cloak. In 1670, Isobel Maitland's 'marriage clothes' included a grey silk negligée, while Sir John Clerk in 1699 presented his daughter Barbara with 'a rich brocade gown' which had belonged to her mother and four hundred pounds Scots which she spent on 'a new gown and other things necessary for my wedding clothes'. On an even grander scale, when the 3rd Duke of Hamilton's daughters married in the 1680s, their trousseaux included not only several new gowns each but petticoats, hoods, embroidered sleeves, silk stockings, shoes, caps, a muff, boxwood and tortoiseshell combs, a powder-box and necklaces.[48]

Not only the bride but the bridegroom viewed the trousseau with intense interest, seeing in it a reflection not simply of his future wife's wealth but of his own status. An inadequate set of clothing or marriage feast would be taken as an unforgivable insult. Sir John Maxwell of Pollok certainly never recovered from his indignation when he saw his bride insufficiently furnished, as one of his later letters to his father-in-law in 1583 plainly reveals. Furious because the old gentleman had neglected to come to his son's christening, he took the opportunity of adding, 'In case of your disremembrance, something I must further write, which I will never forget', and angrily recalled 'in what equipage your daughter, my wife, was in, the time of her marriage and banquet'. The arrangements had been 'not as became your daughter nor my wife' and, what was worse, they did not compare with the provisions made for her young sisters who had since been marrried.[49]

While the bride's family worried about food and clothing, the guests also equipped themselves with new outfits and gave their minds to selecting a present for the bride. In 1693 Margaret Hope listed the wedding gifts she received when she married Patrick Scott of Rossie. Close friends and relations gave her diamond rings, brooches and silver plate. On a more practical note, her mother and sister presented her with bedding, five stones of wool and sixty sheep. The Earl of Southesk provided not only a large silver dish, but sent a cow with a calf, a flock of geese, ducks, turkeys and some pheasants. The Earl of Northesk gave her a horse and Sir James Wemyss, her uncle, sent a load of coal. On a more delicate note, her bridegroom presented her with a gold watch, three gold seals, three diamond rings, a pretty pocket glass, five guinea pieces, a sable tippet, a fine paste necklace, a mirror and a pair of gold buttons.[50]

Whatever the complications, sooner or later the wedding day arrived and the bride was arrayed in her best new dress, usually a garment of white or silver-coloured satin. This was in no special style and would be worn on future occasions. On her leg went a fancy garter and, by the early eighteenth century, a muslin apron was tied round her waist. Thus arrayed, she walked in procession to the church with family and friends. She had her own special attendants for the occasion, and in 1703 there is a mention of the Duke of Atholl's small daughter preparing to act as 'bridesmaid' at a cousin's wedding. Since the celebrating had often begun before the ceremony, the procession was not always the orderly affair it might have been. In 1639, in the small seaport of Dysart, an unseemly squabble broke out between Mrs Margaret Corson and Helen Tailor 'going to kirk with a bride', as a result of which Mrs Corson found herself in court next day, charged with putting violent hands on Helen and tearing her cap.[51]

Once the bridal party arrived at the church, they took part in a service which had been considerably changed by the Reformation. No longer was marriage a sacrament and no longer were the vows exchanged at the church door with the priest simply there to give the blessing. Now the ceremony took place inside the church itself, before the whole congregation, and the participation of the minister was a necessary element. Indeed, there was a set wedding service laid down in the Book of Common Order which followed the service used by the English congregation at Geneva in 1556. It began with the minister making an exhortation. This opened with the familiar words, 'Dearly beloved brethren, we are here gathered together in the sight of God and in the face of His congregation, to knit and join these parties together in the honourable estate of matrimony.' The ensuing words rehearsed how God, wishing to provide Adam with a helper, had fashioned Eve from his rib, thereby giving us to understand 'that man and wife are one body, one flesh and one blood'. The minister then went on to point out that it was the wife's duty 'to study to please and obey her husband, serving him in all things that be godly and honest'. This must be done because 'she is in subjection and under governance of her husband, so long as they both continue alive.' For his part, the husband was reminded that he had no power or right over his

[83]

own body without his wife, for God had knitted the two of them together 'in this mutual society' for the procreation and upbringing of children.

After a short homily on the evils of fornication, the minister asked first the couple and then those others present if they knew of any impediment to the union. If no-one spoke, he proceeded to instruct the man to protest before God and His holy congregation that he was content to take the woman for his 'lawful wife and spouse, promising to keep her, to love and treat her in all things according to the duty of a faithful husband, forsaking all other during her life and, briefly, to live in holy conversation with her, keeping faith and truth in all points . . .' The bridegroom responded with the words, 'Even so, I take her before God and in presence of His congregation.' The bride was then asked to take the man as her husband, 'promising to him subjection and obedience, forsaking all other during his life'. She replied in words similar to those used by the groom, whereupon the minister urged them to live chastely. Psalm 128, 'Blessed are they that fear the Lord', was sung, and after a benediction from the minister, the congregation was free to set off for the bride's home, where the wedding feast would be held.[52]

Ideally, the Reformers would have liked weddings to take place at the ordinary Sunday service, immediately before the sermon, but they were aware that the celebrations which followed would scarcely have been appropriate to the Lord's Day. Weddings therefore continued to take place on weekdays, usually on a Tuesday or Thursday, and sometimes in the evening after the day's work was done. Occasionally, members of the aristocracy held the actual service in their own home rather than in church, but whatever the section of society, a wedding was celebrated with feasting, drinking and dancing to the music of pipers, fiddlers and violers.[53]

As soon as the feast began, the bride's favours had to be distributed. These were bunches of ribbons, sewn loosely to her dress, and all the guests rushed up to try to snatch one. Old Miss Mure, recalling in later years the wedding of Sir Hew Dalrymple's daughter Anne to Sir James Steuart of Goodtries on 9 March 1705, remembered that the bride's favours 'was all sewed on her gown from top to bottom and round the neck and sleeves. The moment the ceremony was performed, the whole company ran to her and pulled off the favours: in an instant she was stripped of all of them.'

[84]

Further romping followed, when the bridegroom's man had to try to take the bride's garter, 'but she dropped it through her petticoat on the floor'. It consisted of a white and silver ribbon and was eagerly seized and cut up into tiny pieces so that they too could be given out as keepsakes. Once this had been done, Lady Dalrymple, the bride's mother, came in bearing a basket of flowers for the bride and groom. Anne's were pink and white while Sir James's were blue and yellow, to match the liveries of the two families. Everyone then sat down to supper, after which there was a ball. The celebrations went on in this way for a week or more, further balls being held at the homes of relatives.[54]

Poor families could not, of course, celebrate on such a grand scale but they nevertheless had several days of feasting and drinking. The guests would bring their own provisions with them, or money to buy food and drink, so the name 'penny weddings' was given to such celebrations. These were well-established by the 1660s and even the fulminations of church and state could not stamp them out. Disapproving of the rowdiness they caused, Parliament went so far as to pass an act in 1681 limiting the number of guests who could attend penny weddings, baptisms and burials, and forbidding bride and groom to change their clothes more than twice during the jollifications. Although this act was reiterated by local courts, it seems to have had no effect whatsoever, except that people were now fined in larger numbers for contravening it.[55]

The term 'honeymoon' was certainly known in Scotland by 1702, when the old Duchess of Hamilton wrote of her son's quarrels with his wife of four years, 'I fear honey month is over,' but there was no question of a couple going on holiday together after the wedding.[56] The wedding night was usually spent in the home of the bride's parents, and it was scarcely a private occasion. The public bedding of the young couple was a necessary part of the entertainment and even by the early years of the eighteenth century, family and friends took a close interest in this part of the nuptials. When a daughter of the Atholl family was married, Lady Nairn told the Countess of Panmure, 'My lord says the new bride is the bashfullest thing can be seen, and the bridegroom no less respectful now than when a lover, for they never speak nor look to one another.' They were late in retiring on the wedding night, and 'next morning, when My Lady Atholl came in to the room, though it was but six o'clock, she found the bridegroom walking softly up and down the room in his nightgown, and mighty careful he was that the bride should not be awakened, and for aught I know, this was his employment all night long, for fear of disturbing the young lady's repose.' Lady Nairn's husband was not impressed, and noted with annoyance that 'they omitted to make the bride give testimony how she liked his behaviour . . . for that part of the ceremony was quite forgot.'[57]

For the sensitive, a wedding could obviously be something of an ordeal, but, sooner or later, one final ceremony was all that remained to be done. This was the 'infare' or homecoming. If the young couple were setting up house in their own establishment, they went there accompanied by the wedding guests and gave the first feast in their new home. This was usually a lavish affair. In 1656 Lord Balgonie was reputed to have spent 24,000 merks Scots on his homecoming, and the Act of Parliament of 1681 had included in its strictures a clause limiting the number of those permitted to attend. Food was plentiful, wine and ale flowed, and it was well into the night before the last guest finally took his departure.[58]

CHAPTER FOUR

Harmony
and Discord

A WIFE 'is in subjection and under governance of her husband, so long as they both continue alive', said the marriage service of the 1560s, and the legal provisions of the time appear to have echoed this restrictive attitude. 'The wife is entirely under the power and subjection of her husband,' was how Sir James Balfour, the eminent Scottish judge, had put it when he compiled his celebrated work on law some ten years earlier, and again, 'The husband is principal and head over his wife.' As it affected the status of women, the law had remained largely unchanged since the Middle Ages. A wife's property was still administered by her husband. He chose where she was to stay and without his consent she could not raise a court action, act as a cautioner or dispose of her goods. As one modern authority has said, 'On marriage, the husband acquired power over the person of his wife, who was considered to have no legal *persona*. As ruler of the house, he had control of her person and conduct, including the assigning of a place of residence.'[1]

Passages such as these give an undeniably gloomy impression of the role of women in Scotland in the sixteenth and seventeenth centuries. Yet were they really so subservient? Portraits of the period show us married couples standing side by side in apparently contented partnership. The pose of the wife never betokens servitude, submission or even respectful veneration. Far from revealing to us a series of poor, downtrodden creatures, these painted records of the past depict self-possessed women of character. This being so, how may we reconcile the two disparate views suggested by the legal records and the material objects? Were the pictures portraying marital amity painted to flatter and conceal, or do the legal texts give a misleadingly harsh impression of life in a former age? Fortunately, the sources for the study of sixteenth and seventeenth-century Scotland are much more plentiful than they are for the medieval period, so that for the first time we may assess directly the quality of the relationship between husband and wife.

Material evidence suggests that wives were not treated as mere ciphers. Lintel stones and carved wooden furniture of the period frequently bear the intitials of both man and wife, as do pieces of silver. Tablecloths and napkins similarly record the identities of both, and so do the designs on bed-curtains and wall-hangings. We know this not only from the surviving objects themselves, but from the documentary evidence. The will of Mr Robert Crichton, an Edinburgh lawyer, reveals that in 1582 he had in his possession a large silver mazer [cup], a silver salt and six silver spoons engraved with the coat of arms and initials of himself and his wife, Isabel Borthwick.[2]

Apart from their lists of goods, the testaments bear witness in other ways to the relationship between men and women. Mr Crichton made Isabel his executor, and wives were frequently nominated to perform this function. He himself did so, he said, because she 'has been to me an honest, loving wife, chaste in her person and one that fears God'. Alexander, Lord Forbes, took the opportunity of paying an even longer tribute to his second wife when he made his will in 1672. 'I have had a most sweet bedfellow and companion of her in every turn of fortune for these forty-six years,' he said. The mother of thirteen children, seven of whom were by that time dead, she had been renowned for her piety, patience, charity and modesty, not to mention her 'scarcely imitable' conjugal fidelity, love and obedience. 'She was the solace and comfort of my youth and I have found by experience that she is the most careful nurse of my old age,' he continued. 'God gave her to me for the comfort of my life and pleasure in affliction. I chose her myself, neither do I repent it, but render infinite thanks to God Almighty for giving me such a consort and companion, who could sweeten all the adversities and bitters of fortune.'[3]

The most vivid illumination of the marital relationship, of course, is to be found in letters between husband and wife. Before 1600, the private letters which have come down to us remain tantalisingly scattered and brief, but they do provide an occasional insight into the domestic life of a famous man. Sir Thomas Ker of Ferniehirst was one of the most powerful and trusted supporters of

Mary, Queen of Scots, yet it seems that even he relied upon his wife's support and assistance. He was twice married, the second Lady Ker being Sir William Scott of Kirkurd's daughter, Janet. By her, he had three sons and a daughter, and in 1583 she was plainly active in his interests outwith the purely domestic scene. Not for the first time, Sir Thomas had been forced to flee from Scotland because of his support of Mary, but Lady Ker remained behind and in September 1583 she was able to give him good news. Addressing him fondly as 'my heart', she wrote to tell him that she had at last heard that he might return to Court. In part as a result of her own efforts, the King was granting him a pardon, so she urged him to come home at once. She ended her letter with that engaging mixture of formality and intimacy which so characterized her time, 'Your humble and faithful bedfellow till death'.[4]

The modern reader is, naturally, struck by the unfamiliar wording of such letters, particularly in the salutation and valediction. The difference, though, is in phraseology and convention rather than in underlying feelings, for affection, jealousy and all the other sentiments one would expect to find within the marital relationship are clearly displayed. When Mr James Hume had to be away from Mrs Hume in 1600, he was obviously nervous of his wife's reaction. Writing her a note, he began, 'My heart, for God's sake forgive me, for I have offended in keeping so long from you, but truly, it is against my will.' What had happened was that 'the Laird of Innerwick continually has had me with him, sometimes shooting and otherwise playing at cards and sometimes riding horse.' As the Laird was none too well, Mr Hume dared not cross him by coming away, but he assured his wife with fervour that he thought of her 'every hour and day' and, for good measure, added a postscript begging her, 'My heart, treat yourself well and be not crabbit [i.e. bad-tempered] at my long tarrying . . . Your heart, Mr James Hume.'[5]

Not all wives were meek and dutiful and not every woman who signed herself 'your obedient spouse till death' really meant it. Dame Juliana Ker, red-haired and quick-tempered, was perfectly prepared to stand up to her second husband Lord Binning, who undoubtedly found her neither humble nor submissive. Himself married twice before, he was by then a man of fifty, an astute statesman and lawyer who later became Earl of Haddington and had already amassed a considerable fortune. However much deference and respect he commanded in public, though, the volatile Juliana was not so easily overawed. When he had the temerity to depart for London in 1613, a few months after their marriage, she plied him with letters rebuking him for his neglect. He was far too fond of travelling, she told him, thereby endangering himself 'so rashly, whenever ye have occasion, both upon the sea and in the waters, to my great grief and miscontentment'. Breaking off a stream of reproaches to give a spirited account of her latest quarrel with a local minister, she took up her original theme again and urged him to hasten home. His return, she said, would be 'welcomer to me . . . nor all the jewels in London'. No sooner had she written these words, than it occurred to her that if he did come away prematurely, he might easily find another pretext for going south again, so she hastily added that he must not be in too much of a hurry. 'Remember,' she told him sternly, 'that London is not at the door. Far better to tarry 8 or 10 days longer, nor go again.'

All her exhortations were in vain, of course, because a man of his standing could not remain at home, and whenever he went away he was pursued by her complaints and cajolings. 'My sweet bird, as ye love me or desires to bring any joy to my heart, mend these faults,' she pleaded when she was in conciliatory mood, declaring on another occasion, 'My desire is to be where you are, whether it be in landward or the burgh's town.' At other times, her tone was less beguiling. 'Your kindness is a proper debt to me, although ye defraud me thereof,' she told him, then added dramatically, 'Ye will not believe this language till I be dead, and then ye will weep for the abuse of such love.' Theirs was certainly a stormy relationship, but she was genuinely fond of him and she was apparently quite sincere when she told him that she had humbled herself so much 'to no man living as I have done and would willingly do to you'.[6]

Dame Juliana was undoubtedly hard to please, but perhaps Lord Binning did not try very hard. Other husbands strove to be more understanding and seem to have appreciated that any woman, left by herself for long periods, could be an easy prey to loneliness, jealousy and boredom.

One husband who laid himself out to create an atmosphere of domestic felicity was John, 16th Earl of Mar, better known to history as 'Bobbing John' because of his frequent changes of loyalty before leading the Jacobite Rising of 1715. That lay in the future, however when, at the age of twenty-eight, he decided to take a wife. His choice fell upon Lady Margaret Hay, eldest daughter of the Earl of Kinnoull. What she felt about his proposal is not recorded, but he did not cut a particularly prepossessing figure. He came from a delicate family and, according to some contemporary accounts, he suffered from a deformity of the spine. He was also twelve years older than Margaret, who was only sixteen.

Presumably the marriage was arranged from the usual practical motives. The wedding took place on 6 April 1703 at Twickenham, for the bridegroom was a privy councillor and in attendance at Court. Whatever his physical defects, he soon proved to be a considerate and understanding husband. Margaret was still a little immature in outlook, easily bored and inclined to be pettish. When she became pregnant, she was all the more unwilling to be left at home by herself while her husband had to go off on business, but he tried to tease her out of her ill-humour. Writing at one o'clock in the morning from his lodgings in Edinburgh, he promised her, 'My dearest life, do not fret yourself and on Monday without fail I will be with you.' He continued in playful tone, 'Since you have delay'd taking another bedfellow since I came away, till now, put it off but two days longer and you'll have one that loves you better than any you can get.' Life had been 'plaguey troublesome' since he left her, and his greatest anxiety was that she would be melancholy in his absence. 'My dear Maggie,' he told her, 'could I transport myself with a wish to you just now, I would be with you all night.' As a small consolation, he sent her the latest book by the Scottish patriot Andrew Fletcher of Saltoun, and 'a famous Tory poem to help to divert you'. She must also be sure to write to him frequently, for he read her latest letter 'every day'.

A son was born to them later that year, only to die in infancy, so Margaret found life even more depressing. In August 1705 the Earl was once more having to apologize for a prolonged absence in Edinburgh. 'Dear Maggie,' he began, 'I know you'll be angry at this and think me unkind, but it was not in my power to help it, so I hope you'll bear it the best you can and forgive me.' He was still worried about her obvious discontent, and felt that, if only she were occupied, she would be happier. She could, for instance, turn her mind to the estate and see if the wilderness was ready to be planted, for, he explained, 'Dear Maggie, if you would look to those things and inquire about them, it would divert you and you would come to take pleasure in them and understand them as well as I, in a little time, which would please me mightily . . . My dear life, put off the time the best way you can and divert yourself from fancies which make you uneasy. We can never get things to go entirely to our wish.'

Apart from Lady Margaret's tendency to depression, there was also room for improvement in her household management. The Earl sent home some shirts and cravats to be washed, but when he got them back they had not been properly laundered. He mentioned this in his next letter, whereupon his wife retorted angrily that they were perfectly all right. 'You must think me very blind or silly that I would have written to you of the linens being ill-washed unless I was sure they were so,' he replied. Time would no doubt have improved her domestic supervision and reconciled her to their intervals apart, but their remaining days together were brief. Their son Thomas was born safely in 1706 but Lady Margaret was already ill and she died the following spring, probably from tuberculosis.[7]

Mar had been a mature man married to a young, inexperienced girl. Given the fact that theirs does not seem to have been a love-match at the outset, it might have been reasonable to assume that they would live on somewhat formal terms, brought together not by passion but by the need to beget an heir. Yet their correspondence demonstrates an affectionate, intimate relationship in which he was far from being a domineering domestic tyrant, a relationship which must have been found in many Scottish homes of the period. Perhaps the neatest combination of homely concern and romantic ideology comes in a letter written by Christian, Dowager Marchioness of Montrose, at the beginning of the eighteenth century. Her second husband, Mr Bruce, was unable to go out and she told an enquirer, 'Mr Bruce [has] been tied to his bed these three weeks, almost, with the haemorrhoids, a disease I believe you have yourself felt to be an intolerable pain and trouble, for indeed a husband and wife that loves one another shares perfectly too with one another in their pain.'[8]

Finally, when a husband or wife died, the surviving partner often gave eloquent testimony of his grief. In 1571, Lord Darnley's mother, Margaret, Countess of Lennox, was referring sorrowfully to the loss of her 'chiefest comfort', her husband having recently been murdered. Old Viscount Tarbat, heartbroken when the Countess of Wemyss died before him, wrote of his 'now saint', while other bereaved widowers referred to 'my dear bedfellow' and 'my dearest and best part of this world'. When the Earl of Cassillis lost

his Countess in the early days of 1643, her friend, Lady Anna
Cunningham, wrote to condole with him on the death of 'that dear
soul that was your other half'. Lady Christian Hamilton sent her
sympathy too, and, knowing that one of his children had also died,
told him she understood perfectly how he felt, 'for marriage
affection is the greatest and then the affection of a parent. I have
had proof of both.'[9]

Even more detailed was the 'history of the life and death of
Elizabeth Henderson, my dear wife', written by John Clerk of
Penicuik after her death in 1683. Accounts of a partner recently
dead are by their nature eulogistic, but it is interesting to see
the qualities particularly valued by a husband of the time.
Presbyterians like John Clerk always set much store by modesty
and a distaste for the worldly values, so he was anxious to record
that 'she had the ornament of a meek and quiet spirit. She looked
not (as too many do) upon gaudy and vain dresses, she neither
liked them nor conformed to them, but went in a grave, decent,
sober and careless attire.' Indeed, she preferred garments of her
own making and although he saw to it that she had all manner of
up-to-date clothes, 'she seldom or never wore them, and at her
death all these were found lying split new, in her chest of drawers,
and she contented herself with what was spun by her own fingers.'

Although she had been only sixteen when he married her, she
had no frivolous tendencies. 'She was far from the gadding
disposition of other talking, walking women.' She disliked town life
and had no time for the idle entertainments held in noble houses.
Rather, 'she was for the most part as a snail within her own shell
and family.' Humble, gentle and tender-hearted, she was 'cheerful
with a becoming severity, she was severe but with a decent
cheerfulness. She was a concurrence and constellation of virtues
and sweetness, a mirror of chastity, a treasure and magazine of
chastity and sobriety.'

In the space of nine years, Elizabeth bore him seven children,
passing the last weeks of her pregnancies reading religious books
and putting her affairs in order in case she should die. She endured
pain and sickness with 'a more masculine patience' and her
devotion to her household duties was commendable. All the
children and her husband as well as she herself were clothed from
the thread she and her servants spun, and she likewise made up all
the tablecloths and bedlinen. If her husband was absent, she put
aside her dislike of towns and went into Edinburgh to look after his

[93]

interests. 'Never man had a more faithful, dear and loving wife,' John declared, and his admiration for her was enhanced by the fact that she apparently agreed with everything he said. 'She had a love so great for her husband, so entirely given up to a dear affection, that she thought the same things and loved the same loves and hated according to the same enmities and breathed in his soul and lived in his presence and languished in his absence and all that she was or did was only for and to her dearest husband.' In the end, it was her devotion to his domestic affairs which killed her. She had recovered safely from the birth of her daughter Sophia, but about a month later she insisted on going to visit her uncle a few miles away at Hawthornden. It was a stormy autumn day, and she came home chilled. Her servants told her that some flax she had ordered from Holland had just arrived, so she immediately went and sat in the unheated gallery of her house to supervise the women who were unpacking it. As a result, she caught a cold which developed into pneumonia, and on 23 October 1683 she died, at the age of 'twenty-five years ten days'.[10]

Happy as many couples were, however, it was only to be expected that there would be others who lived together in discord and strife. Some unions were doomed from the start. There was the sad case of Lord Chancellor Maitland's daughter Anne, for example. In 1603, when she was only thirteen years old, it was arranged that she would marry Robert, 2nd Earl of Winton. The ceremony duly took place, but on the night of the wedding, the bridegroom displayed alarming symptoms of insanity. He had to be forcibly removed from the terrified girl's bedchamber and was kept under restraint for the rest of his life. Anne died six years later, still a virgin.[11]

Less spectacular but equally distressing were the problems encountered by John Kerr, a respectable Edinburgh merchant. In 1690 he met and married Cecily Scott, a lawyer's niece, and proudly installed her in his home. Unfortunately, the girl he took to be a 'modest, virtuous, chaste maid' was five months three weeks pregnant by another man when she married. Her lover was her uncle's lodger and she refused to end her relationship with him. Declaring that she had left a chest of clothes at her uncle's house, she made off there almost every afternoon. Mr Kerr urged her to have the chest brought up to their house. Cecily refused, and at last her husband sent his servants to follow her. They observed her enter her uncle's home. Diligent questioning of the neighbours revealed that she was a regular visitor and that, the better to creep up silently, she was in the habit of leaving her pattens or overshoes at John Grierson's shop at the head of the alley leading to her uncle's house.[12]

If Mr Kerr was disappointed in his bride, equally disillusioned was Isabel McIntosh, a country girl who lived in the Moy area of Inverness-shire. In 1687, she married Angus Mcbean, a soldier in Colonel Hill's regiment at Inverlochy, only to discover that he was 'incapable to perform that duty becoming a husband to his wife'. Try as she might, Isabel's loving persuasions were of no avail, and Angus eventually blurted out the whole sorry story. He had always known that he was an unsuitable husband for any woman, but he was his father's only son and the old man was determined that he should marry. In vain had Angus protested that he would rather his father 'destroyed' him than force him into matrimony. Mr Mcbean refused to listen and Angus at last gave in, with predictable consequences. He stayed with Isabel for three years, but by then the situation was so intolerable for both of them that he rejoined his regiment, to live as a single man once more.[13]

Also deceived, but in another way, was Dame Philadelphia Wharton. Her second husband was the eminent judge, Sir George Lockhart, who died in tragic circumstances in 1689. He was leaving the law courts in Edinburgh one day when he was assassinated by a man against whom he had given judgment in an earlier case. When she had recovered from her initial grief, Dame Philadelphia sought comfort in the companionship of friends, and it was at that point that Captain John Mair came into her life. An attractive military man, just arrived from London, he was charming, persuasive and soon 'insinuated himself' into her favour. Indeed, it was not long before he proposed to her. At first, Dame Philadelphia demurred. After all, she knew nothing of his background. However, he assured her that he came from a respectable family and he was almost suspiciously insistent upon the fact that he was free to marry. She believed him, and as soon as her year's mourning was over, their wedding took place. For three years after that they lived together in apparent amity, but Dame Philadelphia gradually began to wonder about him, until the day when she found among his papers a baptismal certificate which revealed that he already had a wife and child in London. Her husband was a bigamist.[14]

Marriages such as these were patently null and void from the start, and so it was not too difficult to have them set aside. John Kerr, Isabel McIntosh and Dame Philadelphia all succeeded in regaining their freedom, but for others it was not so simple. The Reformation, of course, had brought with it various alterations to the administration of matrimonial law and now all divorce cases had to be heard in the Edinburgh commissary court instead of in the defunct ecclesiastical courts. Canon Law remained the basis of matrimonial law and the Reformers were even more anxious to condemn adultery than their predecessors had been. Indeed, in 1563, Parliament passed an act declaring adultery to be punishable by death. Matters were never taken to this extreme, but persistent adultery remained a justifiable reason for divorce. Because of the relaxation of the regulations governing marriage within the forbidden degrees, people were no longer able to obtain decrees of nullity on the grounds that they had been distantly related, unknown to themselves. However, there was an extension of other reasons for divorce. Before the Reformation, adultery had been the only possible complaint, but in 1573 divorce for desertion was recognized and from time to time divorces were granted in the commissary court because of the husband's impotence.

Obtaining a divorce did, however, remain a lengthy process, requiring both persistence and financial resources. If a woman wanted to divorce her husband for desertion, she had to wait for a year, then she first of all raised an action of adherence in the local commissary court. If her application was successful, the court ordered her partner to return to her. If he ignored the order, the wife then had to go to the Court of Session in Edinburgh to ask for letters of horning. These outlawed the husband. If he still did not return, the Church would admonish him privately and then in public, before the whole congregation. The next step was that he would be excommunicated. Only then, and on the understanding that they had been apart for four years, could the wife institute proceedings in the Edinburgh commissary court.[15]

The reason for such a cumbersome machinery of divorce was, of course, that the Reformers held the sanctity of marriage in high esteem and were anxious to give every possible opportunity for a reconciliation. This system did not militate against women particularly for, after all, there were as many men who were equally anxious to free themselves from an unsatisfactory wife as there were women longing to escape from an undesirable husband. It might be argued, of course, that in a male-dominated society a woman would have neither the courage nor the opportunity to instigate a divorce action, but this was not so. There are many examples of the wronged wife taking her husband to court. Perhaps the most famous of these was Lady Jane Gordon, Countess of Bothwell. Her husband was the celebrated James, Earl of Bothwell, who allegedly abducted Mary, Queen of Scots, and became her third husband. When the abduction took place, Bothwell was still married to Jane and two days later she instructed her lawyers to sue him for divorce, on the grounds that he had committed adultery with one of her maidservants. Bothwell did not allow this to pass unchallenged, but immediately raised a counter-action to have his marriage declared null. He and Lady Jane had been within the forbidden degrees when they married, he said, and so that marriage had no legality. Undeterred, Lady Jane continued with her case and on 3 May 1567, sentence of divorce was duly pronounced against the Earl. Four days later, he obtained a declaration to the effect that his marriage always had been null and void, but Lady Jane determinedly held to the fact that she had won her case and she kept the dispensation permitting her marriage to Bothwell until the end of her life.[16]

Lady Jane was undoubtedly a woman of influence, but she was far from being unique. Records of divorce proceedings in the commissary court before 1658 are intermingled with records of other cases, but after that date they have been kept together and so it is possible to examine them as a coherent series. In this series, there were thirty-five processes of divorce between the years 1658 and 1707. Nineteen of the cases were raised by the wife, sixteen by the husband. Unless the wife was titled, it is difficult to ascertain her social class, but on the whole it would seem that divorces were being obtained not only by the very wealthy but by middle-class and professional people too. The thirty-five wives involved in divorces included four peers' daughters, four knights' daughters and the daughters of two merchants, an apothecary, a mason and a bailie. Similarly, the husbands included one peer, six soldiers, five merchants, two surgeons, a minister, a storekeeper and a periwig-maker.[17]

The section of society which had access to the divorce courts was therefore not as narrowly limited as one might at first suppose, but how did women fare when their cases were actually heard? Did masculine prejudice allow them little opportunity of putting their side of the story? The answer seems to be that they were given a fair hearing. They did not personally argue the point, of course, but were represented by lawyers, some of whom seem to have specialized in such suits. In the 1690s the name of John Smart frequently occurs as procurator for wives in such hearings, and he obviously argued with great success before the judges, who were themselves professional lawyers.

Indeed, it seems that the wife's situation was carefully examined even when it appeared that she was very much in the wrong. An interesting case came before St Andrews Kirk Session in the early months of 1560, before the new system of commissary courts had been established. William Renton accused his wife Elizabeth Geddie not only of committing adultery with several men but of plotting to murder him. At first, the case against Elizabeth seemed black. Alexander Simpson, a neighbouring maltman, gave evidence that he had seen one of Elizabeth's alleged lovers, Alexander Ruddiman, frequently visit her house, there to be entertained to meals and an over-intimate friendship. A local woman, Margaret Graham, said she had seen another man, Andrew Oliphant, 'cast his cloak about Elizabeth Geddie and kiss her upon [her] own stair'. Worse was to follow. Margaret Moncur and her sister had been lodging with the Rentons, and they too were called as witnesses. Margaret testified that one night when she had risen from her bed at nine o'clock 'to ease herself', she had noticed a light in the chamber leading to the gallery. Peering through the keyhole to see what was going on, she beheld the figure of a man. At first she thought it must be Mr Renton, but then she realized that this person had 'red hose and a dusky beard' and was, in fact, Andrew Oliphant. By this time her friend Agnes Lessells had joined her, and, the better to view the proceedings, had climbed on a chair to watch through a small window. When Margaret finally observed Mr Oliphant drawing off his hose, she retired modestly to bed.

Evidence such as this was presented to the minister and Kirk Session over a period of several days, but it did not deceive the men who sat and listened to it. On 21 March they declared Elizabeth to be totally innocent of the charges laid against her, and ordered William to treat her properly 'as becomes a husband on all behalfs to treat his wife, in bed and board and all other things, according to the law and commandment of God'.[18]

It also seems clear that when a woman was divorced as being the guilty party, she really had given cause for complaint. George Preston, the Edinburgh surgeon, was able to produce letters written by his English wife, Mary Boghurst, telling her Scottish lover, 'Thou fillest my soul with raptures of joy inexpressible and gives me life, who without thee cannot live . . . thou art my thoughts all day and dreams all night . . .' Lady Elizabeth Gordon really did run away with a Frenchman called Monsieur Lavallet, following him around the continent until he finally cast her off, and when Alexander Milne's wife, Isabel Gordon, went in 1697 to be a wet-nurse to a farmer's wife, she had an affair with a servant at the farm. When the time came for the baby to be weaned, she and her lover slipped away together, setting up house as man and wife in the parish of Meigle. Two children were born to them before their true situation came to light, whereupon Isabel's husband promptly divorced her.[19]

In a clear-cut case of adultery and desertion such as this, the way out was obvious and, given the necessary proof, the injured party would obtain the dissolution of the marriage. The number of actual divorces was, however, minute, and it remained impossible to seek an end to a marriage on the grounds of cruelty, so many distressing domestic situations went without redress. The best a wronged wife could do in these circumstances was to seek a judicial separation, and so in the seventeenth century a long procession of women came before the Scottish Privy Council complaining of domestic violence. The Council listened carefully and demanded proof. In their final judgment they too were always anxious to uphold the sanctity of marriage, and so they tried to effect a reconciliation wherever possible. Sometimes the woman failed to prove her case. In July 1629, Agnes Arnot was complaining that her husband Lawrence Thomson, an inhabitant of Leith, had on several occasions tried to murder her, one day attempting to drown her in the well at the back of their house. She could not produce any witnesses however, and so the case was dismissed. Similarly, Dame Janet Sutherland, Lady Banff, failed to convince the Privy Council that her husband had locked up her and two of her children in one room, allowing them only 'dusty bread' and water by way of nourishment, and had later 'trailed her up and down the house by the feet', striking and punching her. The Lords were sympathetic, all the same, and although they decided that nothing could be proved against the husband, they bound him over to keep the peace, under pain of being fined 3000 merks.[20]

Elizabeth More was likewise treated with understanding in 1662. Her husband, Thomas Rocheid, had been ill-treating her and had actually left her, but she came before the Council to beg them to order him to return. They agreed, telling Thomas to live with her as a husband but warning him that he must never raise a hand against her. In other cases, an immediate reconciliation was impossible. When the Council heard that John Dawling of Leith had abused his wife Jean Lyon, attacking her in the Pleasance, one of Edinburgh's crowded streets, punching her and trampling on her 'as if she had been a very dog', they expressed grave concern. This type of behaviour was 'a great crime' they said, and they ordered John to stay away from her. He must pay her 600 merks a year for her upkeep, and if he either threatened or molested her again, he would be given a heavy prison sentence to deter others from committing similar outrages.[21]

Sir Alexander Forbes of Tolquhoun, in Aberdeenshire, who regularly beat his wife and put her out of their house 'to lie in the fields in the coldest winter night' and attacked her 'to the effusion of two Scots pints of blood', was similarly admonished in 1690 and told that he must support her during their separation. Husbands could even be put in prison for assaulting their wives, as David Bowman had discovered in 1631. He had attacked Bessie Lindsay with a stick, then slashed at her forehead with a sword when she tried to defend herself. She fell down unconscious and was ill for many weeks. Further episodes of violence followed, until the Privy Council ordered him to be kept in prison, in irons.[22]

Direct assaults of this kind were not the only form of cruelty. Jean Duke's husband was an improvident drunkard and so she was granted a legal separation in the 1630s, but William Sutherland, who in 1659 married Barbara Dunbar and eight days later began drinking day and night in alehouses, was judged to be more foolish than wicked, and simply admonished. Other incidents reveal wives actively resenting their husbands' interference in their own concerns. By 1631, Agnes Arnot, living apart from her husband, was supporting herself by making starch. He and she were involved jointly in the business, although they were still on no good terms. Agnes herself borrowed money to buy the wheat needed for the making of the starch, then sold the final product to the Edinburgh merchants, intending to pay her creditors from the profits. Unfortunately, as soon as her husband heard that some money had come in, he arrived home and appropriated 3000 merks Scots, broke up some of the equipment Agnes had locked in a shed and attacked her when she protested. The Council ordered him to restore the stolen money and told Agnes that she could sue him further for other things he had taken. For his part, he was to leave her alone to carry on the business in peace.[23]

Walter Thomson likewise interfered in his wife's business affairs. She had inherited a merchant booth, where she sold clothing, so when they quarrelled, Walter took her keys and kept them. This meant that she could not get into the booth, and she feared that her wares would be 'eaten by rats and mice'. A legal separation was arranged and Walter was told that he must return the keys at once and pay for his wife's upkeep until they agreed to cohabit once more.[24]

Finally, there is an interesting detail in the complaint of Mary Kellow, wife of the Edinburgh merchant Patrick Ainslie. They were married in December 1632, with a proper contract agreed and signed, but before twelve months had passed, Patrick was ill-treating Mary in every way. He called her names, threatened to murder her brother, an English parson, and declared that he had married her, not to be his wife, but because he needed a slave and a servant. Also, he interfered in all her household concerns, especially in the running of the kitchen. Just as the man had his sphere of activity outside the home, so was the woman's right to manage her household recognized at law.[25]

Whatever the reasons for separation or divorce, the results were always painful. Innocent or guilty of breaking her marriage vows, a woman suffered emotionally and economically. The life of Lady Barbara Erskine epitomizes the misery resulting from an unhappy marriage. The eldest daughter of the Earl of Mar, Lady Barbara married the 2nd Marquis of Douglas, but it was not long before they began to disagree. The Marquis, a morose and immature young man, was completely dominated by his principal chamberlain, William Lawrie, known locally as the Laird of Blackwood. Lawrie was a much older man, but he seems to have resented the Marchioness's growing influence over her husband and he set out to destroy her. By subtle insinuation he soon turned the Marquis against her, so that he completely ignored the piteous letters she wrote to him, begging for a hearing. 'It is in your power, my dear lord, to make me happy or miserable,' Lady Barbara told her husband, explaining that 'to deny me your favour and countenance is enough to embitter to me the greatest earthly enjoyments I can propose to myself.' She could not understand his hostility, but 'if I have offended you in word or deed, I am ready, in the most humble and submissive manner you can prescribe, to crave pardon.' Even if he did not believe her, 'my dearest, I must beseech you seriously to reflect upon my deplorable condition . . . it's but a hell upon earth daily to observe my misery in your countenance when you cannot look upon me but with aversion, if not contempt, and to think of absence from you and my dear child is a terror next unto death.'[26]

Her pleas were in vain. The Marquis insisted upon a separation and from 1681 they lived apart. Lady Barbara's unhappiness was so well-known that her story was commemorated in several ballads, one of which, published shortly after her death, makes her lament:

> 'Martinmas wind, when wilt thou blaw
> And shake the green leaves off the tree?
> O gentle death, when wilt thou come?
> For o' my life I am weary.'

Her death took place in 1690, and after her funeral her mother could only write to the Marquis begging him to pay her debts and asking for news of her grandson, with the hope that he would be 'as happy as her life was unfortunate'. In fact, he was killed in battle in the Netherlands just two years later.[27]

Emotional repercussions apart, the financial implications of divorce or separation were far-reaching. True, the husband was supposed to maintain his wife throughout the divorce action, and if she had brought to the marriage a tocher, her yearly aliment was based upon that. There might also be a division of property or furniture, but the trouble lay in persuading the husband to pay the agreed sum. The Privy Council was constantly hearing complaints from wives about husbands who did not support them as agreed, and if a man had deserted his family, there was no practical way of ensuring that he did pay for their upkeep.

When a wife was eventually granted a divorce, she was put in possession of her jointure lands and was free to marry again: to all intents and purposes, her position was comparable to that of a widow. If the divorce was on the grounds of the husband's desertion, some authorities believed that the tocher was to be restored to the wife too, but there was a good deal of doubt about this and it seems uncertain whether or not the injured wife ever did regain the tocher. In cases of divorce for adultery, it was definitely to remain with the husband. If the wife were the guilty party, she forfeited the jointure and, of course, lost any claim to her tocher, so her circumstances could be very difficult. The position was made even worse by the fact that she was forbidden by law to marry any man who had been named as co-respondent in her divorce suit, although in practice women did marry their lovers after they had gained their freedom. Whatever the background to the divorce, the children of the marriage usually remained in the custody of their father. Only if he was found to be unfit to have charge of them or if his religious beliefs were not satisfactory would he lose custody.[28]

A woman involved in divorce or separation thus lost her children, much of her economic security and her masculine protector in a world which still had its share of physical violence, lawlessness and aggression. It was, indeed, the lack of a strong central government which caused both Church and State to place so much emphasis upon the value of the family as a stable unit. Be this as it may, it is obvious from the correspondence and the other documentary sources of the time, that women did not meekly accept a passive, subordinate role within marriage, silently enduring their husbands' ill-treatment, ready to accept blame for faults not their own, and piously observing their marriage vows although their husbands felt no such obligation. Undoubtedly the double standard existed, but it was not a sign that marriage was a cold-blooded arrangement which resulted in the wife occupying a subsidiary, even subservient role. The Church did teach that woman was the frailer vessel, but although Eve had been created from Adam's rib, she had come into the world to be a companion to him, not a chattel or a slave. Men obviously did seek support, solace and physical pleasure from their wives, relying on their assistance in a wide variety of ways.

It is equally clear that, in return for her loving assistance of her husband, the wife herself had certain rights and expectations. As the Privy Council commented on one occasion, 'It is the duty of husbands to provide for their wives and families, suitably to their fortunes, and to act dutifully, such as do not so being characterized by Scripture as worse than infidels.'[29] Marriage was generally regarded as being a desirable Christian state and there was much disapproval, both public and private, when vows were broken. Possibly a wife was more relieved than anything else when her husband took a mistress during her frequent pregnancies, but he was expected to be discreet about it. Dame Juliana Ker was therefore absolutely furious when her son Patrick openly flouted convention and installed a woman named Barbara in his home in place of his young wife. The poor wife was 'worth twenty of such a slut as she is', Dame Juliana declared, describing it as 'a great presumption' on the part of the 'arrant whore' to 'usurp his wife's place', and thereby make the rightful partner lack much 'which is her prerogative'. To her erring son himself, she dispatched a letter beginning, 'Son, I protest to God I know neither what to say nor do nor what to write to you in regard to your carriage and misbehaviour to your half marrow [*i.e.* wife] that God has joined you with.' This did not prevent her from penning a lengthy dissertation to the effect that he must surely be unaware of the gravity of the sin he was committing in quarrelling with 'your own wife, whom God has bidden you love as yourself'. She was under no illusions about the effectiveness of her intervention, telling him, 'As for my counsel and contentment, ye do no more care for it nor I were a Turk or pagan,' but she felt it to be her Christian duty to try to bring him to his senses.[30] Fortunately, such episodes were not the norm. Most women could expect from marriage not merely the narrow existence set down in legal precept but a much more complete relationship in which both partners experienced the love, respect, jealousy, anger, passion and delight familiar to husbands and wives in our own time.

CHAPTER FIVE

Motherhood

ACCORDING TO the marriage service, the principal purpose of matrimony was the procreation of children, and many a woman found that she was pregnant within a few months of her wedding.[1] Her principal reaction was usually one of apprehension, and this was not surprising, in view of the attendant dangers. Of course, a large family was, in theory, desirable. Everyone knew that death would carry off perhaps half the sons and daughters before they reached adult life, so it was prudent to have as many children as possible. By this means, the number of godly, right-thinking people in the country would increase. James Smith expressed this outlook succinctly when he wrote to Lady Anna Wemyss, Countess of Leven, in 1695. Sending his good wishes for her health, he prayed that God would make her 'the mother of a numerous blessed progeny, to be patterns of holiness to future generations'.[2]

Again, there was the notion that the husband's family would be strengthened as its size grew. Anna, Countess of Rothes, was thinking along these lines when she wrote to her cousin the Countess of Findlater in 1667 to congratulate her on being pregnant. 'I am always glad to hear of you being with child,' she said. 'The Lord give you comfort of them you have and send you many more, that your posterity may be continued and spread throughout the country.' George Allardyce's thoughts on a similar subject were more chillingly expressed. When his wife presented him with a second son in 1701, he wrote to tell a friend that Mrs Allardyce 'begins to make amends for her many daughters, for she has given me two boys in a year, so that if she hold on, I hope she will strengthen my name, which hath been this long time very weak.'[3]

Fortunately, few husbands betrayed such a callous indifference as this towards the welfare of their partners, but there seems to have been no particular concern about the fact that too-frequent childbearing undermined a woman's health. When Mary, Countess of Traquair, gave birth to a daughter at the beginning of March 1695, her friend the Duchess of Gordon gaily wished her 'much joy of the little lady, and that a young lord may follow at the year's end', while Lord Basil Hamilton commented that his much-loved wife's achievement in producing five children before the age of twenty-two was 'very fair'.[4] Wives themselves were anxious to provide their husbands with sons and daughters, but there is no doubt that their pleasure in being pregnant was overshadowed by fear. They knew full well that medical science could do little to help them through the perils of childbirth, and they all had relatives and friends who had died during pregnancy or labour. The Countess of Dalhousie, visiting London in the 1690s, discovered that she was with child and wrote home dolefully to say that pregnancy was 'no rarity' for her, adding, 'I could wish to be well quit of my big belly in this place, for I am in a great fear' and a few years later Margaret Clerk was telling her nephew that his sister 'hath a fancy she will die of this child'.[5]

In spite of their terror, however, women accepted that it was God's will that they should bear children and they awaited the outcome with a fatalistic fortitude. 'Pray for me that I may bring forth this child and live to deserve your innumerable kindnesses,' the Countess of Eglinton begged Mrs John Murray in 1616 and a few years later Lilias Grant, wife of Sir Walter Innes of Balvenie, was expressing similar sentiments. Telling her mother that she thought she had been pregnant since Yule, she said, 'It is not quick but within these eight days, so that I cannot speak of it yet. God preserve me and it both.' She then went on to hope that she could visit her mother 'once, before I be in danger of death' – in other words, before her delivery.[6]

Women found comfort in their religious faith and also in the encouragement of relatives and friends. The Earl of Lothian was distinctly bracing when his wife confided her fears to him in 1679. He reminded her that she had been safely delivered 'many times' in the past, so had no cause to view her impending confinement with alarm. In a similar vein, he remarked a few years later when their daughter was pregnant, 'It is a very natural thing she is about to do, so she needs not be out of heart.'[7] Younger husbands could display a more tender and imaginative concern for their pregnant wives. David, Earl of Leven, a professional soldier who married the

Countess of Wemyss's daughter Anna in 1691, confessed to her that he felt guilty because 'it's your love to me that has been the occasion of your sickness,' and he begged her constantly to look after herself. When she was carrying his second child, they referred hopefully to the coming baby as 'little Davy' and 'Jock in the Low Cellar'. 'I cannot think of being a fortnight without seeing my dearest, dearest heart,' the Earl said at this time, 'especially when you are so oft sick, but I hope it's for a brave lad.' They were both delighted when the desired son was born, and the Earl was just as attentive during later pregnancies, writing regularly to his 'dear Nanny' when he was absent and sending his blessings to their 'dear babes, seen and unseen'. In like manner John, 16th Earl of Mar, told his pregnant wife, 'I hope our little friend is well. I assure you, I long to find it stir with my own hand.'[8]

Expressions such as these of a husband's loving concern for his wife must have been a consolation at a difficult time. Some young, healthy girls sailed through pregnancy with no trouble, but for many others it was a period of wretched discomfort. The Countess of Northesk, for instance, found that she was expecting a second child in the 1690s and did not want her relatives to know until she had the opportunity of telling her absent husband. However, she had a hard time concealing her condition for, as she told her sister, the Countess of Leven, she was 'tormented all day long with heavy sickness and violent pains in my head, and my being at pains to cover it from the family makes me the worse, but I fear they begin to suspect the truth, for yesterday was eight days [*i.e.* eight days ago] I went out of the church half dead'.[9]

There was nothing to be done but to swallow the herbal potions advised by doctors and friends. Some medical books were available, like Dr Hew Chamberlen's translation of Mauriceau's *Traité des Maladies des Femmes Grosses*, but for the most part, women relied on their own concoctions. Recipes were passed eagerly round among friends, but most of them seem to have been of limited efficacy, despite the claims made for them by their users. In 1642, for example, Anna Hepburn, a relative of the Laird of Grant, was ready with advice about how to prevent a miscarriage when her nephew's wife found herself pregnant after losing two previous babies. What she must do, said Anna, was to wear round her neck a small taffeta bag filled with saffron. The vapour from this, breathed in all day, did the world of good in preventing miscarriages. She also recommended that favourite remedy of the time, blood-letting. She had personal experience of its efficacy, she said, 'for I parted with two [children] myself before ever I kept any, and there was nothing I thought so sovereign a remedy as the drawing of blood'. She did recognize that this should not be done too often, 'for it weakens the bairn', but it did not seem to occur to her that it would make the mother seriously anaemic.[10]

Even at the beginning of the eighteenth century, blood-letting was still being recommended as a preventative measure in pregnancy. After her marriage in 1687 Margaret, Countess of Panmure, tried time and time again to bear a living child, but each pregnancy ended in miscarriage. Friends and relations sent her advice and her aunt, Margaret, Lady Belhaven, gave detailed recipes including one for pearl, gold and coral ground down and mixed with plantain juice. She was in advance of her age in that she advised Margaret not to be bled. After all, she reminded her, previous experience during other pregnancies had shown that this had been no help. William Eccles in Edinburgh, on the other hand, did advise bleeding when he sent the Countess lengthy directions. Some of his recommendations would still be made today. The Countess was, for instance, to do no stretching and lifting in the first three or four months and she was to be careful about what she ate. Spicy foods were to be omitted, and he prescribed a somewhat spartan diet of tea and toast for breakfast, weak broth and a little boiled meat for dinner, with a milk pudding or some calf's foot jelly for supper. All fish was to be avoided except for whiting or raw oysters. Drinks of rose leaf mixture and poppy seeds in water he believed to be beneficial and if a miscarriage seemed imminent, the Countess must at once be bled. In view of her medical history, however, he felt it his duty to point out that perhaps some physical defect meant that she never would have a child and in this he was probably right. Only in the twentieth century have doctors devised a method of helping women with an incompetent cervix and the Countess never did carry a child to full term.[11]

For those without such problems, the 'reckoning' fast approached and preparations had to be made. Sometimes there was 'a false alarm', with the pains beginning several weeks too soon. The Marchioness of Argyll was thrown into a panic in 1674 when her daughter found herself having signs of labour a month before her time. A man was at once dispatched from Roseneath to Greenock to fetch the midwife, and the Marchioness waited anxiously, worrying that she might not arrive in time, for 'the weather is very stormy and the way evil'. On other occasions, the baby was late, or seemed to be so, because the mother always had difficulty in calculating when she had conceived. The Countess of Leven found herself in this situation before one of her children was born and her husband had to write from a nearby town to tell her cheeringly, 'We have several women in this place that has gone by their reckoning. One of them was delivered yesterday and had a very good labour. She was much as you have been, for she has had pains these 9 weeks and is a lean small woman. It's like you have seen her here. She is the schoolmaster his wife. Lord make you as well as she is.'[12]

When the baby was overdue, the mother was given honey boiled with mint water to drink as a means of 'hasting delivery'. This would probably be administered by the midwife who, in the larger country houses, came to stay until the birth took place, charging a fee which in the 1660s was usually about £66 13s. 4d. Scots. In poorer homes, an experienced neighbour or relative would assist at the birth, instead of a professional midwife. Sometimes a woman would go to her own mother's house for the confinement, but more often the mother and other female relatives would gather at her home to lend their moral support. Sir John Maxwell of Pollok had some observations to make on this subject when his wife was expecting her second child in 1576. His mother-in-law, Lady Cunningham, had refused to attend the previous confinement, thereby causing Sir John such annoyance that he still remembered the occasion with rage long after the event. His neighbours must have thought his wife had no near relatives, he told Lady Cunningham angrily, for everyone knew that it was 'the custom that either the daughter is with her parents the time of her birth, or else the mother with her'. He did not hesitate to attribute the fact that there would be a space of six years between his children to his wife's distress at her mother's behaviour, and when the second confinement approached he wrote to tell the older lady that this time she must be present. His wife had already 'taken her chamber, abiding the time when it shall please God appoint', so Lady Cunningham must set out at once, 'not that I mean that ye should be her keeper, but her comforter and overseer in her great extremity'. The custom of the woman 'taking to her chamber' several days before the birth seems to have died out in the seventeenth century, and certainly by 1700 Elizabeth Gerard, the young Duchess of Hamilton, was alarming her mother-in-law by setting off in a coach to travel from Hamilton to Edinburgh on the very day that her baby was due to arrive.[13]

As the old Duchess of Hamilton remarked, Elizabeth was lucky that she did not have to lie in on the way but instead was able to have her child with Edinburgh's leading doctors in attendance. That was an unusual feature of the birth, however, for in most households the services of a doctor were not sought unless something went wrong. Instead, the midwife took charge and went to work with an expertise based on experience and oral tradition. The techniques she used were still those set out in the teachings of the famous gynaecologist Soranus, who had worked in Rome in the first century AD. By one means or another his writings had been circulated throughout western Europe and provided the foundation for midwifery in the sixteenth and seventeenth centuries.[14] The first book of midwifery printed in English, *The Byrth of Mankynde*, had been published in London in 1540. Since it enjoyed remarkable popularity, it was probably available in Scotland. Translations of various continental works were circulated during the seventeenth century and in 1668 Nicholas Culpeper's *Directory for Midwives* was published in Edinburgh. It is impossible to assess how many practising midwives themselves read these works, of course, and, given the state of female literacy of the time, it would be rash to suppose that many had done so.[15]

Even so, midwives were reasonably efficient. They knew how to speed up contractions and although there was no way in which they could relieve the pain of labour they did try. In the Highlands, magical girdles were fastened round the mother, and elsewhere there were still spells and prayers thought to help, despite the censure of the Church. The contractions could be endured as long as the birth went normally but what every woman dreaded was that the baby would lie in an awkward position. When that happened, or when the woman herself had some malformation of the pelvis, a tragic end to the proceedings was all too frequent. Descriptions of the suffering which resulted make dreadful reading. A protracted labour could last for days until the woman died with her child still unborn. Sometimes it was possible for a doctor to save the mother by sacrificing the child. In extreme cases the doctor might be willing to attempt a Caesarian section, but the mother invariably died in the process.[16]

By the end of the seventeenth century, progress was being made and it seems likely that the obstetric forceps was introduced into

Scotland at that time. Dr Peter Chamberlen, a doctor of French origin working in London, had soon after 1600 devised a special forceps to assist birth and had used it in strictest secrecy, jealous of the advantage that it gave him over his rivals. Successive generations of his family improved upon the instrument, never divulging what it was, and eventually Dr Hew Chamberlen came to Scotland to attend to the leading noble families of the day, presumably bringing the famous 'secret' with him. The Chamberlens prided themselves on being able to deliver children otherwise doomed to death, but the forceps was not in general use in Scotland and, in any event, it did not work the miracles claimed for it by its devisers.[17]

In view of the number of women who did die in childbed, it was not surprising that those who recovered expressed heartfelt relief that they had come through the ordeal safely. 'It hath pleased God to give me a safe delivery of a living daughter,' wrote Lady Christian Lindsay in 1666, 'though I had fears of the death of both her and myself before I was brought to bed, I was so extremely sick,' and her sentiments were echoed time and time again in the letters of her contemporaries. Husbands naturally shared in the sense of thankfulness, and the Earl of Leven told his wife after the birth of their first child, 'You are dearer to me now, since you have suffered so much for me and my child, than ever you was, and it's indeed but just that so good a wife as you are should have as loving and affectionate a husband as is, my dearest heart, yours.'[18]

Urging her to grow strong again quickly, the Earl remarked to his Countess, 'It's fit you be so before the young laird be gotten, so pray be careful of yourself.'[19] The context makes it clear that he intended this as a piece of playful badinage, but like Mr Allardyce he was anxious for a son. Titled and landed families would always desire an heir to ensure the succession, and when Sir Thomas Steuart's wife presented him with twins in 1685, he commented that it was fortunate that the son had been born first, 'for the daughter suffered much more in the birth and is the weakest'. Outwith these special circumstances, a healthy baby was welcome whatever its sex and in July 1654, Lilias, Countess of Tullibardine, could express complete satisfaction with her new daughter. Writing to her brother soon after the birth, she reported, 'I am again on the mending hand and hopes yet to live and do you service,' adding, 'Your little niece is a very fine child and I hope shall be a very handsome woman. She hath good signs of it.'

Indeed, so pleased had their father been 'that it was a girl', that he had travelled from Stobhall for the christening. Finally, no less an authority than Nicholas Culpeper himself condemned any lingering notion that a son was preferable. In his *Directory for Midwives* he told the cautionary tale of a woman determined to have a male child. She did so, and he proved an imbecile, whereupon her husband tartly remarked, 'Wife, thou wast never contented till thou hadst a boy, and now thou hast gotten one that will be a boy all the days of his life.'[20]

Whatever the sex of the child, it was prudent to arrange the christening as soon as possible, in case death intervened. Parishes therefore held special sessions for baptism on Sundays and sometimes on weekdays too, so that the newly-born baby could be taken to church as soon as possible. Archibald Johnston of Warriston, the man famous for his part in devising the National Covenant, noted in his diary that his wife 'began to cry' before midnight on 19 April 1637, gave birth to a son between ten and eleven the following morning and had the child baptized in the local church that same afternoon. When a baby was weak, it was customary to have the baptism done privately. Knox and some of the other Reformers disapproved of this, because they felt that baptisms should always follow the sermon, but in Aberdeen in 1599 the Kirk Session specifically allowed private baptism provided the midwife certified that the child was delicate, and in 1611 permission was given for baptism to take place in private at any time if the infant's health made it advisable.[21]

The name chosen was usually that of a close relative or friend. The Countess of Tullibardine would have liked to call her daughter after Lady Drummond, 'for she was very kind to me', but felt that duty required her to choose her mother-in-law's name instead, so the baby was called Elizabeth. The 3rd Duchess of Hamilton was one of many women who named a daughter after her own sister, and in 1646 the Earl of Lothian selected Margaret when his daughter was to be christened, 'as I had one formerly that died'. When Sir Thomas Steuart's twins arrived he knew at once that the girl must be called Margaret, 'after her great-grandmother, my Lady Colingtowne, who assisted and was witness to her birth and christening'. People were always flattered when a child was given their name and so sometimes the traditional family names were abandoned, as when John, 8th Lord Elphinstone, had his daughter baptized Mary Beatrice Anna

Margaret Frances Isabella after Mary of Modena who was visiting Scotland in 1680 when the child was born.[22]

Because the christening took place so soon after the birth, the mother could not attend, but the father had for company a number of godfathers and godmothers, known in Scots as gossips and cummers. At the baptism of Lord Basil Hamilton's five-day-old son in 1692, 'My Lady Panmure [the baby's aunt] carried the child to church. My Lord Panmure, Sir William Maxwell, Earnock, Barncluith and Barnton were gossips.'[23] The party then returned to the parents' home to celebrate. In this connection, there is often mention of 'the butter saps'. Literally, butter saps was a concoction of oatcake or wheaten bread soaked or fried in melted butter and sugar, and it gave its name to a celebratory meal held after a baby's birth. Whether the butter saps were served immediately after the arrival of the child, to those who were present, or whether they appeared at the christening is not altogether clear. The documentary evidence does make it seem more likely, however, that it was at the former occasion. In 1622, Robert, Lord Melville, was apologizing for the fact that his mother could not go to Glasgow for Lady Ross's 'butter sap' because she was unwell, and it seems more probable that she would have gone for the confinement. The Earl of Leven told his Countess in 1695 that nothing would prevent him from being with her 'when you draw near your time', and he added, 'therefore persuade yourself that, God willing, I will help the cummers at the butter saps.' As he announced on another occasion that he hoped to be the first person to see the new baby after the midwife, he probably had the delivery in mind rather than the baptism. Again, the Dowager Countess of Montrose, hoping that she and two friends would soon be pregnant, commented that if only they all were, then 'what with buttered saps and sick possets we might grow fat.'[24]

Certainly, the friends who went back to the house after the christening expected to be served with something more sustaining than saps. In 1614 the Marquis of Hamilton gave his servants £60 Scots to buy extra 'wildfowl' for his baby's christening, and that same year when the Countess of Eglinton was arranging her son's baptismal feast, her sister obtained 'wild meat' for the banquet and also promised to send 'some kids and sucking lambs thereto'. On a lesser scale, Sir John Lauder, the Scottish judge, laid out £28 Scots for confections and wine his wife bought for their daughter Isabel's christening, and gave a further £18 for baked meat.[25]

Although the mother saw to the domestic arrangements, she was usually still in bed after the birth. Ordinary women had to get up as soon as they could, to take over their household duties once more, but great ladies were still expected to recuperate for a month afterwards. Of course, the days immediately after the birth were anxious ones. The many women who suffered from after-pains had to drink antispasmodic potions of seven bay leaves beaten to a powder and mixed up in wine. Others suffered minor ailments such as painful breasts and sore throats, but the real danger was from puerperal fever, an infection spread by lack of hygiene. This illness took a sad toll of women in childbed and was all the more upsetting because the first symptoms did not appear until perhaps a fortnight after a perfectly normal birth. The mother would seem to be in good health, then fever would set in, with delirium and convulsions. There was often a brief intermission, then the symptoms grew worse and the woman died. A medical description of the last illness of Anne, Countess of Arran, in 1690 records the classic signs of the illness, and although she had the best doctors from Edinburgh in attendance, she was dead within the month.[26]

Frequent tragedies such as these naturally made people nervous, and even if there were no tragic complications, a woman who had endured a difficult labour needed time to build up her strength again with claret wine and nourishing food. The 4th Earl of Perth knew the wisdom of this, and in July 1675 was writing anxiously to Grizel Steuart, the wife of Sir John Drummond of Logiealmond, to ask if she could send any partridges for his Countess. She had been brought to bed the previous day and was recovering well, so, 'God willing, the 7 day after her delivery, she will venture to eat a bit of one.'[27]

Rest and quiet were equally important, as the Earl of Lothian pointed out in 1694. He had been anxious for weeks about his daughter's pregnancy, and when he heard that the child had arrived he remarked with satisfaction, 'I always thought she would be delivered about the middle of the month, as it hath fallen out.' The reason he was writing to his wife was to urge that the new mother should be 'kept in silence and quiet' as had been their habit with his own wife. Equally anxious about the lying-in period was Margaret, Countess of Wemyss. When her daughter, the Countess of Leven, sent word that she was recovering so quickly that she was up and about again, the Countess was more worried than relieved. It was alarming to know that Anna had been able 'to walk through

your room 15 days after you was delivered', she said, adding, 'I
pray God continue you in health, but it's not the way to be soon
very well and strong, to try your strength too much. In this cold
weather your bed had been better for you, I think.' Husbands, of
course, were somewhat *de trop* during the lying-in period, and even
the attentive Earl of Leven took himself off on a hunting trip to
Moffat once his first child had safely arrived. 'You know,' he
remarked to his wife, 'there's never less need for the husband's
being at home than when the wife is in your condition,' then told
her playfully a few days later, 'I hope you will be kirked at the end
of my hawking – *vous m'entendez bien.*'[28]

The old notion of purification being necessary after childbirth
lingered on and the churching or kirking of the woman was
supposed to take place a month after her child's birth. Knox
objected strongly to this service but in fact it was no more than its
proper name, 'The Thanksgiving of Women after Childbirth'
suggested, whatever its more primitive origins. Only after the
churching could the mother take up normal life again and resume
marital relations with her husband, as the Earl implied. If a
woman was strong and healthy she was usually impatient to return
to her customary activities, and so the interlude was often
shortened in practice. In 1703 Susan, Lady Yester, was reported as
having decided 'to go to church yesterday, though her month was
not out, that she might go to Edinburgh before the Parliament sat
down', and a few years later Sir John Clerk's daughter Sophia
announced, 'Tomorrow I design, God willing, to be kirked at Airth
kirk,' although her new son was only eighteen days old.[29]

When she was fully active again, the care of the new child was
obviously one of the woman's most important tasks. Even in the
great houses there was no question of handing the baby over to
servants to be brought up in a nursery remote from the public
chambers. Marchionesses and countesses seem to have retained a
close and intimate interest in their children, not merely seeing
them for an hour or so each day. Their correspondence makes it
plain that they involved themselves in all aspects of childrearing,
anxiously discussing their offspring's progress with other mothers.
Many of the methods employed were, of course, traditional and
were accepted without argument. In the sixteenth and early
seventeenth centuries, mothers swaddled their babies as a matter of
course, doing what they had seen their own mothers do. Only in
the mid-seventeenth century was there any discussion about the

advisability of swaddling, and that came from a few theorists and medical men.

There is no doubt that the twentieth-century mother would view the swaddling process with surprise bordering on disbelief. First of all, the new baby was placed on a large square of woollen material which was folded up over his feet to form a bag enclosing his lower limbs. Technically, this was known as the 'bed', and it was held in place by long strips of cloth, called bands or rollers, which were wound tightly round his legs. This done, a piece of cloth, known as the waistcoat, was placed round his chest and arms, then further rollers were bound tightly round his upper half. Another band, known as a stay, went over his head to keep it from wobbling from side to side and the head itself was protected by one, or, sometimes, two caps. Thus cocooned, the baby spent the first few weeks of his life. Only when he was nearly two months old was the upper swaddling left off, but even then he spent a further period with his legs still bound into the 'bed'.[30]

Most mothers made the swaddling clothes themselves, from woollen and linen material which they had at hand. Occasionally, however, an aristocratic lady would buy her child's swaddling and in 1634 the Countess of Panmure noted in her account book that she had purchased in London for her new-born twins not only two cradles but 'blankets and swaddlebands and sleeves and waistcoats and gloves'. The sleeves were for the babies' arms once the first swaddling was abandoned: they were detachable, and were pinned to the infant's chemise. Thirty years later Anne, Duchess of Hamilton, paid £1 2s. Scots for '1 child's swaddling band', but this is the only such item in all her voluminous accounts. From the mother's point of view, swaddling must have been a time-consuming performance, but presumably repeated practice would render her adept. Tales of it taking two hours are surely grossly exaggerated, nor is it feasible that the swaddling was not changed for days on end. The real objection is the effect it must have had upon the baby himself. Seventeenth-century mothers and doctors firmly believed that they were acting for the best, of course, as one medical authority explained. The child must be thus swaddled, he wrote, 'to give his little body a straight figure, which is most decent and convenient for a man, and to accustom him to keep upon the feet, for else he would go upon all fours as most other animals do'. Swaddling was also believed, erroneously, to prevent rickets, and presumably the fact that this type of constriction produces a lethargic child had its advantages too, for a busy mother. At any event, although the philosopher John Locke was now seriously questioning the wisdom of swaddling, it seems to have continued unabated in seventeenth-century Scotland.[31]

If the method of clothing a baby went unchallenged, the best way to feed him did not, and just as twentieth-century mothers debated the relative merits of breast and bottle feeding, so did their earlier counterparts discuss the advantages of feeding the baby themselves or employing a wet-nurse. The practice of wet-nursing was an ancient one, and because of the lack of early sources it is impossible to say when it was introduced into Scotland. Presumably in any society a baby whose mother has died, or who cannot feed him, will be handed over to a woman with enough milk to care for him. At any rate, in sixteenth-century Scotland it was an accepted fact that aristocratic and middle-class women would employ a wet-nurse.

Often this was done for entirely practical reasons. The young Countess of Eglinton in 1618 had to seek the services of a wet-nurse because she did not herself have sufficient milk, as a letter from her mother-in-law makes clear. 'As concerning your daughter Eleanor,' the older lady wrote, 'I am very glad that you have gotten a young milk woman for her, seeing her mammy proved not sufficient. You have done very wisely in doing the same.' Probably many of these young mothers gave up too quickly, not realizing that it is the baby's sucking which stimulates the milk supply and that the colostrum produced at the beginning is just as important for him. Even in the late twentieth century a surprising number of mothers mistakenly believe that they have not sufficient milk to feed their infants, when more frequent sucking would solve the problem. Some women, of course, were advised against breast-feeding because of the state of their own health. Alexander Forbes of Ballogie's wife was in 1692 'very desirous to have given suck to her child', but her husband and relatives 'dissuaded her from it as being very unfit for her at this time'.[32]

Husbands may also have argued against breast-feeding out of sheer self-interest. Apparently it was generally believed that a nursing mother must not engage in sexual intercourse, otherwise her milk would be spoiled. Some feared too, that if they became pregnant, their milk would dry up and they would not be able to go on nursing the existing child. William Hay mentioned this theory in his lectures on marriage in the sixteenth century and presumably a notion generally current in England and the rest of western Europe would prevail in Scotland too. As for women themselves, probably some of them shunned breast-feeding because they felt it would tie them down too much, and a recipe of about 1690 gives instructions 'for putting back the milk in those that does not intend to give their child the breast'. By anointing her breasts night and morning with oil of elder and applying special opium plasters, the mother could 'put away the milk without any pain or trouble'.[33]

Whatever the reason for deciding to hire a wet-nurse, women always gave careful thought to the selection of a suitable person. Friends could sometimes recommend someone reliable from personal experience, and when Alexander Macdougall's baby died, he suggested that their wet-nurse could go to his sister-in-law, Mrs Colin Campbell, for her new daughter. Anne, Duchess of Hamilton, always felt that a young, fresh woman should be employed in this capacity, but her contemporary, the Countess of Melville, did not think that age was so important. Seeking out a woman for her daughter-in-law, the Countess of Leven, she reported in May 1695 or 1696, 'My dear daughter, I caused Isabel Webster go to Letham to see that woman I spoke of to my son. She is six week brought to bed of a daughter. She is 36 years old and hath had five bairns. Two of them is dead. She is a well-favoured woman, very lean. You may cause the doctor come here and see her milk if you be not provided already.'[34]

The medical authorities of the day were also quick to give advice about the best type of woman to employ. Nicholas Culpeper advised one 'of middle stature, fleshy but not fat; of a merry, pleasant, cheerful countenance and ruddy colour, very clear skin that you may see her veins through it. She loves company, cannot endure to be alone: not given to anger but infinitely to playing and singing, she delights much in children and therefore is the fittest nurse for one.' Dr Chamberlen was equally emphatic. 'As the nurse is, so will the child be, by means of the nourishment which it draweth from her,' he said, 'and in sucking her it will draw in both the vices of her body and mind ... She ought to have a sweet voice to please and rejoice the child, and likewise she ought to have a clear and free pronunciation that he may not learn an ill accent from her, as usually red-haired nurses have.'[35]

The wet-nurse eventually chosen by an aristocratic lady would go and stay in the great house, there to be given board and lodging and a fee as well. This meant that the baby would not have to go away to socially inferior surroundings, the mother would still be in constant touch with him, and the nurse herself would be kept away from masculine society.

Other families could not, of course, afford to install the nurse in their own home and so their children were sent out to stay in the women's households. Sir John Lauder noted in his expenses for 1671 that he had given two and a half dollars to his wife 'when she went to Waughton to see her son', then an infant, while the Duchess of Hamilton's secretary, David Crawford, recorded in his personal notebook that on 25 July 1692 'my son went to Netherliberton to be nursed.' In like manner, George Hay who lived in Edinburgh in 1694 had a daughter about ten months old 'at nurse in the country', William Legatt that same year had 'a sucking child . . . nursing with John Johnston, mason, his wife', and James Penman the goldsmith's youngest was 'at nurse in the country'. The context makes it perfectly clear that these babies had been put out to a wet-nurse, and indeed some accounts even distinguished between a baby's wet-nurse and his dry-nurse, who looked after him in other ways.[36]

Well-entrenched though the habit of wet-nursing undoubtedly was, it was not without its critics. As early as 1612 the French doctor, Jacques Guillemeau, declared that under no circumstances would he permit wet-nursing. In a translation of his work, published in London in 1612, he stated, 'Aulus Gellius (in my opinion) did not amiss in putting no difference between a woman that refuses to nurse her own child and one that kills her child as soon as she hath conceived, that she may not be troubled with bearing it nine months in her womb.' The four reasons he gave for condemning that practice are illuminating. In the first place, he explained, there was the danger that the nurse might substitute a different child for the one given to her. Secondly, the practice led to a diminution of affection between the mother and child. The third and fourth reasons were the dangers or a bad condition of an illness being transmitted to the child by an unhealthy nurse.[37]

Interestingly enough, the documentary evidence suggests that towards the end of the century, more and more aristocratic women were becoming anxious to feed their children themselves. In part, this was probably occasioned by anxiety lest a nurse of inferior social status have an adverse effect upon the child, but the tone of the correspondence also suggests that there was a genuine concern for the baby and a real desire to supply his wants personally. It has been observed that in England it was often the more puritanical mothers who undertook breast-feeding, the argument being that those of their religious persuasion evinced more affection and concern for their families.[38] Whether or not this is so, it is certainly intriguing to note that this growing desire to breast-feed coincided with a period when women were becoming more and more divorced from the other domestic tasks of the household. Perhaps this in itself was a factor: a woman with leisure to sit about her house might contemplate breast-feeding more readily than one who was always busy with the domestic chores.

Whatever the underlying motives, it is interesting to read the evidence for this new trend in maternal behaviour. Her correspondence makes it clear that Anne, 3rd Duchess of Hamilton, did not nurse any of her own thirteen surviving children herself. Even when her second son's wet-nurse failed to arrive in time, a payment had to be made 'to two women who gave Lord Charles the pap before his nurse's entry'. Her daughters, however, were eager to feed their own children. In July 1685 Lady Katherine Murray, her eldest, was writing to her sister Susan, Countess of Dundonald, to explain why she could not be at the latter's confinement. She hoped Susan would 'be strong against [the time when] you cry, which I'm heartily sorry I cannot be a witness to, for my being a nurse renders it altogether impossible'. Indeed, she had so much milk 'that I give my lord and my son sometimes a drink, for I'm forced to milk my breasts, my little girl not being able to suck it all, though she thrives very well and is little or no trouble to me. This is good heartening to you if you design to nurse yours, which I wish you may come as easily to as I did by my last.' Strange as the idea of having others drink the milk may seem to us, it was perfectly acceptable in Katherine's time, for it was thought to have fine medicinal properties and was often recommended as a strengthening tonic. She herself believed that the actual business of nursing did her good too, and a fortnight later she was telling Susan, 'I am grown so fat with being a nurse that I believe you would hardly know me. I never had so good a stomach [i.e. appetite] as I have now.'[39]

Susan was indeed encouraged by her example, and, in 1688, their mother was telling Katherine, 'Your sister Dundonald and her lord and their son on her breast came here on Monday. He has 8 teeth and is a fine, lusty child and she is a good nurse.' Her daughter-in-law, Lady Mary Hamilton, was there as well and advised Susan to wean the child. An animated discussion then ensued, for Duchess Anne 'was for his sucking until September', although she conceded that 'many speaks against it, [so] that I know not what to advise, my skill being less than others'.[40]

Inexperienced in weaning Duchess Anne might be, but her suggestion that it should not take place until the baby was over a year old was by no means unusual. Uncomfortable and inconvenient though it must have been for the mother, most babies were not weaned until they were that age. The general custom in sixteenth and seventeenth-century England was to give the baby milk until his front four teeth had come in, then to introduce him gradually to bread, chicken and eggs. On the continent, the weaning seems to have been a much more abrupt process and it appears from the contemporary correspondence that Scotland followed the continental, rather than the English, model. Certainly, weaning was feared as a dangerous procedure. 'I am very glad, my dear, that George was at first so easily weaned and made little noise,' the Countess of Wemyss told the Countess of Leven in 1696, then went on to warn that various digestive upsets were liable to occur a month after weaning had taken place, so 'for God's sake advert to it, and let his drink in the night be milk and boiled water with a little cinnamon in it, for they agreed best with yourself. Let me know if he likes broth and if he eats a little flesh sometimes.'[41]

Such apprehension was not without good cause, for a horrifying number of children did die in infancy. The parish burial records for the period provide a sad catalogue of early deaths, and the most vivid impression of all comes from the epitaphs of the time. 'Twice five times suffered she the childbed pains, yet of her children only five remains', were the words inscribed on the tomb of the Laird of Enterkin's wife when she passed away in 1676. George Foulis of Ravelston 'left six sons surviving and as many daughters: he had five sons dead before himself and one daughter', while Grizel Scott was buried in the Howff cemetery of Dundee beside 'children six, sprung from her fruitful womb: as many live'.[42]

It would be a mistake, however, to imagine as some writers have done, that those brief lives passed unmourned. Because a woman had twelve children it did not mean that she was indifferent to their fate or that she calmly waited for half of them to die. Just as she stoically accepted childbirth and other suffering as the will of God, so would she try to submit if He chose to take away her sons and daughters, but her grief was very real. Many of the surviving letters show the terror and alarm of parents when their children fell ill with measles, colds, whooping cough, enteritis or the dreaded smallpox. When the worst did happen, parents tried hard to accept it with Christian resignation, but it was no easy task. Many women had very strong religious convictions and they strove to regard death not as the end but as the 'glorious change' which would be the culmination of their life on earth. Their writings make it plain that they were often able to see their own death in this light, particularly if they were older women, but it was much more difficult to reconcile themselves to the death of a child.

A letter of condolence written by the Countess of Rothes to the Countess of Findlater sums up the contemporary attitude very clearly. 'I am sorry for the bad news that your letter brought me of the removal of your sweet little lady,' she wrote. 'The Lord sanctify that trial to you, for to part with a beloved child is no small difficulty, but it ought to be our daily exercise to be endeavouring to get our affections raised off things here, that we may set them on things that are above, where Christ is, at the right hand of the Father. I confess it is no easy matter as strangers and pilgrims to be using the world as if we used it not, and because this is so contrary to our forward nature, therefore the Lord trusts [*i.e.* tries] his people with crosses, that they may seek after true happiness where it is to be had, and be kept in mind that this is not their rest.'[43]

These poignant words in many ways epitomize maternal attitudes in the sixteenth and seventeenth centuries. Whatever her social status, a woman was generally involved directly with the upbringing of her sons and daughters, and if some of her methods of dealing with them seem strange to modern eyes, her sentiments of anxiety and affection are perfectly comprehensible. For perhaps twenty years of her life, a woman's activities were circumscribed and her consciousness preoccupied with the care of her children, but she accepted without question that motherhood was one of her principal functions in life. The bearing of children was both her Christian responsibility and her duty as a wife. In the accomplishment of her role she would suffer pain, tribulation, grief and even death, but she would not seek to evade it. Indeed, the saddest letters of all are from those wives who tried in vain but never did succeed in bearing a living child.

CHAPTER SIX

Education and Leisure

BECAUSE OF THE EMPHASIS on a woman's domestic role, it was only to be expected that the education given to the daughters of the family would be strictly vocational, fitting them to be capable wives but making no attempt to transform them into educated women. At one time it had seemed as though this state of affairs might alter, for the mid-sixteenth century saw the emergence of a number of cultivated, well-educated ladies whose learning was apparently accepted without question by society. They owed their erudition to the spreading of Renaissance ideas throughout western Europe and, of course, they were the ladies of the Court. Indeed, one of the most accomplished women in Scotland must have been Mary, Queen of Scots, herself. Sent for safety as a child to France, she studied Latin, Spanish, Greek, drawing, dancing and singing. She came back to Scotland in 1560 a typical Renaissance princess in upbringing, her library at Holyrood containing many Latin and Greek books as well as Italian classics and French poetry.[1]

Some of Mary's ladies had been brought up in France with her and presumably shared in her education but, because the sources are lacking, we have no more than a hint here and there of feminine learning. Margaret Haliburton, born in 1526, delighted in later life 'to talk of old histories, knew the whole genealogy of her father's house as also of her mother's'. Mary, the daughter of Sir Richard Maitland of Lethington, one of the Lords of Session, acted as her father's secretary upon occasion and had someone compile for her a volume of Scottish poetry: her name and the date 1586 on the title page at one time misled readers into imagining that she herself had composed the poems. Sir James Melville of Halhill's daughter

Elizabeth did actually write poetry as well as being 'remarkable for her piety and intellectual accomplishments'. In 1598 Alexander Hume dedicated his own book of poems to her, telling her that he did so 'because I know ye delight in poesie yourself, and as I unfeignedly confess, excel any of your sex in that art that ever I heard within this nation'. Not only did he know her reputation but he had seen her 'compositions so copious, so pregnant, so spiritual, that I doubt not but it is the gift of God in you'.[2]

A masculine tribute of this nature was not particularly unusual, for there seems to have been no identifiable prejudice against educated women of the time. When John Knox thundered against the Court of Mary, Queen of Scots, it was the religion and morals of the Queen and her ladies which he criticized, not their intellectual pretensions. In England a number of enlightened men thought that an education was a positive advantage for a woman and Sir Thomas More went so far as to declare that a wife should be learned if possible, 'or at least capable of being made so', nor were his famous daughters the only women to be celebrated for their knowledge of the classics and of foreign tongues.[3]

Of course, these cultivated ladies came from the aristocracy and the landed families, but there was at that time every reason to suppose that higher standards of education for women as well as for men would gradually permeate the rest of society, and this was important. While no-one today would argue that education is the key to happiness or the solution to all problems, it does affect how women are regarded by their contemporaries and, indeed, how they see themselves. Given a similar standard of education, they can meet men on an equal footing, but if their literacy is noticeably lacking, it is all too easy for them to be treated as inferiors.

The coming of the Reformation at first sight seemed to hold out the promise that women as well as men would continue to advance educationally. The Reformers themselves, including Knox, were most anxious that women should enjoy their rightful share of religious enlightenment. The ability to read was accordingly an important asset. No longer were the people to be at one remove from the word of God, hearing passages from the Bible read out in Latin in church or seeing episodes enacted in plays or depicted in paintings. Instead, men and women should be capable of studying the scriptures and the catechism for themselves in their own tongue, a practical possibility since the earlier invention of the printing press.

In pursuance of this ideal, the Reformers' intention was to set up a school in every parish, and although for financial reasons this did not immediately materialize, new schools were founded and some of the old song schools were transformed into grammar or parish schools. Indeed, the seventeenth century saw great progress. An act of Privy Council of 1616 clearly stated for the first time the aim of a separate school for each parish, and in 1633 Parliament passed an act intended to make landowners pay for the endowment of schools. Most managed to avoid doing so, but in 1646 Parliament effectively ordered the landowners to provide premises for schools and pay the teachers' salaries. Of course, the pattern was uneven: some parishes had schools, some did not, but as well as their grammar schools, the burghs now often had private schools set up by individuals.[4]

Apart from its encouragement of schools, the Reformation made a less obvious difference which should have had a beneficial effect upon female education. Ministers of the church and all professional lawyers were now allowed to marry and so could have legitimate children. We have already seen how women like Christine de Pisan owed their intellectual interests to paternal encouragement. There must now have been educated Scotsmen who sought as their wives women who could share their enthusiasms and who fostered their daughters' interest in learning. By 1580, for example, Robert Whitelaw of Fentonbarns was leaving forty pounds in his will to ensure that his daughter Margaret would be 'sustained with the rest of my bairns at the school in reading, writing and sewing' for two years. Likewise, he gave careful instructions that her sister Isabel was to remain at school until she 'can perfectly read and write and sew'.[5]

Be that as it may, girls did not benefit as they might have done from this new educational activity. By the mid-sixteenth century they had drawn level with boys in literacy: a hundred years later they had fallen far behind. Despite the increasing educational facilities, the number of girls attending school remained small. Statistics are rarely available, but we do know that, for instance, in the parish of Lochwinnoch, Renfrewshire, in 1697, of the nineteen children attending the local school, only four were girls. The number sank to six boys and no girls at all that autumn, though the following summer the thirteen pupils did include three girls.[6]

The reason for this low attendance was that girls were much more useful to their parents at home than sitting in a classroom.

Not only were they needed to help their mothers but, in the country areas where most of them lived, they were required to take part in the seasonal work of the land, especially at harvest time. Economic circumstances made their assistance a necessity and it seemed a waste of time to send them out for lessons in extraneous subjects. For a boy it was different: literacy was a distinct advantage and already it was becoming a tradition that an intelligent lad would go to school and from school to university no matter how humble his circumstances. If he was clever and hardworking he could enter one of the professions, thereby improving both his financial and social standing. No such means of advancement existed for girls. Their method of rising in the world was to marry well, and everyone knew that what interested a prospective husband was domestic competence not academic achievement. Accordingly, those town authorities interested in encouraging female literacy had an uphill task. In 1618, Paisley Town Council was trying to insist that 'none be put to the sewing-school till they can read perfectly', a stipulation which was echoed in 1688 by the Baron Court of Stitchill, in Lanarkshire, decreeing, 'None of the said tenants or cottars that have daughters shall send them to any sewing school within the barony till they have been two full years reading at the said public school.'[7]

In towns where there were more professional people and where prosperous merchants and tradesmen aspired to improve themselves and their families, there was more chance that girls would go to school, but here too there were difficulties. The very idea of educating girls along with boys seemed to some to be fraught with danger. Ever-vigilant on questions of moral welfare, the Kirk Session of Edinburgh decided that there should be a separate school for each, and that three masters should be employed 'to have the sole teaching of the lasses'. Three years later, the magistrates of Ayr opined that 'it is not seemly that such lasses should be among the lads,' although they agreed soon afterwards that girls could go to the music school, which already had boys as pupils.[8]

Segregation of this kind was discouraging, and it also tended to reduce a girl's opportunity of receiving the kind of education given to her brothers. If she went to the same school and shared the same teachers, it was possible that she could receive at least some lessons in subjects like mathematics or foreign languages, should she show any aptitude for them. As soon as separate classes or separate schools were set up, however, the argument that education should be strictly vocational came into force and girls were given special subjects like sewing, washing and cookery. The mistresses who taught them were often of a poor standard educationally themselves and the more academic subjects were entirely left out of the curriculum. In 1642, for example, when Lady Gordon of Rothiemay gave a sum of money for 'teaching young women and lasses in the town of Aberdeen', the subjects she laid down for them were 'reading, writing and sewing and any other art or science for which they may be capable'. In practice, the mistress employed taught only reading, writing, sewing and music.[9]

The aristocracy themselves were no better placed. With their financial resources and their greater opportunities for leisure, the ladies of the peerage should have been the best-educated group but instead their writing was laborious, their spelling phonetic and their syntax erratic, and this at a time when their husbands could pen a letter with perfect ease. The Scottish nobleman of the period was usually much more literate than his grandfather had been: why had his wife and daughters not made a similar advance?

The answer seems to be that the male members of the Scottish aristocracy were being affected much more directly by the changes around them than were the women. Undoubtedly society was undergoing a series of shifts and alterations, principally because Scotland was growing closer and closer to England. For hundreds of years the two neighbours had lived in enmity, with Border feuds and full-scale warfare a frequent occurrence. Scotland sought her allies in France and made her mercantile contacts with the Low Countries, while England remained 'our auld enemy'. With the Reformation, however, Scotland was transformed into a Protestant country which had in consequence far more in common with Protestant England than with Catholic France. Friendly contacts became frequent, then in 1603 the Scottish King, James VI, inherited the throne of England and moved his Court to London.

This dynastic accident was to have a profound effect upon Scotland. Many male members of the nobility now found it necessary to visit the south each year, spending the winter months at Court. Formerly the centre of power and patronage had been in Edinburgh: now it was four hundred miles away in London, a fortnight's journey in a jolting coach. Moreover, a Scot who was an important man at home appeared at Whitehall or Hampton Court as an unknown figure, a nonentity who had still to make his reputation in the highly competitive circle surrounding the monarch. Sensitive about his status, his appearance and his accent, he was anxious to meet his English counterparts on equal terms, eager to converse about the latest play, speak a foreign language or two and join in agreeable reminiscences about continental travel. He therefore made sure that his sons went from grammar school to university and from university to a modified version of the Grand Tour, studying classics, languages, philosophy and mathematics as they did so and returning from the continent ready to take their rightful place in society.

By contrast, the nobleman's wife remained at home in Scotland, looking after his estates when he went south. Because of the expense and the difficulties of travel, even the wealthiest peeresses visited London at most perhaps twice in their lives. They did not aspire to be ladies of fashion: quite the reverse. Many of them had strong Presbyterian convictions and as the years went by their outlook became more and more strict. The vanities of the present world were to be shunned: no thought should be given to outward show, sumptuous clothes or frivolities such as dancing, playgoing or the reading of fiction. The Court was a centre of temptation and vice, their husbands' visits there a necessary evil. A woman must aim to be a virtuous wife before all else, living modestly at home, dressing unobtrusively and reading only theological works. Removed for much of her time from the stimulating companionship of the educated men she would have met at Court, she was thrown back upon the company of children, servants and local neighbours. The domestic sphere was truly hers and she had little incentive to change her ways. Anxious to protect her daughters from temptation, she kept them at home. There was no question of sending them to the local school along with their brothers. If necessary, a writing or arithmetic master could be brought in for a few months to give lessons, but there the formal education of the daughters of the aristocracy ended. Lessons were haphazard and usually of short duration. There was no attempt at a schoolroom routine: the hours of study were simply fitted in here and there to the normal activities of the day, and it was not surprising that results were poor.

Reading, of course, was the first skill to be taught, so that a girl could study her Bible. This is neatly exemplified in a letter the Marchioness of Argyll wrote to her daughter in 1674. The quotation is given in the Marchioness's original spelling, so that her own attainments may be judged. 'The littell children heir ar all in health,' she recorded carefully. 'I bles God Marie's eie [*i.e.* eye] is much better then it was. I hop it shal be perfectly well. She can reid the bibell pretie well and Anna is reiding the psalme book. Jean is not entered to any lesson.'[10]

It is noticeable that the Marchioness does not mention the children having lessons in writing. Indeed, quite a few ladies still did not learn until fairly late in life. Lady Anna Cunningham was one of these. Born about 1590, she married the 2nd Marquis of Hamilton when she was still in her early teens. Her husband was a favourite at Court. Elegant and sophisticated, he spent much of his time after 1603 in London while his wife, plain, intelligent and energetic, stayed behind in the west of Scotland to run his estates for him and, when he died, for their son. When she was in her forties she began keeping accounts of her expenditure, written in a large, vigorous, italic hand. The spelling is undeniably phonetic and many of her words and phrases have a distinctly Scottish ring to them. She did her arithmetic in what must have been a confusing mixture of Roman and Arabic numerals, and amongst the carefully noted payments was one 'to Mr John Queen that teached me to write'. Obviously this was a fairly recent achievement.[11]

As the years went by, more and more girls of landed families did learn to write in childhood, though not at such an early age as boys did. The latter went to school at six but, for girls, lessons at home did not usually begin until they were seven or eight. They were then taught an italic style of writing, imitating either the letters set out in a copybook or a sample of writing done by a friend or relative thought to be especially proficient. Even so, as late as 1670, the eminent Scottish judge, Sir John Lauder, had to pay £4 8s. 'for a man for teaching my wife writing and arithmetic'.[12]

English and arithmetic presented problems enough, so few early seventeenth-century ladies ventured upon the study of a foreign language although boys were learning Latin, Greek, French and sometimes Italian. Anne, 3rd Duchess of Hamilton, was taught French when she was a girl in the 1640s, but then her father was a great friend of Charles I and his French Queen, and indeed her sister Susanna was later to be a member of Henrietta Maria's household in France. Duchess Anne forgot most of her French in adult life, but she was still rather proud of the fact that she had once been able to speak it. When her own granddaughter, Lady Mary Hamilton, was sent to be brought up in her household, the Duchess decided that she too should learn. Mary was a precocious child and by the time she was seven she could read and she was learning to write. Soon she was being provided with 'the newest and best edition of a French grammar' and attention was to be given to her accent. Her grandmother decided to employ a Frenchwoman who could act as Lady Mary's maid while at the same time teaching her the language. Duchess Anne hoped to engage a woman who was already in service in Edinburgh but this was not done unless the Mrs Anne Twyford who was paid £36 Scots 'for teaching Lady Mary to speak French' was more foreign than her name suggests.

Not only did the little girl embark upon French, but at the same time she began lessons in Latin. A book of the rudiments of Latin grammar was purchased for her just before the French grammar was sought. Sad to relate, however, she caught smallpox a few weeks later and died.[13] The reference to her Latin grammar is the earliest direct mention found so far of a girl studying the classics in the seventeenth century, but it is possible that her aunt, Lady Margaret Hamilton, had done so a generation earlier. The historian of her husband's family has recorded that 'her acquaintance with the classics . . . is evinced by the remarks and notes in her own handwriting which appear upon Latin books in the Panmure library.'[14]

If Latin was an unusual subject for a girl to study and Greek was virtually unknown in feminine circles, much more customary were the playing of music, singing and dancing, and this despite the strictures of the Presbyterian ministers. The ability to play and sing was to be prized in an age when entertainment had to be provided by individuals themselves. The guitar, the virginals, the harpsichord and the lute were the favourite instruments of the seventeenth century and at least one father had very definite ideas about which his daughter should study. Sir Hugh Campbell in 1677 had sent his children to school in Edinburgh, employing his agent there to oversee their education. That winter he wrote to tell the man that he intended keeping the children in town until at least the following March. 'If I find Maggie [to be] an extraordinary player on the virginals, she shall have a pair of the best harpsichords that England can afford,' he declared, 'and therefore let her take much pains. I do not fancy the viola da gamba: the citar or cittern is more proper.' Maggie obviously had her own ideas, however, for two years later Sir Hugh was paying £18 Scots

'To Mr Chambers for teaching Mistress Margaret, a quarter, of the viola da gamba', and had just bought a set of virginals at a cost of £66 13s. 4d.[15]

Once a girl could read competently, sew and play an instrument, her lessons ceased: how, then, did she herself feel about this standard of education? It is difficult to tell, for women were still not accustomed enough to expressing themselves on paper to want to confide their thoughts to a journal or even to put down their feelings in letters to friends. There was a good deal of inhibition about committing anything personal to paper. Letters went astray and could fall into the hands of political or personal enemies. Men and women alike continued throughout the century to be wary about what they wrote and preferred to keep to the old medieval habit of sending any confidential message by word of mouth, with a trusted friend or servant. As Mary Stewart, Countess of Mar, explained to a friend whom she wished to employ in her husband's business, 'This bearer will say that to you which were both longsome and grievous to me to put in write.'[16]

Whether the Countess had in mind the painfulness of her subject or her own lack of ability with the pen is not altogether clear, but most people were perfectly well aware of women's educational shortcomings, not least themselves. Commenting on her sons' Grand Tour in the 1660s, the Countess of Crawford told a friend, 'Their governor says they are both very free from vice, which I look upon as a great mercy, and he would also have me to believe that they have profited by their travels, but I can say less of that, being an ill judge.' The Duchess of Hamilton was equally conscious of her own shortcomings. When her sons were being educated in Glasgow, she had cause to upbraid her eldest for the poor standard of his letters home. Not only was his writing deplorable but, she told him with engaging honesty, 'You spell worse then I doe.' Her contemporary, Margaret, Countess of Wemyss, begged a friend to 'burn all my letters they are so ill writ' while yet another lady declared that her correspondent would be unable to make sense of her letter, 'it is so broad Scots'.[17]

Of course, underlying most of these confessions of inadequacy lay the feeling that the ladies themselves were not really too ashamed of their ignorance. Sometimes it was irritating to have difficulty in formulating a message but there was nothing humiliating about it. A seventeenth-century Countess would draw attention to her own bad writing in much the same way that a mid-twentieth-century woman would confess that she did not understand the workings of a car engine: ignorant she might be, but it was a rather appropriate ignorance of something which rightfully pertained to the masculine sphere. Women were simply not expected to be highly educated and no-one thought any the worse of them if they could not spell. The Earl of Findlater was typical of his contemporaries in his expectation of feminine abilities. In 1687, his son James married a fifteen-year-old bride, Anne, the daughter of Sir William Dunbar of Durn. The following year, the Earl was agreeably surprised when his new daughter-in-law actually replied to a letter he had sent her. 'I will truly say I did not expect to have seen one of her breeding [*i.e.* upbringing] write such sense in such well-connected terms,' he remarked to his son, condescending but impressed. 'I did see three other letters of hers,' he went on, 'all of different subjects, to very good purpose. God Almighty bless her to you and grant that ye and she may be to my family as Jacob and Rachel were to the Israelites.'[18]

The Earl had not expected Anne to be fluent on paper, but when he met her, he would expect her to be presentable in public, and by the 1680s this was taking on a new meaning. The old Presbyterian emphasis on virtue was fading into the background and instead there was a new consciousness of the social graces, of a girl's manner, appearance and accomplishments. Hitherto religious prejudice and the day-to-day difficulties of living in a country torn by warfare had made these considerations of minor importance, but attitudes were changing. The Restoration of 1660 brought to Scotland a degree of lasting domestic peace and, in a reaction against the years of warfare, thoughts turned away from religion and self-denial to entertainment and recreation, pleasure and a comfortable life. This change was reflected in building styles, for example, as houses finally lost their defensible character and owners pulled down their old fortresses to replace them with mansions modelled on the great houses of England and France. In this tranquil environment, habits and values altered and there was more time to think about fashionable clothes, new dances and the latest card games.

The older generation of aristocratic ladies, while continuing to uphold their lifelong religious principles, were more tolerant with their daughters than their own mothers had been with them. After all, they reasoned, if a young man was used to Court ways, he would never take an interest in their daughters unless the girls were fashionably clad and able to play an instrument, sing and dance as the English ladies could. A little innocent pleasure of this kind was surely no sin if it gained a girl a wealthy, respectable husband.

So it came to be that, by the end of the seventeenth century, the ladies of the peerage were beginning to modify their outlook and where they led, the ambitious middle-class mothers would follow, adopting their habits and imitating their manners. Moreover, the polite accomplishments could not really be learned at home. It was all very well if a family lived in Edinburgh, but for those whose home was in the country there was little possibility of employing local teachers who were sufficiently *au fait* with the latest styles. Daughters would either have to be sent to Edinburgh for the winter, or they would have to attend school there. As early as 1662 an enterprising lady by the name of Mistress Christian Clelland was setting up an establishment in the city to teach 'reading, writing, singing, playing, dancing, speaking of the French tongue, arithmetic, sewing, embroidering'.[19] A few years later Isabel Gray was urging her brother-in-law to send his daughter Helen to her so that lessons could be arranged to 'perfect her of her playing and writing' and, when the 3rd Duke of Hamilton's household stayed in their apartments in the Palace of Holyroodhouse, the daughters of the family went to Mr Edward Fonteine and later to Mr William Maclean for dancing lessons.[20]

By the turn of the century the emphasis was firmly on the accomplishments, and the sort of regime prescribed by Lady Grizel Baillie for her daughter must have been repeated in many other homes. Young Girsie was to rise before seven in the morning and begin the day by reading, presumably theological works. Breakfast was at nine, after which she would put in about two hours of practice on the spinet. From eleven until twelve she was required to read and write French. From two until four she had to sew her seam, then a brief period of learning arithmetic intervened before she danced and played on the spinet once more until six o'clock. From then until supper she was allowed to amuse herself, before being sent to bed at nine.[21]

The reaction of girls themselves to the tedium of this undemanding routine goes unrecorded, but it was obviously well below the level of ability of some of them. John Clerk's description of his late wife, Elizabeth Henderson, reveals that she would obviously have been capable of much more. She was possessed of an excellent memory, and after reading a chapter of the Bible over two or three times she could repeat it exactly. Moreover, 'in the acquiring of all other things, such as sewing, playing, singing, etc. she was so smart that what others with difficulty attained to in a month, she became completely master of in a day, upon which account none of her overseers [*i.e.* teachers] tied her to the keeping of any diet [*i.e.* regular school hours] as the rest were, but were content she should come and go from schools at her pleasure.' On Saturdays, when the other pupils were hastily studying their catechisms and psalms, she did not set out for school till eleven o'clock and then it was a matter of an hour or two to learn passages which it took the others a whole week to memorize. In addition to the work set by the mistress, she regularly learned five or six psalms and a similar number of religious poems selected for her by her father. She excelled 'in all her exercises, but more signally in music, in playing on the virginals and sewing. She was so great a master in the theory of music that in a month's space she learned to play at sight upon the thorough bass, [in] all of which she has left many choice monuments of her skill and industry.'[22]

Even if one attributes most of this praise to the bereaved young husband's partiality, the memoir does point to the fact that the kind of education offered to most girls made few demands on their intelligence. They were not, after all, being educated with a view to allowing them to develop their intellects or earn their own living. The accomplishments they sought to acquire would make them attractive as potential wives and would allow them in later life to pass their leisure hours in an agreeable manner.

Leisure indeed was to gain in importance as the years went by, reflecting the same changes in society which influenced female education. In the Middle Ages, there had been little time for real leisure except in aristocratic circles, and this was to remain true throughout the sixteenth century. Most women were still much occupied with the practical tasks of life, but at the Court of Mary, Queen of Scots, in the early 1560s there was a good deal of light-hearted recreation. Young and energetic, the Queen liked deer hunting at her palace of Falkland and in 1564 went on a spectacular hunting expedition to Perthshire, organized for her by the Earl of Atholl. Two thousand highlanders were employed for two months on that occasion, driving deer into the selected area. On a less grandiose scale, Mary and her ladies held archery contests at Holyroodhouse, where butts were set up in the gardens. She played golf on the sands at Seton, enjoyed a game of pall-mall (a type of croquet) and was fond of long walks as well as of riding.

Music was another passion. She had a pleasant singing voice and she played both the lute and the virginals. She liked to dance, too, and after she married Lord Darnley they enjoyed performing pavanes and galliards together. The recently introduced puppet plays amused her, and in the evenings she could be found playing chess, billiards and backgammon. She had inherited her mother's love of card-games and gambling, but most famous of all was her fondness for needlework. Although the number of existing pieces of embroidery attributable to her has been much exaggerated, it was an occupation she always enjoyed. In her early days as Queen she used to take a piece of sewing with her to the meetings of her Privy Council and during her later periods of imprisonment she found solace in the working of elaborate birds, animals and symbolic motifs for wall-hangings.[23]

Another enthusiastic needlewoman was Lady Campbell of Glenorchy, the daughter-in-law of Katherine Ruthven who had produced the colourful embroidered hangings of the 1550s. Lady Campbell by 1598 had hemmed 98 linen serviettes then in use in her household, along with a further three dozen 'marked with blue silk'. Katherine Oliphant, the wife of George Dundas of that Ilk, worked a table carpet which still exists at the house of Arniston. The design in this instance consists of two medallions, one showing St Paul urging Timothy to take a glass of wine, the other depicting a gentleman giving a loaf to a beggar. Sewing remained perennially popular, and although by the late seventeenth century many furnishings were being imported from abroad, ladies still liked to work bed hangings and cushions as a relief from the more monotonous tasks of making up nightgowns and shirts for their husbands and children.[24]

The reason why so many girls were taught music was in order that they might entertain themselves and friends in later life. By the late seventeenth century, keyboard instruments were to be found in most large houses. The 2nd Marchioness of Hamilton possessed virginals and regularly purchased books of music for herself and her daughters in the 1630s; Spynie Castle, near Elgin, had a set of virginals in 1640; and in 1693 Lucy, Dowager Countess of Nithsdale, was having virginals brought to her home in Dumfriesshire.[25]

Although it has been suggested that the virginals purchased by Sir John Foulis in 1680 might have been made in Edinburgh, it does seem that most keyboard instruments were imported from England. The customs books of the period reveal regular imports, such as the five sets of virginals ordered by an Edinburgh merchant from London in March 1667, and one of the Countess of Leven's friends certainly sought her harpsichord in the south. 'I went this day into the city,' she wrote from London to tell the Countess, 'and enquir'd for harpsichords. I chanced to fall on John Bolton, who made these in the Wemyss [the home of the Countess's mother]. He has 2 pairs, one lesser, at five pounds (which I do not much like) of the ordinary fashion, the other larger, at 8 pound, which has 3 rows of footrails. (You know 2 is ordinary.) By pulling the piece of wood at the side you may use 1, 2 or all 3 as you please, so that the sound is softer or higher as you have a mind. He has none made of the fashion of these which you have, the fellow whereof is at the Wemyss. You know there is a vast difference betwixt these two your mother hath, though Bolton makes none of the price and he says he can make them in 3 weeks. If you need either of the 2 sorts, be pleased to show me which you like best and I shall take care to get them as good and cheap as I can.'[26]

Apart from playing keyboard instruments, ladies could now accompany themselves on the lute as well as the guitar. The guitar or cittern had been known since the Middle Ages, but the lute, although popular in sixteenth-century Italy, was not introduced into England until the last years of that century and came to Scotland at about the same time. It was by then a firm favourite throughout Europe and a great quantity of music was being written for it at the continental Courts. Indeed, it was in the seventeenth century the principal instrument for entertainment at home. Many portraits depict English ladies holding a lute and there is at least one of a Scottish lady of the 1670s, Margaret, Lady Kerr, similarly posed.[27]

As for guitars, although they were not so popular in the seventeenth century as they had been earlier or as they were to be later, they were still to be found in many households. To take but one example, the Countess of Melville was in 1692 having lessons from a German to whom she paid £8 4s. Scots a month 'to teach me the guitar'. She seems to have been an enthusiastic musician, if perhaps a little heavy-handed: at the same time she had to spend £3 12s. to have her guitar mended and another £12 'to Alexander Adam for mending my virginals'.[28]

Dancing to music in the home was another pleasant and continuing diversion and when Lady Margaret Hamilton visited Edinburgh in the winter of 1684 she lamented the fact that she was not getting so much exercise as she had done at her parents' castle of Kinneil, for there she and her sisters called in the daughters of their neighbour Walter Cornwall of Bonhard 'and several other gentlewomen and danced sometimes'. Outdoor activities provided a better source of exercise, of course, and at least until about 1640 ladies enjoyed falconry. The 2nd Marchioness of Hamilton was often to be found 'at the falconing in Avendale', high up above the Clyde valley, and once she paid £3 Scots for a lark net. However, there is no sign that her granddaughters ever went out with hawks although their husbands certainly did. More to the taste of ladies of the 1660s and 70s was bowling. Many of the larger houses now had a bowling alley in the gardens where the game could be played in the company of visitors. In the summer of 1667, the 3rd Duchess of Hamilton played bowls frequently, on one occasion losing the great sum of 18s. Scots to her cousin, Lady Bargany. She likewise gambled away small sums of money at cards, on 3 September 1657 providing herself with £12 Scots before she went into her Great Hall to play with friends. Interestingly enough, even very upright Presbyterian ladies like the Duchess were quite willing to lose small sums at cards and other games with no hint of disapproval of such an activity, although their views about other forms of pleasure could be very rigid.[29]

By Duchess Anne's time, one new source of recreation was readily enough available, and that was reading. Printed books had been on sale since the late sixteenth century in the Edinburgh shops and, by the end of the seventeenth century, newspapers were being printed in Scotland too. We must remember, of course, that a significant number of women still could not read at all and those who did so limited the subject matter of their books severely. Almost without exception, when a lady wished to pass some time reading she would pick up a theological book. Lilias Grant, the wife of Sir Walter Innes of Balvenie in the north of Scotland, was entirely typical in her tastes. About 1630 she carefully wrote out 'the names of my books'. She owned twenty-eight of them, beginning with *A Book to learn to Live and Die*, including the *Imitation of Christ* and ending with a work entitled *The Ambassador between Heaven and Earth*.[30]

Knowing his customers' tastes, the Edinburgh merchant John

Bonar was in the 1640s importing '6 unbound Bibles for women' at 9/- Scots each and when Lady Margaret Kennedy in 1679 wanted to give a friend a special gift she sent her *The History of the Reformation of England*. The Duchess of Hamilton once distinguished herself by purchasing no fewer than '100 books against popery' and when the Duchess of Atholl asked her husband to buy books for her in London in the early eighteenth century, her list noted *A Rebuke to Backsliders or a Spur for Loiterers* by R. A., *The Soul's Preparation for Christ* by Mr Hooker and Newcome's *Sermons of acquaintance with God*.[31]

Other subjects occur only occasionally. In 1677 John Clerk of Penicuik's wife possessed four books on midwifery, one on general medicine and one on cookery, as well as the usual selection of theology. A few years later Lady Eleanor Montgomerie's only secular book was a modern version of a medieval Scottish chronicle and at the turn of the century Lady Cawdor owned a book on palmistry, another on arithmetic and *The Rules of Civility*. Presumably in similar vein was *The Guide to Gentlewomen* Sir John Lauder bought for his wife in the 1670s, not long before providing himself with a rather more daring volume entitled *For the Art to Make Love*. Men were much more adventurous in their literary tastes, but it would be reasonable enough to suppose that at least some wives and daughters read the romances acquired in London by the men of their household.[32]

Certainly, ladies' tastes widened as time went on and in the first years of the eighteenth century at least one of them was well-read in philosophy. Margaret, Lady Nairn, wrote to a friend reflecting that whether 'all the actions of us mortals are only links of the inevitable chain of fate, or proceed they from a free will guided by unstable passions and various interests, most part of the world appears so unstable, one thing today and another tomorrow, that I confess I cannot think their motions are fix'd or decreed for all eternity'. The source of such musings was made explicit in a later letter to the same friend. Describing her trials and tribulations with a weaver who was making her some cloth for a gown, she confessed that this 'has vex'd me more than one would think for, but with reading Epictetus's *Morals* I've learn'd so much of the philosopher as to make the best of what happens [to] me, even in the smallest matters, so I comfort myself that tho' my gown shall not have so much fine flowered work, yet if I can get it wrought at home, which I'm put in hopes of, it will be both cheaper and last longer'.[33]

Reading her theological books or working at her bed hangings was a pleasant way for a lady to pass quiet hours at home, but occasionally something more exciting was desired. The problem was that the limitations of transport still very much restricted mobility and limited the circle of people a woman saw regularly. If she wanted to travel any distance at all she had to be able to ride. That was all very well if she was healthy and energetic, but it posed problems if she was pregnant, elderly or in poor health. The rich did have coaches by the end of the seventeenth century and public coach services were even being introduced in some parts of the country, but roads were poor and the jolting and danger of accidents deterred many women from travelling far afield.

The exigencies of travel therefore dictated the form of entertaining which could be undertaken by women living in the country. They could exchange visits with near neighbours easily enough, but anyone from farther away had to be asked to stay for a few days in order to make the tedium of their journey worthwhile. Families would gather for marriages and funerals, but otherwise a girl who moved far away from her own locality often saw very little of her own relatives and could feel extremely isolated.

Even when ladies did go to town, Presbyterian sentiments coloured their feelings about public entertainment. Playhouses, balls and masquerades came under frequent censure and it was only towards the end of the century that these became acceptable forms of diversion for wives and daughters. In the 1690s, the Countess of Wemyss's daughter Margaret went south for the first time and her letters home reveal something of an untravelled girl's reactions to the unusual range of leisure pursuits to be found in London.

Margaret was young, eligible and attractive, so friends took her about a good deal. Soon after her arrival, she reported to her sister, 'There was plays acted here and I was at 3 of them, but they are gone now.' Not only had there been plays. 'There has been frequent balls. I was at 4 and danced at two. We have no other diversions but to walk in the Meads.' Some weeks later she declared, 'I am disappointed of this place, for I both thought it was finer than it is and much cleaner and I think it as dirty as Edinburgh.' Even appearances at Court failed to arouse her enthusiasm. She was invited to the lodgings of her fellow-Scot, the Countess of Dundonald, when Princess (later Queen) Anne paid a call. The Countess was ill at the time, and 'was laid on the top of her bed; when we heard the [Princess] was coming we ran all down and stood like so many of the guards at the door and then conducted her upstairs where she sat a little, then went away, we all running after her.' A fireworks display for the King's birthday received equally short shrift. 'I expected,' complained Lady Margaret, 'to have seen some wonderful show . . . but all [that] was to be seen was the mob throwing squibs' and the Lord Mayor's Show was no better. 'I've heard music of all kinds then they made a parade on the streets where I could hardly see them.' The only part she really enjoyed was the moment when a squib singed the cravat of Sir William Douglas, her unwelcome suitor. Of course, Lady Margaret was writing deliberately to amuse. 'My dear,' she had told her sister, 'all I beg of you is that you may not let anybody see this nonsense, which is only to divert you.'[34]

Even so, most Scots were anxious to show friends at home that they were not being corrupted by the decadent allurements of the city, and the Earl of Wemyss boasted, 'As for the rattle and pleasures of London, nobody is or can be less affected with those than I am, and my wife has as little taste of them as one could wish. Plays and operas and park are places either of us are very seldom seen in,' and he added somewhat implausibly, 'We live as retir'd as if we were in the highlands of Scotland.'[35] Equally immune to the sophisticated pleasures of the city was Lady Nairn, who visited London in difficult circumstances in 1716. Her husband had been imprisoned for his Jacobite activities and so she went to Court where she interceded successfully for him. This major preoccupation apart, she was determined to make good use of her time in the south and she announced her intention of finding out an improved method of making candles. Many Scottish households still made their own, but she felt that there must be a better method than laboriously dipping the wick into hot wax time and time again until the candle was formed.

She explained to her friend the Countess of Panmure that she had also made enquiries about the bleaching of the wax, 'which is done by being melted into very thin casks and laid in the sun and constantly watered. The hotter the sun, the sooner bleached.' As an aside, she added, 'Your Ladyship sees I forget no part of housewifery by being at Court. When we meet, I'll divert Your Ladyship with telling you how, just after coming from Kensington, I went to a tallow chandler's, who was to give me some instructions about making the moulded candles, and I assure you, I found it much more difficult to get spoke to the greasy fellow than to His Majesty, for to the last I was always readily admitted, but the first would only see me when I came at such proper times as he thought fit, which was very rarely . . .'

She likewise busied herself with arranging to have cloth dyed, but she was well aware of how such domestic activities would be regarded by the English aristocracy. 'Lord,' she exclaimed, 'How would our courtiers despise me if they knew I were taken up with such unfashionable things as this: but everyone according to their mind. For my share, I never was so weary of any place as of their beloved London. I pray God send my lord and me well home to poor old Scotland again. It puts me in mind of a verse,

> "O happiness of sweet retir'd content,
> To be at once secure and innocent."'

The new tide of fashionable activities had not yet transformed the mode of life of the upper and middle-class women of Scotland, and Lady Nairn knew that she and her friends could still enjoy there the peace of the countryside and the happy security of old ways.[36]

CHAPTER SEVEN

Activities

A ROUND OF VISITING, theatre-going and dancing might occupy the English ladies at Court while their servants looked after the menial tasks of the home, but in Scotland the situation was rather different. There, the mistress of the household continued to involve herself in the daily activities of the domestic sphere, and this was true even in the most wealthy families. Many of the large estates were virtually self-supporting, the occupants of the castle receiving dairy produce, meat, poultry, eggs and cereals from their own lands, sometimes in the form of rents in kind from the tenants. There were chamberlains to see to the gathering in of this produce, and a master household to organize all the catering, but even so, the great lady was to be found inspecting the supplies as they came in, rejecting those of inferior quality and keeping a careful record of what was used. Luxury goods had to be purchased elsewhere, of course, but it was usually the mistress of the household who decided what was to be bought and who sent the order to the Edinburgh or Glasgow merchants. A small scrap of paper bears witness to the 2nd Marchioness of Hamilton's activities in this respect. 'John,' she had written one day in the 1630s, 'I pray you, cause help these men up the brae with the wine.' Not only had she personally ordered the wine from France, but it was she who dealt with the carriers and sent for the coopers to make barrels when it arrived.[1]

No matter how wealthy the household, its mistress was always anxious to obtain a bargain. As soon as the Marchioness of Argyll heard in 1674 that 'William Johnston has caster sugar, right good of the kind, and cheaper than I have known him to sell it, 30 shillings the hundredweight,' she wrote off excitedly to tell her daughter Lady Kerr about it. She would indeed have sent a consignment herself, she declared, 'but the transport of those things is very fashous [*i.e.* tiresome] and he may do it with less trouble'.[2]

Commercial transactions apart, ladies were always ready to help each other out in a domestic emergency. They were constantly sending each other goods, sometimes as gifts, sometimes in response to explicit requests, as well as passing on advice and information, and in this way once more demonstrated their own involvement with their domestic concerns. In the spring of 1613, Lady Jane Drummond was writing to thank her 'sweet sister' Anna, Countess of Eglinton, for her offer of linen and aquavitae. The Countess's kindness was much appreciated, Lady Jane replied, but she must not put herself to such trouble, for 'you have many houses to furnish, and it were a pity to give too much ado at once'.[3]

This domestic interchange continued to flourish until the end of the seventeenth century. Margaret, Countess of Wemyss, in about 1698, was preparing to pass on to her daughter, Anna, Countess of Leven, some muslin in her possession and she also allowed her to choose one or two woollen table covers from her own supply. 'I forgot the tablecloths I promised you, of the star knot [pattern],' she wrote to explain. 'The best and biggest, I believe, will suit your fine napery, for tablecloths are never so fine as napery.' The cloths had an embroidered or woven design incorporating the letter 'W', but Lady Anna could alter this. 'You may cause take out the W and put in L,' she suggested helpfully, adding, 'It was never used although it is washed, for it was dirtied in shearing and very ill-bleached, and also ill-washed, but when you cause bleach it with Balgonie water it will look much better. I have but one of the same and your sister has the third.'[4]

At about that time, Lady Anna received from her sister Margaret 'a little cut of my Inchtuthill linen to be your morning aprons', together with the promise of a pot of walnuts and cherries and a choice Bonchristian pear. Lady Anna's fondness for fruit was well-known to her family, and after her recent visit to her sister, Margaret had written to say, 'I could not but laugh to find your two great apples under the cushion of the easy chair some days after you went from this.'[5]

On a less frivolous note, ladies frequently not only exchanged medical advice but sent remedies of their own purchase or making. In 1657, when the Countess of Airlie heard that her grandchild was ill, she lost no time in sending off herbs to make a special broth, and instructions to boil them with chicken and some raisins. The Marchioness of Argyll was able to supply 'green ointment and eye salve' needed by her daughter Lady Kerr in 1674, and six years later Lady Mary Campbell, Countess of Caithness, was dispatching some of her well-known ointment to Sir Thomas Steuart of Grandtully, with the assurance that it was 'a sovereign cure for all stitches and pains in any part of the body'. When summer came and more herbs were available, she would let him have some more, but in the meantime he could try 'a pot of oranges and a few orange and lemon cakes, which are much commended for the scurvy, to be eat now, in the spring'. She added, 'I made them last week, a purpose for you,' and if he liked them 'I can at any time make more of them.'[6]

In her own particular way, the great lady was obviously much taken up with household management, and her less comfortably placed contemporaries continued to spend their time cooking, baking, washing and spinning as they had done for hundreds of years. Woman's traditional role was accepted and understood, but even so there were always occasions when she was involved in activities beyond the strictly domestic, usually in her capacity as her husband's helper and representative. At a humble level, this meant working in the fields in place of him when he was away, or helping him in his trade or business. In the upper echelons of society, it meant supervising the running of his estates and his legal affairs. Great ladies had always undertaken these responsibilities from time to time, but now they found themselves called upon to do so even more frequently. Before 1603, husbands would go to Edinburgh for several weeks at a time to attend Court or Parliament, but in that year the King inherited the throne of England, and although Parliament remained in Edinburgh, all those who sought the favour of the monarch had to go south.

In law, of course, a woman could not administer her own property, let alone her husband's, unless specific arrangements for her to do so were made. Even a great heiress like Anne, 3rd Duchess of Hamilton, who had been running her estates for several years before she married, had to hand over her inheritance to her husband. However, within weeks of their wedding in the spring of 1656, a special commission was drawn up by which he empowered her to act by herself without his consent, in uplifting rents, granting leases and in 'sundry other things concerning the managing of her affairs'.

Admittedly, this was a very unusual occurrence. More conventional was the document her husband caused to be drawn up just after the Restoration, on the eve of his first visit to London. Narrating that their business 'cannot be well managed without [*i.e.* unless] the said Lady Duchess our said spouse be authorized with our commission and power for that effect, as the person who is not only chiefly interested but is also most careful, dextrous and able to manage and govern her own and our affairs', he named her as his legal representative.[7] Unlike the other, this is not an unusual document, but a perfectly normal arrangement of the kind made by the vast majority of husbands who had to be away from home for long periods and had important property or business affairs which would require attention during their absence. To take but a handful of other examples, when James, 5th Lord Ogilvy, went to France in 1572, he made his wife his 'factor and commissioner'; the 1st Earl of Buccleuch constituted his wife Mary his commissioner when he set off for the Low Countries in 1627 and Sir John Dick delegated similar responsibilities to his wife when he had to be out of Scotland for several weeks in 1684. 'Being very confident and having the experience of the fidelity of Dame Anna Paterson, my beloved spouse, and of her good government and ardent desire to promote my interest', he appointed her his 'actrix, factrix and special errand bearer and plenipotentiary', with powers to collect his revenues and generally run his estate on his behalf.[8]

As wives acted for their husbands, so did widows often manage their sons' affairs until they came of age and even after that. Himself a married man, the 6th Earl of Eglinton always left his business in the hands of his mother and one or two of his own advisers when he had to be away. His wife played no part, for all his fondness of her, and in 1612 she was apparently quite happy to report, 'As for your ados at this time, my heart, I will assure you of my lady your mother's great care for the weal of all your affairs,' while the Dowager Countess herself wrote, in similar words, 'As for your ados here at this term, they are at a reasonable good point.' She had succeeded in gathering in some forty thousand merks from people who owed him money, and she was busy paying off his own debts and the interest from them.[9]

Widows also had their own jointure lands to consider, and perhaps it was only to be expected that someone of Dame Juliana

Ker's forcefulness would continue to keep a keen eye on the estates left by her first husband. Indeed, she insisted on retaining for herself lodgings in all his houses, in addition to her jointure proper. Her son George must have read with a sinking heart her letter to him of 3 May 1634. Certainly she would hand over for his use the house of East Mains of Polwarth, she said magnanimously, but on one important condition. She would retain 'the laigh [*i.e.* low] chamber, which I will keep for my own use and pleasure and will keep the key thereof and have my bed and coffer therein, to come there when I please . . . which, I trow, will be sooner nor ye believe'. Anticipating his reaction, she added briskly, 'Do not storm at this, nor think not that it comes of any other [person], for of my conscience it does come of no living creature but myself only, who will not for nobody denude myself altogether of some house to come where I please.'

Not only her son but her chamberlain and her neighbours were the objects of her wrath. 'The devil reward Master Robert,' she declared of the former, when he ordered the thatching of a house contrary to her wishes, and when he sent her fifteen dead fowl in a consignment of living poultry, she at once instructed her son, 'Tell Master Robert that I am little obliged to him, for he has begun the new year with me as he ended the old, with scant and want of money.' The better to drive home the message, she added, 'I protest I live like one that had nothing, for of conscience I may not command this night one Scots turner [*i.e.* a small coin] and I am sure forty sundry [creditors] craving me, but he does not care a whit.' Lack of money did not prevent her from engaging in frequent litigation, suing her neighbours for what she regarded as encroachments on her property. 'God's curse light upon him for the trouble and vexation he brings to me,' she declared of one such gentleman who fought her allegations in court, telling her son picturesquely that the only direction anyone would help her in was 'backwards'.[10]

It would be a mistake, of course, to suppose that every landowner was browbeating his tenants or hounding them for money. There are frequent incidences of ladies complaining to the Privy Council on behalf of their tenants, protecting their interests and generally overseeing their welfare in a kindly manner. To take but one or two examples, when a dispute arose between James Glen and Andrew Logie at Cortachy, it was to the Dowager Countess of Airlie that James's mother turned for help, asking her to effect a reconciliation, and at the turn of the century Anne, Duchess of Hamilton, regularly gave back rents to her tenants 'in respect of the bad and calamitous years bypast'.[11] There are frequent examples of ladies encouraging the building of bridges, schools and almshouses on their lands, not to mention improving their tenants' houses.[12]

Sometimes their concern for the successful running of the estates also led women into rather more unusual spheres of activity. Marion, the wife of Mr George Douglas of Parkhead, not only examined her husband's contract to work the lead mines on his land, but herself went and spoke to possible miners, with the satisfactory result that twenty men declared their willingness to enter her employment. Anne, Countess of Lothian, was more interested in coal. Her mine prospered to such an extent that, when she died, her husband noted that she had been 'excellent in . . . augmenting the estate of her house in the revenues of the lands, with the addition of winning of coals by long labour and much charge and expenses'. Costly the operation might have been, but it was well worthwhile, for she was able to leave to her children the gold she had accumulated 'when I had a good coal [mine] going'.[13]

Apart from their dealings with tenants and their day-to-day estate administration, ladies were frequently active in improving their own residences. After Sir Walter Scott's castle of Branxholm was destroyed by the English in 1570, he decided to rebuild it, and upon his own death his widow completed the task, setting up a stone on the façade to record her own part in the reconstruction. In 1618, the Earl of Moray's wife, Lady Anna Gordon, and a neighbouring lady were busy quarrelling over some lime needed by both of them for their separate building activities, and Sir Robert Lauder's daughter Jane apparently occupied her time during her husband's absence abroad by erecting a fine new house for him.[14]

The Countess of Lothian made improvements to her house and busied herself 'beautifying the entries and accesses by many walls and enclosures and plantation of trees of all kinds'. Gardens had always been a source of pleasure for ladies, and as the seventeenth century progressed, more and more of them took to the fashionable new diversion of planting trees. Lady Anna Cunningham, 2nd Marchioness of Hamilton, was one of the first to show an interest, and in the 1630s she asked her friend Sir Colin Campbell of

Glenorchy to send her some fir seeds. As she explained when she received them, 'Believe me, I think more of them nor ye can imagine, for I love them more nor I do all the fruit trees in the world.' Moreover, she could boast, 'I have already a four or five hundred of my own planting that is pretty trees.'[15] Her granddaughter, Anne, Duchess of Hamilton, had all manner of fruit in her famous orchards; the Countess of Caithness, now married to her second husband, Sir John Campbell of Glenorchy, grew apricots in the gardens at Balloch and Viscountess Tarbat laid out new lawns at Castle Leod, while Margaret, Countess of Lauderdale's accounts for 1701 record her purchase of young fir trees from the Highlands, and lime tree seed and filbert nuts from London, for the gardens at Kinnaird.[16]

The great lady's involvement in activities such as these arose from her sense of duty and her desire to help her family and dependants. For women from poorer backgrounds, it was sheer economic necessity which took them beyond the confines of the home. Eight or nine out of ten women still lived in the countryside and life for many of them was very hard indeed. A glimpse of the activities of cottars' wives is afforded by a document drawn up by the justices of the peace in Midlothian in 1656. This laid down the duties not only of agricultural labourers but of their wives too. The latter had to 'shear daily in harvest, while [*i.e.* until] their masters' corn be cut down'. They were to help their husbands to gather in the hay, cut peats and attend to the lime kilns. They must assist in the carting and spreading of manure. They were to carry stacks from the barnyards and the barns for threshing, take food to the animals, clean the byres and stables and help to winnow the corn. At the end of an exhausting day out of doors doing such hard physical labour, they must have had little energy left for preparing food, looking after the house and bringing up the children. Yet their lives depended on this work, for it was the money brought in by the wives' wages which paid the rent of the cottar houses in which they lived. The actual wages paid were, of course, low. In the summer of 1674 Margaret Richieson and her husband Thomas Vair in Lanarkshire were earning not quite forty shillings for eight and a half days' work harvesting Agnes Lillie's corn, while, twenty years later in the same locality, Isabel Hoggart made only £5 8s. Scots for one summer's work.[17]

If an estate had not only agricultural land but also coal mines, women were to be found working as bearers. Much has been written about the serfdom of miners in Scotland, but this did not really come into being until after an act of Parliament of 1606, which stated that a collier could be employed only if he produced a testimonial from a previous master, stating that he was free to take up work. From this arose the system prevalent by the end of the century, in the east of Scotland in particular, whereby miners and their families were regarded as being the property of the mine owner. The men hewed the coals and the wives and daughters were employed to carry them. The pits were not very deep, but to reach the surface, the unfortunate women had to climb steep turnpike stairs bearing baskets of coal on their backs. At the salt pans too, women acted as bearers, carrying salt from the pans to the storehouses. The financial rewards for this type of work were very low, the physical demands excessively high. A woman coalbearer in 1700 would earn only 4d a day, but as long as her husband was employed in the mine, it was required that she should help in this way.[18]

Only a small number of women were actually employed in the mines at this period. By far the most common method of supplementing the family income was to enter domestic service, a straightforward extension of the woman's work in her own home. As had been the situation in the Middle Ages, all but the poorest households had one or two female servants who lived in and were paid a money wage, sometimes supplemented by shoes and items of clothing, as well as having board and lodging. By undertaking such work they were no longer an economic burden on their parents and in 1694 James Denham, a customs official at Bo'ness, was able to report with satisfaction that he had none of his children still at home, 'being all at service'. When in 1694 a record of the people in the propertied households of Edinburgh was drawn up for taxation purposes, the names of dozens of female servants were listed. They earned, on average, £10 to £12 Scots a year, their employers ranging from prosperous advocates and merchants to widows in reduced circumstances.[19]

Relatively few girls found employment in aristocratic households, where the majority of the servants continued to be men. Not only were men employed in the gardens and the stables, but the kitchens were entirely staffed by men, the master household [i.e. steward] was a man and there were footmen and pages to usher in visitors and run errands. Those women who were employed fell into two distinctive categories. There were several well-born gentlewomen, who acted as companions to the mistress of the household and whose role was akin to that of ladies-in-waiting at Court. They certainly never undertook any domestic duties of the more menial kind. Gentlewomen apart, there were one or two other female servants indoors. The nursery was obviously run by women and the role of the wet-nurse has been discussed elsewhere.[20] The dry-nurse was a more permanent feature of the household and was often recruited from the wives of the male servants. She saw to all the child's other needs and generally supervised his upbringing. As befitted her responsible position, she was well paid. Lybra Granger, who took care of the Duchess of Hamilton's young daughters in the 1660s, was paid £200 Scots a year, a sum equalled only by the amounts paid to the master household and the tutor to the sons of the family. This would seem to have been a typical situation, and in the smaller town households listed in the 1694 Edinburgh poll tax returns, the family nurse was paid three or four times as much as the other women servants.[21]

Apart from nurses proper, there were various nursery maids. During the period 1704–8, the 4th Duke of Hamilton's young children each had a nursery servant, his son and heir being provided with two. These women were paid from £8 to £12 Scots a year each. Often, they were quite young girls, and it is said that Mary Macleod, the celebrated Gaelic bard of the early seventeenth century, was first employed as a nurse in Dunvegan Castle at the age of nine. Thereafter she cared for no fewer than five infant chiefs of the Clan Macleod.[22]

So much for the upper servants. Elsewhere in the household, women were employed in tasks of inferior status. There was always at least one washerwoman, sometimes with a laundry maid to help her. In 1682 the Marquis of Tweeddale's two washers were receiving £15 Scots each a year, while the Duchess of Hamilton's washer, seventeen years later, had £18 Scots. These women washed not only the shirts, underwear and night clothes of the family, but they were responsible for laundering sheets, pillowcases and tablecloths. In 1670 the Duke of Lauderdale's washers were buying pins to pin out the linen and glue 'for making up the napery'. An extra woman was brought in to help at Hamilton Palace if there was especially heavy work to be done, and in 1690 the Duchess was paying £1 4s. Scots 'to a hired woman for scouring 2 suits of hangings and 20 pairs of blankets and helping to wash sheets and other linens at several times'. Women were also employed in the dairy, while both the Hamilton and Lauderdale households included a woman who bore the delightful title of 'necessary lady'.[23]

Out of doors, the only female servant was the henwife who attended to the poultry. Usually she was an old woman and something of a character in the establishment. During the period of the persecution of witches, henwives were sometimes identified as dealing in mysterious cures and having converse with the Devil: indeed, in a list of religious delinquents in the parish of Drumelzier in 1684, there is mention specifically of Agnes Stewart, the poultry woman at Traquair, 'an old hen witch wife'. On that occasion Covenanters, not witches, were being sought, and so she was allowed to continue her life undisturbed.[24]

In towns, there were also opportunities for women to hire out their domestic skills for the use of others. The number of domestic servants in town houses has already been noted. Other women were attached to no particular household but offered their services to those who needed them. At the end of the seventeenth century, Widow Hamilton and Widow Guthrie were both in business as bakers, supplying dozens of rolls to the palace of Holyroodhouse and the Earl of Panmure's establishment respectively. Even more enterprising had been the wife of an Edinburgh skinner, who in 1588 was apparently engaged in a flourishing catering business. In that year her husband was admitted to the merchant guild, an organization which placed great emphasis on the social standing of its members. The skinner was accordingly allowed to become one of them only on condition that his wife would no longer undertake 'common cookery outwith his house'. She was also to promise not to carry 'meat dishes or courses through the town' nor were she and her servants permitted in future to appear on the street wearing their aprons.[25]

Other women set up in business as washers. When the aristocracy came to Edinburgh for parliamentary sessions, they did not bring a full complement of servants with them. Footmen, grooms and secretaries came, but the humble washerwoman remained at home. In 1670, therefore, Margaret Marshall was employed by no less a personage than the Duke of Lauderdale 'for the washing of his linens for his own body' and in like manner, every other day Margaret Fletcher, wife of John Douglas in the Canongate of Edinburgh, received bundles of muslin cravats,

handkerchiefs, linen and cotton shirts, linen drawers and night
cravats to wash for the Duke of Hamilton and his family. Seven
years later, Mrs Douglas was still hard at work, laundering cravats,
cuffs, stockings, shirts and sleeves for the Earl of Panmure.[26]

For the most part, outer clothing was made by male tailors, but
in the late seventeenth century there is the occasional mention of a
seamstress. A list of Covenanters in Roxburgh in 1684 included the
name of Agnes Dalyell, 'seamster', while the Edinburgh poll tax
records ten years later note that, lodging in the house of Mr Patrick
Mowbray, lawyer, was Jean Montgomery, 'seamstrix'.[27] These
women probably made up shirts and headdresses rather than
dresses and suits. Many others, of course, were involved in the
making of cloth by spinning. They would receive the raw wool
from their customers, spin it into thread, give the thread out to a
weaver, then give back the finished cloth once he had done his
work. In 1698, Elizabeth Hamilton, wife of a Hamilton merchant,
received nine stones of white wool and two and three quarter stones
of black wool from one of the Duchess of Hamilton's servants. This
she spun and had made up into $71\frac{1}{2}$ ells of black cloth which she
delivered back to the palace.[28]

Cooking, washing and spinning were accepted parts of a
woman's traditional work. By the sixteenth century it had also
become a recognized tradition that a wife would help her husband
with his business and, if widowed, would earn her livelihood by
continuing that business. The Edinburgh tax roll of 1565 includes
among its 327 names eight women, three of them widows, and the
contribution levied from them suggests that they were making
substantial profits. Similarly, the Edinburgh stent rolls of 1605 and
1614, also drawn up for taxation purposes, record a number of
wealthy widows of merchants who were probably themselves
engaged in commerce. Again, Sara Brown, whose testament was
registered in 1634, was described as being 'merchant burgess of
Ayr' and when Margaret Bisset in 1660 sold cloth to Lady Ogilvy,
she designated herself 'merchant in Perth'. Likewise, when Janet
Scott's testament was registered in Edinburgh in 1707, her
occupation is given as 'shopkeeper'.[29]

Scattered references such as these in official records are an
indication of the general situation. Further details of women
involved in commercial transactions are to be found in their
individual accounts and receipts. These reveal that a number of
women were involved in the sale of clothing and cloth. When the

Earl of Panmure visited Edinburgh in 1687, he purchased ruffles, shirts, nightshirts, cravats and caps from Janet Douglas. Two years later, his Countess was buying more ruffles, muslin, lace and crêpe from Mrs Mary Campbell, and Indian stuff, linen and gloves from Anna Wallace. That same year, Anna Chiesly, shopkeeper in Edinburgh, was able to supply Sir Charles Erskine of Cambo with cravats, and on another visit to Edinburgh four years later, the Countess of Panmure was purchasing ribbon, gloves, lace, shirts and a muslin headdress from Mrs Robert Lightbody, who had actually made up the shirts and headdress herself.[30]

Apart from selling clothing, many women were occupied with the purveying of food. In 1665, Katherine Kennedy was able to supply the Countess of Airlie with currants, sugar, salt, sack, aniseed, liquorice and vinegar, as well as sending her soap. Since the Countess paid part of her bill for £561 19s. 4d. Scots in wool, Katherine probably did spinning as well.[31] Some women supplied only one commodity, possibly selling it at an outside stall or going from door to door. Thus George Skinner's mother, Christian Weir, 'an ancient woman of 60 years of age' was 'a butter wife' in Edinburgh in 1694 while Margaret Stevenson in that same year was a 'fruit wife'. When Anne, Duchess of Hamilton, bought fruit from Agnes Dallen and Agnes Salmon in the 1680s, both were described as 'fruit wives'. She bought her fish from 'Janet Harper and Bessie Hempseed, fishwives'. Bessie, who lived in Fisherrow at Newhaven, also numbered the Marquis of Lothian among her customers, supplying him with such delicacies as oysters, lobsters and flounders. Moreover, she was quite capable not only of signing her own name but of writing out her own receipts.[32]

The fishwife was a familiar figure on the streets of sixteenth and seventeenth-century Scotland and equally well-known were the many female taverners, brewers and tapsters. In January 1580 James Moncrieff was told that he must pay all the local taxes because 'his wife holds an open tavern and hostelry' in Edinburgh, 'and thereby enjoys the privilege of a freeman'. Three years later, the tax roll of the town mentions eight female brewers, seven tapsters and a taverner, only two of whom were apparently widows. Several disputes involving women employed in taverns came before the Privy Council in the 1630s, with Nancy Haddock complaining that her employer Janet Robertson, taverner, had unlawfully had her thrown into prison on a charge of keeping back money paid by the customers. Janet was obviously in business on her own, for her husband David Dalrymple had employment as a wright. Other women seem to have supplied wine to private households: Sara Ingram and her servants were paid £43 18s. Scots in 1651 for wine bought on behalf of the 2nd Duke of Hamilton, and when the Hamiltons' master household died in 1680, the sack, wine and brandy drunk at his funeral had been purchased from Mrs Gibb in Edinburgh. Finally, there was the unfortunate case of William Livingstone's widow, Helen Wilson, who kept an inn near Edinburgh Castle. It was well-stocked with liquor of every kind, but during the siege of the castle in 1689, Helen was forced by the firing of the guns to close her doors and evacuate both the tavern and her own comfortable house beside it. When peace was restored and she was able to return, she found not only that her house had been destroyed but that the soldiers had drunk her entire stock.[33]

Suppliers of other goods encountered less dramatic problems, although their wares covered a surprisingly wide range. In 1702, Widow Henderson in Leith was supplying coals to Holyroodhouse. Barbara Mutter sold candles in the small Lanarkshire village of Cambusnethan in 1691 and Margaret Jamieson was apparently carrying on her late husband's business as a candlemaker in Edinburgh in 1696. Other women kept dishes and cooking utensils. The Bo'ness customs books reveal the import of large quantities of pans in the 1660s for Bessie Gibb, Agnes Gibson, Janet Wilson and Elspeth Gibb. Such were the quantities involved that these cannot have been for private use and must have been destined for sale. Perhaps this Agnes Gibb was the same woman who in 1684 was able to supply the Earl of Panmure with large English dishes, trenchers and ashets. The Earl also patronized Mrs Grisel Edmonston, from whom he purchased such valuable items as a gold seal, a gold sweet box, a crystal bottle and a wooden box decorated with filigree work. This was probably the same 'Mrs Edmiston' who had fine beds and bedding for sale in the 1680s and 90s.[34]

Of course, unlike the butterwives and fishwives, most merchants and shopkeepers did not limit themselves to one type of goods but sold the wide variety of commodities found in our own century in village shops. When Isabel Young, widow of John Norwell, died in Edinburgh in 1584, her merchant booth contained a mixture of items including ten boxes of whitewood combs, half a pound of 'gross stocking silk', six sand glasses and several books. Similarly, the Countess of Panmure was able in the

1690s to obtain from Jean Seton in Edinburgh not only lace, flannel, a pin-cushion and pins, but gloves, sweet oil and anchovies.[35]

Shopkeeping was a conventional enough activity for wives, but some women found themselves drawn into less usual occupations because of their desire to assist their husbands in business. The late seventeenth century saw the setting up of post offices in Scotland, to facilitate the sending of mail and packages. By 1685 Agnes Brown was acting as postmaster at Haddington. Her husband, William Seaton, had occupied this position and now that he was dead she carried on his activities, petitioning the Privy Council for the post horses she needed. Three years later the Privy Council found it necessary to issue a letter to an unnamed 'post mistress' instructing her to take special precautions, since certain rogues had been intercepting packets coming from England, and in 1690 a postmistress herself was at fault. Abigail Gibb, widow of the postmaster at Holyroodhouse, had been found guilty of breaking open the seals on packets coming from London and had to be reproved by the Privy Council.[36]

Women by now were not only able to keep accounts and look after postal packets: some were engaged in businesses which required a high standard of literacy. In 1693 Edinburgh had a female bookseller, Martha Stevenson, the widow of Alexander Ogston, who had kept a bookshop in the town. A letter she wrote to the Earl of Findlater on 22 September of that year reveals her personal involvement in the business. She had, she reported, sent off his lordship's order, which included a dictionary, an edition of *Don Quixote*, *The Gentleman's Recreation* and four volumes about a Turkish spy. At the moment she had nothing new to offer, save for a life of the Duke of Lorraine, a discourse on natural and revealed religion, and a defence of episcopacy. However, more books would be coming in and she was able to promise him a fifth volume of the spy in the near future.

A few months later she was sending the Earl a biography of the Duke of Lorraine and the discourse on religion, along with Sir William Temple's essays. A further selection from London would be forthcoming and she was apparently knowledgeable enough to pick out what she thought would interest him. In that same letter she spoke of dispatching, presumably on approval, 'all the new books I have at this time which I think fit to send Your Lordship' and later sent him Locke's *Essays*, Aesop's *Fables*, some sermons and some poetry as being 'the choicest new books I have got, the which I thought would most fit Your Lordship'. Their relationship was only slightly clouded by the Earl's suspicion that she was charging him too much, but she was able to reassure him that 'I do not exact one farthing more from Your Lordship than what I sell to others for ready money.'[37]

Her business continued to flourish, and when the poll tax was imposed in 1694 Mrs Ogston claimed that it was worth between 5000 and 10,000 merks. As the majority of the richest merchants declared their stock to be worth 10,000 merks, Martha was obviously among the most prosperous. She had four children to support, but she was able to keep two apprentices and two female servants. She was still prospering in 1704 and 1706, when she numbered among her customers the 4th Duke of Hamilton. She was able to supply him with such works as Clarendon's *Memoirs* at £20 Scots, *The Dutch Gardener* at £2 2s., a set of parliamentary minutes and, for his frivolous young Duchess, his unlikely choice of a life of Pythagoras and a volume entitled *Reflections on the politeness of Manners*.[38]

Akin to the activities of Mrs Ogston was the career of Agnes Campbell the printer. Agnes was the daughter of an Edinburgh merchant from a minor landed family. Born in 1637, she married at the age of nineteen Andrew Anderson, whose position as royal Printer allowed him a monopoly of certain publications. His work was much criticized by his contemporaries, but it seems to have been of no poorer a standard than their own. However, when he died in 1676, he left Agnes with a huge burden of debt and at least eight children, the youngest of whom was only five weeks old.

Unable to support her family in any other way, Agnes resolved to continue his business. A clever woman with great strength of character, she was to need all her determination in a field in which rivalry was bitter. It is not possible to assess how much technical expertise she acquired: the fact that she took the rather unusual step of employing a 'corrector' may be an indication of lack of skill but may equally well have been the result of the fact that, with a family to raise as well as a business to look after, she could not do everything herself. Certainly a surviving letter from her gives an impression of capability. Writing to Baron Clerk of Penicuik, she granted two requests he had made on behalf of the local minister. She declared that he was welcome to have 'a pass key to the fountain at Penicuik' and went on, 'The second request, which was that he should have as much paper as he might write his sermons upon, I am as willing to grant as the former, so entreat he may acquaint me what sort of paper he would have and what quantity and it shall be readily sent to him, for I am very sensible of his great care of and his good service done to my men there, and I heartily wish they may improve aright [by] his most edifying doctrine.' She had also sent the Baron some paper 'of the same size with your enclosed before it was cut, and also with the same mark and of equal fineness'. The fact that Agnes dictated this letter is another indication of preoccupation rather than of incapacity, for her signature at the end is neat and competent.

By the time she wrote to the Baron, Agnes had married again. This union with a widowed merchant eleven years her senior was not a success, and they agreed to separate. Resuming the name of Mrs Anderson, Agnes succeeded in becoming Printer of the Acts of the General Assembly and defended her monopolies with great determination. Styling herself 'His Majesty's Printress', she was ready to complain to the Privy Council whenever her rights were infringed. Her business flourished and she was able to acquire the lands of Roseburn, near Edinburgh, henceforth styling herself 'Lady Roseburn'. Her office of King's Printer expired in 1716, but after a fierce struggle with her principal rival, she succeeded in having it renewed. Eighteen days later she died, at the age of eighty, leaving over £78,000 Scots, several warehouses in Edinburgh and a collection of religious and legal books.[39]

Booksellers, printers and the schoolmistresses who were beginning to establish themselves in Edinburgh were eminently respectable. At the other end of the spectrum came the prostitutes who continued to offer their services in the large towns in spite of the fulminations of both Church and local authorities. Any harlot apprehended in vice, declared Edinburgh Town Council in 1578, should be wheeled through the streets in a cart and banished from the town. Nevertheless, prostitution flourished and nearly a hundred years later the magistrates were receiving complaints that the town was 'filled and pestered with a number of thieves and whores', many of whom had already been scourged and banished on several occasions, to no avail.[40]

Generally speaking, women's activities did not bring them into conflict with the law. There was always a fair number of trivial squabbles which resulted in women appearing before the local courts, charged with verbal abuse, minor assault and rowdiness.

Neighbours both male and female, officials and the local landowner were the most frequent targets for slander, and the offender was usually fined or made to stand in a public place in the jougs, an iron contraption resembling a collar which was fixed to a wall of a building, usually the church, and which was fastened round the offender's neck.[41]

From time to time, more serious crimes came before the courts. The incomplete records of the High Court of Justiciary between the years 1570 and 1700 include fifteen cases of women charged with murder. A further seven were prosecuted for serious theft, there was one instance of fire-raising, one of perjury and one of counterfeiting coins. Similar cases came before other courts, but although the high court records are not comprehensive, they do serve as an indication of the pattern of female crime. Apart from those general cases, there were other groups of offences which pertained particularly to women. Some of these were of a sexual nature, with thirteen of the women being tried for adultery, eight for incest and one or two others for similar offences. There were also those women who appeared in court as a result of having murdered their newly-born children. This was a consequence of the Church's harsh attitude to extra-marital sexual activity, for an increasing number of girls who bore illegitimate children were fearful of the consequences and made away with the baby, often in collaboration with their own mothers. Tragic cases of infanticide came before the courts more and more often after 1690, when Parliament passed an act declaring that any woman who suppressed a pregnancy and could not produce the living child was guilty of a capital offence.[42]

The other charge against a horrifyingly large number of women was that of witchcraft. It has been calculated that between 1560 and 1707, over 3000 people were executed for this crime, most of them women. This did not mean, however, that dozens of women were actively practising sorcery. The charges were, rather, a reflection of the outlook of the time. Before the Reformation people had lived happily in the belief that they shared the world with spirits, both good and evil. The saints could intervene in daily life and so could a variety of fairies, water horses and other mischievous creatures. The Reformers were anxious to stamp out superstition, and so they not only condemned the veneration of saints, but set out on a pursuit of evil spirits which had originated in a more minor way in the fifteenth century. Witch-hunting gained an increasing hold on the public imagination, and there were four periods of vigorous persecution of alleged witches.

Some of the women who appeared before the courts were genuinely deluded, imagining themselves to have held converse with the Devil. Often led by a male warlock, who promised them a better way of life in the service of the Prince of Darkness, gave them new names of startling banality – 'He said I was to be called not Margaret but Janet' – and introduced them to a degree of sexual intimacy, they did meet in covens. For the most part, however, the unfortunate women appearing before the courts had done nothing more than offer a herbal cure to a sick neighbour or by chance lived next door to someone who died suddenly. Any unpopular, unprotected woman, especially an aged widow, was liable to be accused of sorcery. Formal charges were laid by the community, she was tried and then tortured until she 'confessed'. Sometimes a pricker tested her with a long needle, seeking the tell-tale spot on her body which was insensitive to pain and proved conclusively that she was a witch.

Very often the women subjected to this treatment in desperation admitted to crimes they had never committed, and at the urgings of their tormentors, implicated perfectly innocent neighbours. One wretched woman awaiting execution, finally admitted in confidence to Sir George Mackenzie, the eminent judge, that 'she had not confessed because she was guilty, but being a poor creature who wrought for her meat, and being defamed for a witch, she knew she would starve, for no person thereafter would either give her meat or lodging, and that all men would beat her and hound dogs at her, therefore she desired to be out of the world.' Like all the others found guilty, she was strangled at the stake and then burned.[43]

The unhappy women who perished in this way had found themselves at the centre of public attention by accident. Usually, they had not been acting out of any great sense of purpose or from any driving principle. Their private concerns had led them along a disastrous path which ended in death. Other women, however, from all sections of society were willing to endanger their lives out of a firm belief that they must act according to conscience. During the first decades of the period, it was Roman Catholic women who found themselves in difficulties. Excommunicated by the established church and often imprisoned for harbouring priests, women like the Countess of Abercorn, Elizabeth Maxwell, widow

[159]

of the Town Clerk of Dumfries, and Janet Ogilvie, wife of an Aberdeenshire miller, all refused to renounce their manner of worship, in spite of the penalties of both church and state.[44]

Later in the seventeenth century, the authorities were more concerned with prosecuting Covenanters, those strict presbyterians to whom the episcopal form of church government was anathema. Feelings ran high, and determined ladies were to be found on both sides in the struggle. It was said that Lady Anna Cunningham, Marchioness of Hamilton, led a troop of armed men with a pistol in her belt, threatening to shoot her own son if he opposed the Covenanting cause. Women from all backgrounds refused to attend normal church services, instead going to alternative gatherings held out of doors and known as conventicles. Unlike the Marchioness, Anna Keith, Lady Methven, a generation later was a vehement opponent of the Covenanters and when she received word that a conventicle was meeting on her lands, she rode at the head of sixty armed men to disperse the participants.[45]

During Charles II's reign, women frequently appeared before the Privy Council charged with attending conventicles, or simply with staying away from church. Under such circumstances, it was once again easy for the vindictive to raise charges against perfectly innocent women, who had been prevented by force of circumstance from attending regular services. A number were able to produce certificates explaining that pregnancy, miscarriages or extreme old age had rendered them unfit for the journey to church. Undoubtedly there were many others, however, who deliberately participated in conventicles because they could not accept the King's ecclesiastical policies. There is ample evidence that many of them did so entirely of their own initiative, and in direct defiance of their husbands. At the beginning of the century, the government had pointed out that husbands were responsible for their Roman Catholic wives' ecclesiastical misdemeanours, and the Privy Council now found it necessary to reiterate this responsibility and declare that husbands must pay any fines imposed upon their Covenanting wives. The urgent public debate which resulted was an indication of the number of husbands who felt this to be unfair. Quite unable to persuade their wives to go to hear the local minister, they were most unwilling to pay the fines. Eventually, the opinion of the King himself was sought, but His Majesty upheld the traditional view: husbands must continue to be liable for their wives' 'ecclesiastical disorders'.[46]

Janet Scott, wife of Sir Thomas Kerr of Ferniehirst, 1593,
by an unknown artist.
(*The Duke of Buccleuch and Queensberry, K.T., V.R.D.*)

Mrs Esther Kello,
calligrapher, 1595, by an
unknown artist.
(*National Museum of
Antiquities of Scotland*)

Juliana Ker, Countess of
Haddington, 1625, by an
unknown artist.
(*The Earl of Haddington,
K.T., M.C.*)

Rachel Chiesly, Lady Grange, by Sir John Medina.
(*The Earl of Mar and Kellie*)

The Henwife of Castle Grant, 1726, by Richard Waitt.
(*The Earl of Seafield*)

Right:

A Glasgow Shopkeeper of the 1790s, by an unknown artist.
(*The People's Palace Museum, Glasgow*)

A Highland Wedding by David Allen (Engraving)
(*The Earl of Stair, K.C.V.O., M.B.E.*)

Jane Welsh, Mrs Thomas Carlyle, by Kenneth Macleay.
(*Scottish National Portrait Gallery*)

Mary Fairfax, Mrs William Somerville, by Thomas Phillips.
(*Scottish National Portrait Gallery*)

Flora Drummond, 1936, by Flora Lion.
(*Scottish National Portrait Gallery*)

In danger of financial penalties, imprisonment and even death, women continued to attend the conventicles and harbour men who did so. A series of executions resulted, notably that of the famous 'Wigtown martyrs'. In 1685 an eighteen-year-old girl named Margaret Wilson and a wright's widow in her late sixties, Margaret McLaughlan, were found guilty of Covenanting activities and sentenced to death. They were to be tied to the stake within the floodmark at the mouth of the River Bladenoch, near Wigtown, so that they would drown as the waters rose. That same year, six other women were branded and transported to New Jersey for similar offences.[47]

Finally, women were prominent among the Quakers, when the Society of Friends came to Scotland during the Cromwellian period. Condemned by both church and state, they persisted with their meetings and at the end of the century one of their most prominent preachers was Margaret Miller, wife of the gardener at Holyroodhouse. When frequent public attacks led to the closing down of the Edinburgh meeting house, Margaret preached in the open air, guarded by her husband on one side and her son on the other.[48]

When their religious convictions were called into question, women from all sections of society were willing to take action, from the ordinary wives who rioted when the Prayer Book was introduced, to the great ladies who defied both their husbands and the local presbytery. Similarly, when their homes or families were threatened, they hastened to the rescue by whatever means they could. A surprising number of women, for example, were able to arrange daring escapes when their menfolk were held in prison. James, Lord Ogilvy, certainly owed his life to the ladies of his family, after he was captured at the battle of Philiphaugh in 1645. Taken to the formidable castle at St Andrews, he was cast into a dungeon and tried for his royalist activities. His judges found him guilty and he was sentenced to death. 'The Maiden', the guillotine used for executions, was transported by sea from Edinburgh and, by the beginning of January, was in position. On the very eve of the execution, he was permitted a final visit from his mother, his wife and his sister. By the time these ladies entered the castle to make their farewells, they had devised a desperate plan. Lady Margaret, Lord Ogilvy's sister, was very like him in both size and colouring. Somehow or other, she contrived to change clothes with him in his prison cell. He donned her skirt and cloak, while she climbed into his bed, pulling the covers well up over her head.

When the little party of visitors left the castle, none of the guards was surprised to see the supposed Lady Margaret weeping into her handkerchief, presumably overcome by grief. Once they were safely out of sight, Lord Ogilvy put on his masculine attire, leaped on his waiting horse and made good his escape. Meanwhile, his sister spent the night in his place. When morning came and she knew that concealment was no longer possible, she sat up in bed, boldly greeted her guards and plucked off her nightcap. Down tumbled her long hair, and the deception was revealed. For two days she was held in the castle and questioned unceasingly, but her mother's family were influential and after that she was released. In spite of the price of £1000 sterling on his head, her brother was not betrayed and in 1639 he was pardoned.[49]

It was not so common now for women to have to defend their castles against the enemy, although it did still happen. Sometimes, the situation arose because of local feuds: in 1581, David Lindsay of Vayne's wife was besieged by the Grays of Dunninald in her tower at Redcastle after a dispute. On other occasions, there were wider issues at stake, and during the Civil War and the Cromwellian periods, various ladies found themselves left behind in the family fortress when their husbands went to serve King or Covenanters. Lady Margaret Scott, second wife of the 6th Earl of Eglinton, was just one of those ladies. Her husband was captured at the battle of Worcester and she was anxious to garrison her small fort on the island of Little Cumbrae, off the west coast of Scotland. She therefore wrote to the Marquis of Montrose, begging him to send her forty soldiers, because without them, she explained, 'I shall not be able to maintain it in such a posture as is necessary to oppose our enemy.'[50]

Defending fortresses, rescuing men from certain death, dying for their religious convictions, running successful businesses and toiling at hard, physical labour: the range of feminine activities was wide indeed, giving ample proof of the courage, energy and capability of the women of the time. Restricted they might be by the legal provisions of their day, but they nevertheless found it possible to engage in all manner of occupations which gave them the opportunity to use their intelligence, organizing ability and domestic skills. Of course, they were playing a supportive part, and if they had to earn a living outside the home they did so in an extension of their role as wives and mothers, cooking, cleaning or nursing for someone outwith their immediate family. It was an exceptional woman who was able to find a different outlet for her creative talents and a mere handful were able to do so. In 1586, when she was only fifteen, Esther Inglis was beginning her career as a calligrapher. Daughter of a French schoolmaster who fled to Edinburgh after the Massacre of St Bartholomew's Eve, she apparently learned calligraphy from her mother and became its most distinguished exponent in the Scotland of her time.[51] Mary Macleod combined her work as nurse in Dunvegan Castle with the composition of the works which earned her the description of 'most original of all our Gaelic poets', while in the early eighteenth century Mrs Batherston found a more limited fame by making death masks in wax.[52]

These women were exceptions, however. The limited education women received did not encourage self-expression, nor did it allow them to be in the position of competing directly with men. The wife helping in a business or the woman running estates was merely fulfilling her traditional role as man's helper, and even the widow engaged in commerce did not normally meet with public disapproval, because it was accepted that she was doing so for the support of her family and would presumably retire when she had a son old enough to take over from her. Only very occasionally is there a hint of censure. Mrs Anderson the printress is said to have incurred particularly bitter opposition because she was trespassing on the distinctly male world of printing, and there are some indications that in post-Reformation Scotland restrictions were being placed on women's business activities which had not existed in the Middle Ages. By the late sixteenth century it was no longer possible for a woman to become a bonnet-maker burgess, a position previously open to her, and the minutes of various other incorporations in the same period record women in subservient positions only.[53] The significance of these developments is difficult to assess because of lack of evidence, but they may well have been the first signs that when women did begin to compete directly with men, they would incur the hostility and alarm of the opposite sex.

PART THREE

1707-1830: WOMEN IN SOCIETY

CHAPTER EIGHT

The Woman of the World

IN THE WINTER OF 1790, Lady Helen Hall wrote enthusiastically to a male relative, describing her family's recent doings. Installed in Edinburgh for the winter, they were finding the current entertainments quite excellent. 'The horsemanship, rope-dancing etc. at Parker and Jones's circus is very diverting,' she noted. 'There is a better company of players at the theatre than any that have been seen here for the whole season together, for the manager in general used to bring a good actor down for a few nights and away again. The private balls have been innumerable and the whole people seem vastly well-disposed to gather together and make merry . . .' She, her husband and their two boys were all well, 'each at our sundry and several pursuits, *he* philosophising, *I* running into dissipation, one brat learning to speak and the other attempting to walk'.[1]

A seventeenth-century lady like Dame Juliana Ker or Margaret, Countess of Wemyss, would have stood amazed at the new social climate. In their day, women lived their lives at home in the country. They saw their own families and their neighbours, but difficulties of travel separated them for years at a time from other relatives and friends. Visits to Edinburgh did not take place with any regularity and even when they were in town their outings to shops and to other households were made in the decorous company of mothers and sisters and servants. Moreover, public entertainment was all but unknown.

At the beginning of the eighteenth century, however, a quiet revolution was taking place. For many years the great barrier to public entertainment had been the Presbyterian disapproval of idle frivolity. Dancing in public places and attendance at

[167]

playhouses were anathema to ministers and strict churchgoers alike, but by the 1670s this puritanical fervour had begun to wane and the visits to Scotland of James, Duke of York, at the end of that decade gave new impetus to the demand for more sophisticated pleasures of the kind available in London. The Duke's residence at the palace of Holyroodhouse, where he virtually held court, was the opportunity for all manner of celebrations and it was no coincidence that, at this very time, Edward and James Fonteine the dancing masters were allowed to assume the title of Masters of the Revels in Edinburgh. This enabled them to hold public balls and masquerades and to license any other dancing masters inspired to follow their example. When this monopoly was constantly infringed, they sent bitter complaints to the Scottish Privy Council but, not to be outdone, their principal rival, William Maclean, made a counter-plea criticizing their interpretation of their powers and was told that he could continue to organize balls and lend out masquerading clothes as long as he did not do so in return for money.[2]

In the south, publicly arranged balls finally received the royal seal of approval when Queen Anne visited Bath in 1703 and, as well as taking the waters, attended an 'assembly' arranged for her diversion. This took the form of an evening devoted to card-playing and dancing. So popular did assemblies immediately become that they spread rapidly, and in 1710 Scotland's first opened in a house at the West Bow in Edinburgh. It was not until 1723, however, that the Edinburgh Assembly proper was established in a large hall off the High Street, in a lane which was later to be named Old Assembly Close.

Margaret, Countess of Panmure, was one of those who viewed the new development with interest. Her husband, a Jacobite, was in exile on the continent but she had stayed on in Scotland to look after his interests and she spent the winters in town with her friend Lady Orbiston. Writing to amuse her husband with the latest gossip, on 24 January 1723 she recounted, 'There are not many company here this winter, but we have got a new diversion here which is an assembly, which I believe will take very well in spite of the Presbyterian ministers railing at it. I have been at one. The young folks dance and the elder ones looks on. They are to play at little [card] games, I mean, for little money, but I am to be no gamester and I believe shall go but seldom. The President of the [Court of] Session, I am told, was there this night to be an encouragement to it, so at last you may imagine Auld Reekie will grow polite with the rest of the world.'[3]

The Countess was being somewhat self-effacing, for she herself was the moving spirit behind the entire enterprise. She and several of her friends, including the indispensable Lady Orbiston, had decided that an assembly would be the ideal method of providing a respectable diversion while at the same time raising money for charity. The organizers were known as Lady Directoresses, and one of them presided at each evening's proceedings. Under their aegis, tickets were sold for two shillings and sixpence each beforehand to a select group of young people, the proceeds going to a good cause. There would be no unseemly changing of partners during the evening, and a strict etiquette was enforced. Indeed, it was common practice for the Lady Directoress to quiz any new arrival unmercifully about her origins and social standing before she was allowed on to the dance floor.

Far from discouraging attendance, this formality helped to make the assembly an immediate success. Reassured that their offspring were not going to mix with any unsuitable companions, aristocratic and middle-class parents gladly allowed them to attend. Each Thursday at four in the afternoon, the ticket-holders accordingly hurried to the hall. At a signal from the Lady Directoress, dancing could begin. A small ensemble struck up and people took their partners for a series of minuets. Half way through the evening, tea, coffee, chocolate and biscuits were served, while the dancers rested and chatted together. Contrary to Lady Panmure's expectation, the Edinburgh Assembly never did include card-playing in its programme. Revived by the refreshments, the participants were then ready for a period of energetic Scottish country dancing which continued until eleven o'clock at night. After that, the gentlemen strolled home by the light of flambeaux carried by their servants and the ladies were borne away in their sedan chairs.

Despite the vigilance of the Lady Directoresses, it would seem that the dancers were ready enough to enjoy themselves in a boisterous way. In 1746, the organizers found it necessary to hang up in the lobby of the hall a set of rules which included the following prohibitions: 'No lady to be admitted in a nightgown [*i.e.* a negligée] and no gentleman in boots . . . Each set not to exceed ten couples to dance but one country dance at a time . . . No dancing whatever to be allowed but in the ordinary dancing place

. . . No misses in skirts and jackets, robecoats nor staybodied gowns to be allowed to dance country dances but in a set by themselves. No tea, coffee, negus nor other liquor to be carried into the dancing room. It is expected no gentleman will step over the rail round the dancing place but will enter or go out by the doors at the upper or lower end of the room . . .'[4]

The assembly continued to flourish throughout the century. Lady Orbiston took over as principal Lady Directoress when the Countess of Panmure died, and in 1736 fine new premises had been opened. By 1747 a sixth Lady Directoress had to be pressed into service, and smaller assemblies were opening in country towns like Haddington. A further refinement came into being in 1755, when Comely Gardens behind the palace of Holyroodhouse were opened in imitation of the celebrated Vauxhall Gardens in London. Two dancing rooms and four drawing rooms were available, with no fewer than sixteen arbours, 'all elegantly furnished for the recreation of company, and a good band of music'. Lamps lit the gravelled walks after dusk; fruit, wine, sweetmeats, tea and coffee were served, and every Wednesday and Saturday evening there were dances from 6 p.m. until 10.30. Perhaps the Scottish climate was not so well-suited to such diversions as the warmer south, for some people complained that on leaving the dancing rooms for the gardens they caught cold from the night dews, and there were those who alleged that the sound of the dance music drowned out the concerts which were held at the same time, but on the whole the venture was a success and in his journal for 1769 James Boswell recorded a pleasant visit there with several ladies.[5]

From being an exciting novelty, public dancing had become an accepted mode of entertainment, and despite all the rules and regulations of the assemblies there is no doubt that they introduced an element of greater freedom into the lives of well-to-do young men and women in the eighteenth century. For the first time, girls had the opportunity of meeting eligible men in surroundings outwith their own family circle. Limited this freedom might be, but it had been unknown a hundred years before, and as old Elizabeth Mure of Caldwell remarked, because of the assemblies, society 'now came to be more enlarged'.[6]

Dancing, of course, was not the only public recreation. The eighteenth century saw the introduction of regular theatrical performances. Plays and pageants had been perfectly acceptable before the Reformation, but ever since then, ecclesiastical censure had seen to it that any enterprise in that direction was shortlived. Strolling players came up from the south every two or three years, only to be banned by Edinburgh's magistrates, at the instigation of the clergy. When the Duke of York was in residence at Holyrood, he summoned from London part of the company of actors who enjoyed his patronage, but after that there had been little activity. Those occasional performances which did take place seem to have done so in inconvenient circumstances. Writing from Edinburgh about 1715, Eleanor, Countess of Stair, told her husband that the Duke of Argyll 'was at our playhouse tonight, where all the fine ladies in town was. 'Tis the tennis court, which is the coldest place in the world. I was there this day sennight and got so great a cold that I have not been able to stir since.' Bearing in mind that the court was a covered one, for real tennis, it still fell far short of the comfort expected from a normal playhouse.[7] In 1733, however, an advance was made. The Company of Players leased the Tailors' Hall in one of the town's most fashionable streets, the Cowgate. They began their season on 6 June with *The Beggars' Opera* by John Gay and in ensuing years there was a short series of plays each winter.[8]

From the start, ladies were among the most enthusiastic members of the audience. In 1743, *Richard III* was performed 'at the desire of several ladies of distinction' and feminine taste also ran to comedies. *The Careless Husband* by Colley Cibber was put on 'in response to the wishes of several ladies' and when Rowe's *The Fair Penitent* was produced in 1744, the stage was 'ornamented and illuminated by wax light' specially 'for the better accommodation of the ladies'. Women frequently took boxes in their own names, for although girls had to be chaperoned to public entertainments, they did not necessarily have to be escorted by men but could go with female friends. In the 1770s James Boswell's eminently respectable wife often went with a woman friend to see the latest play and when Mary Somerville was a girl in the 1790s and had no-one to accompany her to the theatre, she thought nothing of calling at the box office on the morning of a performance to ask if any ladies of her acquaintance had booked seats. She then sent round a message to one of them asking if she might join her party. 'Of course, I always paid for my place,' she noted carefully, and in this way she saw all the best performances of the day, admiring Mrs Siddons, Charles Kemble and the other leading actors who came north.[9]

Ladies continued to show a preference for Shakespeare and light comedy, but they were equally intrigued by some of the more novel entertainers presented to them. In the 1720s Signora Violante, the famous Italian rope-dancer, was still giving regular performances in a house at the foot of Carrubbers Close and fifty years later the Venetian Company of Tumblers was in town, offering such entertainments as Signor Carlino's leaps on a rope five feet from the ground and Mrs Colpi's 'surprising equilibres in full swing', which involved balancing a sword on the edge of a wine glass while on a tightrope. Nothing if not versatile, Mrs Colpi interspersed her athletic feats with the rendering of favourite songs, a musical performance on glasses, and her celebrated hornpipe.[10]

More conventional were public concerts, which existed in their own right as well as being a cloak for theatrical performances. Originally, group music-making was a strictly masculine preserve. The instruments favoured by ladies were usually those played alone – the virginals, lute and later the harp. No doubt this was a reflection of their lack of opportunity for getting together with friends. Men, however, seemed to prefer those which could be played in a small ensemble – recorders, violins and cellos. Less talented companions were happy to listen to their gifted friends, and so in 1693 the enterprising Mr Beck, a German music teacher employed by the Earl of Balcarres, arranged a short series of concerts in Edinburgh. A more ambitious event took place on St Cecilia's Day two years later, when the master of the Edinburgh music school appeared on the public stage with a choir of his pupils, a trumpeter, several professional string players and a group of amateurs on the recorder, violin, cello and viola da gamba. The lengthy performance combined both English and Italian music, thereby demonstrating the players' modern tastes. The success of that particular occasion led to the establishment of several series of concerts in the years which followed. By 1762, Edinburgh had its own concert hall, St Cecilia's, in the Cowgate, and although performers were exclusively male, the audience included a large number of enthusiastic female music-lovers.[11]

Public balls, plays and concerts were attractive novelties in the early eighteenth century, and in private entertaining too, an exciting new development had come into being: the tea party had been invented. At first, tea was a highly expensive beverage which had to be imported specially from the East by way of Holland or London, but by 1710 both black 'bohea' tea and 'green tea' were on sale in the Edinburgh shops and more and more ladies discovered the joys of tea-drinking.[12] Now, instead of having friends come to a more formal meal, ladies in town summoned their guests to take tea with them. Cakes of all kinds were served too, and Henry Mackenzie the writer recalled that when he was a boy in Edinburgh, a baker named Scott made a fortune by selling 'milk bakes'. Each afternoon, at about five o'clock, all the servant girls in the district converged on his shop in Forrester's Wynd to purchase newly-made baking for their mistresses. Once their guests had arrived, the ladies sat at ease with their small, china bowls of tea, gossiping, exchanging novels and, in the 1750s, playing with the small, jointed paper dolls which had become such popular adult toys. Dressed in harlequin costume, these were called after Monsieur Pantin, a fashionable French dancer, and ladies seem to have gained endless amusement by making them go through all manner of droll antics.

After the meal was over, one of the ladies would be urged to sing. Scottish folk songs, sung unaccompanied, were particularly popular, and when Allan Ramsay published a collection called *The Tea Table Miscellany*, it was an immediate success. So well-known were the songs, indeed, that although he used over seventy different tunes, he did not find it necessary to print the music of any of them.[13] When young men were present, as they often were, there would be dancing. Scots reels were particularly liked, and while the younger people danced, the older ladies sat at the card table playing whist or vingt-et-un. The evening was rounded off with supper, which could be an elegant occasion. When Boswell supped at eleven at night at Captain Schaw's house in 1774, he remarked not only upon the 'very genteel company' but admired 'the most brilliant table that ever I saw in Edinburgh: a row of crystal lustres down the middle of the table; fruits and flowers interspersed in gay profusion'.[14]

Towards the end of the century, tea parties were eclipsed in polite society by the growing preference for dinner parties. Dinner had originally been eaten shortly after mid-day. By 1790 or so its hour was three or four. In the 1820s, no-one would consider having dinner before six, and so a dozen people were invited for that time instead of for tea. Dinner parties were held in Edinburgh from the late autumn until Christmas, then in January were replaced by a series of private routs and balls. The routs were large evening parties where cards and good conversation were the principal entertainments. At the balls, country dancing remained the central feature until 1816, the year when the quadrille was introduced from France. The older generation were vociferous in their disapproval of the new dance, but soon everyone was taking lessons and since smaller rooms and orchestras sufficed, this cheaper form of programme was adopted with alacrity by hostesses.[15]

The big, public balls continued to be very grand affairs indeed and elegant new assembly rooms were built in Edinburgh's New Town. Harriet Scott sampled the splendour of these formal functions when she visited Edinburgh with her daughter in the winter of 1826. Writing home to describe one such occasion, she reported, 'There were near 800 people there, and seats difficult to obtain.' The ladies were magnificently clad, the Lord Provost's wife cutting a particularly fine figure. She 'looked rather like one of her husband's great chairs, in her green velvet embroidered with great gold roses and thistles'. Harriet and her daughter retired exhausted at 2.30 a.m., but she was told that 'the thorough bred Scotch people, who are quite indefatigable, danced on till *nine* o'clock this morning.'[16]

Mrs Hamilton-Dundas had a similar experience when she launched her daughter Mary into society at about the same time. Mary 'really looked remarkably well,' she thought, and was very nicely dressed, but Mrs Hamilton-Dundas was 'opprest with the heat' and suffering horrible doubts about her own appearance. 'The dresses were in general white silk net over white satin, and plumes of feathers,' she confided to a friend. 'I felt quite uncomfortable in my gown, which was an old peach blossom; it seemed so showy beside the net.' The Edinburgh of her day was undoubtedly the centre of Scottish fashion still, and during the winter season the range of activities was positively bewildering. Margaret Mackintosh's letters home to her sister Anne in about 1802 are full of reports of an unceasing social round. On Monday of her first week in town with her friend Eliza Gloag, the two girls went to call on some of Eliza's relatives. On Tuesday, they dined with a group of friends at Mr Kerr's. Wednesday morning saw them visiting the Fergussons, then they entertained Mr and Miss Stewart to dinner, dancing reels in the evening. On Thursday, they called on Miss Wilson and her sister in Leith, then drove back into town with them to see Mrs Dewar. Supper at Lord Hermand's was Friday's entertainment, while on Saturday there was the excitement of a trip to a performance by Mr Boaz, the famous conjurer, who performed tricks with cards, eggs and birds. After a brief respite on Sunday, when they went to church twice, they dined with Lord Hermand again on Monday and then went on to the assembly in the evening. For this occasion, Margaret was elegantly turned out in a white gown trimmed with gold knots and gold net. Her shoes were white and on her head was a spray of white feathers. It was only a pity that 'there was very little pleasure in dancing . . . and the room was so excessively hot' because so many people were present. However, with commendable stamina Margaret was up and out visiting again the very next day.[17]

In 1819 the Laird of Barcaldine's sister, Miss Caroline Campbell, was equally active in pursuit of entertainment. Edinburgh now had its own musical festival and so, staying at 50 Great King Street at the end of October, she was able to attend a whole series of concerts. 'Edinburgh has been extremely gay and very full of company during the Festival and race weeks,' she told a friend. She had been to an excellent morning concert where Handel's *Messiah* was sung in a manner 'most sublime'. Evening concerts were held in a theatre which was on the small side, with the result that people who arrived late did not find good seats: in fact, 'Lady Wemyss and some other ladies were one evening in the one shilling gallery and some that I know of who were there came home such figures, their faces so blackened with the smoke of the lights.' Shortly before she wrote, Caroline had been down to Shrubhill, between Edinburgh and Leith, to view a huge balloon which was 'in the form of an old woman and labelled Meg Merrilies'. Large crowds of people had gathered to see it, assembling too on the Calton Hill and Salisbury Crags, the better to follow its progress. 'I thought it did not ascend to a great height,' Caroline remarked, 'however, it seemed to gratify the multitudes.'[18]

It was, perhaps, only to be expected that at the end of the eighteenth century the capital would enjoy a glittering social life to match its fame as a centre of intellectual activity, but smaller towns followed suit not only with theatricals but with concerts and private entertaining. Glasgow was for many years regarded as something of a cultural desert. Still a comparatively small port, its great days of trade with America were to transform its life in the last decades of the century but in Alexander Carlyle's youth he complained, 'There never was but one concert during the two winters I was at Glasgow, and that was given by Walter Scott,

Esquire, of Harden [an amateur] who was himself an eminent performer on the violin, and his band of assistants consisted of two dancing school fiddlers and the town waits.' According to him, 'The manner of living too at this time was coarse and vulgar,' for there was little large-scale entertaining, although he did admit that a dancing assembly was held once a fortnight.[19]

Shortly afterwards, the situation improved. Concerts were held regularly from the mid 1740s onwards and by 1750 Mr Burrell's Dancing Hall was being used for the production of plays. Two years later, a temporary theatre was started up and by 1764 there was a permanent structure for performances. Other towns could also boast flourishing entertainments. In 1748, Aberdeen had a musical society of its own, founded on the Edinburgh model and giving regular concerts featuring the works of Corelli. Dundee Musical Society was well attended in the late 1750s and by the end of the century concerts were being held in small places like Forfar, Greenock and Peterhead. As for theatricals, visiting companies toured both the Highlands and the Border areas.[20]

New styles in private entertaining were adopted too. Tea drinking spread rapidly throughout Scotland, despite the strictures of the ministers, who considered, not without reason, that the habit encouraged idleness and gossip. Glasgow tea parties were not at first the elegant affairs held in Edinburgh. The lady of the house simply asked a few friends in to take tea in her bedroom at four in the afternoon. From this informal arrangement, however, rather grander tea parties developed and by the 1740s a dozen or so guests of both sexes were being invited. After tea, they played whist and quadrille until about nine at night, when supper was served. The wives went home after the meal, but the husbands stayed on drinking with their host.[21]

In addition to the recreations available in Scotland, aristocratic and very wealthy ladies were now able to take part in the London season. By 1783, sixty coaches a month went from Edinburgh to the south and new modes of travel were coming into fashion. In 1800, Lady Elizabeth Murray was full of praise for a novel type of carriage called a sociable, although Elizabeth Grant was not so impressed when she and her family travelled from London to Inverness-shire in one, four years later. It had 'a cane body, a roof of four supports hung round with leather curtains, which we were continually letting down or tying up, according to the weather' and which always let the rain in. It was pulled by four horses. In 1808 they made the same journey in a barouche landau and found it 'a great improvement upon either the old heavy close coach or the leather-curtained sociable', while other ladies continued to travel by post chaise.[22]

The birth announcements of the eighteenth century bear witness to the increasing number of Scottish ladies going south. Lady Cathcart, the Countess of Ancram, the Marchioness of Tweeddale, Sir Henry Erskine's wife and the Countess of Sutherland were but a few of those who produced babies while they were in London in the 1750s and 60s and groups of Scots could be found at all the public entertainments as well as many of the private parties. When James Boswell went to breakfast at Lord Eglinton's town house one day in 1762, he found a most elegant company which included not only three English dukes but the Duchess of Hamilton and her son, Lord and Lady Garlies and Lady Margaret Macdonald. A number of Scottish ladies were also to be found in the Royal Household. The 2nd Lord Bellenden's beautiful daughter Mary was a maid of honour and Lady Harriet Campbell served as a lady of the bedchamber.[23]

London life was not to everyone's taste, of course, and when Jane Maxwell, Duchess of Gordon, was asked by George III how she liked the city, she apparently replied, 'It's frizzle-frizzling aw the morning and knock-knocking aw the night' – a comment upon the fact that forenoons were spent at the hairdresser's and evenings at balls and parties. Those most anxious to go to London for the winter season were the mothers of eligible daughters. When Lady Betty Hamilton was about to make her debut in 1768, the whole family and her mother's man of business were involved in the preparations. He was noting that 'the sum requisite for her outfit will be £200', adding, 'This sum, it is proper, should be raised out of her portion, which is £5000 or £6000.' Whatever happened, he was anxious that she should 'appear *comme il faut*', for she was 'a fine girl, very handsome, and I think it will not be long before she arrives in some good harbour'. He was quite correct: in due course she married an English peer, Lord Derby.[24]

The daughters of the Scottish aristocracy as well as the sons were now involved in the London marriage market and by the beginning of the nineteenth century almost half the total number of Scottish peers' daughters were marrying Englishmen. These were arranged marriages, for when large estates and ancient titles were at stake, fathers still insisted on making the choice of a partner for their daughters. As Lord Kames remarked in 1782, 'Young women in high life are married at the will of their parents, without any personal attachment.'[25]

For other young women, however, the new social climate brought a greater freedom. Although rules of etiquette were strict, perfectly respectable young ladies were now able to make up mixed parties for the theatre or give intimate suppers for their men and women friends. As Mary Somerville later recollected, no chaperones were needed for a function in a private house, the hostess's presence being enough to guarantee propriety. 'Girls had perfect liberty at that time in Edinburgh,' she said. 'We walked together in Princes Street, the fashionable promenade, and were joined by our dancing partners. We occasionally gave little supper parties and presented these young men to our parents as they came in.'[26] This new interchange between the sexes bred a new self-consciousness, a pleasurable awareness of the differences between the roles of man and woman. Pamphlets with such titles as *Woman unmask'd and dissected* and *Female qualifications, or, Jilts and hypocrites portrayed* laid stress in a flirtatious way on the allegedly feminine qualities of empty-headedness, inconstancy and garrulousness. There were jocular warnings about the dire fate of those who entered into matrimony: *Celibacy: or good advice to young ladies to keep single* could be bought for a shilling. There were also enjoyable literary debates: *Man superior to woman*, followed swiftly by *Woman not inferior to man*.[27]

With new opportunities for flirtation and gallantry, a new social etiquette came into being. Provided they accepted the conventions, strangers or near-strangers could pay extravagant compliments of a kind which would have been ill-received by the more prosaic ladies of earlier centuries. Of course, personal relationships did not remain at this light-hearted and superficial level, and parents soon found that in allowing their children greater freedom to go about in society, they were taking a serious risk. Hitherto, marriages had been arranged within the context of the family, with solemn consideration of financial assets, status and religion. Now, however, young people met and became ac-quainted with members of the opposite sex from a much wider circle.[28]

Assemblies, concerts and theatres all provided opportunities for men and women to meet and eligible young ladies now basked in the flattery of competing suitors, gossiping interminably with friends about the merits of their prospective husbands. The initial stages of courtship would take place under the indulgent eye of sympathetic aunts and cousins, while employers, neighbours and even servants all joined in the merry game of throwing eligible young people together. Such intrigues could enliven an otherwise dull existence, and quite often they were successful. Lady Barbara Drummond was in 1732 confiding to her sister, 'We are to have Widow Weir this summer within two miles of Drummond, which will be a fine lover for Master John,' and Sir William Weir's widow did indeed marry 'Master John' Stewart as a result of their meetings.[29]

Many girls thoroughly enjoyed playing one suitor off against another, but it was inevitable that mutual attraction would carry relationships beyond the level of flirtation and passing amusement. Encouraged by novels and by the general preoccupation with matrimony, young women were now looking for romantic love rather than for a partner selected on a strictly practical basis. It became quite acceptable for a man to admit to a passionate attachment and as well as gossiping about a girl's tocher or a man's reputation, it was customary for the bystanders to note with approval the evident signs of romantic involvement. When John Steuart wrote in 1721 to his brother, Sir George Steuart of Grandtully, seeking approval for his proposed marriage, he explained that his fondness for the young lady who had 'thus captivated' him had arisen 'from no less than a violent passion of love'. Four years later, the Countess of Bute was aware that her son John was deeply in love with the Earl of Traquair's daughter, although he was doomed to disappointment: in the end she married someone else and he died a bachelor.[30] James Boswell was perpetually falling in and out of love with a whole succession of young women of varying suitability, so it would surprise no one when he remarked in 1767, 'Love is a perfect fever of the mind.'[31]

Love at first sight was a recognized phenomenon. When James Mackenzie of Craig Park, near Glasgow, was sitting in church one Sunday in 1805, he espied Miss Louisa Balfour of Pilrig in a nearby pew and immediately lost his heart to her. Similarly, Hugh, Earl of Marchmont, a middle-aged widower, was instantly attracted to the young lady who became his second wife. Visiting the theatre in London not long after the death of his first Countess, he saw a beautiful girl of about seventeen sitting in one of the boxes. The effect upon him was startling. 'His raptures were so undisguised, his looks so expressive of passion, his inquiries so earnest, that every person took notice of it.' He was not in the least deterred when he discovered that the object of his affections, Elizabeth Crompton, was the daughter of a bankrupt linen draper. Next morning he wrote to her father, asking if he might pay his addresses. Needless to say, Mr Crompton was delighted and within a short space of time his daughter became Countess of Marchmont.[32]

Women in particular now expected to 'fall in love' before they married and young girls who had not experienced the sensation nevertheless recognized its existence. One of Boswell's friends, an eighteen-year-old heiress named Catherine Blair, explained to him when he urged her to reveal her feelings, that she had no special liking for him and 'never had felt the uneasy anxiety of love for any man'. In similar vein, when Thomas Carlyle first wooed Jane Welsh, she recoiled from his more enthusiastic advances, telling him, 'Positively I cannot fall in love – and to sacrifice myself out of pity is a degree of generosity of which I am not capable.' Carlyle wrote back sympathetically, but he assured her that 'the time *will* come indeed when you must "fall in love" and be wedded as others have been: it is the general law and must be fulfilled.'[33]

For all her delight in their intellectual friendship, Jane remained impatient with his amorous advances. Nonetheless, he persisted, and in January 1825 he sent her a long letter proposing marriage. 'Speak then, my Angel!,' he urged her. 'How say you? Will you be mine? or am I a fool for having hoped it? Think well; of me, of yourself, of our circumstances; and determine.' Jane's reply was somewhat dampening. She loved him as she would a brother, she said, 'but I am not *in love* with you – that is to say, my love for you is not a passion which overclouds my judgement and absorbs all my regards for myself and others'. Fond as she was of him, she believed it was 'a duty which everyone owes to society, not to throw up that station in which Providence has assigned him, and having this conviction, I could not marry into a station inferior to my own'. All the same, from that time forth she regarded herself as being betrothed to him, and, by the end of the year, was addressing him as 'my dearest' and quoting *Paradise Lost* to him. It did not matter where he went to live, she said, as long as she was with him, 'for "thou art to me all things under Heaven, all places thou." ' She was now ready to boast to her aunt that he was 'among the cleverest men of his day, and not the cleverest only but the most enlightened'. He possessed all the qualities she considered essential in a husband, 'a warm, true heart to love me, a towering intellect to command me and a spirit of fire to be the guiding star-light of my life'. To Carlyle himself, she wrote that he had always been destined to be 'the chosen only Partner of my heart and soul'.[34]

A hundred years earlier, no unmarried man or woman would have dreamed of writing in such impassioned terms. Few people were possessed of the Carlyles' literary fluency, but the letters of their contemporaries reveal equally deep feelings, and, written assurances apart, the late eighteenth century was the age of the grand romantic gesture. One of Lady Elibank's suitors is said to have given her proof of his devotion in a manner which she must have found disconcerting, to say the least. After she had told him playfully that she did not believe he would part with the joint of his little finger for her sake, he returned the following day and handed her a small parcel. When she opened it, she found reposing there that very thing, the top part of his little finger. Recoiling in pardonable disgust, Lady Elibank told him sensibly that she could have no more to do with him. 'The man who has no mercy on his own flesh will not spare mine' was her terse comment.[35]

Disappointment in love could also provoke extreme reactions. When Jane Welsh refused the advances of young Dugald Gilchrist, 'He threw himself down on the sofa and wept and sobbed like a child.' In spite of Jane's attempts to console him – which included kissing him on the forehead half a dozen times – he refused to be comforted and 'lay in bed and cried' for three days. It was with much relief that the Welshes finally saw him depart.[36]

The Earl of Wemyss's daughter Betty allegedly took to her bed and spent the last twenty-six years of her life there after suffering a similar disappointment, and even the sensible Elizabeth Grant of Rothiemurchus attributed her long illness in the winter of 1816 to the fact that her parents had broken up her romance with a young student, who had proved to be the son of an old enemy of their own. Rather more practical in her approach to love and marriage was Miss Ann Pitcairn. Spurning the advances of Dr Carnegy, a man much older than herself, she had second thoughts when he left for India. The year was 1812, and young ladies did not normally set off on long journeys unchaperoned, but Ann followed him to Gosport. Upon her arrival, she discovered that his vessel was about to sail. Somehow or other, she managed to get a message aboard and in reply he sent word that he would marry her if she followed him to

Bombay. Nothing loath, she took passage aboard *The Union*, having persuaded her parents to let her little sister go along with her for company. Presumably Dr Carnegy kept his promise, but Ann's initiative caused a good deal of criticism as well as much mirth among her friends.[37]

In countenancing Ann's expedition, her family were being unusually compliant. Most fathers and mothers retained strictly conventional ideas and continued to look for the solid, traditional virtues of status, wealth and sobriety in their young people's partners. When Anne, Countess of Seafield, urged her son James to marry in 1707, she told him he should choose 'the daughter of a good family – I mean a sober, sensible people. And I cannot deny but I would wish you to marry in a family of quality,' she added. 'I do not mean by quality only the nobility. I would not have her much above your own age, but above all, soberly and religiously educate.' She did allow, however, that he should also be satisfied as to her 'personal qualities, both as to wit and inclinations.' Four years later, Lady Mary Hamilton noted with satisfaction that her daughter Nellie had married 'a man of good sense and very sober, with a competent fortune' while Winifred, Countess of Nithsdale, was in 1731 approving of her son-in-law, Lord Bellew, as having 'a sufficient estate and the best character from everyone that speaks of him that I have heard'. As an article in the *Scots Magazine* in 1764 put it, 'Sobriety, prudence and good nature, a virtuous disposition, a good understanding and a competent fortune, are qualities never to be dispensed with in this matter.'[38]

Given the traditional attitude of parents, combined with the new emphasis on romance, it was hardly surprising that conflict between the two generations arose. Indeed, the number of elopements and clandestine marriages in the eighteenth century increased so much that a later statistician estimated that no fewer than a third of all marriages were now irregular.[39] Of course, this did not mean that these were all runaway matches. Many of those who married clandestinely did so only in so far as they were not members of the established Church of Scotland and sought the services of a clergyman of a different church, be it Roman Catholic, Episcopalian or Quaker. Others perhaps wished to avoid the expense of a formal wedding or simply shrank from the fuss. There still remained many, however, who sought to evade parental control by eloping.

Baron Clerk's sisters, for example, showed a deplorable

tendency to make up their own minds about marriage. In 1724, Peggy announced her intention of marrying Mr Belsches, a widower with six children, 'all of them excepting one elder than herself'. To add insult to injury, she had originally been wooed by his eldest son, but nothing the Baron or anyone else could say would have any effect. Four years later, it was Christy's turn. In April 1728 she was telling her friends all about her secret wedding in Leith although, when taxed with it by her mother, she denied any such thing. She kept up the pretence for several weeks after the ceremony, while her husband visited Fife, then slipped away to join him.[40]

An even greater stir was caused by the elopement of the 4th Earl of Wemyss. Having fallen in love in 1720 with Janet Charteris, a wealthy heiress, they both feared that she would be forced to marry one of his rivals. They therefore thought it best to meet secretly one September evening at nearly ten o'clock at night, when they were duly married. No-one knew a thing about it until the next morning, when Mrs Charteris went to her daughter's room and found her gone. The whole household was thrown into a state of alarm, then a messenger arrived with letters from the Earl and his bride. Privately charmed to find herself the mother of a Countess, Mrs Charteris at once sent a civil reply, although her husband took longer to come round.[41]

A letter announcing the marriage of the writer to the recipient's daughter cannot have been easy to compose, but Lord George Murray managed rather well in 1728. Better known to history as the famous Jacobite general of the 1745 Rising, he secretly married Amelia, the daughter of Mrs James Murray of Glencarse and Strowan, in the presence of his elder brother, the Duke of Atholl. With a fine diplomatic turn of phrase, he began his confession with the words, 'Madam, the greatest happiness I aimed at in this world was to marry Your Ladyship's daughter and to have your approbation. But when I found that my most sincere endeavours to persuade Your Ladyship of the uprightness of my intentions was altogether ineffectual and all that I could say or do was of no use to bring Your Ladyship to hearken in any way to my proposal, I then indeed, with the greatest earnestness that I was capable of, entreated your daughter to take the opportunity of my brother's being in town to put an end to that affair [i.e. business], and now, since we were married last night, I take this first opportunity to ask Your Ladyship's pardon and blessing.'

Modestly acknowledging that she might have 'cast your eyes upon many who had advantages which I want [*i.e.* lack]', he nevertheless stressed his affection and love for her daughter, declaring that he would make it 'the constant study of my whole life to approve [*sic*] myself worthy of her'. He begged her forgiveness with an appealing mixture of confidence and contrition, signing himself 'Your Ladyship's most dutiful son and faithful humble servant'. His marriage did indeed prove to be a happy one.[42]

Sir Alexander Lindsay of Evelick was the father of two pretty young daughters. In 1751 the elder, Margaret, fell in love with Allan Ramsay the portrait painter. Allan was a perfectly respectable widower some years older than she, and he had already begun to establish his extremely successful practice in London. To Sir Alexander, however, he was not good enough, and so Allan and Margaret ran away together to Edinburgh, where they were married. They then moved south to London. Sadly, the twins born to Margaret less than a year later died at birth, but her marriage was a happy and successful one, clouded only by the breach with her own family. From the beginning, both she and Allan were anxious to make their peace, but Sir Alexander was deaf to their pleas. He told one of his friends coldly, 'The world is much mistaken if it's thought that I despise Mr Ramsay, though an utter stranger to me, yet I never heard anything in his character but what might have entitled him to my daughter.' His disapproval was based entirely upon the fact that he had been defied. 'That I have cause to be displeased with my daughter is undeniable,' he observed, 'as she has done the most undutiful act was in her power to do. Should I pass this over without making her sensible of her fault, it were too great an encouragement to my other daughter to do the like. I therefore think I am bound to do the duty of a parent in letting her see that an affair of that consequence if done without consent (even though otherwise reasonable) is not to be too easily forgiven.'[43]

Nor did he forgive. Five years after her marriage, Margaret wrote to her mother from Rome, to tell her, 'You and Sir Alexander's displeasure has been long the occasion of great concern to me, and there is nothing in my power that I would not have undertaken in order to have removed it, but was afraid of doing anything for fear of being troublesome. That fear of offending has been the reason of my never venturing to write . . .'

Only a message from Lady Balcarres saying that she was interceding on the Ramsays' behalf had emboldened Margaret sufficiently to take up her pen. After emphasising that her husband 'has always acted in every relation of life with uprightness and generosity, to the best of his knowledge and circumstances', she added some touching family news. Her little daughter was by now 'a most engaging child . . . She has got nine teeth and has walked quite alone ever since she was a year old. She has a great stock of half words by which she makes herself understood for everything she wants.' Even this failed to melt her father's heart and to his dying day he refused to have anything to do with her. Only after his death was she able to effect the much-desired reconciliation with her mother.[44]

Even James Boswell, more noted for his hot-blooded pursuit of women than for his support of convention, came down heavily on the side of parental authority. 'If a daughter is so lacking in respect for her parents and in confidence in them as to engage in the most important of contracts without consulting them,' he said, 'ought she to be surprised if her parents lose a little of their affection for her?' He was sorry when a marriage of that type succeeded, for it gave encouragement 'to girls of impressionable hearts and light heads to forget the weakness of their sex, to scorn the sage maxims of prudence and to disturb the settled order of society'.[45]

Nor were these merely the idle vapourings of an immature young man. Society's disapproval of those who offended against its canons is demonstrated all too vividly in his chilling attitude to his sister-in-law some eleven years later. When she fell gravely ill with consumption, Boswell grudgingly permitted his wife to go and see her, 'as the feelings of natural affection may be indulged towards an unworthy object when dying'. It appeared that the unfortunate girl had married beneath her. 'Her debasing herself by a mean marriage ought, from a just regard to preserve the honourable distinctions of a civilized society, to prevent her from enjoying the countenance of her relations in cheerful intercourse. But sickness and the approach of death may be indulged with a humane attention.' When her sister died the following year, Mrs Boswell was greatly upset. Boswell himself, who was, after all, her cousin, as well as being her brother-in-law, admitted, 'Though I could not regret that a woman who had disgraced herself by a low marriage and was by that estranged from us, was removed, the recollection of former days made me be a little affected with some sort of tenderness on hearing she was no longer in life. But stern reason soon resumed its influence.'[46]

The new emphasis on romance and individual attraction does not, of course, mean that love was invented in the eighteenth century. Strong feelings of passion and attraction had always existed between men and women. What had altered was the way in which society regarded these feelings. In previous years, love between husband and wife was fully recognized but it was not taken to be a necessary prerequisite for marriage. People might feel drawn to each other but it was their duty to marry for practical reasons and it was to be hoped that deep affection would grow between them after they had become man and wife. In the eighteenth century, new ideas of individual freedom and the hitherto unknown opportunity for people to meet beyond the family circle, led to the acceptance by many that love should precede marriage and that it was wrong to tie oneself to a partner to whom one was not attracted.

We can observe these changes of attitude in the letters of upper and middle class Scots of the period, but their feelings were not unique. There was a much more general recognition of the importance of personal preference, and Rousseau in his influential work *Emile* argued strongly for freedom of choice. 'It is for men and women to suit themselves,' he said. Mutual inclination must be the principal consideration. 'Their eyes, their hearts ought to be their first guides, for as their primary duty after they are joined together is to love one another, and as to love or not to love doth not depend on us, their duty necessarily implies another, namely to begin with loving one another before marriage.'[47]

Girls who had the leisure and the opportunity to enjoy the new delights of light-hearted dalliance and the excitements of the Edinburgh season came, of course, from a very limited section of society, and it is their feelings which are revealed by the documentary sources of the period. It is no more possible to find correspondence from poor women expressing their innermost thoughts in the eighteenth century than it is to discover personal letters from medieval ladies. The standard of female literacy was still such that these girls could not put down their feelings on paper. It is therefore much more difficult to assess the attitudes of people from poorer circumstances.

As a starting point, however, we do know that girls without property had always been able to exercise a far greater element of personal choice than had their wealthy contemporaries, and there is no reason to suppose that this had changed. Servant girls, farm labourers' daughters and the children of lesser tradesmen and shopkeepers associated much more freely with members of the opposite sex, so the new opportunities for social encounter enjoyed by middle class and aristocratic women were no novelty for them. Nor did women play a passive role. Scottish folk songs of the period frequently include an independent-minded heroine, ready to take the initiative in courtship and looking for both romantic love and strong physical attraction in marriage.[48]

Family conflicts there were, of course: not because estates and titles were involved, but because girls associated with men whom their fathers personally disliked or because they anticipated marriage and found themselves pregnant. It was not only the aristocracy whose defiant sons and daughters made clandestine marriages. The records of the Kirk Session of South Leith demonstrate this very clearly. A seaport just outside Edinburgh, the town had a regular military garrison, and with its changing population of soldiers and seamen was an obvious place to find people in trouble for marrying irregularly. In the twenty-five years between 1708 and 1732, thirty-one soldiers, twenty-five sailors, thirteen servants, a number of landed gentlemen and a variety of tradesmen ranging from wheelwrights to candle-makers went through clandestine ceremonies in the town. There are fewer references to the social status of their brides, but five were servants, one was a merchant and those others designated were the daughters and widows of tailors, shoemakers, weavers, gardeners and the like. Most, indeed, were marrying partners from backgrounds similar to their own: the five female servants married a soldier, a servant, a refiner, a tobacco spinner and a sailor respectively, while a carter's daughter married a carter, a brewer's daughter married a maltman, and a shoemaker's daughter became the bride of a shoemaker.[49]

Perhaps some of them had become imbued with the current romantic ideas of elopement, for there is no doubt that new ways of thought spread throughout society. Critics had been quick to notice that the daughters 'even of tradesmen' were imitating the manners of the aristocracy, and by 1793 a gardener, albeit an unusual one, was able to view his own courtship in a manner familiar to the peerage at the beginning of the eighteenth century. With remarkable sang-froid, Donald Fraser wrote to his employer's wife, reporting on his amatory progress. Anxious to find him a suitable partner, her friend Miss Cooper had suggested that he might pay court to her maid Hannah, while another acquaintance urged him to consider Kathy MacKay. 'Kathy and Hannah are one equal in size and shape,' he observed, 'only Kathy is rather more blooming and young.' He, of course, preferred Kathy, though he did admit that Hannah was 'certainly more experienced and knows more of the nature of life than the other'. When he did propose to Kathy, however, she refused him. (He discovered later that she was secretly engaged to a soldier.) Not in the least downcast by this reverse, he 'then tript off as hard as I could drive to Aldowie, with flying colours'. After a few words with Miss Cooper, he marched in and proposed to Hannah, who accepted him with alacrity. Philosophically accepting his fate, he remarked, 'Now, I (thank God) have obtained the consent of the very girl I love best . . . The poor gardener is tied up as round as a turnip.'[50]

Donald's general approach was very similar to that of the young men of fashion who 'laid siege' to rich heiresses, nor was the exchange of terminology in one direction only. The old Scots folk songs of love and courtship enjoyed great popularity with middle and upper-class ladies who sang them at their tea parties in the 1770s and 80s. In some respects, these well-to-do women were sharing in the general aristocratic conceit of identifying with peasants and amusing themselves by pretending to enjoy a pastoral mode of life. Yet a direct comparison with, say, the ladies of the French Court who played at being shepherdesses, is hardly fair. The Scotswomen who enjoyed their country's traditional music were far closer to their heritage than were Marie Antoinette and her circle. For many of them, the vernacular was still their natural form of speech and their grandfathers or even their fathers had been part of the rural community. The gulf between the social classes might be increasing, but Scotland was still a small country where the rich and poor mingled together in daily life, not entirely set apart by barriers of wealth and status. The old songs dealt with the loved one's charms, the desire to be in his company and the anguish of despair felt at parting. Permitted now to experience such feelings for their future partners, even those young women destined for arranged marriages could find a natural expression of their own feelings in the traditional lyrics of the old folk songs.[51]

CHAPTER NINE

The Marital Bond

IN 1741, READERS OF the *Scots Magazine* were able to peruse a piece reprinted from *The Universal Spectator*. Purporting to relate a conversation between Mrs Modish and her unmarried friends, the article satirised current London attitudes. The friends took up the subject of matrimony, envying Mrs Modish's freedom to do exactly as she pleased now that she had escaped from the supervision of her mother. While denying that she could do whatever she chose, their hostess nevertheless admitted that she was trying her best 'to obtain universal monarchy and unlimited power' over her husband. He still showed an unfair tendency to be obstinate at times, but, as she put it, 'I don't mind him.' Asked if she ever dared go contrary to his wishes, she gave a merry peal of laughter and embarked upon a long speech of advice. 'My dear,' she said, 'when you marry, you must not be afraid of not *daring* to contradict your husband's whims and humours; what you have a mind to do yourself, you must *dare* do. We should have a fine time of it indeed if we were to *obey* all our dear spouses' solemn commands. You may say at church that you'll *obey* and be *obedient* and I don't know what, but that is only a matter of form and perhaps not ten women in England pay any regard to it.'[1]

Intended to amuse, this piece nevertheless had an underlying vein of seriousness. Men were becoming nervous of growing feminine independence. At one time, their wives had remained safely at home, tied down by the cares of the household. Now, with long hours of leisure, the lady in town was apt to go her own way, spending her days in a round of pleasure which took her out to theatres and balls and friends' houses and gave her ideas about doing as she pleased and flouting her husband's wishes. Of course, in law a wife's position remained unchanged and she was still treated as though she were a minor. Obedience to her husband remained, in theory, her chief duty and many women accepted this without question. Lady Grizel Baillie's daughter saw nothing amiss in the fact that her mother's 'principal and sole delight was to watch and attend everything that could give him [*i.e.* her husband] pleasure or make him easy', and Lady Grizel was far from being a cipher. Some women were naturally meek, of course, and for all that the Earl of Marchmont had fallen romantically in love with the young girl he saw at the theatre, he domineered over her once she was his Countess. According to Alexander Carlyle, who met them in 1753, the Earl's three daughters by his first marriage 'were all under due subjection, for His Lordship kept a high command at home'. They were clever and spirited, though, and stood less in awe of him than did his young wife, who, 'had it not been for her only child, Lord Polwarth, then an infant, would have had but an uncomfortable life'.[2]

Even more submissive was Sir Thomas Dick Lauder's wife. She was not ashamed to merge her personality completely with that of her husband. Elizabeth Grant of Rothiemurchus encountered her in 1809 and noted that 'Her merit was in implicitly following his lead; she thought, felt, saw, heard as he did, and if his perceptions altered or varied, so did hers. There never was such a patient Grizel.'[3] Elizabeth's amusement was tinged with contempt. Like many of her contemporaries, she preferred to believe that clever women manipulated their partners in a subtle manner, while allowing them to think that they were masters in their own home. Undoubtedly the husband had the legal right to command; this was not directly questioned. During an argument with her stepson, Baron Clerk, in 1723, Christian Kilpatrick alluded to this aspect of the marital bond. She told him with some heat, 'I will ever think it my duty to ask your advice, but you cannot expect I should be in such subjection to you as to a husband, to go in everything you please, nor will I promise it, for I do not owe you such subjection.' Similarly, Lord Eglinton in 1768 voiced the belief that 'a woman had a right to be courted as much as a husband, after marriage, had a right to command', but neither Christian nor the Earl would have denied the woman's right to influence her husband. The eighteenth-century attitude was well put in another article published by the *Scots Magazine* in 1765. Amanda, the ideal wife described in 'A picture of true conjugal felicity', always put her husband first and devoted all her efforts to making both their home and herself attractive to him. As a result, she was able 'to enjoy the amiable female privileges of ruling by obeying, of commanding by submitting, and of being perfectly happy from consulting another's happiness'. In marriage, the husband's duty was to give protection and support, while the wife provided the 'alleviating sweetness and exhilarating delight'. In short, 'she must subdue by obedience.'[4]

Lord Kames took up the same theme in 1781. 'Women, destined by nature to be obedient, ought to be disciplined early to bear wrongs without murmuring,' he began sternly. 'A man indeed bears rule over his wife's person and conduct: his will is law.' That was not the end of it, though. 'Providence . . . has provided her with means to bear rule over his will. He governs by law, she by persuasion. Nor can her influence ever fail if supported by sweetness of temper and zeal to make him happy.' As Rousseau had so perceptively put it, 'Hers is a sovereignty founded on complaisance and address: caresses are her orders, tears are her menaces. She governs in the family as a minister does in the state, procuring commands to be laid on her for doing what she inclines to do.'[5]

These passages came from theoretical writings, of course, but they found their echo in the letters of individuals. Thomas Carlyle expressed his views cogently in 1826. Discussing her suggestion that they might begin their married life in her mother's household, he told Jane Welsh, 'The man should bear rule in the house, and not the woman. This is an eternal axiom, the law of nature herself which no mortal departs from unpunished. I have meditated on this many long years and every day it grows plainer to me: I must not and cannot live in a house of which I am not head.' Fearing that she might take this amiss, he went on to explain further, 'Think not, darling, that this comes of an imperious temper; that I shall be a harsh and tyrannical husband to thee – God forbid! But it is the nature of a man that if he be controlled by anything but reason, he feels himself degraded; and incited, be it justly or not, to rebellion and discord. It is the nature of a woman, again, (for she is essentially *passive* not *active*) to cling to the man for support and direction, to comply with his humours and feel pleasure in doing so, simply because they are his; to reverence while she loves him, to conquer him not by force but by her weakness and perhaps (the cunning gypsy!) after all, to command him by obeying him . . .'[6]

The behaviour of various couples likewise bears out the contemporary belief that a sensible wife quietly managed her husband. Before her marriage, Elizabeth Grant's relative, Mrs Cumming of Logie, had been the beautiful Miss Baillie, not only an heiress but 'one of the cleverest women of the age'. Her husband, who had married rather late in life, was 'ugly, ungainly, kindly, simple'. Their union was a great success because he 'looked up to her without being afraid of her' and she exerted herself to be agreeable. In spite of her superior understanding, she gave herself no airs and 'indeed she set out so heartily on St Paul's advice to be subject to her husband that she actually got into a habit of thinking he had judgement.' Elizabeth's mother clearly remembered a whole roomful of people being hard put to it to maintain their gravity when, after giving her own opinion in some debate, Mrs Cumming declared, with the manner of one clinching the matter, 'It's not my conviction only, but Mr Cumming says so.'[7]

One of the most long-suffering wives was undoubtedly Mrs James Boswell. After many years of amorous adventure, the diarist finally proposed to his own cousin, Margaret Montgomerie. An eminently sensible woman, she dealt with his vagaries in an admirable manner for she understood him perfectly, but even she rebelled occasionally, resenting his drinking, his womanizing or simply his patronizing attitude to her. 'My wife, with great justice, complained that my conversation with her was never rational, but merely childish nonsense,' he noted after one such disagreement. 'The reason of it may be partly indolence, to avoid thought: partly because my wife, though she has excellent sense and a cheerful temper, has not sentiments congenial with mine. She has no superstition, no enthusiasm, no vanity: so that to be free of a disagreeable contrarity I may be glad to keep good humour in my mind by foolish sport.'[8]

Mrs Boswell's complaint was that of many women over the centuries, who have felt that they were not being taken seriously by the men of their acquaintance. For the most part, she was prepared to flatter her husband's vanity and overlook his indiscretions, but there were occasions when she could no longer 'command by obeying', but felt impelled to contradict or stand out against him. That so many women did pretend compliance while secretly manoeuvring to obtain their own way may seem to the modern reader to be depressing, demeaning or even downright deplorable. It is possible to interpret the remarks of Lord Kames or Thomas Carlyle as pieces of masculine propaganda designed to make women accept their subjugation without complaint. As long as they believed that their influence mattered, they would rest content, making the best of a sorry situation which left them economically dependent upon husbands and fathers and in consequence afraid to defy them.

On the other hand, the women's reluctance to challenge masculine authority may be interpreted as the inevitable outcome of the female nature. Gentle and unaggressive, women may not have wished to voice their own views in an open manner, preferring to give way to the superior male, either because life in an authoritarian society dominated by men had conditioned them to be submissive or because they were, by their biological nature, less assertive. Certainly they themselves have apparently subscribed for generations to the belief that their most effective means of influencing their husbands was to allow the latter to believe that they decided everything while privately smiling at masculine credulity. This is an attitude still found in the late twentieth century, and it had probably originated long before Thomas Carlyle ever put pen to paper. Presumably the ladies of the Middle Ages confided to each other that they could make their husbands do exactly as they wished, by means of a little clever management.

In the event, both these views are probably too extreme. Men did not subjugate women completely in a brutal and unfeeling manner, nor did women continually manipulate their gullible husbands. The truth was rather more subtle. Some wives were domineering by nature, others were submissive, and the marital relationship was governed as much by the personalities of the individuals as by the letter of the law. The balance between husband and wife was always a delicate one, and in the Middle Ages it had not really been a matter for public debate. By the eighteenth century, however, the climate of opinion had changed and so indeed had the physical circumstances of life. Most women no longer required masculine protection against actual danger, and there was a shift in the parts played by husband and wife. Hitherto, each had assumed a vital and complementary role. The man not only supported his family economically, but provided defence in times of trouble. The woman ran his home for him, undertaking the domestic work personally and bearing his children. By the eighteenth century, the situation had changed. The wealthy woman enjoying the Edinburgh season was divorced from her domestic concerns. Servants did her cooking and her cleaning and looked after her children, while she went to the theatre, mingled with friends of both sexes and read new ideas in recently published novels and journals. The men she met were

similarly removed from their original role. The young man of
fashion was not seen to be defending his home or even earning his
living. He had not yet taken up his family responsibilities, and as he
sat and debated with married women temporarily removed from
theirs, it was not surprising if the conversation turned to their
respective functions in society, nor was it unexpected if a witty and
mature woman who could win a battle of words and share in many
of the masculine pleasures of town life, began to question her
traditional subordination to men. While recognizing that her first
duty was to her husband, she nevertheless began to question the
fact that the law treated her as if she were a child, and it may well
be that the fashion of the time for recognizing male dominance
while acknowledging feminine influence provided a compromise
which suited both sexes at a period of unsettling change.

There is no doubt, however, that for all the artificiality of life in
polite society, the love between husband and wife remained as real
as ever it had been, and their expressions of attachment to each
other are in tone very similar to comparable declarations of an
earlier period. 'My dearest soul,' Janet Inglis wrote to her husband
Baron Clerk early in their marriage, 'I cannot describe it [sic] to
you, my dearest life, how much liking I have for you, oh my dearest
life . . . If ever you leave me, as God forbid, it should be seen to God
and the world that I should never love another while the breath of
life were in me . . .' In later years her style was somewhat calmer,
but her affection was undiminished. 'Let not the kindness you meet
with [in London] keep you too long from Tuckie,' she was writing
in 1727, employing his pet name for her, and the following month
remarked that 'a large, easy bodice for a woman big with child
would be a great present to Tuckie'. Her unsophisticated letters
reflect very clearly the happy intimacy of her domestic life, and
with equally touching affection, Robert Dundas of Arniston was in
the habit of addressing his wife as 'my dearest pleasure' and 'my
dearest kind obliging comfort' when he had to be away from her in
the 1740s. 'God bless you and send you safe to your doting Mary,'
William Rose's wife was telling him some forty years later and
Lord George Murray left a whole series of letters evincing his love
for the girl with whom he had eloped.[9]

As in the previous centuries, tributes to a spouse recently dead
reveal further proof of devotion. When Lady Jean Montgomerie
died in 1725, leaving her husband with three sons and four
daughters, he wrote sadly in his day book, 'We was fourteen years

and five months married. Never two lived more happily together. Never man had so great a loss of a loving, virtuous wife and faithful friend and companion, endowed with the greatest ornament and qualities of body and mind, capable of the greatest affairs, the best counsellor I ever had, indefatigable about any business she was engaged in.' Not noted for his tender feelings, Simon Fraser, Lord Lovat, was in 1729 lamenting the loss of his lady in childbirth with the words, 'The universe could not produce a better wife for my circumstances and temper, the most affectionate and careful wife that ever was born, whose chief care and greatest happiness was to please me in everything.'[10]

In somewhat ungallant manner, Boswell's father, Lord Auchinleck, regretted the death of his own partner in 1766 by declaring that 'she was no *bel esprit*, no wit, no genius' but hastened to add that she had possessed much more important qualities, for she 'endeavoured to make her husband, children, friends and all round her happy . . . Her exit has left me in a most desolate state.' Even more inconsolable was Mr Luke Fraser of Edinburgh High School, who lost his young wife in 1775. 'We had lived together but a short, short time,' he wrote, 'but in the most pleasing and uninterrupted unity of heart. Now all my schemes are broken. I am twenty years older than when you saw me. I feel no desire after [*i.e.* for] long life. I have a mother, indeed, with me and two infant daughters. Perhaps in life I may be of some small service to them. Yet I find it proper to compose myself, if possible, with a decent posture of dying, and they, now orphans, will be the care of the Father of the fatherless.'[11]

Not all marriages ended so tragically, although there were those which came to a premature conclusion by means of separation or divorce. Contemporary observers in the second half of the eighteenth century tended to believe that in their freer society, marriages were more unstable, and, comparing attitudes in 1783 with those twenty years earlier, one Scottish observer decided that 'separations, divorces, recriminations, collusions, separate maintenances are becoming almost as frequent as marriages.' Moreover, 'the known adulteress has been, by people of fashion, again received into society notwithstanding the endeavours of our worthy Queen [Charlotte] to check such a violation of morality, decency, the laws of the country and the rights of the virtuous.'[12]

In the new atmosphere of social freedom and with the new

emphasis on romance and the preference of the individual in seeking a partner, it would hardly have been surprising if divorce had become more frequent and indeed the records of Edinburgh Commissary Court prove that this was so. During the period from 1708 until 1800, 347 people sued for divorce in the court, which was still the only one in which such actions were heard. Fewer than twenty cases a decade came up before 1760, then the figures suddenly showed a sharp increase. There were twenty-four cases from 1761 to 1770, sixty-one from 1771 until 1780, eighty-eight from then until 1790 and in the last decade of the century, no fewer than one hundred and seven. In other words, 26% of those obtaining a divorce did so before 1770, and the remaining 74% did so in the last thirty years of the century.[13]

When examined in more detail, it soon becomes obvious that, although the numbers increased, the background to the cases remained much the same. Divorce did not, for instance, become suddenly easier for those married for a short time. The average duration of a marriage which ended in divorce before 1770 was twelve years, and after that date it was eleven years. Moreover, both the earlier and the later periods included extremes of length or brevity. There was Dame Alice Paterson, daughter of the Archbishop of Glasgow, who remained married to Sir Alexander Dalmahoy of that Ilk for thirty-two years before she sought a divorce from him in 1720, and at the opposite extreme Margaret Hamilton, daughter of a Dumfries lawyer, was in 1724 granted a decree after being married to a servant named Henry Johnston for less than two years. Similarly, when Elspeth Lambie divorced the Glasgow cabinet-maker Joseph Hewitt in 1798, they had been man and wife for forty-five years, and by contrast Sally McNish was granted her divorce after only two years.[14] It must be remembered, of course, that a marriage of forty-five years did not necessarily mean that the couple had stayed together for that length of time. Often they had parted years before and the divorce simply regularized a separation which had long existed.

The average duration of marriage prior to divorce did not, then, alter significantly, nor did the social class of those involved in divorce. The range remained wide throughout the century, with 12% of the total 347 husbands involved being soldiers. This was not surprising, given the amount of time they spent away from their families, for it was all too likely that either husband or wife would find someone else who attracted them. The second highest figure, however, was for merchants: 10% of the total were thus employed. A further 9% were servants and 7% were sailors, both groups with a higher than usual degree of mobility. Landed gentlemen, lawyers and weavers came next with 6%, carpenters accounted for 4% of the total and the remaining 46% comprised a very wide selection of occupations including among the 159 men concerned six doctors, five tailors, four labourers, three peers, two dancing masters, a butler, a dentist, a periwig-maker, a hatter, a fisher, a painter and a miner.

The wives came from a similar social range. Of the total 347, 6% were the daughters of merchants. A further 4% were the daughters of farmers and another 4% were daughters of lawyers, who included Lord Braxfield the famous judge and two of his colleagues. The daughters of shoemakers accounted for 3% and, again, there were daughters of many other workers ranging from candle-makers to colliers and from locksmiths to labourers. Several of the women had occupations of their own. Seven were servants, two were mantua-makers, Sara Dolphin was an Edinburgh shopkeeper, another girl had been a seamstress and, occupations apart, one of those involved was a Duchess. They came from all parts of Scotland, both urban and rural, and it seems that people from all but the very poorest families were liable to end their marriages by divorce.

Social background apart, there appear to have been several factors which predisposed a couple to go their separate ways. A marriage which had begun with an elopement often came to grief when the initial infatuation passed off and practical difficulties loomed large. Sophie Clerk and Gabriel Rankin engaged in constant arguments from their earliest days together, and their life was fraught with scenes, separations and indignant messages from both of them to Sophie's father. In October 1718, Gabriel composed a civil letter to Sir John Clerk announcing that 'After mature deliberation and advising with friends, my resolution is that your daughter, my wife, should not come home to me again, in regard her humour is so cross and inclinations so vicious and everything about her so unfit for cohabitation that it will render both her life and mine weary and uncomfortable.' Sophie's letters of the same period contain many counter-charges against her husband, along with some incoherent denials of drunkenness. However, a reconciliation was effected and by December she was claiming that 'there is nothing now but love and peace in our family.' Such harmony was unlikely to last, and by the autumn of 1720 the complaints had begun again. 'He never allowed one farthing in my pocket,' Sophie raged, adding, 'They must run whom the devil draws. He came home yesternight from Airth Church like a monster.' Six months later, of course, Gabriel was writing her a perfectly amiable letter, ending with the assurance, 'I am, dearest, your affectionate husband.' They quarrelled energetically with each other for the rest of their lives.[15]

Another match which ran into difficulties was that of the Earl of Wemyss, who eventually separated from Janet Charteris, the heiress he had been so anxious to marry in 1720. Again, Christian Farquhar in 1744 sought a divorce from her husband, Captain John MacNeill, whom she had married in very romantic circumstances. She had been a pupil at a boarding school in Bloomsbury Square, London, when she met him, and to the horror of her family she ran off with him, marrying him in a secret ceremony in a tavern on Ludgate Hill. Archibald Nisbet's secret marriage to Amelia Provan likewise came to grief, but not before they had six children. In 1795 a Dumfriesshire girl ran away to Gretna Green with a Lancashire merchant but he soon tired of her and went away to America, while Deborah Kelly, who had married George Morrison in presumably dramatic circumstances in London's Fleet Prison, also rued her decision and came to the divorce court in 1734.[16]

Partners from widely differing backgrounds were also likely to experience difficulties, and it was perhaps no surprise to their friends that Mary Rodgerson, daughter of a sober Dumfries merchant, did not get on well with her husband Alexander Stevenson, a dancing master, or that Captain William Jardine of Applegirth eventually sought to end his marriage to Barberie de la Motte, the wedding by then lying so far in the past that he could not recall the year, let alone the month when it had taken place. Unconventional marriages were sometimes unstable, but so were those where the husband and wife appeared to be from perfectly compatible backgrounds. Alexander Herbertson, a Glasgow looking-glass maker, divorced Marion Stuart, daughter of a Glasgow wright. John Morrison, weaver in the Pleasance in Edinburgh, ended his marriage to another Edinburgh weaver's daughter, and a stay-maker parted from his mantua-maker wife, a musician from his music master's daughter and an earl from his aristocratic lady.[17]

Throughout the eighteenth and early nineteenth centuries, the grounds for divorce remained unchanged and many of those suing in the court alleged that their partner had committed adultery. Propinquity obviously accounted for a large number of extra-marital affairs and a significant proportion of those who were unfaithful were attracted by someone in their own immediate circle. An army wife, for example, was liable to fall in love with a soldier. This happened to Lord Ruthven's daughter, Elizabeth Maria. She was married for eleven years to Major Robert Lawrie of the 7th Dragoons, but in 1774 he divorced her because of her relationship with Lieutenant Hatton Flood. Similarly, General James Lockhart Wishart lost his wife Mary Ann to Captain Evan Baillie after thirteen years of marriage, Harriet Charlton left her husband Captain John Forster Hill of the 65th Foot to run off with an ensign in her husband's regiment, and Colonel David Robertson was cited as co-respondent when Colonel John French divorced his wife in 1800.[18]

Even more humiliating was the experience suffered by the distinguished soldier, General John Scott of Balcomie. When he was about sixty he married a beautiful young girl of sixteen, the Earl of Errol's daughter Lady Mary Hay. His happiness appeared to be complete when a child was born within the year, but he was oblivious of the fact that Mary had fallen in love with his own cousin, Captain James Sutherland. This young man was twenty-six and had been brought up by the General as a beloved son. As soon as Mary had recovered from the birth of her child, she and Captain Sutherland crept out of Balcomie House by night, crossed the Firth of Forth, passed through Edinburgh and set off for London. It was ten o'clock the following morning before the General awoke and found that she had gone. Furious, he set off at once for Edinburgh and there collected two legal advisers. They piled into two coaches and took up the chase. At three o'clock in the morning they reached the house in Barnet where the eloping couple were spending the night. A servant ran upstairs to warn the pair, who were in bed together. In alarm, the Captain leaped out of the window without a stitch of clothing on and ran away to hide in some bushes. Meanwhile the General forced the door of the chamber, ordered Mary to dress and took her to London with him where he consulted Lord Mansfield, one of the leading legal authorities of the day. He then escorted his faithless wife back to Scotland and rapidly divorced her. Meanwhile, Captain

Sutherland, who had eventually emerged from his bushes shivering and covered in scratches, fled to France and there Lady Mary joined him. According to Mr Steuart, the contemporary whose letters give details of the episode, some people blamed the General for his 'morose behaviour to so young and fine a woman' while others condemned the Captain's base ingratitude and declared that Mary's behaviour resulted from the effects of a London education upon a weakened head. Perhaps the whole sorry story was best summed up by Mr Steuart when he quoted the saying, 'Auld age and young never agree together.'[19]

Not all instances of adultery involved people from the same family or social stratum, of course, for there were always those who felt a sudden violent attraction for someone from totally different circumstances. Mary Mackenzie married a respectable landed gentleman and lived as his wife for twenty-two years, bearing seven children. However, she then had an affair with a servant and found herself divorced. Sir Alexander Maxwell of Monreith's daughter Margaret was also divorced for adultery with a servant, while Lady Augusta Murray, daughter of the Earl of Cromartie, was unfaithful to her husband, Sir William Murray, with a local surgeon. Susannah Cunningham, wife of James Dalrymple of Orangefield and mother of his three children, disgraced herself by running away with a comedian named Henry Mills. She had a further three children by him and was eventually divorced many years later, by which time both Henry and one of his children were dead. Finally, the lure of the exotic proved too much for Barbara Moodie, a minister's daughter married to a military servant. She was found to have committed adultery with 'a man who was exhibiting wild beasts in Edinburgh'.[20]

The other ground for divorce was, of course, desertion, and actions for desertion frequently involved adultery too. Complicated situations could arise when the deserted partner sought another companion, as in the case of John MacMillan, a Lanarkshire distiller. In the 1740s he married Anna Marshall, daughter of a local tenant, but after nine years he left her and their four children. He then cohabited with various women in Edinburgh, Dundee and Fife before forming a more permanent relationship with a servant girl called Catherine Imrie. Deciding that they would like to stay together, they passed themselves off as husband and wife and finally departed for England, never to return. In the meantime, Anna made an irregular marriage with a neighbouring farmer and had one child by him. The local kirk session knew that she was already married, and summoned her to appear before them. Needless to say, she could produce no evidence that her rightful husband was dead and so she was referred to the commissary court. After hearing her story, they allowed her to initiate divorce proceedings against John and in the end she was given her freedom from him.[21]

Anna's case demonstrates a sympathetic attitude on the part of the authorities, who might easily have dismissed her as an adulteress deserving of punishment, nor was their behaviour unusual. The commissary court went into all the cases heard before it in great detail, and there is no evidence that they were prejudiced in favour of the men who came to complain to them. However, one of the most interesting features of eighteenth-century divorces is the ratio between men and women suing for divorce. In the seventeenth century it seems that men and women were equally likely to initiate proceedings, but in the later period sixty per cent of those suing for divorce were men and only forty per cent were women. From 1711 until 1720 six women and four men sought divorces, but in every other decade there was a preponderance of men, the greatest disparity coming in the 1770s when forty-two men and only twenty women sued for divorce. Presumably it was easier for a man with his economic resources and social contacts to contemplate raising an action than it was for his dependent wife.[22]

A total of three hundred and forty-seven people in a country which by 1800 had a population of around 1,600,000 inhabitants is very small and there was obviously much more marital discord than this figure would indicate. The impossibility of suing on the grounds of physical or mental cruelty continued to give rise to all manner of tragically unhappy domestic circumstances. Perhaps the classic case is that of Lord Grange, the leading lawyer, and his wife Rachel Chiesly. Lord Grange was a man of complex character, introverted and self-doubting. As a law student in Holland he embarked, by his own account, upon a period of debauchery, then on his return apparently had an affair with Rachel. He was deeply in love with her and made many promises to marry her, but, as his family were swift to point out, there could be no more unsuitable wife for a rising young lawyer. Rachel's father, upon losing a lawsuit, had assassinated Scotland's foremost judge as he left the Court of Session. Prudence and ambition gave Lord Grange pause, but when Rachel threatened him with a pistol he thought it wisest to remember his promises, and he married her.

This incident was to be typical of their life together. She was a beautiful, passionate woman, given to violent rages, but at first they settled down well enough and their three sons were followed in rapid succession by four daughters. According to Lord Grange himself, he gave up his pursuit of other women, turned to religion and struggled to restrain his fondness for drinking and swearing. Life in his family was never dull, though, and on one occasion, when his eldest son was nine, Lord Grange was indignant to find a diary kept by the boys' governor in which the man declared that his situation was intolerable because of the 'imperiousness and unreasonableness of Lady Grange'. Admitting that he knew 'there are some things in my family which I wish were more easy,' Lord Grange was nonetheless indignant on his wife's behalf.

As the years went by, however, Lady Grange's behaviour became more and more flamboyant and her own children went in fear of her. Alexander Carlyle remembered meeting her when he was a child of six or seven, about 1729. He was out playing on the road when she stopped in her coach. She was 'gorgeously dressed: her face was like the moon, and patched all over . . . she appeared to me to be the lady with whom all well-educated children were acquainted, the Great Scarlet Whore of Babylon.' He was later invited to take tea with her daughters. They had a charming room with a maid to serve them, and the afternoon began well. However, the serenity of the scene was soon to be disrupted by the sound of Rachel screaming for one of her daughters to attend her. Alexander noted that 'The girls seemed frightened out of their wits, and so did the maid.' They made the boys stand guard in the doorway and though cakes and sweets were brought in the occasion was ruined and Carlyle had 'by contagion caught a mighty fear of my lady'.

A young child was perhaps easily intimidated by a noisy woman, but there was more to it than that. By now Lady Grange was obsessed with the idea that her husband kept a mistress in London. Certainly, this seems to have been common gossip at the time, although it is difficult to assess its accuracy. Carlyle, whose father was a close friend of Lord Grange, certainly believed it. Lord Grange, he said, had a long-standing affair with 'a handsome Scotswoman, Fanny Lindsay, who kept a coffee house' in the Haymarket, and this did not surprise him. Lord Grange had frequently engaged in long sessions of prayer and religious discussion with Mr Carlyle senior, but he often disappeared for months at a time, causing the elder Carlyle to conjecture 'that at these times he was engag'd in a course of debauchery at Edinburgh'.

Whatever the truth of the matter, Lady Grange now made life a misery for everyone who came into contact with her. She followed her husband about, abused him in public, swore at his relations and terrorized her household. In an attempt to pacify her, Lord Grange gave her the management of his estate, making her his official factor, but she proved so extravagant that he had to replace her with Mr Thomas Elliot. This move provoked terrible scenes, and her grown-up sons and daughter were soon exhausted by her emotional demands. Lord Grange by now had sought refuge in London, and his family's letters to him retail in painful detail the stormy arguments which roused the neighbours in the Cowgate by night. Lady Grange shouted, screamed and raged, constantly threatening to follow Lord Grange to London, there to confront him with his evil deeds. It is often said that she threatened to reveal his involvement with the Jacobites, but this particular issue is never mentioned in the surviving correspondence. Lady Grange was much more taken up with his personal attitude to her, though she was undoubtedly ready to say anything in public, true or otherwise, if it would make trouble for him. More and more of his friends, including his own family, were convinced that he could never live with her again, and indeed some began to wonder if she were not deranged as she shrieked and cursed, changed her mind twenty times a day and eventually ran about the house in her nightclothes threatening to kill herself. This, she told the servants the following day, was because she had decided that to feign insanity was the only way she would gain her husband's attention.

If that was her idea, it enjoyed a hideous and unlooked-for success. In July 1732, she was threatening once more to set out for London and had actually booked her seat on a coach when, late at night, a party of Highlanders burst into her room, trussed her up, gagged her and carried her out into a sedan chair. After a short journey, during which she was blindfolded, she was lifted out and put up on a horse behind a rider. That was the start of a long journey westwards, which was to take her to the deserted Castle Tioram, on Loch Moidart in the West Highlands, then to the lonely island of Heiskir, off North Uist. There she spent two years as a prisoner, until the family who lived on the island refused to put up with her any longer and she was moved to the remotest island of all, St Kilda. For four years she was a captive in a little house with only a young girl to look after her, and everyone speaking Gaelic, a language she did not know.

Obviously, her disappearance from Edinburgh had not gone unnoticed, but Lord Grange and his family let it be known that she was insane and, for her own safety, had been taken to a place in the Highlands. In 1738 a letter, said to have been smuggled by her to the mainland, came to light. It described her seizure and imprisonment, and an expedition set out to rescue her. By the time the ship arrived at St Kilda, however, she had been moved elsewhere. In the months which followed, she was kept in various places on Harris and Skye. By this time she was very obviously deranged and in 1745 she died.[23]

Both Lord and Lady Grange were complicated, difficult people of conflicting temperament. Much public sympathy over the years has been directed at Lady Grange, in the mistaken belief that she was the young, innocent victim of a cruel husband. The truth was rather different. Although Lord Grange himself was hardly an attractive character, it is perhaps more just to see them both as the victims of circumstance and of the marriage laws of their time. Since Lady Grange had not committed adultery or deserted her husband, there was no way in which he could divorce her, so he had to remain tied to her until his friends came up with their drastic solution. For her part, it seems likely that Lady Grange was, at the very least, emotionally disturbed and unfortunately there was no such thing as psychiatric medicine or even an understanding treatment of the insane in her time.

CHAPTER TEN

The Learned Lady

THE INCREASING ANGLICISATION of fashionable Scottish society in the eighteenth century owed much to the Union of the Parliaments in 1707, and although Scotland retained her own educational and legal systems, and her own established Church, far more people generally had to travel south on business than ever before. Since public stage coaches were making transport easier, it was more feasible for a wife to accompany her husband on his journey to London so that she could share with him the pleasures of the winter season. One result of this increased contact was that Scots became much more conscious of what was socially acceptable in London. Before 1707, for instance, it had been virtually unknown for any Scot to be educated in England, but now more and more aristocratic families were sending their sons to Eton or Westminster School. As one nobleman remarked in 1716, admittedly with some exaggeration, 'all the peers are breeding their sons at London.'[1] Having accustomed themselves to the idea that the best education was to be obtained in the south, it was a short step for aristocratic parents to decide that the English boarding schools would most benefit their daughters. However, there were other factors to consider. Mothers were often unwilling to be parted from their girls by such a distance, especially if they had already agreed to allow their sons to go to London. Again, there was the question of expense. Susanna, Countess of Eglinton, had an optimistic view of the English establishments when, planning to take one daughter to Bath for the sake of her health, she decided to 'take Christie and Peggy along and send them to a boarding school: they are much cheaper in London than in Edinburgh.' However, it was not long before her illusions about cost were shattered. Even in Bath, Peggy's singing lessons were horribly expensive and, the Countess lamented, 'I don't find her hundred pounds will go a great way.' If the entire family was to be in London anyway, the additional expense was not so large. Sir James Grant accordingly took the opportunity of putting his daughter Sophia to a school near London when he took his family to the city for several months. There Sophia would study French, dancing, singing, writing, and playing on the spinet.[2]

For most parents, however, Edinburgh provided a more economical alternative, so the eighteenth century saw a great proliferation of the boarding schools in the city, each one taking perhaps six to ten pupils. The daughters of the upper peerage were not sent away to school in normal circumstances, their parents preferring to bring in suitable instructors or let the girls have lessons when the family was in town.

Boarding schools varied very much in standard, but the curriculum formed a set pattern. At first, practical skills were combined with the much-desired social accomplishments. Cooking and sewing were taught along with dancing and singing, and if the mistresses resident in the school were not qualified to teach everything themselves, then special masters were hired or the girls were sent as pupils to the local day schools which taught particular subjects. From about 1690 onwards, there were 'pastry' or cookery schools in Edinburgh, and the enterprising Elizabeth Clelland who kept a pastry school went so far as to publish in 1755 a book entitled *A New and Easy Method of Cookery . . . chiefly intended for the benefit of the Young Ladies who attend her School.*[3] On a more exotic note, a dancing academy was kept by none other than Signora Violante, the Italian rope-dancer. Her classes for young ladies were very popular and when she needed partners for her senior girls she even permitted a few select boys to attend. One of these was Alexander Carlyle. He much appreciated the opportunity to dance 'with her grown-up misses, weekly, at her practisings'. Such was Signora Violante's fame that her obituary even appeared in the *Scots Magazine* when she died in 1741.[4]

Carlyle also had some interesting comments to make on education in Glasgow in the 1740s. For boys, the town had little to offer, 'and in this respect, the females were still worse off, for at that period there was neither a teacher of French nor music in the town. The consequence of this was twofold. Firstly the young ladies were entirely without accomplishments, and in general had nothing to recommend them but good looks and fine clothes, for their manners were ungainly; secondly, the few who were distinguish'd drew all the young men of sense and taste about them, for being void of frivolous accomplishments, which in some respects make all women equal, they trusted only to superior understanding and wit, to natural elegance and unaffected manners.' In the domestic sphere, Glasgow was rather better equipped, for in 1740 James Lochhead was promising to teach young ladies 'pastry, confectionery, candying, preserving and pickling, making of milks, creams, syllabubs, jellies, soups and broths of all sorts, and also to dress and order a table and make a bill of fare'.[55]

Generally, as the demand for boarding schools increased, more were established outside the capital. The site chosen was usually a healthy one, where the pupils could benefit from the sea air while acquiring their accomplishments, and by the end of the century Alexander Carlyle's parish of Inveresk, a few miles from Edinburgh, could boast no fewer than three such schools, run by Miss Grant, Miss Primrose and Miss Neilson respectively, while an establishment in Ayr could offer 'everything taught as complete as at Edinburgh'.[6]

As time passed, not only did the number of schools grow, but the balance of the curriculum altered. Because ladies were abandoning housewifery to their servants, they no longer had to learn how to cook and wash and sew. It has been calculated that of sixty-eight schools advertising in the Edinburgh papers during this period, forty-two mentioned either needlework, millinery, lace or gummed flowers. Nineteen offered tuition in French. Nine gave music lessons and eight had cookery courses. Four spoke of drawing and geography and three taught dancing and bookkeeping. English, writing and arithmetic were mentioned but seldom. The young lady was now learning not so much how to run her home, but how to take her place in society and fill the long hours of leisure thrust upon her by convention. This explained the vast range of handicrafts which had become so popular. These are well listed in the testimonial of Miss Betty Forbes of Edinburgh, who decided to open a school in Aberdeen and came before the magistrates there with her certificates and references. Not only did Miss Forbes have 'integrity and gentleness of manners, joined to the most rigid modesty and morals', but she would teach 'white seam and samplers, washing and dressing, coloured work of various sorts, Dresden work and Dresden marseilling, gum flowers, pongs [*i.e.* decorations] in silver, silk and enamel

[207]

embroidery, shell-work, drawing patterns for sewing, painting flowers and water-colours in silk and paper, illuminating
prints, working fringes, tassels, jump-straps, watch and cane-
strings, cords and looping of all sorts, with several other things of
the like nature'. Suitably impressed, the magistrates concluded
that 'all ladies and gentlemen may depend upon having their
children sufficiently taught at Aberdeen in all genteel parts of
education.'[7]

This change of emphasis in female education did not go
unnoticed by contemporaries. In the summer of 1766, one of the
Scots Magazine's reviewers forcibly expressed his opinion of current
female instruction. Founded in 1739 and still in existence today, in
a rather altered form, this popular periodical concerned itself
mainly with politics and foreign affairs, frequently reprinting
letters and articles from the London journals. The reviewer of 1766
was, however, a Scot and he complained bitterly that 'parents
nowadays, almost universally, down to the lowest tradesman or
mechanic, who to ape his superior, strains himself beyond his
circumstances, send their daughters to boarding schools. And what
do they mostly learn there? I say, mostly, for there are exceptions
that do the mistresses real honour. Need I mention that, making
allowance for those exceptions, they learn principally to dress, to
dance, to speak bad French, to prattle much nonsense, to practise I
know not how many pert, conceited airs and in consequence of all,
to conclude themselves accomplished women.'[8]

Almost twenty years later, one of the *Magazine's* correspondents took up the theme once more. Pointing out how
female education had altered since 1763, he alleged that in those
days 'people sent their daughters to Edinburgh to be accomplished
in their education and to give them urbanity of manners. An
Edinburgh education was thought the most likely to procure them
a good marriage . . . In the best families in town, the education of
daughters was fitted not only to embellish and improve their
minds, but to accomplish them in the useful and necessary arts
of domestic economy. The sewing-school, the pastry-school, were
then essential branches of female education, nor was a young lady
of the best family ashamed to go to the market with her mother.' By
1783, however, things had changed for the worse. Frivolity was
now the order of the day, the daughters 'even of tradesmen'
would not think of doing any domestic chores and instead relegated all the work of the home to the servants. Left with long

hours of leisure, they filled them with idle amusements.[9]

Forty years on, nothing had changed. Sir John Sinclair, writing in 1826, remarked that 'the education of females, when it is considered only as a preparation for fashionable life, seldom leads to a happy result, for . . . the great objects of attention too often are merely to hold up the head, to point the toes, to learn a smattering of French and Italian, to play on some musical instrument, to draw and to receive instructions in the more useless and flimsy parts of needlework to the almost total neglect of mental attainments and of moral and religious principles.' To sum up, an education of that nature was better calculated to inspire girls with 'a love of admiration and of trifling amusements, than to give them the means of acquiring useful accomplishments or fit them for the important duties of wives and mothers'.[10]

Here in this last phrase was the real reason for educating women at all, as far as most people were concerned. Men had always tended to see training as an efficient wife and mother as the only end of female education, and their viewpoint had received support in the late eighteenth century from Jean-Jacques Rousseau. In his famous treatise *Emile*, Rousseau declared that the evils of sophisticated society could only be escaped by a return to nature. The 'noble savage' was his ideal, and as part of his belief he held that women's 'entire education should be planned in relation to men', their principal duties being 'to please men, to be useful to them, to win their love and respect, to raise them as children, care for them as adults, counsel and console them, and make their lives sweet and pleasant'.[11] Rousseau's writings were avidly read throughout Western Europe and, twenty years later, his views were echoed by the eminent Scottish judge Lord Kames, when he published in Edinburgh his own *Loose Hints upon Education*. In his section on girls, he points out that their role as future mothers was all-important. The task of bringing up their children was one 'with which females only are charged by Providence, a vocation that ought to employ their utmost sagacity and perseverence', and one 'not inferior in dignity . . . to any that belongs to the other sex'. Women must be virtuous and right-thinking. They were all too liable to roam around the town seeking idle amusement. Instead, they should realize that 'the dignified occupation of educating their children would be their most charming amusement'. A knowledge of human nature and history and a general familiarity with science would allow them to fulfil their true role in life and there would be

[209]

the added benefit that 'a woman of sense, prudently educated, makes a delicious companion to a man of parts and knowledge.'[12]

The same attitude pervaded the education of girls from other sections of society. Parents continued to brush aside literacy in favour of the practical skills and, of course, there was no question of instructing these girls in the accomplishments which they would never need and which would have been regarded as inappropriate to their station in life. When new schools were set up, they therefore concentrated on a narrow range of subjects. In 1719, for example, Dumfries had a school where 'shaping and sewing all sorts of white and coloured seams, embroidering and pastry' were taught. Further north, Brechin in 1722 resolved to employ a mistress to instruct girls in the 'arts of sewing and working of lace' while Elgin appointed a mistress 'skilful in needlework and pastry'. Stirling in 1726 had a woman who taught the sewing of white and coloured seams, shaping and washing. Nine years later, the fishing town of Arbroath set up a school where instruction in sewing and lace-making was given, while the small burgh of Forres in Morayshire hired a teacher whose principal qualification was that she was expert in sewing.[13]

Apart from the desire of the Lowland town councils to provide useful schools for girls, the eighteenth century saw a move towards expanding education in the Highlands. The aim in view was the general improvement of conditions, and in 1709 the Society for the Propagation of Christian Knowledge had embarked upon a campaign of establishing schools of industry, where spinning and sewing mistresses could instruct not only the local girls but adult women too. These efforts met with strong resistance. Highland women disliked and mistrusted the industrial schools and the Society's report for 1774 shows that only twelve sewing mistresses were needed that year. Not until the 1790s did the campaign meet with success. Gifts of spinning wheels and reels to girls willing to attend encouraged an interest, and by 1802 the SPCK inspector was able to report that those formerly employed in labour in the fields 'most unsuitable to their sex, are now occupied in spinning, sewing and knitting stockings and the like appropriate employ-ments', thereby gaining a considerable source of income.[14]

After the Jacobite Risings of 1715 and 1745, the commissioners appointed to manage the estates forfeited by those who supported the Stewarts took a hand in education. They hoped that by spreading the Protestant faith to formerly Catholic areas and by establishing the English language in Gaelic-speaking communities, they would eradicate support for the Jacobite cause. They therefore set up schools in Highland parishes where these had not previously existed and improved the facilities in others by erecting new schoolhouses and paying better salaries. Once again, spinning and sewing mistresses were employed along with the school-masters. For the girls, of course, the emphasis of these schools remained vocational: the spinning and sewing mattered far more than the reading or the writing. In the charity school of Glenartney, near Comrie, for example, none of the twenty-one girls attending in 1776–7 could write, and about the same time, in Monzie school in Perthshire, only one of the fifteen female pupils could write although all of them could read. The fact that Gaelic was the native language in the Highland areas was obviously a disadvantage when it came to acquiring these skills, and travellers in the Highlands frequently commented on the fact that the people they encountered could speak no English, or at least claimed to speak none.[15]

In the Lowlands, the position was not much better. Throughout the second half of the eighteenth century, town councils were still noting the need for schoolmistresses and doing their best to employ them. Social and economic advantage was the aim. Girls were better kept in school than being allowed to roam the streets, and spinning and sewing could usefully supplement the family income. By 1756, however, Dunfermline Town Council was still lamenting 'the great loss caused to the town through the want of a proper schoolmistress to teach the girls', and twenty years later, Forfar Town Council received a petition from some of the local inhabitants declaring that girls were 'shamefully neglected and seldom or never in this town receive the proper rudiments of education, finding the loss thereof all the days of their lives'.[16]

Few educationalists stopped to discuss the requirements of girls from poorer backgrounds, but one author who did was Mr George Chapman, master of an academy near Crieff. Declaring himself to be 'incapable of advising on the education of ladies of higher rank', he humbly offered in 1784 'a few hints on the education of women in the lower stations of life'. Like Lord Kames, Mr Chapman emphasized the importance of woman's role as the preceptor of her own children. Religion and morality were of the greatest importance in life and so future mothers must learn to read the Bible, sing hymns and write, 'and to this may be added the common rules of arithmetic, if they discover an inclination to learn them'. Girls ought to attend the parish schools, 'either in company with the boys, as at present, or rather by themselves and at different hours'. They should also be instructed in cooking, sewing, spinning and knitting, all of which would help to recommend a girl to a husband and serve as compensation for a lack of fortune. Both men and women would benefit from the results, for a pleasing wife will encourage a man to 'regularity and decency of behaviour' and, after all, 'our truer and more lasting happiness' was to be found in 'a married state, as it can arise only from the possession of a virtuous and amiable woman, the friend and companion of life'.[17]

Mr Chapman was willing to admit that 'the fair sex are capable of a very high degree of improvement' and later went so far as to say that 'they are capable of instruction as well as the men.' Discussing their need to be taught morality, he asks, 'Are they not endued with the same powers of mind [as men]?' He was quite convinced, however, that these powers should be devoted entirely to the welfare of the woman's home and family. The effect that this attitude had on intelligent young women from ordinary backgrounds is well illustrated in the life of Jean, the sister of Thomas Carlyle the historian. A talented girl, she was unable to go on with her education because her duty was clearly seen to lie in the home. Her father was a stone-mason turned farmer in Dumfriesshire. His able sons were allowed to go to school and university, but his able daughter had to help in the house and on the land.

When she was twelve, her brother and his wife Jane encouraged her to study Latin. Jean was eager, but her domestic duties took up most of her day and she simply did not have time to persevere. Her sister-in-law understood very well that 'it *is* impossible for you, sure enough, to make any great attainment of scholarship' in her present circumstances, but urged her not to give up. Perhaps an opportunity for further study would present itself. She and Carlyle did their best to make this possible. They took Jean to stay with them in Edinburgh for a few weeks and taught her, but word soon came that she was needed on the farm again and so, as another brother put it, she 'grew up a peasant girl, got no further special "education", tho' she has since given herself, consciously or otherwise, not a little both of the practical and of the "speculative sort"'. She married a house painter in Dumfries and settled down happily enough with him, recognized by family and friends as being 'a superior woman; superior in extent of reading, culture, etc., and still better in veracity of character, sound discernment and practical wisdom'. Whether she ever yearned for her Latin books and the knowledge she might have gained, remains unknown.[18]

In view of the attitude of parents, educationalists and burgh authorities, it seemed that the demand for anything beyond the usual curriculum would have to come from women themselves and, on the face of it, this seemed unlikely to happen. Economic necessity deprived most of them of the time to study, and many of those who did have hours of leisure were perfectly content with what education they received. Balls and concerts were enjoyable, sewing and handicrafts could be creative and satisfying, and matrimony was an attractive prospect. Thirteen-year-old Anna Rose, who attended Miss Drysdale's boarding school in Edinburgh in 1798, was able to tell her mother with pleasurable pride, 'I began artificial flowers last week, and have made a bunch of white roses and am now making a hawthorn wreath.' When the time came for her to leave the school, she did so with genuine regret.[19]

By her day, a new method of educating wealthy girls was coming into fashion, although the curriculum remained un-changed. The early nineteenth century saw the installation of governesses in the large country houses. Hitherto, girls at home had been taught by their mothers, with some help from their brothers' tutors or the local schoolmaster. Now, however, it was judged more fitting to employ a female teacher in the English manner and many of the governesses employed were English by birth, venturing north of the border in some trepidation to instruct their charges in the customary subjects. Lord Arbuthnott, for example, had in his employment in the early nineteenth century a certain Miss M., who, when she left him, advertised her services in the following terms: 'A native of England wishes a situation in a nobleman or gentleman's family, who reside part of the season in Edinburgh. She can instruct her pupils in English, French, music and geography. Likewise useful and ornamental work.'[20]

Like her colleagues, Miss M. expected to be in sole charge of her pupils when the family were at home in the country, but she envisaged that the household would move to Edinburgh in the winter, where her own efforts would be supplemented by those of hired masters. Elizabeth Grant of Rothiemurchus, who later wrote the much-loved *Memoirs of a Highland Lady*, knew this type of situation at first hand. The daughter of a Scottish advocate, she was seventeen when her father took over a house in Edinburgh's fashionable Heriot Row in the early years of the nineteenth century and installed his family there. As Elizabeth later recalled, 'Six masters were engaged for us girls, three every day; Mr Penson for the pianoforte, Monsieur Elouis for the harp, Monsieur L'Espinasse for French, Signor something for Italian and Mr I forget who for drawing, Mr Scott for writing and ciphering and oh! I was near forgetting a seventh, the most important of all, Mr Smart for dancing.'[21]

Although many girls were perfectly delighted with this type of curriculum, there were others who were not so satisfied. As early as February 1740, the *Scots Magazine* was publishing a letter purporting to be from 'Mary Lizard' in the small Scottish port of Bo'ness to her friend 'Jenny'. Mary gave news of her successful progress in society, then proffered some advice. 'I understand you have a turn for reading,' she noted. 'You must by all means lay that aside; meddle with no books, unless they be love-epistles or novels: you will else render your turn for gallantry insipid and unjustly encroach upon a prerogative of knowledge due only to men. Nature has endued them alone with the faculty of reflection, while she made women only for their amusement and domestic conveniency. So whenever one shows a capacity for more than this, she becomes despised and ironically gets the character of a learned lady.'[22]

The true identity of the author of this piece of satire is not important. What does matter is that the *Scots Magazine* would hardly have published it, had it not thought that it would find a sympathetic audience among its female readers. Even if the intention was only to provoke a titillating argument about the roles of men and women in society, it would not have been couched in such terms had no women ever resented the part assigned to them by men. Some women did object to the remarks of Rousseau and Lord Kames and, more important, there were those who felt a real need to exercise their intellect regardless of the conventions of society.

An extremely illuminating account of current attitudes is to be found in the reminiscences of Mary Somerville, the brilliant Scottish mathematician. At the end of her long and successful life, she wrote down an account of her career, and it is worth looking at this in some detail. Mary was born in 1780, the daughter of a naval lieutenant. She was brought up in the small port of Burntisland on the River Forth and in early childhood she was more or less allowed to run wild. When she was ten years old, her father returned from one of his lengthy trips abroad and was dismayed to observe that, although Mary could read, she could not write, and was quite uneducated in any other subjects. He therefore decreed that she should be sent to Miss Primrose's school in Musselburgh, on the other side of the Forth. Her mother agreed to this somewhat reluctantly, commenting that she would be quite content if her daughter learned nothing more than to write well and keep accounts, 'which was all that a woman was expected to know'.

In the event, the year at school achieved little. 'I was utterly wretched,' Mary recalled, and this was not surprising. Miss Primrose took the social graces with a deep seriousness and Mary discovered that the pursuit of accomplishments could be painful as well as tedious. 'A few days after my arrival, although perfectly straight and well-made, I was enclosed in stiff stays with a steel busk in front, while above my frock, bands drew my shoulders back till the shoulder-blades met. Then a steel rod, with a semi-circle which went under the chin, was clapped to the steel busk in my stays. In this constrained state I, and most of the younger girls, had to prepare our lessons.' Such contraptions were by no means unusual, for great emphasis was always placed on deportment.

The lessons themselves afforded little mental stimulation and, at the end of the year, Mary returned to Burntisland still unable to write or spell properly. Nevertheless, her intellectual curiosity had somehow been awakened. Domestic duties, relieved by working on a sampler, were not enough for her, and she found herself thinking it 'unjust that women should have been given a desire for knowledge if it were wrong to acquire it'. She worked her way through her father's small library and taught herself to read Latin, but her real moment of revelation was to come from a most unlikely quarter. On her return home she was invited by a Miss Ogilvie to visit her house and inspect the fancy-work this lady had produced. This was a normal enough occasion in a dull round of tea-parties and social visits. In the course of conversation, Miss Ogilvie produced a magazine which contained some embroidery designs. Glancing politely through its pages, Mary found her attention caught by several arithmetical puzzles, then, as she recorded later, 'On turning the page I was surprised to see strange-looking lines mixed with letters, chiefly Xs and Ys and asked, "What is that?" "Oh," said Miss Ogilvie, "it is a kind of arithmetic: they call it Algebra, but I can tell you nothing about it."'

For some reason, Mary was afire with enthusiasm. She returned home determined to discover everything she could about those strangely seductive symbols. Excitedly hunting through her father's books, she could find nothing on the subject. She pounced on a manual of navigation, but it proved disappointing. There seemed no way in which she could find out more, hedged about as she was by the conventions of her day. She did not encounter organized prejudice, but the accepted ideas of her time were an equally difficult barrier to surmount. 'Unfortunately not one of our acquaintances or relations knew anything of science or natural history, nor, had they done so, should I have had the courage to ask any of them a question, for I should have been laughed at.' However, a chance conversation gave her the information she needed. Alexander Nasmyth, the popular landscape painter, opened an academy for ladies in Edinburgh and Mary was allowed to attend. She enjoyed herself painting copies of his works and listening to his well-informed conversation. One day, as he discoursed on the rules of perspective, he remarked to two of the other girls, 'You should study Euclid's *Elements of Geometry*, the foundation not only of perspective but of astronomy and astronomical science.' Here, at last, was what Mary needed to know. Even so, her problems were not over, for 'as to going to a bookseller and asking for Euclid, the thing was impossible!' Once again, she had to bide her time until the day came when she persuaded her brother's new tutor to buy her Euclid and an algebra textbook. He was able to explain the first few pages of these to her, and that was enough. Her serious study of mathematics had begun.

She sat up late each night, poring over her books. To her dismay, the servants then complained that she was using up the household supply of candles too quickly, and she overheard her father say to her mother, 'Peg, we must put a stop to this or we shall have Mary in a straitjacket one of these days.' Mary told this story with relish in her memoirs. By now, nothing could stop her pursuit of learning. When her mother took her to Edinburgh again she rose at daybreak to read algebra until breakfast time. She was now eighteen, and her days continued thus until, six years later, she married her cousin Samuel Greig. A captain in the Russian Navy, he was completely out of sympathy with her, 'as he had a very low opinion of the capacity of my sex and had neither knowledge of, nor interest in, science of any kind'. He died three years later, leaving her with two sons. She spent the next four years in her parents' home, then she married another cousin, Dr William Somerville. He was the complete opposite of Samuel Greig. He advised, supported and aided her in every way. He took her to London, introduced her to the best intellectual society and travelled with her on the continent. She met and impressed all the leading French scientists of her day, winning their unstinted admiration for her superior understanding. She published no fewer than four influential books on astronomy, science and physical geography, along with three famous papers recounting experiments with light. Her works sold well and were translated into many languages. The Royal Society recognized her researches by placing a bust of her in their Great Hall, an honour rare enough for any living person but unknown for a woman. The Royal Geographical Society presented her with its Victoria Gold Medal, the Geographical Society of Florence awarded her its Victor Emmanuel Gold Medal and a Liverpool shipbuilder amused and delighted her by naming a merchant vessel after her. Throughout her long life she was always a staunch supporter of the cause of women's education and when she died on 29 November 1872, at the age of ninety-two, she had been at work until the day before, revising a paper on quaternions.[23]

Mary was exceptional, but she was not alone in her intellectual turn of mind. Other girls also felt a desire for knowledge, although all too often they tended to pursue their studies in an undirected way, obviously eager to learn but not knowing quite where to begin. Mary Scott of Harden and her cousin Margaret Scott had a notion to study foreign languages and searched their fathers' bookshelves for inspiration. There were grave disadvantages in such a method, for the books were very specialized and, not content with the more usual subjects, the girls were attracted to the exotic. 'My Icelandic fever is rather cooled for the present,' Mary was writing in 1828, 'partly because the grammar is in manuscript and is therefore difficult to read, particularly as what should have been English is Latin, and partly because I have taken a still greater fancy to learn the language of the troubadours – the French call it *La Langue Romaine* which I cannot translate . . . it is a mixture or perhaps a sort of middle language between Latin, French, Spanish and Italian.' Full of enthusiasm, she announced, 'I have begun to write an abbreviated grammar of it for you – just enough to give a general idea of the most important parts of the language.' As for her cousin's own plans, 'You must *not* learn *Russian*,' she advised. 'Papa says that the Slavonic dialects *stand alone* and will not assist one in learning anything else but themselves, and we know that their literature is not in a very advanced state – they have no great authors, or at least one has not heard of them, so if you will learn a new language there is Persian, Arabic, which can surely be more worth learning, and above all, *Chinese* . . .'[24]

It would be easy to laugh at these girls' attempts to continue their own education, but the very fact that they took the trouble to search their fathers' bookshelves for suitable reading, or spent their hours of leisure translating foreign languages rather than paying calls, is an indication of a growing desire in women to receive a more academic education. As long as they had no instruction they would not hanker after intellectual pursuits, but once introduced to the pleasures of the mind there would always be some who would respond eagerly.

One young woman who particularly longed for encouragement in her studies was Jane Welsh, whose early life in many ways parallels that of Mary Somerville, although her talents lay in a different sphere and she tried to solve the problems they brought her in a different way. Born in 1801, the only child of a Haddington doctor, Jane was highly-strung, extremely intelligent and possessed of a sharp, sarcastic wit which often made difficult her dealings with the people she met. Her father loved her, understood her and planned out her education for her, intended her to develop her literary gifts. She attended the local school before spending a little time at one of the Edinburgh boarding schools, but she also received private tuition in Latin and was reading French and German with her father. His sudden death in a cholera epidemic left her utterly bereft. Becalmed in the intellectual backwater of a small country town, she tried desperately to pursue the studies planned for her by her father, but she felt that she had lost 'the pole-star of my life' and she often 'wept to think the mind he had cultivated with such anxious, unremitting pain was running down to desolation'. Even in her studies she had 'neither the same pleasures or the same motives as formerly – I am *alone* and no-one loves me better for my industry – this solitude together with distrust of my own talents, despair of ennobling my character, and the discouragement I meet with in devoting myself to a literary life' plunged her into depression.

The discouragement largely emanated from her mother, with whom she was completely out of sympathy. However, at this low ebb, Jane made the acquaintance of Thomas Carlyle, later to become the celebrated historian. They talked together, he appreciated her conversation and she begged him to send her a reading list. This he did, recommending the works of Voltaire, Tasso and De Stael, along with other histories and biographies. Admiring Jane's capacity, he did not attempt to patronize her in any way, and indeed the list was much the same as one he had given to a young male friend a few weeks before. Determined as she was to follow the regimen he had laid down for her, she was continually frustrated by the demands of convention. Her mother enjoyed an active social life and expected Jane to play her part. For Jane, tea-parties and social chit-chat were the acme of boredom and even at home her time was not her own, for Mrs Welsh received a constant stream of callers and expected Jane to help to entertain them. An aunt was horrified to discover her niece's attempts to avoid visitors when she paid a visit to Haddington that April. 'Mother tells me,' Jane wrote to Carlyle, 'that whenever I take myself off to my place of refuge, she sets to work to rail against learned ladies and expatiate on the utter detestation which they are held in by the gentlemen. God grant that her ignorance may recommend her to their good graces.'

Strangers could be even more hurtful. On a visit to the Highlands one year Jane made the acquaintance of a pleasant, older woman who seemed to like and admire her. When they went their separate ways, they promised to write to each other, so of course Jane sent one of her fluent, entertaining letters. To her dismay, the reply she received was 'cold, short and formal', and was accompanied by a postscript from the woman's husband, an English army officer, beginning, 'If you choose to be a blue-stocking, do you think or expect we common people can answer you in the same style?' The rest of his message was filled with unpleasant allusions to her 'blue-stocking talents'. Fortunately, Carlyle understood when Jane related the episode to him, and was able to offer consolation. He knew that her melancholy was caused by the fact that she had to live 'shut out, absolutely shut out, from all communication with minds like your own'. He had long been in love with her, and in the end she came to return his feelings, escaping at last from the dreariness of her mother's house by marrying him.[25]

By Jane's time, the expression 'blue-stocking' had joined 'learned lady' as a favourite term of abuse for any woman with intellectual aspirations. At first the epithet seems to have been applied to ladies who were not genuinely learned but who, as a fashionable fad, chose to scatter their conversation with literary allusions and supposedly erudite remarks. It was not long, however, before it became a name applied indiscriminately to any woman who showed a scholarly turn of mind. The trouble was that the climate of opinion made it seem that erudition in a woman was entirely unnecessary, even undesirable, whether or not she felt a deep need for learning. At the end of her long life, Miss Elizabeth Mure of Caldwell commented that, in the 1720s, 'domestic affairs and amusing her husband was the business of a good wife.' Girls were not expected to study literature or philosophy. 'The women's knowledge was gained only by conversing with the men, not by reading themselves . . . whoever had read Pope, Addison and Swift, with some ill-wrote history, was then thought a learned lady, which character was by no means agreeable. The men thought justly on this point, that what knowledge the women had out of their own sphere should be given by themselves and not picked up at their own hand in ill-chosen books of amusement.'[26]

Men who were ready to criticize the boarding schools as producing frivolous, empty-headed women were equally ready to castigate those girls who aspired to more intellectual pursuits, for they were guilty of neglecting their appointed role in life as wives and mothers. It is noticeable that neither Lord Kames nor any of the other writers on female education criticized the boarding schools on intellectual grounds. A woman was to be educated for her domestic vocation, not because she had inherent mental abilities. Virtue and capability in the home were her desired attributes, and the attainment of accomplishments was censured because they were thought to encourage immorality, not because they failed to utilize a woman's intelligence. Lord Kames admitted that 'females have a flexible tongue and acquire earlier than males the use of speech,' but he went on merely to observe that women have sweeter voices and talk more. 'A man says what he knows, a woman what is agreeable: knowledge is necessary to the former, taste is sufficient to the latter.'[27] Sir John Sinclair was equally dismissive. Reflecting that a husband could only consider his wife a fit companion if she were capable of conversing with him on equal terms, he declared that 'when women are properly educated they are very far from shewing any mental deficiency.' However, since a classical education could not be acquired outside a public school, it was necessary only for those men who intended to go into the professions and it was 'not at all desirable that women should waste their time in making an acquisition which may supersede accomplishments of a more feminine description and more likely to be useful'.[28]

Even Sir Walter Scott referred to the writer Mrs Grant of Laggan as being 'proud as a Highland woman, vain as a poetess and absurd as a blue-stocking'. He was usually more sympathetic. When his own daughters criticized a young and pretty poetess, he declared that 'they call her *blue*, but I think they are hypercritical.' Indeed, he was to come to the rescue of his friend Lady Anna Maria Elliott when she was condemned for her witty conversation. 'It is the fashion for women and silly men to abuse her as a blue-stocking,' he said, continuing, 'If to have wit, good sense and good humour, mix'd with a strong power of observing and an equally strong one of expressing the result be *blue*, she shall be as blue as they will. Such cant is the refuge of those who fear those who, they [think], can turn them into ridicule – it is a common trick to revenge supposed raillery with good substantial calumny.'[29]

Understanding very well the current prejudice, Dr Gregory of Edinburgh in his advice to his daughters warned, 'Be cautious in displaying your good sense. It will be thought you assume a superiority over the rest of the company. But if you happen to have any learning, keep it a profound secret, especially from the men, who generally look with a jealous and malignant eye on a woman of great parts and a cultivated understanding. A man of real genius and candour is far superior to this meanness. But such a one will seldom fall in your way; and if by accident he should, do not be anxious to shew the full extent of your knowledge. If he has any opportunities of seeing you, he will soon discover it himself, and if you have any advantages of person or manner and keep your own secret, he will probably give you credit for a great deal more than you possess.'[30]

One reason why Mary Somerville was so popular with her contemporaries was that she always retained her femininity, concealing her intellect beneath a mild, diffident exterior. She did not scorn the feminine graces, excelling at music, producing exquisite needlework and making talented drawings. As her old friend Maria Edgeworth the novelist remarked, Mary's natural modesty and soft voice added 'a prepossessing charm to her manner', which quite took away 'the dread of her superior scientific learning'. So long as a girl hid her true interests behind a façade of innocent femininity, her companions were reassured: she was no different from them after all. As Francis Jeffrey, the famous judge and critic, once remarked, 'There was no objection to the blue-stocking, provided the petticoat came low enough down.'[31]

Francis Jeffrey and Dr Gregory were perspicacious. From the beginning there were enlightened men who, like Dr Somerville, approved of women using their brains, but there were still more who criticized, jeered and found fault. Nor is narrow-mindedness the prerogative of one sex or the other, and as many women as men sneered at girls who genuinely wanted to spend their time reading, instead of idling their hours away in gossip. Trivial as many of the criticisms of them were, these found their mark and depressed the young women at whom they were levelled. It needed strength of character to go on learning Latin or reading philosophy or working on mathematical problems when mothers, sisters and aunts condemned such pursuits as a positive disqualification for matrimony. The advance of female education was significantly obstructed by petty spite.

CHAPTER ELEVEN

The Home
and Beyond

WHATEVER THE INTELLECTUAL ASPIRATIONS of eighteenth-century women, most were still tied down by family obligations and for them there was no escape from the perpetual business of childbearing. Moreover, maternal mortality remained distressingly high. The discovery of anaesthesia lay many years ahead and surgical techniques were slow to advance: no successful Caesarian section saved any mother in England until the very end of the eighteenth century and there is no reason to suppose that the Scottish record was any better. A prolonged and difficult labour still resulted in death and it was not surprising that women approaching their confinement went in fear of 'the terrors of that dreadful hour'.[1] Ignorance of the physical facts, combined with bitter experience of previous sufferings, made women a prey to all manner of alarming thoughts, and the situation was not improved when medical men began a lengthy debate about the powers of imagination on the unborn child, arguing that monsters were born to women who had suffered frightening experiences during pregnancy. Old wives' tales abounded and it was widely believed that poor Lady Aboyne died in childbirth of sheer apprehension after an Italian fortune-teller had predicted a fatal outcome to her pregnancy: the woman's prophecy was later found written on a scrap of paper pinned to the inside of the unfortunate lady's stays.[2]

The eighteenth century was, however, a period of advance in the sphere of gynaecology and obstetrics. Perhaps the most obvious change was that, after the 1730s, midwives finally abandoned the obstetric stool and women were delivered in bed. There was more to it than that however. Many male doctors were now deeply interested in the subject of childbirth and strove to improve methods of delivery. At one time, of course, confinements had been the concern of the female midwife, but the seventeenth century had seen the gradual increase of 'men midwives', who alone had the anatomical knowledge to use surgical instruments. Their presence was bitterly resented by the female midwives, who would call them in only when all other methods had failed, but it was a series of brilliant male midwives who finally reduced the dangers of childbirth. There was William Smellie, for example, a Lanarkshire doctor born in 1697 and educated at Glasgow University. Early on in his career as a general practitioner he became involved in midwifery as a normal part of his duties, although the local midwives showed the customary reluctance to summon him. In spite of their hostility, he became more and more interested in that branch of medicine and determined to develop the medical forceps. When a paper he wrote on the subject was received with acclaim he decided to move to London, there establishing himself as a noted teacher. Students were soon flocking to see him demonstrate methods of delivery with an ingenious dummy representing the mother and a doll serving as the child.

His lectures and publications brought him international fame, and he continued his experiments with instruments, becoming the first doctor to apply the forceps to the following head of a baby in the breech position. In spite of these experiments, he always taught his students that it required more skill to avoid than to perform an operation and he was anxious to conceal from his patients whenever possible that he was having recourse to instruments. He therefore devised forceps first in boxwood, then with leather coverings, so that the mothers would be less likely to realize what was happening to them than if he used forceps of steel. He was the first person to revive an asphyxiated infant by inflating the baby's lungs with a silver catheter and his studies of pelvic measurement at last enabled doctors to calculate in advance when the size of the mother's pelvis was going to make her labour difficult. By the time of his death in 1763, he was the foremost man midwife in Britain, and his works were read as eagerly by doctors in Scotland as they were elsewhere.[3]

One of Dr Smellie's first pupils, and his most successful, was a fellow Scot, William Hunter. Also from Lanarkshire, Hunter became Surgeon-Man-Midwife to the British Lying-in Hospital in London and treated hundreds of women, ranging from Queen Charlotte and Mrs William Pitt to destitute mothers from the poorest parts of the city. A popular teacher and a great anatomist, he demonstrated on Dr Smellie's dummy and dissected all bodies he could obtain of women who had died in pregnancy, labour, or after delivery. His great work, *The Anatomy of the Human Gravid Uterus*, was published in 1774 and amongst his other anatomical achievements was the fact that he was the first person to describe accurately the backward tilting of the uterus.[4]

Not only Scottish doctors interested themselves in childbirth. English, Irish and continental doctors were making important advances and books on gynaecology and obstetrics began to appear in increasing numbers. Sir Feilding Ould's *Treatise on Midwifery*, an authoritative study of the mechanism of labour, was advertised in Scotland shortly after its publication in 1741 and by the end of the decade *The Nurse's Guide or Easy Rules for the Management of Women in Childbed* could be bought in Edinburgh for a shilling, as could Sir Richard Manningham's *Abstract of Midwifery for the use of the Lying-in Infirmary*. Dr Smellie's own *Treatise on the Theory and Practice of Midwifery* had appeared by 1751, as had Dr Brudenall Exton's *New System of Midwifery*, Dr John Burton's book of the same name and Dr William Clark's *The Province of Midwives*.[5]

There was no excuse for Scottish doctors not keeping up with the latest advances in medicine but the trouble was that it was difficult to persuade female midwives to make use of the new knowledge. According to Mary Somerville, the midwife in her part of Scotland when she was a child was 'a person of much consequence', who often had to go 'far into the country by day and by night, riding a carthorse'.[6] Even so, she was unlikely to read any books at all, let alone a weighty work of medical reference. Moreover, most areas could produce horrific tales of midwives who were either drunk or clumsy and did their unfortunate patients damage by rough handling. Much reliance was still placed upon the old herbal possets, magic girdles and strange incantations. Some of the folk remedies had a sensible scientific basis, but the success attributed to others was undoubtedly the result of either coincidence or wishful thinking. As late as 1753 the *Scots Magazine* was solemnly printing a recipe 'To procure an easy delivery to women' in which it was stated that a mixture of pulverised laurel leaves and olive oil, applied to the navel, would cause the baby to present himself for birth in the correct position, whatever his original attitude.[7]

By the middle of the eighteenth century, however, proper training for town midwives was on its way. In 1756 Edinburgh University had appointed Mr Thomas Young as its first Professor of Midwifery and by 1784 the University's Dr Alexander Hamilton was advertising in the newspaper *The Caledonian Mercury* the fact that on 5 May he would 'begin a class for midwives'. Better facilities for the city's mothers were also provided, with the establishment of the Edinburgh Lying-in Hospital in 1793. In its first years more than two hundred women *per annum* had their children there, while a further five hundred and fifty were delivered at home by the hospital staff. By 1833, the number of hospital deliveries had risen to 4970 for the year, with another 8554 home births.[8]

Sad to say, the establishment of lying-in hospitals for poor women did not bring about an unalloyed improvement in their welfare, for there was a tragic increase in the number dying from puerperal fever. When all confinements took place at home, supervised by the local midwife, the disease was not common, although it could be carried from one patient to another if the midwife was attending to more than one case. As doctors were called in, the likelihood of infection increased and with the founding of lying-in hospitals, it reached alarming proportions. It has been estimated that from the middle of the seventeenth to the middle of the nineteenth century, there were no fewer than two hundred epidemics of the disease in Western Europe.

The trouble was that no-one realized that the fever was infectious. Because it often started with a fit of shivering, people believed that it was caused by cold, and concentrated on keeping the patient as hot as possible, excluding every vestige of fresh air from the room. Even well-meaning attempts to investigate the cause could have fatal results. Dr Campbell, an Edinburgh practitioner, performed a post-mortem on a woman who had died of the illness, then lectured to his students, using her organs to demonstrate the points he was making. Without changing his garments, he hurried off to attend a woman in labour. She later died of the fever. The next morning he delivered another woman. She too died, and there were three more deaths in the following week.

Not until the 1770s did Charles White, a Manchester physician, have any success in treating puerperal fever when he insisted on fresh air and cleanliness as important parts of the treatment of a newly-delivered mother. It was more than twenty years after that before a Scottish doctor named Alexander Gordon finally showed that the fever was infectious. His *Treatise on the Epidemic Puerperal Fever of Aberdeen of 1795* emphasized the need to kill the infection by fumigation, and from that time onwards it was possible to fight its terrible toll.[9]

It is difficult to estimate how many women actually died in childbirth in eighteenth-century Scotland, but figures are available for the two Edinburgh parishes of Greyfriars and St Cuthberts. Mortality tables were printed each month and these reveal that in the thirty years 1739–69, childbirth accounted for the deaths of 3.7% of the total number of women who died there. The comparable figure for London at the same period was 2%. This may seem small, but a total of 15,306 women died in these two Edinburgh parishes at that time, no fewer than 557 of them in childbed. Winter and early spring were the worst times: 42% of the 557 died in the first four months of the year, only 25% from May to August then 32% from September to December.[10]

As medical advances were made, there was a noticeable improvement in the grim statistics of maternal death. It has been calculated that in England during the period 1657–81, one woman in forty-three was dying in childbed, whereas by the years 1791–1815, the figure had fallen to one in 108. The Edinburgh mortality tables seem to show a corresponding improvement, with the percentage of women who perished in childbirth reaching a peak of 10% in the 1740s then levelling out at about 2% in the late 1750s and 60s. The development of the forceps, better methods of delivery of both child and afterbirth and the greater understanding of pelvimetry all played their part in this welcome advance.[11]

The patients themselves continued to display a stoical acceptance of what they had to suffer. 'I took my pains on Thursday morning at one o'clock,' Sophie Clerk told her father in 1717, 'and which continued till Friday at six o'clock at night, at which time my forelabour began, which continued till Saturday morning about 9 in the morning, at which time it pleased God, blessed be He forever, to bring me safe to bed of an excellent strong, lively child, a boy.' There is no hint of complaint in this description of her prolonged labour, only relief at the happy outcome. Exactly a hundred years later, the Countess of Leven and Melville's daughter, Lady Jane Pym, bore her labour with fortitude and, on hearing her new daughter cry, exclaimed tenderly, 'Oh, thou dear little thing! Thou art indeed a reward!'[12]

After the delivery, a lying-in period of at least a fortnight was prescribed. Mrs James Boswell, recovering from the birth of her son on 9 October 1775, was well enough by the 18th to dine 'tête-à-tête with her husband in her bedchamber' and the next day was able to eat with the family, though on 21 October she had to retreat to her own room when visitors called, because she 'could not yet dress to appear before company'.[13]

The gradual process of recovery was laid down in minute detail for Mrs Campbell of Barcaldine by her physician, Dr Stewart, in July 1792. For a week after the birth, the house was to be kept as quiet as possible, though Mrs Campbell was to be allowed a constant companion to whom she could chat gently. Each evening at about seven o'clock she was to be helped into a chair so that her bed could be made. Her sheets were to be changed twice a week, her own nightclothes every two days. When she felt like moving about the room, she was to be allowed to do so, provided someone was there to help her. Food during that first week was to be light but sustaining, with chicken broth, bread pudding and tea forming the basis of her diet, supplemented by stewed prunes and nourishing glasses of claret. Whatever happened, 'she should not by any means venture out of her own room before the sixteenth day at soonest, and even then to be extremely attentive against catching cold, and on no account do I think it proper she should expose herself to the external air previous to the twenty-second day.'[14]

Once the mother was safely on the way to normal health, all the old arguments about the best method of rearing the baby could begin again. The battle between those who favoured breast-feeding and those who preferred to employ a wet-nurse continued with increased acerbity, for a new element of social criticism was joined to the old condemnation of wet-nursing on health and practical grounds. Frivolous mothers, it was now argued, refused to feed their own children because they did not want to interrupt their social round or spoil their figures. Much was written on the subject in the general context of condemning fashionable women for neglecting their duties as wives and mothers, and even artists joined in. John Kay, the Edinburgh caricaturist, in 1795 produced a satirical drawing entitled 'Modern Nursing'. This depicted an elegantly clad female wearing a most unsuitable gown strangely adapted to permit breast-feeding.[15]

The arguments put forward in favour of breast-feeding usually concentrated on the suitability of the mother's own milk as food for the child and the desirable emotional bonding between mother and infant which resulted from suckling. An English physician had in 1748 produced a popular essay arguing persuasively that the mother's own milk was of superior nutritional value and would produce a good-humoured, quiet child, while stressing the satisfaction to be derived by 'every woman that can prevail upon herself to give up a little of the beauty of her breast to feed her offspring'.[16]

A later article of 1765 declared that 'It would be happy indeed if all mothers would suckle their children, as so many more would be preserved, since no other woman's milk can be so good' and Rousseau's celebrated treatise on education further urged the practice. By the 1780s the *Scots Magazine* had actively joined in the debate. 'It is the duty of the mother to nurse her own children,' thundered Lord Kames, declaring that this method had been appointed by God and would be ignored at the mother's peril. Breast-feeding was in any event so agreeable, he believed, that 'even the most delicate court lady would take delight in it, were not her manners corrupted by idleness and dissipation'. Willing or not, more and more women began to heed the example of George II's Queen Caroline, who breast-fed all her children, and Jean Hamilton, Lady Cathcart, whose obituary boasted that she had 'nursed seven of her nine'.[17]

In their belief that the mother's own milk was usually best, eighteenth-century writers were medically correct. Child mortality rates remained appallingly high throughout Western Europe in the first part of the eighteenth century, then there was a dramatic fall in the figures. In England in the 1730s no fewer than 437 out of every thousand babies died in their first year of life, but by the 1750s the number had fallen to 360 per thousand and in the last decade of the century it was a relatively low 240. This improvement, it seems, was largely due to the increase in the practice of breast-feeding, for the British Lying-in Hospital was able to report that, when it compelled all its mothers to breast-feed, the infantile mortality rate was cut by more than 60%. Statistics for Scotland are not available, but it would be reasonable to assume that a similar improvement would be found if breast feeding was increasing. Certainly, the country's population rose dramatically in the second half of the century.[18]

Breast-feeding apart, there were other improvements in the treatment of infants. Just as criticism of wet-nurses had increased, so too did condemnation of swaddling. The English physician writing in 1748 had devoted considerable space to the question of babies' clothing. Nothing could be more undesirable, he said, than the binding of infants with 'flannels, wrappers, swathes, stays, etc.' These deformed both limbs and vital organs. Instead, he advocated the wearing of a light flannel waistcoat with a petticoat under a gown of some flimsy material, with only one cap on the head. The author of *Observations upon the proper nursing of Children*, extracts of which appeared in the *Scots Magazine* of 1761, likewise recommended the wearing of a flannel petticoat and shirt under a frock, though he did maintain that buckram stays were still a necessity. Four years later, the magazine's readers were able to peruse an even more strongly worded diatribe against 'the diabolical method of the nurses' who bound the tender bodies of their charges as soon as the babies were born, 'with bandages so tight that neither the bowels nor the limbs have any liberty to act and exert themselves in that free easy way nature designed they should'.[19]

Even as late as 1784, George Chapman felt it necessary to urge that children should not be 'shackled with bandages or confined with ligaments of any kind', but swaddling was by now on the way out. Moreover, mothers could turn to a growing corpus of medical knowledge. Doctors were writing books on such subjects as ruptures in new-born children, fevers and coughs, croup and various other diseases of infancy. In addition, inoculation against smallpox was now available. First tried on a large scale in Dumfriesshire in 1733, it became more usual in the 1770s and in 1780 Mary Campbell of Glenure was calmly arranging for the illness which she knew would follow her son's inoculation. 'My dearest,' she wrote to her husband from Fort William, 'Dunkie was inoculated Wednesday last, must at furthest sicken in five days hence, therefore I wish that you would upon receipt send Little Nanny here with two of the jelly bowls that is in the press of my room and as much fresh butter as you can spare and six good fowls.' The discomfort he would suffer was well worth it if he was protected from the dreadful disease.[20]

No matter how fashionable a lady was, she could not avoid the perils of childbirth or the cares of bringing up her family. Indeed, contemporary letters suggest that most women did not try to escape from their traditional duties in the home. True, writers of the time were not slow to postulate a conflict between frivolity and domesticity, and the London journals were particularly ready to castigate mothers for neglecting their families in the pursuit of pleasure. Scottish writers like Lord Kames added their censures, but in so doing they usually overstated the case. There may have been frivolous Englishwomen who gave themselves up completely to idle amusement, but in Scotland the situation was rather different. Whatever new habits were adopted by the aristocracy in town, even they still reverted to their old-established ways when they moved back to their country homes at the end of the winter season. Thus do we find the Dowager Countess of Mar in 1708 worrying about obtaining stamped wallpaper and black cane stools for her son's chamber in the royal castle of Stirling, where her eldest son was hereditary keeper. Some twenty years later, Eleanor, Countess of Stair, was as busy with spinning and bleaching cloth as any of her predecessors had been, and in 1729 Lady Jean Mackenzie was happily telling her son, 'I always thought your wife was an excellent housewife, but now she betters every day.' In the summer of 1782 Sir Alexander Dick's wife and daughter were hard at work producing two hogsheads of whitecurrant wine, while Philadelphia, Countess of Mar, spent some hours at Alloa in 1829 making strawberry and raspberry jam and blackcurrant jelly.[21]

Ladies not possessed of a natural aptitude for the domestic scene could now purchase books with such titles as *The Accomplished Housewife or Gentlewoman's Companion*, *The Modern Art of Cookery Improved* and *The Experienced English Housekeeper, for the use and ease of ladies, housekeepers, cooks, etc*. Even Elizabeth Grant's mother, who spent long hours in London, lying languidly on her sofa, transformed herself into 'an example of industry' when the family moved north to their Rothiemurchus home. Admittedly, she did not do many of the household chores herself, but she took care 'to see all well done', performed many acts of kindness to the poor and was a beautiful needlewoman who sewed and repaired all the family's linen. She had indeed 'become Highland wife enough to have her spinnings and dyeings and weavings of wool and yarn and flax and hanks and she busied herself at this time in all the stirring economy of a household "remote from

[231]

cities" and consequently forced to provide its own necessities'.[22]

Ladies still kept their own account books, recording the daily expenditure of the household, and they were normally responsible for the hiring and dismissing of servants as well as for the living conditions of the staff.[23] Eleanor, Countess of Stair, was distinctly put out when her military husband proposed bringing his own French cook to their establishment near Edinburgh. 'He will never humble himself to work in such a place as our kitchen,' she declared, adding defensively, 'The cook I have is much better than any I ever had in this country; he, a man and a boy will do all the business of our family. If yours come that will not be the case, for he'll neither brew nor bake nor kill the meat nor, I fear, dress any but for your own table.'[24]

Great ladies had to organize hospitality on a grand scale. When the Duke of Hamilton gave a ball in 1753, the supper served afterwards consisted of '312 dishes, one half of them served up hot and a dessert of 112 dishes more'. While no-one would suggest that the Duchess set foot in the kitchens that evening, this description does give an indication of the elaborate arrangements which had to be made for guests.[25] Moreover, entertaining by means of house parties continued to be a perennial feature of large houses. Certainly transport was now easier than it had been and there was not the sheer physical necessity of having to put up visitors for several nights at a time until they could face the long journey home. However, the tradition of house parties gained increased momentum at the end of the eighteenth century, and hostesses had to offer hospitality to a never-ending stream of visitors, as fashionable ladies used to the variety of the winter season in town set off on a tour of friends and relations to pass the time. In 1813, Miss Campbell of Barcaldine and her companions 'travelled about four hundred miles backwards and forwards' for a period of six weeks, paying visits 'in Ayrshire, Renfrewshire, Stirlingshire, Perthshire, finishing with Taymouth', and in similar manner Isabella Hamilton Dundas contemplated with satisfaction a forthcoming trip to the west of Scotland which would last for a fortnight and during which she would 'pay a great many visits'.[26]

Entertaining guests, supervising servants and sewing linen and furnishings took up the time of great ladies much as these activities had always done, and if the way of life of aristocratic women living in the country went largely unaltered, so too did that of ordinary women. The eighteenth century in Scotland saw a great expansion economically, both on the land and in industry, but the role played by women remained largely unchanged. Whatever improvements were made on estates by the planting of trees, experimentation with crops and the general provision of better conditions for everyone who lived there, to the women fell many of the hard, basic, physical tasks which had always been theirs. Thomas Pennant, travelling through the north of Scotland in 1769, observed when he visited the fishing area of Slains in the north east, that most of the labour on the shore was provided by the women. 'They will carry as much fish as two men can lift, on their shoulders,' he said, 'and when they have sold their cargo and emptied their baskets, will replace part of it with stones: they go sixteen miles to sell or barter their fish.'[27]

Inland, it was still the women who did all the dairy work of milking, making butter and producing cheese, and they too performed the seasonal tasks at harvest time as well as doing other unskilled work. On the Earl of Stair's estate at Newliston in the 1740s, Euphan Wilson, Jean Alister, Agnes Gray and her married daughter Margaret Wills were paid sixpence a day for shearing corn, while Euphan Clelland gathered sheep dung in the garden for a wage of two pecks of meal a week. As the century progressed, women were called upon to do more than seasonal work on the land. When sheep farming came to the Highlands in the 1770s the men gave all their energies to that and so the wives and daughters had to take over more of the work which had been theirs, carrying seaweed manure from the shore in creels, planting and lifting potatoes and generally making themselves responsible for whatever cultivation there was. In like manner, the introduction of turnip-growing meant that women had to be employed on a more regular basis, for they had to hoe and tend the crop for at least six months of the year. Undoubtedly the day wages they were paid must have made a difference to the prosperity of their families, but their labours were tiring, took up much of their time, and forced them to do their own household work in the evenings after a day in the fields. After all, they could not abandon their domestic duties and travellers often noticed the traditional tasks continuing. When Dr Johnson made his tour to the Hebrides in 1773, he and Boswell watched women preparing cloth and grinding corn with a cupped stone, and in Nairn occupied a room below one in which 'a girl was

[233]

spinning wool on a great wheel and singing an Erse [*i.e.* Gaelic] song'.[28]

Work on the land was at least healthy enough. Much worse was the plight of those women who still worked in the coal-mines. In the west of Scotland better conditions prevailed and they were not sent underground, but were either given surface jobs or employed on the mine farm. In the east, however, it was a different matter. Owners were not so enlightened and women still carried the coal for their husbands and sons, bearing loads of perhaps a hundredweight and a half, twenty-four times a day, along galleries and up the steep ladders to the surface. As the demand for coal grew, the mines were dug deeper and conditions progressively worsened. Improvements were slow to come, although in the 1790s the Earl of Dundonald, whose lands lay principally in the west, abolished female labour below ground in his Culross mines in the east and by 1808 horses were being used instead of women to transport coal at Alloa. The emancipation of the miners in 1799 did little to ameliorate female conditions however, and there was as yet no significant public concern about their situation.[29]

The rising demand for coal was, of course, caused by the growth of industry in Scotland. The nation's population increased by approximately two-thirds in the sixty-five years from 1755 to 1820, and as a result more and more people had to leave the land to find employment. Industrialization was a gradual process, though, and even as late as 1825 Scotland was still a predominantly rural country, only thirteen towns having a population of over ten thousand. Moreover, until steam power became cheap and plentiful, mills had to be sited in the countryside, conveniently placed beside streams. Even more important, much of the work of the growing textile industry could be done by women in their own homes. Few were at this stage employed in factories to tend machinery: owners preferred to use children for that work. Instead, women could undertake vital tasks at home. Many hundreds of agricultural workers' wives learned to do tambour work, a form of chain-stitch embroidery which took its name from the large, drum-shaped frame on which the material was stretched. Other women spun for the linen manufacturers, doubling their own productivity if they were able to use the new two-handed wheel. In fact, although Glasgow's cotton industry employed almost 180,000 people in 1795, the vast majority of these were outworkers. The day of factory-filled cities where workers toiled in dreadful conditions still lay in the future, and most women were pleased enough to be able to earn more with their spinning or embroidering than they could have done by spending a day in the fields. There was a general feeling of optimism in the country, a conviction that the new economic developments would benefit the entire nation, so women adapted readily enough to a pattern of work which was only slightly different from that known to their mothers and grandmothers.[30]

For town-dwellers, the traditional modes of earning a living likewise continued without any dramatic alteration. Wives and widows were still to be found in their accustomed areas, purveying clothing and food. To cite but a few examples, Mrs Margaret Stewart was selling linen, plaiding and fustian in Edinburgh in 1730, Eliza Murray could provide sheets and neckwear run up by herself, and a few years later Margaret Robertson was one of several women in the capital who could make and supply shirts.[31] Seventeen women recorded in the Edinburgh Register of Testaments for the period 1701 to 1800 are designated in its printed index as merchants and shopkeepers, with a further twelve in Glasgow during the same era. These figures are far from complete, of course: there must have been many more whose testaments were not registered.[32]

Women were thus to be found in the same occupations which had engaged their energies for many years past. By the early nineteenth century there were, however, various new openings for them, particularly for single women living in towns. *The Edinburgh Post Office Directory* of 1824–5 clearly reflects the combination of traditional services which women had always provided and new occupations which had grown up in response to the demands of fashionable town life. In the *Directory* people advertised their businesses and trades. That year, no fewer than 344 women offered lodgings, a means of earning some money from which they had benefited ever since the Middle Ages. The next highest number of women, however, were dressmakers and this was something relatively new. In the seventeenth century, clothes were generally made by men but not long afterwards women came into their own. As early as 1724, the Countess of Findlater was paying four shillings to 'Mrs Dundas, mantua maker' for that old-fashioned type of headdress, the bongrace. James Boswell's future wife Margaret lived in Ayrshire, but she had her dresses made by Miss Tait of Milne's Square, Edinburgh, and by the early nineteenth century the city's dressmakers prided themselves on providing their customers with the latest styles of clothing. In 1823, Misses MacLagan and Rodger, milliners and dressmakers at 21 George Street, had a printed letterhead which assured their patrons that 'wedding orders and family mournings' would be 'executed in the most elegant style' and in November they were able to tell their customers that Miss MacLagan was on the point of arriving back from the south with 'an elegant selection of London and Paris patterns in millinery and dresses'.[33]

Dressmakers frequently undertook millinery too, although there were also forty-two milliners as such in the *Directory*. Again, this particular type of business seems to date from the beginning of the eighteenth century. Certainly, in September 1710 the Scottish portrait painter John Alexander was writing from London to an Edinburgh friend, 'I doubt not, good sir, but you will make this young gentlewoman Mrs Shepperd (Mr Campbell's niece) welcome, and will keep her in business, so far as it lies in your way, for she designs to merchandise in milliner's wares.'[34] Most dressmakers and milliners were willing to take on apprentices, and so this was a good way of placing an orphaned or illegitimate member of the family: Colin Campbell of Glenure's natural daughter Isabel was in 1761 apprenticed in Stirling to Jean Christie, mantua maker. The indenture signed by Isabel and Mrs Christie notes that for three years the former obliged herself 'carefully and diligently to attend, serve and obey the said Mistress Jean Christie in the aforesaid business of mantua making'. During her first year, Isabel was to be allowed an hour a day 'to attend any school in Stirling for improvement of her writing or otherwise'. If she married during her apprenticeship, the agreement became null and the remainder of her fee would be returned to her. Her uncle was paying sixteen pounds sterling for her training, and in return Mrs Christie was to 'teach, learn and instruct the said Miss Isabel Campbell her apprentice in the whole parts and practiques of the above business and trade of mantua making', giving her bed and board throughout the three years.[35] Lower middle-class parents also looked with favour upon these businesses as a genteel means by which their daughters could support themselves in later life and so Christian Learmonth, daughter of the postmaster in Bo'ness, and Grace Stewart, whose father was an Edinburgh merchant, also took up millinery.[36]

According to the 1824–5 *Directory*, teaching was the third most popular occupation for women in Edinburgh. Ladies were to be found teaching music, drawing, dancing, French and sewing, and there were others who actually ran boarding schools. Mrs Bucknall had her seminary for young ladies in Albany Street, Miss Duncan's boarding school for ladies was in Picardy Place and women kept other boarding schools scattered throughout Edinburgh's fashionable New Town. The only teachers who did not advertise in the *Directory* were governesses, for they either lived with the families who employed them or, if they were between situations, had no settled address. Theirs was, however, the classic occupation for impoverished gentlewomen and, as Elizabeth Grant had noticed, 'Accomplished girls, portionless and homeless, were made into governesses, and for the less instructed there was nothing dreamed of but the dressmaking.'[37] The fate of those young women depended entirely upon the family in which they found themselves and their vicissitudes are well-illustrated in the career of Miss Brandon, who became the governess to the children of Mrs Campbell of Barcaldine.

Miss Brandon was a nervous single lady, rather past her first youth, but in the Campbell household she found a delightful and liberating home. The children usually lived in Argyll, in the west of Scotland, and when their parents were away Miss Brandon was left in sole charge of the growing family. Her letters to her employer on these occasions are full of happy enthusiasm. In November 1805, for example, she and her charges were busy with all manner of enjoyable activities. She took them off on a nut-collecting expedition, 'bottled the 5 bottles of vinegar that remained in your fine new cask, set the maids a-spinning wool which I reeled, killed a sheep and eat [*sic*] the head and haggis and on Sunday began gossiping, for on that evening I had James and his family to drink tea and sup with me . . .' So involved was she with the household chores which would not normally have been her concern that, when her neighbour the Laird of Ardchattan called, 'I was working among the wool in the store room . . . with a dirty bedgown on, but he was so impatient to get home that I was obliged to get Maria to shut him up in the parlour till I passed and got a gown huddled on.'

She enjoyed a happy and uninhibited relationship with Mrs Campbell, asking her, 'Will you buy some marking silk? There is only two bars of brown soap in the house and very few split pease. I hope to be able to brew tomorrow or next day . . . Will you take the trouble if you are getting any flannel for yourself to get for me 5 quarters and a nail for me as I cannot make out my flannel shift without it . . . I am busy getting lint sent to the mill and making blood puddings. God bless you and send you safe back in spite of wind and weather.'

Sad to say, even the happiest of employments came to an end when the children grew up, and the following year Miss Brandon's services were no longer required. She remained on excellent terms with Mrs Campbell, however, and her letters to her former employer reveal the rest of her career. At first she tried to settle down with a relation in Edinburgh, but she found life there such a contrast to the carefree atmosphere at Barcaldine that she determined to seek another post. She was therefore hired by Mrs Hepburn to take her nieces to drink the waters at Moffat, a small spa in the south-west of Scotland. The girls were pleasant enough, though delicate, and they longed to indulge in the lively social life around them. However, Mrs Hepburn had given strict orders to the contrary, declaring sternly that 'she sent them to Moffat for health, not amusement' and so Miss Brandon had to ignore their pleas. 'No, Miss Campbell of Barcaldine's governess wou'd not yield one degree from her rules,' she remarked.

This particular engagement was only for three months, and after that, with fond memories of the Highlands, Miss Brandon took a position as governess to Mrs Campbell of Islay. This in itself presented problems because her new home was so inaccessible, but she set off bravely from Edinburgh in the Glasgow coach, 'where I met a very disagreeable set of travellers'. After a stay of two days in Glasgow, she went on to Greenock, hoping to sail that same evening, but she discovered that there was no boat and she would have to stay alone at the inn until Sunday morning. At long last the weekend passed and she embarked on the sailing ship which was to take her north. The master urged her to go below to the cabin until the sails were put in order but there an unpleasant surprise awaited her, for 'I never heard of such a dirty hole, crammed full of filthy women returning from the harvest.' (The Highland women were in the habit of working on Lowland farms at that time of year.) They plied her with unwelcome questions about her identity and her destination until she fled back to the deck again. There she fell in with a pleasant couple who shared their bread and cheese with her. This fortified her for what lay ahead, for the crew spent the night drinking and next morning discovered that instead of being near their destination they were half-way back to Greenock again. By this time a storm had blown up, the ship was rolling violently, and most of the passengers were seasick. It seemed that they would never reach land but when at last they did, Miss Brandon was confronted with an uncomfortable journey of some ten miles across country to reach the ferry boat which would take her to Islay. Eighteen days after she had left Edinburgh she set foot on the island, where a series of carts conveyed her to Mrs Campbell's home, 'in good health, but much fatigued and very low'. Settling in, she consoled herself in some measure by writing a long letter to Mrs Campbell of Barcaldine relating all that had happened to her and finally reflecting, 'As it was my own doing, I must not complain, nor do I regret yet having left Edinburgh, though I feel as if at the World's End.'

Soon afterwards, she did regret it. Mrs Campbell was a well-meaning woman 'but the temper of my pupil is dreadful and her manner so brutal I may say that I fear I never shall make her such as I wish,' Miss Brandon confided. There was an overbearing elder sister to be reckoned with too, but in spite of these difficulties she stayed on for another two years, lamenting towards the end, 'I have no society, am as great a stranger as the first week . . . Every day appears a month . . . I would with pleasure give up the half of my salary to get away from this horrid place.' By that time, she was determined to make her escape from an intolerable situation where the servants did not even keep her room tidy or wash her clothes and her salary was not paid on time so that 'even snuff I am obliged to get on credit here'.

Probably through Mrs Campbell's good offices, she now found a place with Mrs MacPherson of Cluny's family in Perth. From the outset there were problems there too. 'The children,' she reported, 'though she [i.e. Mrs MacPherson] has taken much pains with them, are like all who are kept under restraint, wild and untractable when out of sight.' Her quarters were comfortable enough, with a very neat bedroom 'entirely to myself' and one of the best rooms in the house as the schoolroom, but she was now in poor health. She was suffering from problems connected with her age, and the journey from Islay in a storm, with twenty miles in a jolting cart, had done her no good. Mrs MacPherson grew jealous, too, complaining that the children sometimes 'shows more love' for Miss Brandon than for herself so once more she had to move on.

She went back to Edinburgh in the winter of 1812, hoping to regain her strength, then look for another situation, but her condition was too serious. A pathetic letter written to Mrs Campbell in the summer of 1814 from Mr Mossman's house in Comely Bank described how she had recently been dangerously ill for ten weeks. Only the kindness of her landlady and of Sir William Fettes, who treated her like a sister, had saved her life and she was longing to have news of the family at Barcaldine. 'Many times in the dead hour of the night, when I could not sleep, I have pleased myself looking back to the happy days I spent with you,' she said. 'I shall never know such again.' Her correspondence ends there, and this sad letter was probably the last she ever wrote to Mrs Campbell.[38]

A governess's life was invariably made difficult by the conflicting personalities of the family in which she lived and by her own equivocal social status: feeling herself to be much better than the domestic staff of the household, she was nonetheless often patronized by the servants. Less complicated from this point of view was the lot of those women in business or providing traditional services. To return to the 1824–5 *Directory*, forty-five of the women there listed were vintners and spirit dealers, thirty-eight were grocers, thirty-seven were midwives, there were thirty-five shopkeepers, seventeen straw-hat-makers, thirteen corset-makers and nine sick-nurses. These formed the main feminine occupations, but the list also includes examples of a woman chiropodist, a butcher, a gardener, a glover, a bookbinder, a glass-blower, a hatter, a wireworker and an upholsterer.[39]

Thus far, the range of occupations was very much as it had been in the seventeenth century, but for the first time there are also significant indications of women taking up what may be termed artistic or cultural activities and seeking to compete with men in these spheres. Men would argue that women were not represented in the arts because they lacked any creative inspiration. This was far from being so, of course, and indeed modern psychological studies are suggesting that women, instead of lagging behind men, have a slightly greater 'creativity potential'.[40] Hitherto, however, they had directed their creative impulses into raising children, looking after the family, and taking up certain feminine handicrafts. In the eighteenth century when drawing was an inevitable component of the polite accomplishments, it was to be expected that some women would excel at it. More than that, however, there were one or two girls who were not content to sketch simply to amuse friends and while away the time, but who actively sought a career in the competitive masculine world of portrait painting.

Their task was not an easy one, as the experiences of Anne Forbes show. The granddaughter of William Aikman, the well-known Scottish portrait painter, Anne won the enthusiastic approbation of her immediate circle for the paintings she produced, and she actually went to study in Rome. On her return, one of her cousins urged her to establish herself in London and seems to have paid for her to settle there with her mother and sister. With high hopes, they took a house in St Martin's Lane and eagerly awaited the patrons they were sure would flock to her studio. Unfortunately, her society friends shunned her when they learned that she was in town on business. As her sister explained, 'When Anne came here she had in view many powerful patrons and who we supposed would not only show her a way as an artist but as a gentlewoman, and that immediately she would have some faces to show that were generally known.' The bitter truth was, however, that 'no-one has ever taken her by the hand or so much as come to see her works.'

With only a trickle of commissions coming in, Anne could not afford to employ a drapery painter as her more successful rivals did, and so she was forced to toil laboriously on every detail of her work. 'To paint a drapery,' she said, 'I must have it put, whatever it is, a gentleman's coat or lady's gown, upon a wooden figure which is set in the place where the person sat and is put in the same attitude as they were in, which figure must not be moved nor one fold of the drapery altered till the whole is finished, which is always the work of several days, indeed, I may say, weeks, when it is a half-length picture.'

She had never been robust, and such long hours wore her down. Her sister commented sadly that Anne did not have the stamina to emulate Angelica Kauffman, who, as well as having 'great facility', was possessed of 'such a constitution that she is able to work from 5 in the morning till sunset in summer and during the whole daylight in winter, whereas Annie cannot rise till eight or fall to work till ten, nor will she attempt it for any consideration, sleep being her only support'. During the first year she made £245, but her household spent almost £500 in spite of living the life of 'hermits'. Losing weight, suffering from fever and wholly discouraged, she decided to move back to Edinburgh. There she set up as a drawing teacher, obtaining commissions for portraits in pastel and oils whenever she could. Her lack of success cannot be attributed to the fact that she met with masculine prejudice: it was rather that although some of her works were pleasing, she had not inherited the full measure of her grandfather's talent and so she could not hope to compete on equal terms with Reynolds, Angelica Kauffman and Nathaniel Dance.[41]

To succeed in the competitive world of portrait painting, a woman needed determination and financial support as well as talent. Proper training was denied them; women could not go to art schools or attend life classes, and they required a studio, equipment and, most of all, clients, before they could establish a career. Slightly better placed were those women whose talents lay in the sphere of literature. They needed no formal training, their only equipment was a pen and paper, and quite often they did not view their writing as a means of supporting themselves financially. Problems there were, however, for the prejudice against learned ladies meant that many of them wrote in secret to avoid the derision and discouragement of their own families. They were tormented by the lack of privacy in which to carry on their work but, nevertheless, those who felt the urge to write continued to do so under all manner of unfavourable circumstances.

Some women writers came from humble backgrounds. One of these was Jean Adam, who was born in Greenock in 1710. She was orphaned at an early age and found work looking after the children of the local minister. She educated herself by reading the books in his library, and soon she began writing religious poems herself. A volume of these was published in 1734, and not long afterwards she set up a girls' school. Her principal interests remained in literature, however, and she interspersed her teaching by giving Shakespearean readings to her pupils. According to tradition, she fainted with emotion as she recited some scenes from *Othello*, and so determined was she to meet Samuel Richardson, author of the famous *Clarissa*, that she closed the school for six weeks and walked all the way to London to visit him. Unfortunately, her published poems brought her little income and after a few years the unsold copies were shipped to Boston and never seen again. She was compelled to give up her school, became a hawker and eventually died in a Glasgow poorhouse.[42]

Religious poetry was hardly a promising source of income at the best of times, and those ladies who wrote for the stage attracted more public interest. Joanna Baillie, the Hamilton minister's daughter, published poetry but soon turned to the writing of tragic dramas. Her *De Montfort* was actually produced at Drury Lane with Mrs Siddons in the cast, although it ran for only eleven nights. At least four more of her plays were staged, *Family Legend* enjoying real success both in Edinburgh and at Drury Lane. Less fortunate was Eglantine Maxwell, sister of the Duchess of Gordon. Her comedy, *The Ton*, when produced at Covent Garden was judged to be 'very dull' and *The Whim* was actually banned from the London stage.[43]

When Joanna Baillie began to publish her work she did so anonymously, as did many of the contemporary female writers. It was not thought fitting by society that a woman should be setting herself up as an author, and so these ladies, as Henry Mackenzie put it, 'are known or shrewdly guessed at, but, like the beauties of Spain, come out veiled'. Caroline, Lady Nairne, a prolific writer of ballads, published her work under the name of 'Mrs Bogan of Bogan' and even her husband did not know that she was the author of the popular 'Caller Herrin' and 'The Land of the Leal'. Lady Anne Barnard composed 'Auld Robin Gray', another popular ballad, and published it anonymously. Various people, including a clergyman, claimed to have written it and she only acknowledged it as hers two years before her death. As she explained to Sir Walter Scott, 'I was pleased in secret with the approbation it met with, but such was my dread of being suspected of writing anything, perceiving the shyness it created in those who could write nothing, that I carefully kept my own secret.' Grace Kennedy, the author of religious tales, published her many stories anonymously and Christian Johnstone, the novelist, was content to produce articles for the journal her husband published, allowing him to take most of the credit for them.[44]

Only a few women were able to establish themselves as accepted literary figures. Mrs Grant of Laggan's writings about the Highlands were well known and acknowledged. Similarly, Elizabeth Hamilton found fame for her educational writings as well as for her novels of Scottish life. Brought up by her aunt in Stirlingshire, she wrote from childhood and published her first article when she was in her twenties. She lived for some time in London, then in Berkshire with her sister, producing a series of historical and educational works. In 1804, she settled in Edinburgh and was sufficiently famous to receive a government pension. Important and influential, she held regular literary gatherings, undertook a good deal of philanthropic work and continued to publish. She was held in high esteem by her contemporaries, and when she died Maria Edgeworth wrote a warm appreciation of her work. It had now become possible for a woman to find fulfilment beyond the domestic sphere.[45]

PART FOUR

1830-1980:
THE
ACTIVE WOMAN

CHAPTER TWELVE

The March
of the Intellect

THE NINETEENTH CENTURY was to be a period of great advance in the education of women, but at first the situation did not look at all promising. Women like Mary Somerville and Elizabeth Hamilton, who were able to use their abilities to make satisfying careers for themselves, were exceptional and it seemed as though the tide of thought was turning against them. In prosperous, Victorian Britain, the feminine role was in some ways becoming more passive than ever before, as the notion that domestic labour was demeaning gained wider and wider currency. Middle-class women finally abandoned any practical household activities and what had been a tendency in fashionable circles in the eighteenth century became a commonplace in the nineteenth. People with any social aspirations now employed a fleet of female servants to do the work of the household and even lower-middle-class families had their resident maid. A leisured life was accepted as the norm for the married woman. She would supervise her household, chatting with the cook about meals and giving the servants their orders, but most of her time was to be spent reading, sewing, visiting and undertaking charitable work. She was to be ornamental rather than directly useful, but ornamental in a moral, pious manner. She would not spend her time in a giddy round of party going and idle amusement, but she would stay at home trimming a bonnet or stitching a firescreen or reading a book of sermons. Cooking, baking and washing were all very well for the wives of working men, but not for those women who had any pretensions to gentility. Times had changed quite drastically since the days when the lady of the great house worked alongside her few female servants in the kitchen or at the spinning wheel. Lady Nairn of the early eighteenth century had patiently studied the best method of making candles and buttons: Mrs Elizabeth Brodie in 1848 was urging her husband to hire a good housekeeper, 'as I don't pretend to be an upper servant, which most of the ladies about us are, though they don't make good ones, judging from their establishments [and] cuisines'.[1]

Some women were content enough to be relegated to a life of virtuous idleness, but others had always found it irksome. Becalmed in her mother's house at Haddington, Jane Welsh had told a cousin in 1823, 'Really, there is nothing at all amusing in one's mode of existence here. A tea-party, a quarrel or a *report* of a marriage now and then are the only excitements this precious little borough affords.'[2] In later years, when she had made her escape and was living with her husband in the Dumfriesshire countryside, she was to write even more eloquently on the same subject. She was herself now happily occupied with a multitude of practical tasks, and she believed that an energetic absorption in such things would ward off the well-known melancholy and depression which she and her contemporaries termed ennui. 'Shame that such a malady should exist in a Christian land,' she exclaimed. 'Should not only exist, but be almost universal throughout the whole female population that is placed above the necessity of working for daily bread. If I have an antipathy for any class of people it is for *fine ladies* . . . Woe to the fine lady who should find herself set down at Craigenputtock for the first time in her life, left alone with her thoughts, no "fancy bazaar" in the same kingdom with her, no place of amusement within a day's journey; the very church, her last imaginable resource, seven miles off. I can fancy with what horror she would look on the ridge of mountains that seem to enclose her from all earthly bliss! With what despair in her accents she would enquire if there was not even a "charity sale" within reach.'[3]

Elizabeth Pringle, who lived at Yair, in the Borders, had reached a similar conclusion about the cure for boredom and low spirits. In a lengthy poem entitled 'Ennui' she described her depression. It was dull and dreary November weather: her books seemed uninteresting, her needlework insipid, a walk gloomy. Her melancholy was only dispelled by the arrival of the 'Damsel Industry' and, once occupied with useful domestic tasks, she forgot her troubles.[4] Other ladies sought a similar remedy in all manner of more or less rewarding pastimes. There was a tremendous proliferation of ladies' work as women gladly took to the new crafts of netting and knotting, tambour work, tatting, beadwork and crochet, and, of course, the universally popular Berlin work which permitted them to copy pictures in coloured wool for firescreens, cushions and slippers.[5]

The bazaars mentioned by Jane Welsh Carlyle were sales of work which served the purpose of raising money for charity, and at the same time provided an outlet for the vast quantities of fancy-work produced by the women of the family. There was, after all, a limit to the number of fire-screens or embroidered waistcoats a lady's relations would require, but the charitable sales gave her a welcome incentive to carry on with her needlework or crochet. The quality of the articles produced varied very much, naturally, as Marion Hamilton's sisters noticed in 1827. 'Of course, you must have heard about the ladies' sale of fancy-work at Glasgow and Mrs Dennistoun's exertions on that occasion,' Marion told her cousin. 'At Mrs Oswald's table, at which Mrs D. and her daughter assisted, there were between 2 and 3 hundred pounds raised. My sisters who were there for a short time say it was a beautiful sight, though there was a great deal of trash mingled with very pretty things.'[6]

An even greater impetus to doing handiwork of this kind was given by the outbreak of the Crimean War. Queen Victoria herself set an example by knitting 'comforts' for the soldiers who were undergoing the rigours of extreme cold at Balaclava, and on 7 December 1854 Margaret Murray of Polmaise wrote to tell her brother John that she and her family were making him comforts, muffatees [*i.e.* knitted cuffs] and socks. 'The whole of the British ladies are working for the same cause at present,' she said. Even John's elderly grandmother joined in, telling him proudly, 'I have adopted the last *new fashion* by knitting a *mask* or *visor* which I am sure will help to keep you warm and cosy. It is a queer looking affair. Put it over your head. It should come over your *mouth* and *nose*, the upper part covers the forehead, all the face is by that means covered except the eyes. It is considered first rate as a defence from a cold exposure.'[7] Women could not help the war effort in any other way, but at least by knitting garments for the soldiers they could feel that they were somehow playing their part.

This form of creative work, limited though it was, could provide some measure of fulfilment. Even so, many women were left with long hours of tedium. Mary Somerville's eccentric aunt solved the problem of what to do with too much leisure by setting up a telescope in the window of her Edinburgh flat and spying avidly on her neighbour across the street. Other ladies concentrated too much attention on their own health. Unable to adapt satisfactorily to a life of inactivity and with too little to think about, they lay on couches in darkened rooms, prostrated by sick headaches and a multitude of other more nebulous symptoms. In the country Elizabeth Grant's mother was healthily busy, but in London 'she very seldom left the sofa in the back drawing-room, a dark and dull place looking on the back windows of a low commercial hotel in Serle Street, the near neighbourhood of what obliged her always to keep the blinds down.'[8] Jane Welsh Carlyle was frequently prostrated by nervous headaches when she lived in Haddington, and, significantly, the newspapers of the period frequently printed advertisements like the one which appeared in *The Daily Courant* on 4 January 1860. Widow Welch's pills, it said, were a sovereign remedy for 'all female complaints, nervous disorders, weakness of the solids, loss of appetite, sick headache, lowness of spirits and particularly for irregularities in the female system'.[9]

Taking little exercise, spending their lives in stuffy rooms, wearing constricting clothing and with their health often undermined by frequent childbearing, it was small wonder that many of these women had little energy. As the well-known English example of Florence Nightingale suggests, however, it was often their mode of life which was at the root of their fragility rather than any physical cause. Florence spent years as a semi-invalid, except for the period when the demands of nursing revealed her as a woman of outstanding courage, resourcefulness and determination. Doctors fairly early on recognized the psychological effects of an overly narrow existence, and when Dr W. A. Finlay remarked in 1887, 'I would submit that much delicate health and lack of energy is occasioned by the want of an occupation fitted to satisfy the desires of the mind,' he was voicing a sentiment not out of keeping with modern psychiatric thought.[10]

As the Victorian age progressed, conventions became more and more restrictive. Girls could no longer go out and meet young men in Princes Street, or make up parties to attend entertainments. Whenever they set foot outside the house, they had to be accompanied at least by a maid. There was a revived preoccupation with theology and a censorship of the books thought unsuitable for young ladies to read. The *joie de vivre* of the eighteenth century was replaced by a gloomy sentimentality, and women turned more and more from dancing and the theatre to doing good works.

Time and again their names are found in this connection. At Inveresk, near Edinburgh, a clothing society was founded in the 1840s 'by a number of benevolent ladies connected with the parish' who distributed clothes to the poor. In Haddington a female society existed 'to visit and afford pecuniary relief to the sick and aged poor, and to minister to their instruction and comfort by reading the Scriptures and giving them suitable tracts'. The members of Greenock Ladies' Association 'visit and converse with the female prisoners six hours in the week', the minister reported in 1840. At Bo'ness, the association of ladies supplied the poor with clothing, meal and coal in winter. Many philanthropic female organizations were in existence in Edinburgh, including the committee of ladies who visited the workhouse each day to read the scriptures and converse with the female inmates 'on religious subjects' and the Ladies' Highland Association, founded in Edinburgh in 1850, sent north clothing as well as raising funds for the northern parts of the country.[11]

Some ladies worked with particular societies: others acted individually. In 1834, for example, Lady Helen Hall of Dunglass contributed £1 1s. to the Edinburgh House of Refuge, presented half a crown to a shipwrecked foreigner, gave a guinea to the Blind Asylum and another to the Destitute Sick Society, sent a pound to the New Town Dispensary, another pound to the Lying-in Hospital and handed ten shillings to 'a German teacher wishing to get home again'. In addition, she had a regular set of pensioners, mainly widows, but including a lame girl and a man 'who cannot get into work'.[12] Genuinely compassionate and caring, these ladies were ready to carry on their philanthropic work in spite of personal difficulties. When Clementina Drummond, Countess of Airlie, died at the age of forty in 1835 it was noted that, although she had been compelled to spend long periods in bed because of 'anaemic debility', she had never neglected her charitable works and was known far and wide as 'The Good Countess'. Mrs Baillie of Jerviswood, although confined to bed for more than thirty-two years, was always ready to send help to anyone who was in need or distress and, in spite of disabling lameness after a childhood illness, the Duke of Argyll's daughter, Lady Victoria Campbell, travelled all over the Western Isles of Scotland from the 1880s onwards, organizing Bible classes, mothers' meetings, local branches of the YWCA, clothing clubs and soup kitchens. In an age long before the welfare state was known, these women did invaluable work.[13]

Not least among their activities was the provision of education for girls. At Pencaitland, in East Lothian, a school for 'Instructing girls in the elementary principles of education and teaching them needlework' had been established before 1850 by Mrs Hamilton Campbell. At Liberton, on the outskirts of Edinburgh, Mrs Trotter of Mortonhall generously endowed a school, and in Linlithgow Mrs Douglas, the minister's sister, set up a special school for poor girls. Mrs Waddell of Stonefield bequeathed money to endow an establishment at Govan, outside Glasgow, and at Stevenston in Ayrshire the girls' school was superintended and managed by 'a committee of ladies'.[14]

The curriculum of these female schools was unvarying. They taught reading, writing and sewing, as did the parish schools and the other local schools. No-one ever questioned the value of the subjects taught because it was perfectly obvious to all concerned that these were what an ordinary girl would need in her future life. The minister of Dunoon reported with considerable satisfaction that a school of industry had been set up in his parish for the purpose of 'instructing the rising female generation in the necessary and useful departments of knowledge' and the vagueness of his phraseology was echoed by his colleagues throughout the country. When they described the facilities in their parishes, they were quite happy to note down that schools taught 'the usual female branches' of education. After all, there was no point in elaborating what everyone knew. Women's education had always been vocational, so what should their schools teach but the traditional subjects?[15]

On the comparatively few occasions when slightly more detail is given, the emphasis is on the moral benefits derived by the pupils. The minister of Loudon in Ayrshire remarked with some satisfaction that the school in his parish 'has been of much service in teaching useful branches of knowledge, industry and habits of neatness'. The girls at Monimail school in Fife benefited from lessons in 'knitting and needlework in its several branches' but also, 'what is scarcely less important, are trained to habits of order and exactness', while the female school at Oban was praised for 'training the female children of the labouring classes in habits of industry, besides imparting to them the elementary branches of a useful English education'.[16]

An education suitable to one's status in life was now as important as an education suitable to one's sex. The ordinary woman ought to know how to sew and wash and cook and read her Bible, but anything further would be inappropriate, unless it were training for some financially rewarding activity. It was recognized that women did have to earn their living before marriage, that they might have to supplement the family income while bringing up the children afterwards, and that as widows they would have to support themselves. This was regarded as being of benefit to the economy in general as well as to the individuals concerned, and Greenock charity school taught its girls 'needlework, knitting and other handicraft occupations *gratis*, preparatory to their going to domestic service'. A school of industry in Ayr taught 'sewing and other simple qualifications' aimed at fitting its pupils 'to become useful domestic servants' and the girls at Kilmarnock school were taught the knitting of stockings, which they would do not only for their families but as outworkers for the clothing industry.[17]

As a result of all this educational activity, standards of literacy increased enormously. In their reports for the *New Statistical Account* the vast majority of ministers declared that all or almost all the girls and younger women in their own areas could read and write, explaining that only a few of the older inhabitants were still illiterate. There were areas where the situation seemed less satisfactory, of course. At Cockburnspath in the south-east of Scotland there were 116 boys aged between five and fifteen learning to read at school, but only 60 girls, and although 75 of the boys were also learning writing, only 30 girls were doing so. Likewise, in Old Monkland, Lanarkshire, 204 boys were learning to read but only 114 girls and at Cambuslang parish school, not so very far away, approximately 60 per cent of the pupils were boys. Occasionally the reason for this discrepancy was indicated. At Dunipace in Stirlingshire where 'many, particularly of the female part of the rising generation, read so imperfectly that they can reap little practical benefit from it' the cause was 'the reprehensible practice of putting mere infants to work in the several manufactories of this district'. Similarly, at Dalserf in Lanarkshire, 'poor parents are often tempted to take their boys and girls alike from school far too early, and to employ them at the weaving loom and tambouring frame before they have been even taught to read properly.'[18] In fact, it was usually the daughters rather than the sons of the family who were removed from school first. In spite of these reservations, however, it seems that literacy was rapidly becoming usual, and a study of the Registrar General's statistics for the 1850s bears out this conclusion. In Banff and Aberdeenshire in the north and in Dumfriesshire in the south-west, more than 95 per cent of the men and from 85 per cent to 95 per cent of the women could sign their own names. Similarly, a survey of Scottish marriage registers for 1855 showed 88.6 per cent of the new husbands signing and 77.2 per cent of the wives; interestingly enough, the English figures are 70.5 per cent of husbands and only 58.8 per cent of wives.[19]

The ability to sign one's name is no more than a test of basic literacy, of course, but once all women were given the opportunity to read and write the likelihood was that some would wish to pursue their studies far beyond that fundamental level. The problem was, of course, that although primary education for almost all girls had been achieved, a secondary education with any real academic content was much more difficult to come by. Middle-class girls were still sent away to boarding school to learn the ladylike accomplishments, while no-one gave much thought to the curriculum of the girls attending the parish schools.

The interesting fact was, however, that more and more girls were attending the parish schools. Many of the female schools so popular at the beginning of the century simply disappeared as the women who had run them moved on, retired or died. The parish authorities were pleased enough for the girls to come to the parish school, although all the old fears about the propriety of educating them along with the boys were revived. The heritors of the parish of Maybole, in Ayrshire, had solved the problem by 1845, deciding that although all the children should go to the local school, the boys should be taught at a different time from the girls. In the early 1850s, the minutes of Irvine Academy, also in Ayrshire, recorded that 'part of the playground, to the south of the Academy' was 'exclusively for the use of the misses', while at nearby Girvan, the school playground was divided down the middle by an upright wooden railing five feet high. Separate entrances and old railings dividing playgrounds are indeed still to be seen in schools erected in the earlier part of the present century.[20]

Artificial barriers might keep the children apart in the playground, but in the classroom it was difficult to teach them separately. Only if a school had plenty of teachers and a large number of classrooms was it practicable to have separate classes, so most schools arrived at a compromise whereby the sexes were taught subjects like English and mathematics together, then went their separate ways for more specialized subjects like sewing or woodwork. It soon became obvious that the girls were perfectly capable of equalling the boys in the performance of the more academic subjects. In the 1860s, many of the girls attending Ayr Academy took French and German and, if they chose, were allowed to study Latin and mathematics. Some did so to such good effect that when an English commissioner came to inspect the school, he commented favourably on a large class of girls who 'passed a very good examination in Virgil, answering the kind of questions he would have put to the boys in an English school and answering them as well'. In like manner the other burgh school commissioners reported that, in the more advanced schoolwork, including English, classics and mathematics, the girls did as well as the boys, and that in modern languages they did even better.[21]

Girls were found in Latin and mathematics classes almost by chance. No-one had decided once and for all that they should receive the same education as boys, and indeed most educationalists, if pressed to give their views on female education, would no doubt have spoken of sewing and cookery and a woman's destiny as a wife and mother. In 1872, though, the authorities were compelled to give serious thought to the manner in which they wished girls to be educated, for in that year an act of parliament was passed reorganizing the entire educational system. New arrangements for funding and administration were made, and henceforth every parent was bound to send his children to school between the ages of five and thirteen. All were to be taught reading, writing and arithmetic, and poverty was to be no excuse: fees would be remitted if the family could not afford them. A child could only be exempted if he obtained an inspector's certificate of proficiency. In 1883 the leaving age was raised to fourteen, although half-time education was allowed after ten, but in 1901 all exemptions were abolished and in 1947 the leaving age was raised to fifteen.[22]

It was obvious that large numbers of girls would master the basic skills long before they reached the appointed leaving age.

There were, inevitably, those people who disliked the new state of affairs and clung to the belief that the ideal wife and mother had no need of French or Latin as long as she could sew and bring up the children. 'The truth is,' said Professor Laurie, writing a report for the Edinburgh Merchant Company in 1861, 'that the intellect of women is a very difficult growth and that it is interwoven with her imagination, her affection and her moral emotions much more intimately than in man. What the world wants is not two men, a big one in trousers and a little one in petticoats, but a man and a woman.'[23]

Fortunately, not all men shared these rigid views. In 1876 James Grant, writing a book about the burgh schools of Scotland, was decidedly sympathetic. True, his chapter on female education comes last, and he admitted disarmingly that he had taken 'advantage of the ungallant decision of grammarians that the masculine is more worthy than the feminine gender' and so had left the girls to the end. Nevertheless, he went on to condemn outright the 'old fallacy' that higher education was unnecessary for women, and noted with approval that 'we are slowly realizing that any knowledge calculated to improve the human mind should be communicated to women no less than men.' He did repeat the traditional notion that women were particularly in need of education because by 'birth and destiny' they would have to educate the future generation of men, but he was quite definite that boys and girls should study the same subjects. Criticizing the 'so-called lady-accomplishments' taught in the boarding schools as being designed 'not so much for purposes of intellectual discipline as for attracting attention', he thought that 'it stands to reason that what is good for educating a boy is equally good, *mutatis mutandis*, for educating a girl, *et vice versa*.' At one time, classics and mathematics were taught almost exclusively to boys, but now, he was glad to see, they were finding their way even into girls' schools.

His views on the moral aspect of mixed schools were equally refreshing. Taking note of the contemporary discussion as to 'the propriety of teaching boys and girls together', he came down firmly on the side of co-education. 'It would indeed seem as if Providence intended that the sexes should influence each other from their birth to their death and at no time is this influence more necessary than when their characters are being formed,' he wrote. Both boys and girls derived benefit from attending the same schools, and so although the mixed system was not without its drawbacks, 'the balance of advantages appears to be decidedly in its favour'.[24]

Grant was forward-looking in that he recognized that through education a woman could find self-fulfilment. He did not, however, see it as leading to any alteration of woman's role in life and indeed he was anxious that his views should not be taken as an encouragement to women to desert the domestic sphere. He urged that more instruction in housewifery should be given to girls, for if they were to be allowed to grow up ignorant of its techniques, then 'bachelors young and old' would be 'thankful to dine anywhere than at their lodgings', and the 'poorer classes' would have to 'resort to cooks' shops for procuring ready-made meals'.

Others shared his views, and it was not long before it was stipulated that girls studying secondary subjects must also take a course in what was termed 'domestic economy'. This subject proved popular with the girls themselves, and although in 1875 the inspector of schools for Renfrew, Bute and Argyll examined only two girls in domestic economy, there were 3648 taking it by 1881 and in the following year in the whole of Scotland more than 24,000 sat the final examination. It was a theoretical course, but when practical cookery was introduced in the 1880s it proved equally popular.[25]

These school classes were aimed at equipping a girl to run her own home. There was no thought that she would later earn her living by means of her skills. Similarly, although colleges of domestic science appeared that same decade, they were not designed to train girls to be, say, teachers of domestic science, but had the aim of improving the circumstances of the poorer families. The Glasgow School of Cookery was founded with the intention of providing courses in cookery 'for the working classes' and only when it failed to elicit the expected response did it widen its curriculum. It then offered courses for middle-class women who would go on to do voluntary social work among the needy in the city. Some years had to pass before the colleges of domestic science admitted school leavers and trained them to teach that subject in schools.[26]

Anxious though the authorities were to encourage girls to fit themselves for their future domestic duties, the growing demand for a more academic education for women could not be denied. One difficulty had been the lack of endowed schools for middle-class girls: benefactors in the past had simply not founded secondary schools for them. However, a reorganization of endowments in the 1870s resulted in the founding of George Watson's Ladies' College in Edinburgh and the transformation of the city's charitable Merchant Maiden Hospital into the Edinburgh Institute for Young Ladies. In Glasgow, Hutcheson's Girls' School was set up in 1876. These schools combined the academic with the more traditionally feminine subjects, and the fact that the principal was usually a man was an indication of how the balance was shifting away from the accomplishments.[27] Even the boarding schools did not now limit themselves to the ornamental subjects. The founders of the famous St Leonards School in St Andrews had the avowed intention of providing the pupils with a first-rate academic education, and so the curriculum included Latin, Greek, mathematics, French and German. Only science was omitted.[28]

In previous centuries, when few women had been able to read and write competently, only a tiny minority had been in the position to entertain any aspirations towards a higher education. The seventeenth-century girl, restricted to reading her Bible, never had any opportunity to discover whether she had an aptitude for languages or mathematics or science. Now that the study of most subjects was a possibility for able girls with the means to stay on at school beyond fourteen, it was inevitable that some of them would find such satisfaction in their studies that they would seek to pursue them at an even higher level. There was, for instance, Sarah Elizabeth Siddons Mair, daughter of an Edinburgh military man. She was brought up in the city and from her earliest days she was known for her love of learning. 'We *read*, but Sally *studies*,' said one of her sisters, and it was with much enthusiasm that Sarah attended history and literature classes held by a Mr Hunter for the benefit of young ladies. In 1865, when she was nineteen, she formed a small literary group which she named the Essay Society. Each Saturday morning she and her young female friends gathered round the mahogany dining-room table in her parents' house and discussed the books they were reading. From this modest beginning grew the Ladies Edinburgh Debating Society, which was to flourish for the next seventy years, presided over by Sarah herself until she was in her nineties. As well as discussing literature, the society took a keen interest in higher education for women, campaigning actively for their admission to the universities.[29]

[258]

One of the most enthusiastic members, Mary Maclean, was particularly committed to the cause of university education for women. The daughter of a Dumfriesshire couple living in England, Mary was educated at one of the famous Edinburgh boarding schools. During her stay there, she met her future husband, a young German merchant named Crudelius. They married, settled in Edinburgh and had two daughters. Mary was delicate, but she proved to be a perfect wife and mother and had ambitions far beyond the immediate domestic sphere. She was firmly resolved to set up an association which would work for the admission of women to the universities and to this aim she devoted all the time and energy she could muster. She began by writing innumerable letters to all whom she thought might support her and, at last, in October 1867, her Edinburgh Ladies Educational Association was able to hold its first meeting in a friend's house. Six people attended, but only six weeks later the membership had risen to seventy, with a further eighty enrolled as honorary members.[30]

At this stage, women apparently had no thought of qualifying themselves for a future career by means of obtaining university degrees. Instead, self-fulfilment was their real motive and their association's constitution stated quite clearly that the intention was 'not . . . to train for the professions' but to give women 'the advantages of a system already acknowledged to be well suited for the mental training of the other sex'. Unfortunately, many men did not see it this way and chose to disbelieve the women's disclaimers, but there were others who understood and were willing to help. Their assistance was indispensable. After all, unless the women could find qualified men to teach them, they could go no further. One keenly interested friend was to be an influential supporter and a most valuable ally for the rest of his life. This was David Masson, Professor of English Literature in the University of Edinburgh for thirty years and later Historiographer Royal for Scotland. An Aberdonian by birth, he published many distinguished works of history and literary criticism and was for a lengthy period the Editor of *Macmillan's Magazine*.[31] From the outset, he was convinced of the need to allow women to study at university, and so he promised the Edinburgh Ladies Educational Association that in the winter of 1867–8 he would give them a course of lectures on English literature, charging them the modest fee of £1 11s. 6d. each. His generous offer was taken up with alacrity, and on 16 January 1868 when he gave his first lecture so many women came along that he was hard put to it to find room for them all. Between four and five hundred had thronged the hall where they were to enrol as students, with some 265 actually putting down their names and paying their fees. Their ages ranged from sixteen to over sixty, but most were young women from twenty-two to thirty-five. At the end of the course, ninety-four ladies sat the examination and Professor Masson had no hesitation in declaring that their papers were 'in the highest degree satisfactory', while Mr Nicholson, the University's examiner, decided that any of the women would easily pass for a Master of Arts degree and some would do very well indeed.

Encouraged by this success, the Association widened its curriculum the following year. Once more, Professor Masson lectured in literature, while his colleagues Professor Tait and Professor Fraser gave classes in natural science and logic and metaphysics respectively. Again, they reported very favourable results at the end of the session and, in the years which followed, the eager students were able to hear lectures in mathematics, Latin, Greek, education, fine art and political economy. Lack of any preliminary examination structure was a problem, for not only did this deprive women of the usual basic qualifications, but it also removed a customary incentive to studying. In reply to a growing demand, however, Edinburgh University in the 1860s established a 'Local Examination', awarding the successful candidates (seven-eighths of whom were women) a certificate which really meant something. The ladies wishing to study with Professor Masson and his colleagues accordingly formed themselves into small groups, hired tutors and sat the Local Examinations so that they could appear at the Ladies Association classes triumphantly bearing written evidence of their abilities. Any disadvantages resulting from a lack of early training melted away, and in 1876 Professor Sellar was able to state that in his Latin class of sixteen female students 'four at least of the ladies would have ranked among the first ten or twelve, had their papers been judged with those of the men.'

Mrs Crudelius herself died at the early age of thirty-eight, but her Association went from strength to strength. Its printed *Calendar* for 1889–90 proudly appeared from the lecture rooms at 15 Shandwick Place, Edinburgh, with the Marchioness of Lothian as president of the executive committee and the faithful Professor Masson as one of the vice-presidents. An average of 250 class tickets were now being taken out each session, and since 1874 it had been generally recognized that the certificates awarded were the equivalent to the degree of Master of Arts.[32]

Edinburgh was not the only place to provide classes of university standard for women. In 1876–7 St Andrews University actually instituted a certificate specially for ladies and gave it the name of L.A., Literate in Arts. This was a deliberate parallel to the M.A. degree for men. Much prized by its recipients, the L.A. enjoyed a high reputation, and it was with indignation that St Andrews saw the initials adopted by other universities to denote an inferior degree for men. The L.A.'s name was therefore changed to L.L.A., Lady Literate in Arts, and thus it remained until its final abolition in 1920.[33] Glasgow was also active. In the 1860s its professors were busy offering lecture series for ladies and in 1877 a branch of the Association for the Higher Education of Women was formed there. Six years later, Mrs John Elder presented to the Association a handsome mansion set in its own grounds. This they named Queen Margaret College, and opened as an institution which could provide women with the genuine equivalent of a university education. There were those who sneered at and patronized the women, of course, like the lecturer who told his men students that his lecture was not up to his usual standard because it had been 'prepared for the weaker intellects of Queen Margaret College'.[34] The ladies could afford to ignore such cheap jibes, however, knowing that by their own determination they had overcome the disadvantages inherent in the existing educational system and were now showing themselves to be just as capable of advanced study as men were.

Unfortunately, their success aroused a growing feeling of masculine alarm. It was all very well for women to amuse themselves in a harmless enough way by holding little classes and enlivening their leisure hours by discussing books and paintings. Once women began to prove their abilities, however, men saw rising before them the spectre of female competition, not only for degrees but for public employment afterwards. Allow a woman to gain academic qualifications and, unthinkable though the prospect was, she might start demanding entrance to the masculine preserves of politics, the law, teaching and even medicine. The whole structure of society would be undermined and man's position of superiority threatened. Confronted with this danger, men produced all manner of reasons for refusing women entrance

[261]

to the universities. Not only did they cite the old arguments of the frailty of the feminine physique and the variable nature of feminine morals, but they now set about a new line of argument and spoke volubly about women's intellectual inferiority. Women's brains must be smaller because they were generally smaller than men. The rigours of intellectual discipline would not only be beyond them but would place an intolerable strain on their minds. They would do themselves actual physical harm if they started reading science or philosophy.

To an intelligent woman, this was nonsense and, hard though it would be to combat this kind of prejudice, there were those women with enough courage and determination to challenge entrenched masculine attitudes. Perhaps the most famous of all was an English girl, Sophia Jex-Blake. Volatile, enthusiastic and quick-thinking, Sophia from her earliest days exhausted her family by her energetic search for intellectual stimulation. The normal, middle-class girl's life at home until marriage was obviously not for her, and she soon determined to study education. In a bold step, she set off in 1865 to visit the United States, with the intention of studying the educational system there, and discovered to her delight that American women could actually make public careers for themselves. In Boston she struck up a friendship with a lady doctor named Lucy Sewell and by the time she returned to England, she was determined that she, too, would study medicine. Having heard much about the reputation of the Edinburgh Medical School she travelled north in 1869, determined to gain admission. Certainly, people had warned her that no woman had ever been considered as a possible student, but she had boundless optimism and the will to succeed. She carried with her letters of introduction to various influential people, and one of the first she saw was none other than Professor David Masson. He felt obliged to point out that she was perhaps being too sanguine about the possibility of being admitted to university classes, but he promised her his warm support.

Encouraged by his sympathy, Sophia embarked upon an exhausting round of visits to professors and other men of influence. The diary she kept at this period provides an illuminating record of contemporary masculine attitudes. None of the medical professors was positively encouraging. The best that could be said was that some were unable to raise any real objections. The Dean of the Faculty, Professor Balfour, thus declared himself to be not unsympathetic, but explained that he had reservations based upon his belief that a woman simply could not dissect. Professor James Syme, recognized as being the greatest living authority on surgery, was perfectly agreeable to women studying, he said, provided it was 'clearly understood' that they meant to practise only in midwifery and uterine diseases. Taken up with academic politics, Professor Hughes Bennett the physiologist declared that he was so tired of struggling against those of his colleagues who opposed everything he suggested that he wanted nothing to do with this new battle. He saw no need for female doctors, though, when pressed, he did allow that they might be useful as assistant physiologists.

Thus far, the reaction had been more promising than Sophia had expected, but there remained a group of professors who were vehemently opposed to the slightest suggestion that women might join their students. Their leader was Professor Robert Christison, the celebrated toxicologist. Now seventy-two, he was the only professor to have a seat on the University Court, and he belonged to every single body which would consider the question of female entry to the university. This was the man who was to be Sophia's implacable opponent, telling her the first time he saw her that the issue of female doctors had already been decided and that there could be no further discussion of the subject.

How, then, was she ever to make any progress with her campaign? Many a girl would have been discouraged, but Sophia's fighting spirit was aroused by such intimidating opposition and, the more defeats she suffered, the more determined to win did she become. That people eventually listened to her was due to her abundant energy, enthusiasm and charm. Another important factor was the support of a number of leading men in public life, and Sophia was to find, at every stage of her campaign, not only obstinate male opposition but understanding male sympathy. Indeed, at the very beginning, the medical professors actually voted to allow women into their classes and the Senatus Academicus agreed. Needless to say, not everyone reacted with pleasure and Professor Christison was furious. Threatening to resign his chair, he persuaded the University Court to reverse that earlier decision. Women were not to be allowed to attend classes after all.

Despite this decision, Sophia was determined to persevere. She was very conscious of the fact that she was fighting on behalf of women generally and she now gathered together a small band of friends who shared her ambitions. They put forward their applications and eventually the university was persuaded to admit them. There was no question of them studying along with the men, and they had to give an undertaking that they did not intend to enter the medical profession.

By the end of the session, they had good reason to be satisfied with their progress. Indeed, Edith Pechey did so well in chemistry that she was third in the entire list of students, male and female. Her success entitled her to a Hope Scholarship, but once more prejudice intervened. The Professor of Chemistry withheld the scholarship and gave it instead to the man who came fourth on the list. There was at once a furious outcry in the national press. *The Scotsman* had long supported demands for female education, and other papers joined in the protests. The Professor defended his decision on the grounds that Edith was not an official member of his class, since she studied at a different time, yet he had already awarded her the bronze medal, which she could claim only if she were a recognized student. The women bitterly concluded that he thought he was compensating her for the disappointment by giving her a special class certificate, which was of no practical use whatsoever.

Professor Masson came to the rescue once more, trying to persuade the university authorities to admit women to their ordinary classes along with the men. His proposal was defeated, but the special, separate classes continued, and the women now gained a valuable ally in the person of Dr Alleyne Nicholson, lecturer in the Extra-Mural School. He agreed to admit the women to his ordinary zoology class, and, as he later explained, the lectures he then gave to the mixed group were 'identically the same as the course which I delivered last winter to my ordinary class of male students. I have not hitherto emasculated my lectures in any way whatever, nor have I the smallest intention of so doing. In so acting, I am guided by the firm conviction that little stress is to be laid on the purity and modesty of those who find themselves able to extract food for improper feelings from such a purely scientific subject as Zoology, however freely handled.'

At long last, women were studying a medical subject along with men students, and although they had to endure some jostling and harassment in the mixed classes, they accepted it good-naturedly. Worse was to follow, however, when in 1870 Dr P. D. Handyside agreed to let the women attend his class in anatomy and dissection at Surgeons' Hall. His consent was a triumph indeed for Sophia and her friends, but immediately student opposition was mobilized. On the day that seven women students arrived for the class, there was a full-scale riot. About two hundred singing and chanting male students surged round the gates of Surgeons' Hall and, as soon as the women appeared, slammed the gates in their faces with much derisive laughter and shouting. The janitor finally managed to open one section of the gate and the women made their way in thankfully, amidst much jostling. Once inside the lecture theatre, chaos broke loose. Dr Handyside was prevented from starting by dozens of intruders crowding in at the door, and someone let loose a pet sheep which grazed in the grounds. 'Let it remain,' said Dr Handyside tersely. 'It has more sense than those who sent it here.'

He finally began his lecture, but the scenes outside were repeated when the women emerged. Determined not to be intimidated, they turned out in no little trepidation for the next meeting of the class. Crowds had gathered to watch the excitement, and there were shouts of, 'You know, they'd never do it if they could get married.' By this time, however, the women had won support among the male students and groups of the men were ready to escort them to and fro for their protection. Moreover, the national press took up their cause with much indignation, and in the face of the public outcry which resulted, the demonstrations gradually died away.

Even so, Sophia's struggle was far from being over. Experience in the wards of the Royal Infirmary was a necessary part of the medical curriculum, and this too was being withheld. Public opinion was now increasingly on the side of the women's cause, however, and in 1871 no fewer than 956 Edinburgh women signed a petition expressing the earnest hope that the managers of the Infirmary would afford all the facilities needed, not only to Sophia and her friends but 'to all women who desire to enter the medical profession'. There was no longer any question of allowing the women to study if they promised never to practise: more and more people saw it as a denial of individual freedom to suggest that women should never be permitted to work as doctors.

Professor Christison, of course, remained as implacable as ever in his opposition, and unfortunately, Sophia's impetuousness sometimes played into his hands. In the aftermath of the Surgeons'

Hall riot she accused his assistant of having been there in a state of intoxication, and using foul language. The Professor immediately urged the man to sue her for libel. At the end of an embarrassing court case, she was ordered to pay one farthing's damages, and men and women from all over Britain sent her money to cover the legal expenses of the action. What had been designed to produce adverse publicity for the women in fact had the opposite effect.

Even when the Infirmary's managers finally allowed women into their wards, Professor Christison persuaded the medical faculty to refuse to allow them to sit the examinations. The Senatus rescinded this decision, but a year later the University was refusing to grant degrees to the female students, no matter how well they did in their examinations. A celebrated lawsuit ensued when the women took the matter to the Court of Session. At first the judges found in their favour, but in 1873 they upheld an appeal against the decision. Undaunted, Sophia and her friends took the case to Parliament. Such was the public interest by now aroused that sixty-five petitions in favour of university education for women came in, one from 16,000 women and another from twenty-six of the professors of Scottish universities. After many setbacks, Parliament in July 1876 passed an act enabling the universities to grant degrees to women, although it was not until the Universities (Scotland) Act of 1889 that the universities were empowered 'to admit women to graduation in one or more faculties and to provide for their instruction'. Two years after that, Edinburgh announced that it would permit women to graduate in medicine, but not until 1916 were they actually admitted to the medical school itself: until then they had to continue to study at the Extra-Mural School.

By that time, Sophia had long since been forced to seek her degree elsewhere, and in 1877 the University of Berne awarded her a doctorate in medicine. She returned to Scotland after that, set up in practice as the first woman doctor in Scotland and taught midwifery at the Extra-Mural School, thereby becoming the first woman lecturer.[35]

Her battle had been long and demanding, but in the end it had been worthwhile. What had begun as the desire of one young woman to study medicine had become a national campaign to improve the educational facilities for women, and it had succeeded. In 1892 Queen Margaret College became an official part of the University of Glasgow. Two years later, eleven women enrolled in the University of Aberdeen. In his first year as Professor of English there, Herbert Grierson, the celebrated scholar, awarded the first prize in his class to 'the most gifted and interesting student it has been my lot to encounter', Miss Rachel Annand. The much prized L.L.A. of St Andrews University was eventually transformed into the Master of Arts degree. At long last, women could be educated to the same standard as men.[36]

CHAPTER THIRTEEN

The Emancipation
of Women

EDUCATION GAVE WOMEN a new awareness of the world around them. This is to deny neither the intelligence nor the perceptiveness of their predecessors, but the fact remains that if a woman had read something of the condition of women in other countries and at other times, she was more likely to question her own role in a society which had altered dramatically since many of the laws and conventions affecting her had come into being. The old days when the husband literally provided food and protection for his family had long since gone. Physical danger was not the ever-present threat in the Victorian era that it had been in the Middle Ages, and the distinction between male and female activities had in many respects become blurred. Fewer and fewer men required physical strength for their work and women were realizing that they themselves were just as capable as their male counterparts of operating a machine or adding up a column of figures. Yet masculine prejudice tried to tell them that they were incapable of doing these things, and the law still treated them as though they were children.

Marriage, of course, remained the accepted destiny for women, and only in relatively minor ways were traditional ideas relaxed. Certainly, it was now generally agreed that a woman had a right to choose her own partner, but there remained considerable family pressure on middle-class and aristocratic girls to marry a man at least approved if not chosen by their parents. Propertied families were as adamant as ever that they should control their daughters' marriage choice, because if the girl were wealthy enough, there was always the danger that a fortune-hunter would manage to insinuate himself into her favour. After all, in spite of elaborate

Victorian conventions which insisted on modesty and chaperones and the limitations of feminine freedom, it was possible that some unscrupulous adventurer would gain admittance to polite society, with only one aim in view.

When Miss Adela Grant fell in love with Robert Cobham in 1885, her brother immediately feared the worst. Their father was dead, Adela had property of her own, and Sir Arthur was convinced that this was her attraction. On May 13, his sister wrote announcing that she had fixed her wedding for 10 June and, she added defiantly, she would go through with it whether or not the prospective bridegroom had made any financial provisions for her future. 'I really intend to marry him then, even if there is risk,' she told Arthur, '. . . and I hope you will come and give me away.' Understandably alarmed, he confided to a friend that he was sure that Mr Cobham 'simply wishes for Addie's money'. His remonstrances were in vain, however, for a few days later Adela was writing to tell him, 'Believe me, I am not acting from obstinacy, but I am of an age to act for myself and I cannot and will not give up my marriage . . . In this case I must judge for myself and I can only assure you that you have a wrong opinion of Mr Cobham.' In reply, Arthur begged her to think again. The idea of 'marrying without settlements is downright folly'. Finally, it was arranged that he should have an interview with Mr Cobham and, to his surprise, he discovered that the latter seemed to have a comfortable income. He therefore admitted defeat. 'You know that none of us like the match and the connection in general,' he told Adela, 'but that is more your business.' As the financial arrangements appeared to be beyond reproach, he could only conclude, 'I have done the best I could for you, and now I hope the marriage will turn out a happy one.'[1]

Adela's choice of an Englishman was not so unusual, for there was now less likelihood of a girl becoming engaged to a man from the same village as herself. In the already cited sample of 150 daughters of the Scottish peerage marrying before 1600, no fewer than 87% had become the wives of Scots, with a mere 2% marrying Englishmen. This was largely explained by lack of opportunity to meet strangers and the financial restrictions which made English husbands expect larger tochers than Scots could provide. In the eighteenth century, the proportions were roughly half and half,[2] and by the period 1800 to 1900, a comparable sample of 150 titled brides showed only 40% marrying Scots, while

55% became the wives of Englishmen. Greater mobility meant that Scottish aristocratic families were now intent on seeking partners of comparable status for their daughters and would do so in England if they could not find a suitable husband at home.

Increased opportunities for travel brought young women into contact with a wider range of people, but of course it did not inevitably follow that a woman would marry a foreigner she met abroad. Travellers tended to congregate together with people from their own country, and when the Duke of Argyll's daughters were staying in Cannes in 1869 they attracted the attention of Sir John McNeill. This 'stately and kind widower' devised all manner of outings and picnics for them, but the girls soon realized that he was doing so as a means of meeting their aunt, Lady Emma, who acted as their chaperone. They teased her unmercifully about 'Uncle John', but the friendship flourished and when they got back to London he lost no time in asking the Duke for permission to marry her.[3]

Not everyone had the opportunity of romantic flirtation on the Riviera, of course, and for girls from poor families increased mobility meant not the occasion to travel but to meet in towns young men from other areas who, like themselves, had left home in search of employment. Working-class women had always enjoyed much greater freedom in choosing their marriage partners and now Victorian writers were constantly moralizing about the behaviour of young female servants who lived away from home and all too easily evaded the watchful eye of their employers. It was not surprising that such a large proportion of working-class girls were now pregnant on their wedding day.[4]

Increased mobility apart, there was a further widening in the range of available marriage partners. After many years of acrimonious debate, the Marriage with the Deceased Wife's Sister Act was passed in Parliament in 1907. There always had been instances of a widower left with young children turning to his dead wife's sister for help. She knew the family, was perhaps taking care of them, and would have provided an obvious second wife had she not been within the forbidden degrees. In fact a considerable number of Englishmen did marry their sisters-in-law, and so in 1847 a collection of petitions was sent to Parliament asking for the law to be changed. As a result, the British government set up a Royal Commission to look into the whole question of consanguinity and affinity. The Commission eventually recommended a relaxation in the law, but such was the opposition to the idea that bills foundered again and again on their way through Parliament and the churches often voiced their condemnation of the proposal. It was, they said, contrary to both scripture and the sanctity of the family. Sixty years were to pass before public opinion altered sufficiently for the bill to become law. Fourteen years after that, the similar Deceased Brother's Widow's Marriage Act followed.[5]

Once the choice of husband had finally been made, most families still proceeded to draw up a marriage contract. In detail, these documents had become increasingly complex, though their basic provisions remained much as they had always been since the seventeenth century. When Lieutenant Lachlan Macquarrie of the Scots Greys promised to marry Miss Isabella Hamilton Dundas Campbell in 1836, their contract began with the familiar agreement to marry. There then followed the arrangements for her should she be widowed. In that eventuality, she would be given £500 sterling a year, a sum which would be reduced by half should she ever remarry. A life rent from her husband's principal mansion-house would also be hers in widowhood, and she would keep the entire household furniture, silver plate, china, linen and wines. If, however, the heirs of the estate wished to reclaim the house from her, they would pay her £1200 sterling with which she could buy a home for herself, along with a further £500 in exchange for the furnishings.

There then followed provision for any children of the marriage. The eldest son would inherit the estate, of course, and a younger child would receive £4000 sterling, payable to a son when he reached his majority, or to a daughter upon her majority or upon marriage. Until then, the children were to be maintained and educated in a manner suitable to their station. Trustees for them were chosen, and it was agreed that Isabella would be provided with a suitable sum of money for her mourning clothes. She herself brought with her a tocher of £2000 sterling, and she made over to her husband all debts, sums of money or lands belonging to her or which she might acquire during the course of the marriage. Unusually, if either party died within a year and a day of the wedding and no children had been born, the terms of the contract were to be fulfilled as if the time had been much longer. Marriage contracts remained the customary arrangement for ordinary people too, although in form they were less complicated, concentrating upon the basic exchange of tocher and jointure.[6]

Before the wedding itself could take place, it was still necessary to have banns proclaimed. However, by 1865 a Royal Commission appointed to look into the state and practical working of the marriage laws in England, Scotland and Ireland could report that the proclamation of banns had outlived its usefulness. There were constant complaints about the expense involved, the growth of more and more different denominations meant that the whole community was not meeting together in the parish church on a Sunday, and it had come to be that, unless more money was paid, the banns were read out three times on one Sunday instead of once on three consecutive Sundays. There was a good deal of argument as to whether banns should be abolished altogether and finally, in 1878, the Marriage Notice (Scotland) Act permitted an alternative procedure. Local registrars had been appointed in Scotland in 1854 and the new act allowed a written announcement of marriage to be published on the registrar's door if the couple preferred not to have the banns called in church.[7]

The circumstances of the wedding itself were also undergoing some modification at this period. Recognizing the ever-increasing number of denominations other than the established Church of Scotland, an act of 1834 permitted priests and ministers of other churches to perform the marriage ceremony. Moreover, weddings were now increasingly taking on the nature of private celebrations rather than public festivities. In the Middle Ages the actual wedding had taken place at the door of the church. In the sixteenth century the early Reformers had been insistent that it should be held in church, before the entire congregation, but by the nineteenth century it was becoming more and more popular to have the wedding in the bride's own home or in the private room of an hotel. The reasons for this alteration were social rather than theological. Middle-class families in particular tended to shun the publicity attendant upon marriage and were anxious that the guests should be their own friends and relations, not just anyone who could come along and pay a penny to join in the fun. By the end of the century the private wedding had become usual throughout society. When the Marquis of Tullibardine married Miss Louisa Moncrieffe on 29 October 1863, the service was held at Moncrieffe House with the bride's seven beautiful sisters attending her, and at a wedding breakfast held at Mellerstain about 1871, an enthusiastic guest noticed that 'there were 33 persons, almost all near relations – 2 very magnificent cakes, one for show and another for eating'. At the other end of the social scale, brides in the village of Wanlockhead in south-west Scotland were usually married in their mother's kitchen, while in Nairn at the beginning of the present century the Seamen's Hall in the evening was the normal choice.[8]

The ceremony itself might be private, but even so the accompanying public rejoicings were slow to die out. When a landowner married, his whole estate usually joined in the festivities. Lady Dunmore's son married in the 1830s and she was pleased to observe that 'the poor dear little village of Dunmore to whom we had only given dinner and a bonfire and a fiddle . . . of their own account they decorated the whole village with boughs and garlands and put up flags at every house and at night there was not a *single window* that was not *illumined*. The very poorest had 2 or 3 farthing candles and I thought that such a pretty *feeling* I was quite delighted with it.'[9]

Obviously, ordinary people could not hope to emulate such lavish rejoicings, but they had their music, dancing and feasting too. In many areas in the 1840s the old custom of creeling continued. Soon after the wedding, the bridegroom's friends caught him and placed a creel or basket of stones on his back. He had to go through the streets thus encumbered until his bride came and cut him free. The infare when the couple entertained friends in their new home persisted too, and so did the practice of going to the church the first Sunday after the wedding. However much the couple themselves might seek privacy, the community as a whole was still insistent that their new change of status be marked in a formal way.[10]

Incidentally, most weddings in Scotland were now regular. The clandestine ceremonies so popular in the eighteenth century died away after the passing of the 1834 act allowing the much wider range of ministers to officiate. It was now a relatively simple matter to find some clergyman to perform the ceremony and it was becoming increasingly desirable to be legally married. The full range of Poor Law relief could only be claimed by those who were actually man and wife, and compulsory education meant that it was embarrassing for children at school if parents had to admit that they were only living together. By 1864 irregular marriages had become very rare, accounting for only 0.1% of the total number.

[273]

In spite of this, the old forms of irregular marriage *per verba de praesenti*, by promise *subsequente copula* and by cohabitation and repute all remained lawful. Legal reformers were trying hard to have them abolished, but every attempt to do away with them brought an outcry from the general public, who saw the proposals as attempts by the English to interfere in the Scottish legal system. Moreover, the end of the century saw a surprising revival in their popularity. There was still no such thing as civil marriage in a registrar's office in Scotland, and so the increasing number of people with no religious beliefs or a determination to marry before no more than the statutory number of witnesses, ignored the church ceremony altogether and resorted to the old, irregular forms. The couple who were living together could have their irregular marriage legally registered if they went to a sheriff and made a formal declaration. He would then issue them with a warrant which they could take along to the local registrar. By 1884, 2.4% of all marriages were technically irregular. By 1894 the figure had risen to 4.2% and in 1913 it reached 9.1%.[11]

However she actually married her husband, the wife found herself hemmed in by all the old restrictions. Educated, intelligent women found it particularly hard to accept the laws which declared that upon marriage all their moveables were made over to their husbands, along with the administration of their heritable property. The laws affecting this aspect of married life had gone largely unchanged since the seventeenth century, when the daily circumstances of life had been very different. One mitigating factor was that, within the home, wives' emotional relationships with their husbands remained much as they had always been. The Victorian husband might expect to be treated with deference by his partner, but he still relied upon her for advice and support. Even Thomas Carlyle, with all his emphasis that women must command by submitting, was far from being a cold domestic tyrant. When a journey to Liverpool in the summer of 1831 deprived him of his wife's company, he told her that when he opened the trunk she had packed for him and found the jujube box she had embroidered, 'it was so beautiful I could almost have cried over it. Heaven reward thee, my clearhead, warmhearted, dearest little Screamikin. If I were there I would kiss thee fondly and whisper that thou wert mine forever.' Nor was Jane shy to respond. She described how she cried herself to sleep on the evening of his departure, and next morning when she opened her eyes and saw 'your nightcap lying on my pillow . . . I fell a-crying anew, and actually kissed it, I believe, though you know I hate *red* nightcaps.' Indeed, so overcome was she when she sat down to her lonely breakfast that she retired to bed and spent the next day and a half there. The fact that the Carlyles' later married life was something less than idyllic was the outcome of their own difficult personalities rather than of any matrimonial conventions of their time.[12]

If attitudes in the home remained unchanged, so too did feelings about female employment. No matter how industrialisation altered the scene, women remained in lower paid jobs with few or no prospects. This was largely because marriage was still the principal object of a woman's life and those women who did work outside the home were for the most part young girls putting in the time before marriage, or widows forced to support themselves economically. One of the frequent misconceptions about conditions during the Industrial Revolution is the notion that large sections of the female population went to work in the factories and that hundreds of married women were to be found with their young children toiling in terrible conditions there. Undoubtedly more adults were employed in factories after the Factory Act of 1833 limited child labour, but from 1851 to 1881 an average of only 25.4% of women were actually out at work. Of this total working population, 11% went into that traditional area of activity, domestic service. It remained as popular as ever, particularly with country girls, because it meant working in a relatively familiar environment, improving domestic skills already acquired at home.[13]

The staff of a house was now preponderantly female. Gone were the days when the cook and the baker and the brewer were men. When Lady Helen Hall paid her domestic servants at Whitsun 1836 she was employing a lady's maid, an upper housemaid, an under housemaid who also did duty as a laundrymaid, a female cook and a footman. The lady's maid was paid £20 a year, the cook £16, the upper housemaid £15 and the under housemaid £11. The footman's wages were £28 a year.[14] Most girls entering domestic service had no intention of moving up the hierarchy of servants. The laundrymaid would probably never be considered suitable to undertake the duties of a lady's maid and she would not envisage her future in terms of a life in service. Rather than attempting to improve her position, she was probably more concerned with finding a husband among the male staff. As a result, when a girl did not like her situation, she would not hesitate to move on elsewhere. Her hours were long, her accommodation sparse and her mistress might be overbearing and unpleasant, but the maidservant was in no way imprisoned in her household and she moved swiftly to another job if her surroundings were too uncongenial.[15]

As for factories, the girls employed there were generally between the ages of sixteen and twenty-three, and they had marriage in mind. The years at work were an interlude during which some money could be made, and more money was to be made in the industrial environment. Girls in the carpet factory at Sanquhar in Dumfriesshire in the 1840s were earning 12s. a week. If they had gone into agricultural work instead, they could only have hoped for about half of that sum, and even in domestic service they would not expect more than three or four shillings a week although they would also have had board and lodging. True, working conditions were often undeniably unpleasant, particularly in the flax mills, where the heat of the atmosphere and the constant spray of water from the machinery generated an almost intolerable humidity. The working day was also some eleven or twelve hours long. Eventually, in 1847, the Ten Hours' Bill was passed, limiting the female working day to that duration, but it was not fully implemented until further acts were passed in 1850 and 1853.[16]

It must be remembered, however, that the women thus employed were not required to undertake heavy manual labour. They were normally engaged in subsidiary processes such as winding thread. In Newburgh, Fife, in 1833 some 329 women were employed in winding bobbins for the linen weaving and in Renfrew in 1836 at least 128 women were winding for the muslin weaving. At Wilton, Roxburghshire in the 1840s, the men in the woollen manufactories attended to the machinery while women prepared the wool for the carding and scribbling machines. Moreover, as machinery became more sophisticated, it was as easy for women as for men to operate it and girls were often employed to work the power looms. This in itself aroused masculine resentment, but women did not retaliate because, regarding their situation as a temporary phase, they saw no point in combining to demand equal opportunities.[17]

In the textile industry there remained a good deal of outwork in spite of technological advances, because this was the great age of embroidered muslin and embroidered shawls. Hundreds of women in the west of Scotland stitched away in their own homes. In Auchinleck, Ayrshire, in the 1830s, it was reported that 'a number of women, both older and younger, throughout the parish, are engaged in flowering muslin. This is not confined to those residing in the village, but many of the farmers' daughters and others find it a profitable employment.' Glasgow employers paid from five to eight shillings a week for the work. White Ayrshire embroidery was now in great demand, not only in Britain but on the continent, so girls in that area were earning from one to two shillings a day. Again, they were mainly young women, because the work required good eyesight. About 150 women in Kilbirnie, Ayrshire, were in 1840 engaged in flowering muslin, earning from seven to ten shillings a week, while the minister of Irvine estimated that about two hundred of the women in his parish prepared thread for the weaver and perhaps as many as two thousand were engaged in ornamental needlework.[18]

Paisley shawls were much in vogue in the 1840s, so in Erskine, Renfrewshire, 'Many of the young women are kept in constant employment by sewing muslins and embroidering crape shawls for manufacturers in Paisley.' They were paid according to the stitch they executed. Victoria stitch on cotton muslin earned them 1s. 3d. a day, as did French opening stitch on muslin. The less complicated French veining was paid at the rate of a shilling a day, a sum also to be earned by girls sewing satin borders on silk shawls or embroidering Tibet wool shawls with twined silk.[19]

Jobs available in towns for middle-class women likewise remained limited in scope and the Situations Vacant columns in the newspapers of the time give a good indication of the range. On 4 September 1874, people were advertising in *The Scotsman* for housemaids, cooks, nurses, schoolmistresses, a governess ('an elderly lady of cheerful disposition and good manners, a good linguist and accomplished musician'), dressmakers, mantle-makers, a milliner, saleswomen for tobacconist's, confectioner's and baker's shops, a darner, a message girl and, more adventurously, a girl of over twenty 'to take an infant to the Cape of Good Hope.'[20]

Some changes there undoubtedly were. More and more women came to prefer working in a shop to domestic service, because, although the hours were long and the wages low, the general atmosphere was more interesting. The clerical world of shorthand and typing rapidly became a female preserve once those skills had come into being, and it was usually women who operated telephones and telegraph systems. Office work was light and pleasant compared with the tasks of the factory, hours were not excessive, wages were reasonably high and there were plenty of potential husbands in the form of male colleagues.[21]

Yet again, however, women were employed in the supportive, subsidiary role. Many were perfectly happy with this situation, but there were other people, both male and female, who saw it as incongruous that, because of their sex, capable and intelligent human beings were debarred from a whole range of activities. As early as 1791 Mary Wollstonecraft had written her *Vindication of the Rights of Women*, arguing vehemently that the education accorded to middle-class girls of her time was restrictive and inappropriate. She placed a high value on women's domestic responsibilities, but she hated the accepted view that woman was man's inferior and she wanted women as well as men to play their full part in society, freed from the arbitrary restrictions imposed upon them by generations of masculine legislators and educationalists.[22]

Mary's language was passionate and emotive, and when her book was published in 1792 it aroused a good deal of outraged dismay. She was, after all, applying the egalitarian principles of the French Revolution to the conditions of her own sex, and those of conservative views reacted fiercely against her arguments. However, people of more radical opinion were sympathetic and impressed. Mary was in many ways ahead of her time, but by the second half of the nineteenth century, the whole climate of opinion was gradually altering and important changes in the matrimonial law of property came into being. In 1861 Parliament passed the Conjugal Rights (Scotland) Amendment Act. Hitherto, a woman who was separated or divorced could still have any moveable property she subsequently acquired taken over by her husband. In other words, if a deserted wife opened a small shop with the intention of supporting herself, her husband could appear and claim everything – her furniture, her stock and her savings. The Act remedied the situation by declaring that when a wife obtained a judicial separation, all property she acquired thereafter belonged to her exclusively. A deserted wife who obtained a protection order from the courts was to be similarly treated. Moreover, if a wife inherited or acquired property by any means other than by her own industry, this would not pass automatically into her husband's control, unless he made reasonable provision for her from the income. The same act abolished the lengthy preliminary procedure for divorce for desertion. Until that date, it was necessary for the person raising the action to go through a long series of ecclesiastical and judicial formalities before anything could be done. Now an action could be raised, as long as four years had passed since the desertion had started. There was still no divorce on any grounds other than desertion or adultery, however, although judicial separations for cruelty could be obtained from the commissaries, then from the Court of Session and, after 1907, from the sheriff court.

This was obviously a step in the right direction, and further legislation followed. The Married Women's Property (Scotland) Act of 1877 gave wives the right to keep their own earned income, unless it came from a business owned jointly with the husband. Three years later, the Married Women's Policies of Assurance (Scotland) Act empowered a wife to take out an insurance policy on her own life, or that of her husband, for her separate use; then in 1881 a second Married Women's Property (Scotland) Act finally abolished the *jus mariti*. Henceforth, 'the whole moveable or personal estate of the wife, whether acquired before or during the marriage shall, by operation of law, be vested in the wife as her separate estate and shall not be subject to the *jus mariti*.' The husband retained his power to administer the wife's separate property, and his consent was necessary if she wished to dispose of it but that, too, was eventually swept away by the Married Women's Property (Scotland) Act of 1920.[23]

This was a major advance, and in another completely different sphere the feminine condition was improving dramatically. It is no exaggeration to say that for centuries women's lives had been overshadowed by the burden of childbearing, their whole attitude to life affected by the knowledge that they would probably spend their fertile years in a succession of pregnancies culminating each time in a painful and life-threatening labour. At long last, however, this suffering was to be alleviated. Significant advances in methods of delivery had already been made by the men-midwives, and in the nineteenth century all aspects of reproduction became the subject of reasearch. The foetal heartbeat was heard for the first time by a Swiss in 1818 and the invention of the stethoscope made it possible for doctors to listen in and hear whether or not the foetus was still alive. The human ovum was discovered in 1832 and seven years later Nicholas Gendrin suggested that menstruation is controlled by ovulation and not by the moon, as everyone had hitherto believed. This better understanding of the female cycle laid the foundation for all manner of advances in gynaecology and obstetrics, and the realization that it was the father and not the mother who determined the sex of the child relieved women of the guilt of failing to bear a son. Most important of all, however, for women themselves were the discoveries of anaesthesia and antisepsis.[24]

Throughout history, women had suffered the pains of childbirth with a fatalistic acceptance. After all, had God not said to women, 'in sorrow thou shalt bring forth children'? The agonies of labour were part of the burden which sinful human beings had to bear, and it was not only useless but reprehensible to seek to evade them.[25] Fortunately male doctors were not willing to stand by and watch what they believed must be unnecessary human suffering, and the man whose name is particularly associated with anaesthesia in childbirth is the Scotsman, Sir James Young Simpson. Born in 1811, the seventh son of a Bathgate baker, Simpson was able to attend Edinburgh University, thanks to the sacrifices made by his family. He almost abandoned medicine altogether when he witnessed the sufferings of women undergoing surgery, but he persevered and at the early age of twenty-eight he became Professor of Midwifery in his old university. His brilliant, concise lectures brought students flocking to hear him, and the midwifery class was soon the largest in the university, for the first time in its history.

Particularly anxious to relieve the pain of his maternity patients, Simpson became eagerly interested in the possibilities of anaesthesia. Laughing gas had been used in dental operations for seventy years past, and in 1846 ether was first used in London in a surgical operation. Unfortunately, ether was not an ideal anaesthetic. Apart from its persistent and unpleasant smell, it tended to irritate the throat and lungs and cause bouts of coughing. Simpson had used it but he was determined to find a more satisfactory alternative and began experimenting with a variety of chemicals. One of these was chloroform, discovered in 1831 by a French chemist, Soubeiran, and a German, Liebig, working independently. Simpson managed to obtain a sample from the Edinburgh firm of Messrs Duncan and Flockhart. The bottle lay in his house for several weeks then, late one November evening, he decided to try it out. He and his two assistants, watched by some ladies of the family and his brother-in-law, inhaled the vapour from a tumbler. To the alarm of the bystanders, the three became suddenly over-excited, then crashed to the floor unconscious. The ladies expressed horror and dismay, but as soon as Simpson recovered, he knew that he had found what he sought. Persuading Duncan and Flockhart to produce quantities of chloroform for him, he pursued his experiments excitedly, then on 17 January 1847 he administered it to a doctor's wife who had previously endured an agonizing delivery resulting in the death of her baby. Dropping chloroform on to the funnel he had made from a pocket handkerchief, he anaesthetized her about three and a half hours after her labour had begun and she gave birth to a healthy daughter. On regaining consciousness, she commented drowsily that she had enjoyed a lovely sleep and was now ready for the work ahead.

A few months later, Simpson reported his experiences in the *Provincial Medical and Surgical Journal* and it was clear that he was delighted with the results he had achieved. 'I have never had the pleasure of watching over a series of better and more rapid recoveries, nor once witnessed any disagreeable result follow, to either mother or child,' he wrote, 'whilst I have now seen an immense amount of maternal pain and agony saved by its employment.'

It is difficult to overestimate the joy and relief felt by women on the introduction of chloroform. Simpson's first patient was so overwhelmed that she christened her baby girl 'Anaesthesia', and women who experienced the benefits of the new discovery could not praise it highly enough. At first, only a few were able to enjoy the relief it brought for, as Simpson himself had foreseen, there was much opposition to its use. Churchmen used the old argument that since pain in childbirth was divinely ordained, it was nothing short of sacreligious to try to prevent it. However, Simpson was equal to them, and when they quoted Genesis to him, he retorted with the verse from the same book, which reads, 'And the Lord God caused a deep sleep to fall upon Adam and he slept, and he took one of his ribs and closed up the flesh instead thereof.' He was convinced that women themselves would insist on the general use of anaesthesia. As he had written in his paper, 'Obstetricians may oppose it, but I believe our patients themselves will force the use of it upon the profession' and he was proved right. When medical men declared that chloroform would cause increased bleeding, convulsions and even paralysis, he was able to demonstrate that pain, shock and exhaustion were far greater dangers. Finally, he found his greatest ally in Queen Victoria herself. The Queen had always shuddered at the prospect of having a large family, and when in 1853 she gave birth to her eighth child, chloroform was used. 'The effect,' she noted in her diary afterwards, 'was soothing, quieting, and delightful beyond measure.' Given her approval, it now came into general use.[26]

Anaesthesia apart, far too many women were still dying because of infection. Doctors were simply not aware that diseases like puerperal fever were spread by germs and so cleanliness did not figure largely in the treatments they prescribed. One young doctor particularly appalled by the toll of human life was Joseph Lister, a Londoner who in 1860 became Regius Professor of Surgery in the University of Glasgow. From his study of the work of Pasteur he learned about organisms floating in the air and he realized the need to destroy them. This would have to be done by means of a chemical agent, and in his search for a suitable substance he came upon carbolic acid. He saw that here was a means of destroying germs and soon afterwards he published his first important paper on antisepsis. Its implications aroused wide interest throughout the medical profession, and although his ideas were not fully accepted for a number of years, he pursued his researches. By the 1880s carbolic acid solution was being used in obstetrics, and as a result, lying-in hospitals found their death rate falling rapidly. There was indeed a diminished mortality rate for every kind of surgical operation, including the hitherto highly dangerous Caesarean section which, thanks to anaesthesia and antisepsis, now became a safer possibility.[27]

Not only was childbirth transformed in the nineteenth century, but the whole attitude towards childbearing was revolutionized. Already by 1798 Thomas Malthus had alerted the public to the dangers of overpopulation and now, with fewer and fewer mothers and babies perishing, the population was rising rapidly. Doctors warned that infanticide and abortion were on the increase because parents simply could not afford to support such large numbers of healthy children, and Sir James Young Simpson had himself noted that 'on the birth of a second or third child, the neighbours will say "so-and-so has another baby: you'll see, it won't live" and that this becomes a sort of joke, in which its mother will join, public opinion expressing no condemnation of her cruelty.' Obviously, something would have to be done, and although it remained a legal offence to disseminate information about contraception, various hints appeared in publications and it was obvious that large numbers of people were anxious for details. By the 1890s even some of the churches, hitherto bitterly opposed to the idea of limitation of family size, were beginning to withdraw their opposition. The new notion that a woman could be largely freed from the burden of childbearing had begun to grow.[28]

In spite of legislative and personal improvements, the rate of progress seemed to an ever-increasing number of people to be far too slow, and in the 1860s the women's cause found an influential new champion in the philosopher and member of parliament, John Stuart Mill. In 1869 Mill published an essay entitled *The Subjection of Women*, and in this he argued powerfully that 'the legal subordination of one sex to the other is wrong in itself and now one of the chief hindrances to human improvement.' Like Mary Wollstonecraft, he was concerned with the good of society as a whole, and he found it totally wrong that half the population was prevented by prejudice and outmoded attitudes from contributing to the improvement of the human condition. One by one he dealt with all the objections raised to feminine participation in public life, defending women's abilities and attributing any deficiencies to the upbringing which conditioned girls to believe that 'the object of being attractive to men' was 'the pole star of feminine education and formation of character'. He wanted women to be allowed to vote, and he organized an impressive petition to Parliament demanding female suffrage. This was denied, of course, and his writings met with a mixed response among women themselves.[29]

Mrs Margaret Oliphant, a forward-looking writer who supported herself and her children by her literary activities, noted on one occasion that she had just finished writing 'a little paper about Stuart Mill and his mad notion of franchise for women'. Mary Somerville, on the other hand, was not only the first person to sign his petition, but wrote to thank him for *The Subjection of Women*, telling him, 'Age has not abated my zeal for the emancipation of my sex from the unreasonable prejudice too prevalent in Great Britain against a literary and scientific education for women . . . I joined in a petition to the Senate of London University praying that degrees might be granted to women, but it was rejected. I have also frequently signed petitions to Parliament for the Female Suffrage, and have the honour now to be a member of the General Committee for Woman Suffrage in London.'[30]

The women's suffrage movement had its origins in London in the 1860s. The aim was not, of course, simply to obtain the vote for its own sake. Women felt that only by participating in the election of members of parliament would they ever to able to bring their influence to bear on the politicians who governed the country. The long campaign which followed was centred on London, because that was where Parliament sat, but activity was not restricted to that city and the suffrage movement found active supporters throughout Scotland. As early as 1866 Sarah Siddons Mair's Edinburgh Essay Society was debating the need for women to have the vote, and indeed Sarah herself eventually became president of the Women's Franchise Association.[31]

That lay in the future, of course, but the following year saw the establishment of formal suffrage societies. The defeat of an amendment to the Reform Bill, which would have enfranchised certain women, led supporters of women's rights to found the National Society for Women's Suffrage and on 7 November the Edinburgh branch held its first meeting. It had as its president Priscilla McLaren, the wife of a radical member of parliament.[32]

For the next thirty years, the campaign was conducted mainly through the organization of petitions to parliament and the holding of meetings both large and small. There were no spectacular acts of propaganda, but public sympathy was undeniable. During the years 1867 to 1876, two million signatures to petitions were collected in Scotland, but they did not have the desired effect and the press often took little note even of the larger rallies. When a Scottish National Demonstration of Women was held in the St Andrew's Hall, Glasgow, after the passing of the Married Women's Property (Scotland) Act, the hall was packed to capacity but *The Scotsman* the following day accorded the occasion one small paragraph only. Under an eleven-line obituary of a Glasgow solicitor, there was tucked away, at the foot of the page, the seven-line report of the rally. 'In spite of the inclemency of the weather,' said *The Scotsman* tepidly, 'there was a large attendance of women.'[33]

Successive governments regularly refused to sponsor any bill granting women the vote, usually because they did not wish to lose support for their own policies, and private members' bills were inevitably defeated. Queen Victoria's own disapproval of the women's cause likewise helped to discourage some who might otherwise have favoured an extension of the franchise. In the 1880s, however, support began to come from a new direction. The Scottish Labour Party was founded in 1888 and both it and other socialist organizations were anxious that the vote should be extended to women. At the same time, the Pankhurst family in England became active and gave the movement fresh impetus, and in 1903 Mrs Pankhurst established the Women's Social and Political Union (WSPU). Soon, branches were established throughout Great Britain.[34]

Among the leaders of the WSPU in London was a Scotswoman, Flora Drummond. A telegraphist from the island of Arran, in the west of Scotland, Flora was now in her late twenties, small, pugnacious and full of energy. Known to her friends as 'The General', she organized huge demonstrations in London and, dressed in a quasi-military uniform, rode on a horse at the head of all the large processions. Throughout Scotland itself, the WSPU held dozens of meetings, and a large demonstration in Edinburgh in October 1907 was followed by an impressive procession along Princes Street. On 11 January 1908 the Scottish headquarters of the organization was set up in Bath Street, Glasgow, and in the months which followed there were lecture tours by such leading figures as Mrs Pankhurst, Charlotte Despard and Mrs Pethick-Lawrence.[35]

That spring, Scottish suffragettes at last had the opportunity to be in the forefront of the campaign when four members of parliament in safe Liberal seats died. There were to be by-elections at Kincardine, Dundee, Montrose and Stirling, so the women decided to campaign against the Liberal candidates. Their particular attention was to be concentrated on Dundee, where Winston Churchill was standing. Two years before, they had been instrumental in securing his defeat when he stood for North-West Manchester. It was not that the Suffragettes had any particular personal antipathy towards Churchill, for he had actually been more or less in favour of the enfranchisement of women, but he had been the only prospective cabinet minister standing in the vicinity of Manchester, where the Pankhursts were based, and so he had become their target. Now Mrs Pankhurst hired halls and theatres in Dundee for mass meetings, and excited suffragettes burst into the Stock Exchange and the offices of one of the local newspapers, the *Dundee Courier*, in an attempt to gain converts to their cause. In the end, Churchill was elected, but as a direct result of the campaign the movement in Dundee had gained a strong organization.[36]

Not all suffragettes believed in such lively action, of course, and in 1907 the Women's Freedom League was founded by those who preferred more passive methods. It too found strong support in Scotland, and women there refused to pay taxes on the classic grounds that there should be no taxation without representation.[37]

Support for the suffragettes came from all sections of the community. There were aristocratic ladies like Lady Frances Balfour, daughter of the 8th Duke of Argyll and wife of Colonel Eustace Balfour. Married in 1879 and the mother of two sons and three daughters, she spent much of her time addressing meetings on the subject of women's enfranchisement and she wrote biographies of Lady Victoria Campbell, an early supporter of the movement, and of Dr Elsie Inglis, one of its leading protagonists. Equally enthusiastic was Ishbel, Marchioness of Aberdeen and Temair. She served on a large number of committees relating to women and their welfare, being President of the International Council of Women from 1893 until 1899, then again from 1904 to 1936.[38]

Professional women obviously had a vested interest in improved conditions, and, as well as including doctors and teachers in its ranks, the suffrage movement recruited women artists and actresses.[39] Working-class women were also quick to give their support. Many were involved initially because of the Labour Party's interest, and for a time the English suffragettes had relied heavily upon them. Later, the Pankhursts severed their direct connections with the Labour movement because they feared that they were alienating other sections of the public, but working-class women continued to do all they could to help. When Flora Drummond led a working women's deputation which went to see Lloyd George in January 1913, a group of fisherwomen from Newhaven travelled down to London in traditional dress to take part.[40]

Gatherings in London were becoming even larger and more vocal. Meanwhile, local meetings on a more modest scale continued throughout Scotland. In the week beginning 21 October 1912, for instance, WSPU meetings took place in Old

Cumnock, Ayrshire, in the Unionist Hall, Prestwick, the Memorial Hall, Airdrie, at 61 Nethergate, Dundee, in the Temperance Hall, Mauchline, and in the Wilson Hall, Catrine. At the five Ayrshire meetings, the speaker was Mr S. D. Shallard, for of course there were men who supported the suffragettes too.

Many of the WSPU meetings took a traditionally feminine form, which at first sight seems a little hard to reconcile with the radical views of the participants. Their activities were often in the idiom of the long-established tea-parties and fancy-work sales so popular with their mothers and grandmothers. In Aberdeen in November 1912, Miss Mackay raised £3 2s. 6d. by holding a sweet-making class. At about the same time, Miss Edith Hudson and the indefatigable Mr Shallard were speaking at 'At Homes' in Edinburgh. In February 1913 the Aberdeen WSPU was planning a whist drive, Dundee organized a jumble sale and Edinburgh had cake and candy stalls. These indoor activities apart, suffragettes were to be found on the streets handing out leaflets and selling copies of *The Suffragette*. Edited by Christabel Pankhurst, this newspaper gave all the latest details of WSPU activities, as well as including advertisements for the newest and most elegant clothes, not to mention notices about electrolysis and training courses for beauticians.[41]

Just as active at this period were the members of the Women's National Anti-Suffrage League. In January 1909, the Edinburgh branch of this society held its first meeting, with a large attendance. Mrs Arthur Somerville addressed the assembled ladies, declaring that the extension of the suffrage to women was not in the interests of the nation. After all, government was based upon physical force, she said, and so women were unsuited by their very natures to playing any part in public life of this kind. Certainly a woman of property was liable for rates and taxes, but what she should look for in return was not the vote but the protection of men.

The anti-suffragettes saw nothing wrong with this somewhat outmoded view, and branches of their society were established throughout Scotland. Those who supported it were mainly drawn from the aristocracy and middle class, but to all outward appearances they were indistinguishable from their opponents, the suffragettes. Lady Griselda Cheape, president of the St Andrews branch and 'an untiring supporter of the anti-Suffrage cause' was active in many charitable works, particularly involving women and children. Still a young woman with a family of three of her own, she had actually trained as a children's nurse. Similarly the Duchess of Montrose, president of the Scottish Women's National Anti-Suffrage League, was also president of the Scottish Council of the Red Cross, interested herself in hospitals and nursing as well as in needlework, and held an honorary LL.D. from Glasgow University. Either of these women might equally well have been found in the opposite camp. Like the suffragettes, they held rallies and printed their own journal, *The Anti-Suffragette*, which appeared each month, but in their defensive position they lacked the impetus which drove on those determined to change the place of women in society.[42]

As time passed, the Pankhursts and their friends became increasingly impatient. By 1909 the government was still refusing to sponsor a new franchise bill on the grounds that it would split the cabinet, and with each successive disappointment the suffragettes grew more desperate. Petitions, processions, pleas and demonstrations had all failed. Although more and more women were demanding the vote, the government would not listen and, to make matters worse, their refusal was based not upon ideological reasons but simply on political factors. A female suffrage bill would interfere with legislation already in hand and might lose each political party some of the support it valued so much. In the summer of 1909, the Pankhursts decided that only militant action would bring them the publicity they needed. On 29 June, Mrs Pankhurst attended a march to Parliament, deliberately assaulted a policeman and had herself arrested. The militant campaign had begun. In the weeks which followed, more and more hitherto respectable, law-abiding women went out deliberately seeking arrest, declined to pay fines and went to prison. Once there, they refused food and embarked on hunger strikes which brought them much suffering, not least through forcible feeding, but which also aroused the public sympathy they desired.[43]

Extreme tactics were taken up by Scottish suffragettes in the autumn of 1912, after yet another franchise bill had been refused. On 30 October, Dundee policemen found a window in the savings bank broken, the hole covered by a sheet of paper bearing the words 'Votes for Women'. Later, Fanny Parker and Alison Gibb were seen breaking the windows of the town's Inland Revenue Office. When arrested, they refused to pay their fines and were sent to prison, where they declined all food until their release three days later. Also on 30 October, two windows were broken in Aberdeen's

Central Telephone Office and a suffragette message was left nearby.[44]

In December, pillar boxes were being attacked. Pieces of metal filled with sticky black liquid were pushed into the Edinburgh boxes to damage the mail and similar attacks on the post continued in the weeks which followed. When Mr Asquith, the prime minister, came to Scotland in January 1913 to receive the freedom of Dundee, the suffragettes turned out in force. On 29 January he visited the small seaside town of Leven in Fife and when he addressed a meeting there the suffragettes held their own gathering outside. Miss Margaret Morrison threw pepper in the face of a policeman, broke twelve panes of glass in the police office, then threw water over the sergeant in charge. Committed to prison in Dundee, she too went on hunger strike.[45]

Further minor incidents took place that spring. Telegraph wires were cut, a glass showcase in the Royal Scottish Museum in Edinburgh was broken, apparently by a suffragette throwing a piece of cable from a balcony, more mail was set alight and suffragettes tried to damage the Scott Monument. Leading English suffragettes came north to speak, and on 13 March 1913 Mrs Pankhurst herself addressed a crowded meeting in Glasgow. The local papers were full of letters denouncing this 'league of insane criminals', but the suffragettes were only spurred on by the increased publicity.[46]

A fortnight later, two elderly sisters, both retired missionaries, were arrested for trying to set fire to the new grandstand at Kelso Racecourse and the militant campaign took on a more serious aspect. The targets now were unoccupied buildings with a high insurance value, the notion being that the insurance companies, if sufficiently hard pressed, would bring their influence to bear on the government in favour of female suffrage. The same night as the Kelso incident, a three-storey club stand on Ayr Racecourse was practically burned to the ground, causing damage of some £2000. Suffragette literature was found on the scene. On 3 May, Ashley Road School in Aberdeen was set alight and a week after that, Farington Hall, a handsome mansion in Dundee, was burned to the ground. A bomb exploded in Blackford Observatory, Edinburgh, on 21 May and Stair Park House, Tranent, was destroyed by fire on 11 June. Later that month the Gatty Marine Laboratory in St Andrews was severely damaged by fire, and a week after that Leuchars Station, a few miles away, was burned down. At Lossiemouth that summer, two suffragettes hid on the golf course and assaulted the prime minister. There were further fires at Fettes College and Morelands House, Edinburgh. In December a spectacular blaze at Kelly House, Wemyss Bay, did £30,000 worth of damage and in February 1914 the medieval church of Whitekirk was set alight.[47]

Mrs Pankhurst received a rapturous welcome when she visited Glasgow again the following spring. She had been released from prison under the notorious 'Cat and Mouse' Act, which freed hunger strikers for the time being but made them liable for re-arrest once they had recovered their strength. Her supporters smuggled her into St Andrews Hall in a laundry basket but almost as soon as she began to speak, police rushed the platform, rioting broke out and Mrs Pankhurst was arrested once more. Further outbreaks of fire-raising followed in the wake of her imprisonment, and Robertsland House in Ayrshire was among those buildings damaged by fire that March. There were violent demonstrations in London, with more arrests and more hunger strikes, and when George V and Queen Mary visited Scotland in July, they were confronted on several occasions by women protesting vociferously. In Perth, a large placard invited the King to 'Visit Your Majesty's Torture Chamber in Perth Prison' and one woman even jumped on to the bonnet of the royal car and tried to smash the window.[48]

So far, the suffragettes had alarmed and enraged their opponents, but they had met with no real success. Rather than gaining support for the WSPU, militancy had alienated many of its most intelligent members, nor had the repeated hunger strikes had the desired effect. Whatever its progress, however, the militant campaign was now about to be overtaken by events. On 4 August 1914, war was declared and the Pankhursts immediately suspended their violent demonstrations, turning all efforts instead to a patriotic defence of their country. Instead of travelling the country addressing meetings about women's suffrage, Mrs Pankhurst, Flora Drummond and the others now spoke solely on behalf of the war effort and their paper, *The Suffragette*, printed nothing but anti-German propaganda.

Some suffragettes openly resented the abandoning of their cause, but in fact the First World War was so to alter society that when it ended their battle had been won. With men going off to the army, women were suddenly called upon to undertake all manner of work hitherto reserved for their masculine contemporaries.

They were now to be found stoking furnaces, rolling out barrels at breweries, acting as bank clerks and bus conductors, and, most notably, working in large numbers in munitions factories. No-one could withhold admiration for their devoted efforts, and particularly esteemed were those women who became directly involved in the conflict as doctors and nurses.[49] The founder of the Scottish Women's Suffrage Federation, for example, was Dr Elsie Inglis, who established the Scottish Women's Hospitals in France and Serbia.[50]

Elsie Inglis and hundreds of ordinary women had given triumphant proof of their capabilities as well as of their patriotism. It was evident that they could be denied the vote no longer, and the political situation had altered sufficiently for all practical difficulties to be swept aside. There was now a coalition government, so the old fears of the different political parties that an extension of the franchise would play into the hands of their opponents no longer held good. Lloyd George had replaced Mr Asquith as Prime Minister, and in 1917 a Conference on Electoral Reform recommended that certain women be given the vote. On 6 February 1918 the Representation of the People Act finally received the Royal Assent, and from then onwards women over the age of thirty who were householders, wives of householders, occupiers of property worth at least £5 a year, or university graduates, were included in the electorate. A few days later, the elated Edinburgh Women Citizens' Association placed an advertisement in the local evening newspaper, announcing joyfully, 'Thousands of Women in Edinburgh have the Vote! Come to the Oddfellows' Hall, Forrest Road, on Monday 17th at 8 p.m. to hear George Simpson, Burgh Assessor, Leith, speak on Qualifications of Women Voters'. The reason why the vote had been restricted to women over thirty was that, unless this had been done, there would have been an immediate feminine majority in the electorate. As Mrs Leslie Mackenzie pointed out to the Edinburgh Women Citizens' Association a few months later, already the total of 76,730 women voters in the city fell short of the masculine total by only just under 6000.[51]

Ten years later, on 3 June 1928, a second Representation of the People Act made women eligible to vote on exactly the same terms as men. Inspired and delighted by their success, they anticipated a new and rewarding future. Men and women alike believed that in their victory against the Germans, they had won the war to end all wars and could now enjoy an undisturbed prospect of peace. If the writings of both the suffragettes and the brave women who had risked their lives in the war seem to us today to have a curiously innocent, naïve quality, their enthusiasm and their optimism were undeniable. 'We cherish an unswerving hope, the possibility of a new land and a new world,' one speaker had said at the celebrations after the first Representation of the People Act, and women now looked forward to an era when they would be educated to the highest standards and would enter any employment they chose, unfettered by the constraints imposed by masculine prejudice. They would become doctors, engineers and lawyers. They would not only vote in elections but would sit in Parliament, and the laws of the country would swiftly be changed to allow them to enjoy true equality with the opposite sex, for the first time in history.[52]

CHAPTER FOURTEEN

The Fruits of Freedom

TRIUMPHANT IN their new-found freedom to participate in public life, large numbers of women flocked to Edinburgh City Chambers on the evening of 9 May 1918. Their purpose was to inaugurate a new society named the Edinburgh Women Citizens' Association, and as the secretary noted in her minutes, 'The hall was filled to overflowing with women who showed keen interest and great enthusiasm in the new movement.' The audience listened intently as the aims were read out. The Association would foster a sense of citizenship in women, encourage the study of civic, economic, industrial and social questions and secure 'an adequate representation of women in local administration and in the affairs of the nation and the Empire'. The Lord Provost struck a sobering note when he warned his listeners against 'too little reason and judgement in their efforts to help solve the many new and grave problems arising because of the war', but even that did not dampen the spirits of the audience. In the years which followed, the Association discussed everything from women in industry to a clean milk supply and from public morals to the price of gas. The mood of interest in all female activities was exemplified in an entertainment produced with the Association's help at the Synod Hall in 1926. Called 'A Masque of Scottish Women' and intended to raise funds for the city's Outlook Tower, this took the form of a succession of scenes involving women famous in Scotland's history. A dignified St Margaret and Mary, Queen of Scots, were followed by lively representations of Jenny Geddes and Flora Macdonald, and the whole evening culminated in a tribute to the work of the Scottish Women's Hospitals.[1]

As well as a great sense of pride in the deeds of heroines of the past, there was a happy confidence in the development of women's role in the future, and it was with satisfaction that women throughout the country were to watch further improvements in their status and conditions follow upon the initial legislation. Indeed, by the late twentieth century, many of their aims have been achieved. In marriage choice, for instance, there is now far greater freedom than ever before, not only because it is an accepted fact that the selection of a partner lies with the girl herself, but because the less formal arrangements for the wedding give her the opportunity of organizing it with no reference to her parents should she prefer to do it that way. The only new restriction is that since the Age of Marriage Act of 1929 no-one may marry before the age of sixteen. Until that date, the old canon law ruling that girls could marry at twelve and boys at fourteen still held good.[2]

From being the normal preliminary to a wedding, the marriage contract is now virtually unknown. The Married Women's Property (Scotland) Act of 1881 had made contracts no longer necessary in most respects by ensuring adequate provision for wives, and there were other reasons too for the disappearance of this traditional legal document. Inflation meant that the kind of fixed annuity settled on a bride rapidly lost its real value as the years went by, so that by the time she was actually widowed what had seemed like a generous income had shrunk to a mere pittance. The growth of the welfare state and the development of life insurance schemes meant that widows would find financial support from different sources. Occasionally, titled or very wealthy families do go to the trouble of having a marriage contract drawn up, but in 1962 only twelve were registered in the Books of Council and Session and several of those actually dated from before 1920.[3]

The arrangements for the wedding itself were much altered by the Marriage (Scotland) Act of 1977 which abolished banns, and ended the need for sheriffs' special licences if the ceremony was to take place with unusual haste. Instead, anyone intending to marry must give notice to the registrar of the district where the wedding will be held, submitting to him the relevant documents – birth certificate, certificate of death of a previous partner or decreet of divorce. If no objections are lodged within the following fourteen days, the marriage schedule is issued, enabling the minister or registrar to conduct the marriage. In an emergency, the schedule can be issued before the fortnight has passed, this procedure replacing the previous sheriff's licence.[4]

Civil marriage has been legal in Scotland since the Marriage (Scotland) Act of 1939 and has become increasingly popular. In 1976 there were no fewer than 14,100 civil ceremonies out of a total of 37,543. Usually, these take place in the registrar's office but since 1977 it has been possible to have a civil marriage elsewhere if there is good reason, such as the serious illness of one of the couple. Religious marriages can now be conducted by the minister of any approved religious body and can take place at any hour of the day or night, in church or elsewhere. Despite the legal abolition of banns, many people still like to have them called at the services preceding the wedding day. All marriages, religious or civil, have to be registered in the district where they took place.[5]

In view of the past history of irregular marriages in Scotland, it is interesting to note that in 1976 none at all was registered. Indeed, the old forms of marriage by declaration *de praesenti* and by promise *subsequente copula* finally became invalid from 1 July 1940, unless they had been entered into before that date. Only cohabitation with habit and repute is still valid in 1981, and occasionally such cases feature in the newspapers when they come before the Court of Session. The couple themselves or their children, even after the parents' death, can bring an action to have the marriage declared valid. It is cheaper for the man and woman concerned to marry in the usual way, so most of the actions heard are where an inheritance or a question of legitimacy is involved.[6]

The legislation of the past hundred years has also altered considerably the position of the married woman, often changing laws which have been in operation at least since the seventeenth century and sometimes since the Middle Ages. Traditionally, the husband has been the head of the household, exercising a degree of personal control over his wife, theoretically if not always in reality. Now, husband and wife are partners, each with an obligation to behave reasonably towards the other. A number of duties do, of course, remain, although at the time of writing these are under review and liable to alteration in the near future. When they marry the couple must live together and it is still the husband who decides where the home shall be. However, he must make this decision with due regard to his wife's feelings, and he has no say over where she chooses to stay during his absence, even on a business trip. Many husbands and wives own their home jointly, and only if he is sole owner may the husband put her out. By the same token, she can eject him only if she is the sole owner. The husband has a duty to provide the basic necessities of life for her – food, clothing and shelter – suitable to their status in life. He must also support their children, and only under very unusual circumstances does this alter. If he becomes incapable of earning his living and she has enough income, then she may become liable to support him and the family but not otherwise, regardless of how wealthy she may be.

When the wife goes out and purchases small household goods, she is still regarded as acting not for herself but as his agent. In all larger transactions, though, she is taken to be purchasing on her own behalf. Any savings she makes from housekeeping money he gives her will belong to both of them equally, but if it is she who earns the housekeeping and gives it to him, then any savings her prudent husband makes are legally hers. Gifts made between husband and wife are now legal, but they are taken to be irrevocable so that a man cannot defraud his creditors by transferring his goods to his wife then taking them back again.

If the married woman's economic position has greatly improved, so too has that of the widow. The Succession (Scotland) Act of 1964 as amended states that, from 1 August 1981, when a husband dies intestate his wife is entitled to their house, up to the value of £50,000, along with certain furniture and household goods up to the value of £10,000, provided that it was her normal home when he died. If there are no children of the marriage, she is also the recipient of the first £25,000 of the estate as well as half of the residue of the moveable estate. The other half share goes to the husband's own relatives. If there are children, the wife has the first £15,000 with a third of the residue of the moveable estate, the rest going to the sons and daughters. These rights are reciprocal, so that a wealthy woman's goods will be divided up in the same way when she dies leaving a husband.[7]

These alterations have come about as part of the law's gradual adjustment to the conditions of an industrialized society and in other ways too women have found their situation changing dramatically. The First World War revolutionized the manner in which middle and upper-class homes were run, sweeping away the long-established system of domestic servants. Town houses built a century ago often still have their 'maid's bedroom' and the bars on the kitchen windows to keep the servants in, but the maids themselves have long since disappeared. Instead, labour-saving devices have taken their place, freeing women from much of the heavy work of the household and making it possible for working

[296]

wives to condense into evenings and weekends much of the cooking and washing for the family. Moreover, men have come to share increasingly in the household chores. Scotland probably lagged behind England in this respect until recently, but the latest generation of husbands usually expect to take their share of work in the home, thereby blurring still further the old division between the responsibilities of husband and wife.

Even more significantly, women have finally been able to shed the burden of inevitable and perpetual childbearing. It is difficult to overestimate the benefits conferred upon women by medical improvements and the development of birth control. Letters written in the 1920s to its great pioneer, Dr Marie Stopes, reveal a harrowing picture of female ignorance and suffering, with women in poor circumstances completely at a loss as to how to avoid the pregnancies which brought them both economic deprivation and severe physical hardship. Even at that relatively late date doctors might advise a woman that a further pregnancy would kill her, yet refuse to give her any information at all about what preventative measures to take. Maternal deaths and abortions with fatal consequences were the all too frequent result.[8]

Many of the letters written to Dr Stopes came from the large English towns, but Scotswomen were equally anxious for assistance. When the American advocate of birth control, Margaret Sanger, spoke publicly in Glasgow in 1920 she attracted a large audience, and about the same time many of the women's socialist organizations began to demand free birth control. Fearing to alienate their Roman Catholic supporters, male members of parliament refused to lend them any assistance, but after 1930 it did become legal to pass on information about contraceptive methods and from that time onwards these became increasingly popular, especially after the development of the oral contraceptive. Criticism of birth control continues to come on religious and moral grounds, but in an age when the rate of child mortality has happily been reduced to very small proportions, the notion of most mothers raising ten or twelve children is economically unthinkable.[9]

For those women who have failed to take the necessary precautions, the Abortion Act of 1967 has made it legal in certain circumstances to have a pregnancy terminated. From April 1968 onwards, a woman could seek an abortion in a National Health Service hospital or other approved place on the grounds principally that there was a serious risk to her own health or a real danger that her child would be born severely handicapped. Again, there has been a good deal of opposition to this act on religious and moral grounds, but many women have been eager to take advantage of its provisions and in Scotland in 1978 there were seven abortions for every 1000 women aged between fifteen and forty-five. The Act has meant that few women are now likely to die from back street operations and indeed there were no registered deaths at all from abortion in Scotland in 1975 and 1976 and only one in 1977 and 1978.[10]

As for the majority of women who do bear children, more and more are choosing to have their families while they are still in their twenties. The country's birthrate has shown a progressive decline since 1964, from 20 live births per thousand of the population that year to 13.1 in 1975. The most noticeable reductions have been in women of thirty-five and over, and in those who already had two children. From being an obligation which preoccupied them from marriage until their mid-forties, childbearing has become an event which many women experience no more than twice in their lives. Moreover, most mothers expect to have their youngest child at school by the time they themselves are thirty-five.[11]

This new freedom apart, childbirth itself is no longer the dreaded encounter with death which it once was. Anaesthesia has developed considerably since the days of Sir James Young Simpson. Ether came back into fashion at the end of the nineteenth century when it was decided that it was safer than chloroform. After the First World War intravenous anaesthesia was introduced, and after the Second World War spinal analgesia was developed, while the use of a mixture of nitrous oxide and air has remained popular. As in the rest of Britain and in the United States, there is an increasing tendency to recourse to delivery by Caesarean section, in spite of the slightly higher risk of death from haemorrhage or the effects of anaesthesia.

Better surgical techniques, the introduction of drugs such as penicillin and the availability of blood transfusions have saved the lives of many hundreds of women. In the early years of the twentieth century there was a maternal mortality rate of from 4% to 7%, but by the 1970s this figure had fallen to 17.5 deaths per 100,000 live births. Presumably there could be a further improvement still, for Scotland ranks eleventh in the table of world statistics. Denmark has the best record, with an average maternal death rate of 4.6 per 100,000 live births, while the figure for

England and Wales is 13.8. Scotland's poorer performance is linked to her generally worse health record.[12]

The long battle against puerperal fever has also been virtually won. Even as late as 1966 there were 131 cases in Scotland, but since 1974 the annual figure has been below 12 and no women have died from the disease. Equally striking has been the reduction in infant mortality, with still births falling from 20.8 per 1000 in 1961 to 11.1 in 1975. Many of these improvements are due to the fact that almost all confinements now take place in hospital, with the proper medical facilities available. Indeed, in 1975, 99.1% of confinements were in hospital. There are enthusiastic supporters of home birth, so it remains to be seen if they, and perhaps more importantly, economic difficulties within the Health Service, lead to a decrease again in this figure. At any rate, recovery from childbirth is now much more rapid than it once was. Even in the 1930s the mother was kept in bed for a fortnight after the delivery but now the average stay of mothers in hospital is as low as just under six days for the third or so of British women in general practitioner beds, and just under eight days for the two-thirds in specialist beds.[13]

If the treatment of women in childbed has changed considerably, so too have methods of child-rearing. The practice of employing wet-nurses persisted until the beginning of the twentieth century and finally ceased only when artificial foods based on cows' milk became readily available during the Second World War. The Welfare Food Scheme of 1940 and the production of cheap, subsidized National Dried Milk made bottle feeding a practical alternative to the breast, and more and more women adopted this method because of its comparative convenience. They have not done so without opposition, for the medical profession have been anxious to point out that human milk is a much more suitable food for babies and gives invaluable protection against infection.

In 1972 the Committee on Medical Aspects of Food Policy in Britain set up a Working Party to consider the question, and in the resulting survey they found that although 51% of the 2103 mothers interviewed did breast-feed, many persevered for only a relatively short time. The reasons they gave for desisting make fascinating reading, so akin are they to the reasons given by the seventeenth-century mothers for employing a wet-nurse. More than half said that they did not have sufficient milk. About a fifth suffered from painful breasts, while over a tenth complained that their baby was either too sleepy to suck or could not master the technique. In a few cases the illness of mother or baby prevented breast-feeding from taking place. Whatever the reasons given, a third of the women in the sample stopped in the first fortnight, over half had stopped by six weeks and only a quarter were still nursing at four months. As for weaning, the age is very much younger than it was in the past. Most of the babies in the survey were starting solids at six to eight weeks, long before the recommended age of four months. This is a striking change from the seventeenth-century practice of breast-feeding the child until he was over a year old.[14]

A final significant point is that none of the women in the survey who had stopped breast-feeding by six weeks said that they had done so because they wanted to return to work, and only 5% of those who persevered for from four to six months mentioned this as being the cause of their finally giving up nursing. In the future, this state of affairs may well alter in view of the fact that recent legislation has made it possible for women to go back to the same job after having a baby. Under normal circumstances, no woman can be dismissed because she is pregnant. She is allowed to take reasonable time off during her pregnancy to visit her doctor, midwife or ante-natal clinic, provided she shows her employer her appointment card and a certificate stating that she is expecting a child. If various conditions are satisfied she can claim maternity pay when she does stop work, and she has a right to return to her old job within twenty-nine weeks of her baby's birth, provided she has been in that employment for two years and has given notice in writing on three different occasions to the effect that she does intend to return.[15]

Advances in medicine and innovatory legislation have combined to free women from any of the previous disadvantages of motherhood, so that a twentieth-century girl's view of matrimony is rather different from that of any of her predecessors. She is also aware that her union is much less likely to last for the rest of her life. By the 1980s one in four Scottish marriages ends in divorce – not because people are more fickle in their affections but because divorce is much more readily available. The Divorce (Scotland) Act of 1938 at long last introduced new grounds for suing, in addition to the customary adultery and desertion. That Act added incurable insanity, sodomy, bestiality and, most importantly, cruelty, to the list. The insertion of cruelty was of immeasurable benefit, and naturally resulted in a rise in the number of people seeking an end to their marriage. In 1900 a total of 142 people sued for divorce in Scotland: by 1950 the number was 1957 and by 1975 it had reached 8677.[16] These men and women continued to come from all classes of society. The vast majority of Scottish divorces, at least since the seventeenth-century onwards, had been sought by people from what the nineteenth-century Commission on Marriage called 'humble circumstances' and the Legal Aid (Scotland) Act of 1949 helped to maintain this breadth of range.

A further rise was experienced after the Divorce (Scotland) Act of 1976 made it simpler still to terminate a marriage. From that date onwards there has been only one ground for divorce, the irretrievable breakdown of marriage. Adultery, desertion, cruelty and abnormal behaviour are all comprised within that term and a divorce can now be granted to a couple living apart even if the person who would at one time have been termed 'the innocent party' does not wish it to take place. With consent, the divorce can be granted after two years 'separation'; without consent, five years have to elapse.[17] A deserting wife can eventually gain her freedom even if her husband wishes the marriage to continue. This might seem a relatively unlikely situation, but it is instructive to note that Scottish wives in the late twentieth century are much more likely to raise divorce proceedings than their husbands are. In 1951 there were 1037 actions at the instigation of wives and 920 by husbands. By 1966 almost twice as many women as men were suing and by 1978, 6405 women sought a divorce, compared with 2377 men. This is not to say that all these women were deserting wives. In the 1960s the most frequent reason for divorce was adultery, but after that more actions were raised because of cruelty, a fact which would suggest that wives are more often the victims in marital discord than men are. At any rate, many of the women do not risk matrimony a second time: in 1978 some 58.6% of divorced husbands remarried, but only 17.8% of the divorced wives did so.[18]

Not only have the grounds for divorce changed, but its consequences have also been altered by law. The Succession (Scotland) Act of 1964 abolished the old rule that an innocent wife received on divorce a half of her husband's moveable estate if she had no children, a third if she did. Instead, the courts now make a discretionary award to the wife, either in the form of an allowance or a capital sum, or even both. The difficulty remains in enforcing payment.[19]

In a variety of ways, the woman in late twentieth-century Scotland therefore enjoys much greater freedom than ever before. She has increased economic independence as well as a lessening of domestic responsibilities, and she is also better educated than any of her female forebears. Ever since the Education Act of 1872 most girls have attended mixed secondary schools. Indeed, by 1914 no fewer than 186 of the 195 secondary schools in Scotland were mixed, just two taking boys only and seven, all Roman Catholic, taking girls only. The separation of the sexes was more common in private and grant-aided schools, possibly in part at least because they modelled their curricula on the English pattern, and it was in these establishments that at least some concentration on the lady-like accomplishments lingered on.[20]

There was never any real demand in Scotland for the extension of single-sex education. The subject was raised briefly in the 1930s, not so much out of concern for the pupils but because women teachers had so few opportunities for promotion. The principals of secondary schools were almost invariably men, and so the lady teachers felt that their only chance for advancement would be in a school where all the staff were female. With this in mind, the Women's Educational Union were in 1930–1 urging that separate establishments in the charge of female headmistresses should be brought into being for the education of girls. The arguments put forward by the lady teachers in support of their demands had an old-fashioned ring to them. They said that after the age of twelve, an adolescent girl needed special care. This was vital 'for her future development as a citizen and as a mother'. She required opportunities to study child welfare, housewifery and needlework, subjects which could only be accorded their proper status if taught in schools exclusively for girls. The omission of these subjects, it was thought, 'has warped the nature of many of our young women of the rising generation and is the cause of much of the discontent and the badly-governed homes of today'.

In response to the Association's pleas, the Scottish Education Board set up an advisory committee to hear the views of individuals. These proved to be entirely predictable. The heads of the single-sex fee-paying schools considered that their own type of institution was best, while those in charge of mixed establishments were firm believers in co-education. A girls' school, said one lady headmistress, has 'an indescribable atmosphere – *a finer feeling* which has a most valuable influence upon the pupils', while the headmaster of a large Edinburgh boys' college agreed that separation was desirable since 'The outlook of boys and girls is essentially different. The boys' job in the world is to get on with things, that of the girls is to conduct the home and influence the family . . .' In contrast, the headmaster of a mixed, non-fee-paying school in Leith professed a strong preference for co-education. This, he believed, was both healthy and socially advantageous, a view with which a colleague in Lanarkshire agreed. Even if finance permitted the creation of single-sex schools, he would still prefer co-education, he said.[21] In the end, the committee decided diplomatically that it would be unwise to upset the traditional system, and so co-educational state schools continued, with a relatively small number of private schools existing alongside them. The female teachers for their part were to some extent satisfied by the creation of the post of lady adviser in secondary schools, the holder acting more or less as a headmistress of the girls although the headmaster remained in charge of the school.

The age-old debate about what girls should learn continued to exercise the minds of teachers and parents alike. Obviously, education provides a training for the future, but were girls to be taught the housewifely skills which would prepare them for marriage, or should they acquire qualifications which would equip them for what would in all probability be a short-lived career outside the home? The nineteenth-century opponents of female education had done their work well, and many people still had reservations about women's mental capacity. In 1921 the Board of Education Consultative Committee on Secondary School Curricula decided to examine the comparative educability of boys and girls. Noting that there were now 252 state secondary schools, all but eight of which were mixed, they found that in many the classes were subdivided according to sex. Moreover, they were able to identify two main attitudes prevalent among both teachers and educationalists. There were those who believed that sex differences were mainly the result of conditioning, and there were those who were convinced that the differences were innate and unalterable.

This controversy has raged ever since. The 1921 committee hesitated to come down firmly in favour of either point of view, but its members did feel that there were significant differences in rate of growth between adolescent boys and girls. More importantly, English and American psychologists had been suggesting that, although there might be no difference in general intelligence, boys and girls did have special aptitudes. Girls were superior in languages and literature while boys excelled at mathematics. However, the committee were of the opinion that such innate sex differences were 'astonishingly small', and they concluded that what really gave boys the advantage were their superior masculine powers of concentration and their scope of thought.[22]

Since the committee's day, girls have gone a long way towards demonstrating their abilities, and they have certainly disproved once and for all the Victorian notion that women were incapable of serious study. To look at fairly recent figures, in 1962 girls were gaining as many Scottish Certificate of Education Highers passes in their fifth year as boys and they have done so ever since. Upon closer examination, certain differences in performance do come to notice. An analysis of the Scottish figures for the 1970s shows that half the boys sitting O Grade examinations sat physics but only 10% to 12% of the girls did so, and while 60% of the boys sat mathematics, only 44% of the girls did. This divergence is in no way peculiarly Scottish, for similar results have been found in England and Wales, and in the USA, although Scottish girls have studied slightly more chemistry and considerably more mathematics than their English counterparts have done in the past. Again, there is a difference in the number of passes acquired at Higher level. In 1977–8 a total of 4435 girls and 3793 boys passed one or two subjects in the Scottish Certificate of Education Higher examinations. A further 4419 girls and 4010 boys gained passes in three or four subjects, while 3378 girls but 4264 boys achieved five or more passes. The figures for the previous decade and those for O Grade examinations show a similar pattern.[23]

Again, these findings are repeated in girls' performance at university. Sophia Jex-Blake and the other early pioneers who fought for the universities to open their doors to women would have been depressed and disappointed to have known that, more than a hundred years later, only a little more than one third of all university students are women. At first the advance had been rapid. By 1921, 27.7% of the students at Scottish universities were women, the actual number being 3162. Moreover, these women were easily proving their suitability, graduating with first-class honours, gaining higher degrees and taking prizes and medals in subjects ranging from mathematics to mercantile law.[24]

Throughout the 1920s, the number of women students rose steadily to 36%, but with the economic difficulties of the 1930s, it dropped back again to 25%. A similar level prevailed immediately after World War II and only in the late 1950s was there a slight increase. Not until 1964–5 was a figure of 30% achieved once more and, despite a gradual and continuing rise, women formed only 38% of the university population in 1977–8.[25] Fewer women than might have been anticipated have so far taken degrees, and those who have done so have tended to take ordinary rather than honours courses. In Scotland the tradition has been that the ordinary degree is a separate, general degree which students can choose to take from the very start of their university careers. This ordinary degree has been a popular qualification with those who intend to take up teaching, and it has consistently attracted female students. In 1977–8, while two-thirds of the men studying Arts and Pure Science took honours, only a third of the women did so. Indeed, even among those women who initially intended to take honours, far more were liable to finish with the ordinary degree instead.

It seems unlikely that women suddenly fall back dramatically in ability at the age of eighteen: after all, in the 1970s the women entering the arts and pure science faculties had, if anything, slightly better Scottish Certificate of Education qualifications than the men, and some of them went on to do outstandingly well. It is more probable that cultural factors are at work, and this would seem to be borne out by the distribution of women in the various classes. In the 1970s women were still concentrated in the arts and social sciences, with very few indeed studying engineering, dentistry, architecture, business or economics.[26]

Of course, it could be argued that this is due to some inherent difference in mental skills, but this seems unlikely. Certainly modern studies do suggest that girls have the superior linguistic abilities observed by the psychologists in the 1920s, while boys do have greater spatial skills. Evidence about differences in the structure of the male and female brains is difficult to come by, although physiologists do believe that sex differences in cognitive ability exist. However, more and more writers are now arguing that these differences are not so much physical as the result of conditioning. Psychologists and sociologists in the 1970s have returned with energy to this debate, and much attention is now given to the alleged effects of sex-role stereotyping. It is pointed out that if girls are brought up to believe that women perform poorly in certain subjects, they will not only make a deliberate effort to avoid them, but they will insensibly do less well in them if they do have to study them. To take a notable instance, society has long regarded science as being a particularly masculine subject. Most girls accept this judgement and profess a distaste for it. At the same time, those who do study it find it more difficult because of their less favourable attitudes and because they are in any event more easily discouraged than boys.[27]

The evidence of school and university results is strongly suggestive that cultural expectations do play a significant part in girls' educational performance, and an important element in this must be their future aspirations. A girl's intended career obviously affects her choice of school or university course, and conversely her career is largely determined by the education she has received. Many women have inherited traditional ways of thought and still did not have in mind a lifelong and satisfying career in the outside world when, as girls, they had to consider their future. Because marriage remained their principal goal, they and their parents regarded higher education as an unnecessary luxury. In any case, many girls had no desire to give up evenings to study when their contemporaries were already out enjoying themselves and forming relationships with possible marriage partners. The schoolgirl was, in fact, making a choice between marriage and a serious career. For many years this was a choice which had to be made, because in the 1930s, for example, when a woman married she was compelled to retire from most occupations. Others did have ambitions outside the home, but for many these lay in the traditional fields of feminine activity, such as teaching. In the Scottish Colleges of Education the students have been predominantly female: in 1976 the proportion of women was very high, 4249 of the 4661 students being female.[28]

Not all women, of course, chose marriage, and a high proportion of the early women pioneers in the professions remained single. Some did so deliberately, determined not to distract themselves from their chosen course, others failed to meet a partner who could be their intellectual equal, and a number had been unfortunate enough to lose fiancés and friends in the First World War.[29] The outlook of these early career women can be conveniently examined by looking at those who feature in the pages of *Who Was Who 1961–70*. This volume of some 1242 pages with over 7000 entries gives brief biographies of the eminent men and women who died during those years, and many of whom belonged to the generation who were being educated at the beginning of the century.

Thirty-eight of those who appear were eminent Scotswomen. Of these, more than a third found fame in the arts: seven were authors, three were artists, two were sculptors, one was an actress and one was an opera singer. A further third took up the traditional careers of teaching and medicine in one form or another. Five became high-ranking nurses, three worked as university lecturers, three as headmistresses and two were eminent doctors, one a dermatologist and the other a professor of gynaecology and midwifery. Five of the women in the sample were members of parliament and four were aristocratic ladies whose social standing had given them the opportunity to involve themselves in public life. Finally, one women had risen to a high position in the Women's Royal Naval Service and another had become a celebrated botanist.

Obviously this sample is very small, and the selection of people included in *Who Was Who* is not entirely objective, but the careers of these women do draw attention to certain attitudes which were prevalent at the time. Most noticeable is the fact that so many of the thirty-eight were employed in traditionally feminine areas: the nurses, the teachers, the writers and even the botanist. Certainly it was new to have women members of parliament, but in a way they and the aristocratic ladies in public life were carrying on the old tradition of those women of earlier centuries who had looked after the tenants on the estates and done philanthropic work while at the same time making their influence felt indirectly in politics.

Not all the women included gave details of their background when their biographies were originally drawn up for *Who's Who*, but six of them (three of the authors and three of the public figures) came from titled families, and thirteen had professional fathers. Interestingly enough, only one actually followed her father into the same profession. The authors were not the daughters of authors, the doctors did not have medical men as fathers, the MPs were not the children of politicians, but Jean Forbes-Robertson the actress was the daughter of the famous actor Sir Johnston Forbes-Robertson and his actress wife.

Again, not all the women gave details of their education, but eight said they had gone to girls' schools and five mentioned that they had been educated privately: Dorothy M. Stuart the novelist announced that she had been taught at home, 'mainly by her mother'. The nurses and the artists had undertaken professional training, and the headmistresses, lecturers and doctors had of necessity gone to university. In fact, eleven of the thirty-eight women had been to university, and ten of them took up professional careers, the other marrying but becoming a writer.

The marriage and childbearing pattern of these early achievers is particularly interesting. Only 50% of the women in the sample married and only 31.5% had any children. Both these figures must have been well below the average for the population in general. Moreover, the element of deliberate choice becomes more obvious when the different occupational groups are separated. None of the five nurses married, nor did any of the three headmistresses or the three lecturers. One of the doctors, Professor Margaret Fairlie, did not marry and the other, Agnes Savill the dermatologist, married but was a widow for fifty-four years. As for the other occupational groups, all four aristocratic ladies in public life were married and so were all three artists. Five of the seven authors and three of the five MPs were likewise married.

Obviously it is easier to combine marriage with some careers than with others. The nurses and teachers felt a sense of dedication and involvement which took priority over everything else in their lives. The WREN could not have reached her senior position had she married, nor would either the Professor of Gynaecology or the opera singer. It was easier for the authors and the artists working at home to combine both sides of their lives, and all the committee ladies and some of the MPs devised a practical solution for their divided interests. Mrs Jean Mann the MP managed to have five children as well as a parliamentary career – but it was the unmarried Florence Horsburgh who rose to the rank of Minister of Education and became a life peer. The inference is clear. Women with a particular sense of vocation were foregoing marriage, and in areas with formal career structure it was usually only the single women who achieved eminence.[30]

It would be wrong to give the impression that these early career women sailed through life encountering neither masculine prejudice nor deliberate obstruction. Many women had a hard struggle to establish themselves and so in the 1970s new legislation was introduced with the specific aim of preventing discrimination. The Equal Pay Act of 1970 had the stated intention of preventing 'discrimination as regards terms and conditions of employment between men and women' and said that from 1975 onwards a woman employed on the same work as a man in the same organization would have to be paid at the same rate.[31]

Furthermore, Parliament in 1975 passed 'an act to render unlawful certain kinds of sex discrimination and discrimination on the ground of marriage and establish a Commission with the function of working towards the elimination of such discrimination and promoting equality of opportunity between men and women generally'. Known as the Sex Discrimination Act, this long and detailed piece of legislation makes it illegal for employers to treat a woman less favourably than a man because of her sex or less favourably than another woman because of differing marital status. This latter part is aimed at preventing employers from regarding married women as secondary staff whom it is not worth while training or considering for promotion. All women must have the same training facilities and opportunities of advancement as their masculine counterparts, and discrimination in the sphere of education and job advertisements is also made unlawful. As its full title indicates, the Act set up the Equal Opportunities Commission. This body has the general purpose of working towards the elimination of discrimination and making possible real equality of opportunity. It publishes an annual report and investigates particular problems, keeping under review the working of the Act itself and of the Equal Pay Act. Certain inequalities do remain, in the operation of the taxation system, but by 1981 these were under review.[32]

Such legislation is obviously an encouragement to women to take up work as a serious, long-term commitment, and, of course, it applies throughout Britain. In Scotland, however, there seems to be less awareness of the workings of the Commission. Only 8% of all equal pay cases and 7% of all sex discrimination cases in 1979 were heard there. This was not because Scotswomen were better placed as far as equality is concerned than were their sisters in the south;[33] far from it, for the traditional pattern of female employment still persists throughout Britain. In 1978, women formed 42% of the civilian labour force in Scotland, but they continued to be concentrated in low-paid work with few prospects. In Britain as a whole in 1979 more than half the female manual workers were employed in catering, cleaning, hairdressing or other personal services, while more than half the female non-manual workers were in clerical or related occupations.

To turn to Scotland once more, a New Earnings Survey made

in April 1979 found that 20% of the women doing full-time work in Scotland were earning less than £40 a week. Almost half of them had under £50 a week, and only 3.4% earned more than £100 a week. In this they actually did slightly better than women in Britain as a whole, but compared with men, their position was very unfavourable. A mere 6.1% of the men earned under £50, only 47.9% had less than £80 and 27.8% were above the £100 a week level. This disparity was evident in all categories of work, non-manual as well as manual. Professional women and those in related posts in education, welfare and health were paid on average £71 gross each week while their male colleagues made on average £105.2. Clerical women were receiving £49.9 a week whereas men earned £70.1, and women in manual work were paid an average of £50.2 compared with the men's £81.4.[34]

These figures do not mean that women were illegally being paid less for doing the same job as men, but that they were concentrated in the lower grades. In industry as a whole, the New Earnings Survey of 1979 found that only 12% of managers were women and even in a traditionally feminine field like teaching there are relatively few women in promoted posts. By July 1979 there were still no female Directors of Education in Scotland nor were there any in Deputy Director posts. Of over 430 head teachers of secondary schools, only thirteen were women and there were only thirty-three female deputy head teachers compared with more than 400 men.[35] Similarly, women professors have been rare indeed.

It might be tempting to suppose that this unhappy state of affairs is the result of direct masculine prejudice, but the reasons are much more complex. Feminist writers have tended to perceive in the employment situation a cynical exploitation of cheap, dispensable female labour by unscrupulous employers, but most have recognized that women's own attitudes have also played their part. For many thousands of women, matrimony and motherhood do remain the principal aims in life, and so employment outside the home is a secondary consideration. Many married women go back to work not because they have a burning compulsion to do the job for its own sake, but because they see the additional income as a means of raising their family's standard of living and, to a lesser extent, because they miss the feminine companionship they enjoyed before they resigned to have their children. Naturally enough, their first loyalty remains to the family and so they are ready to leave an employment which does not suit them and will not look for a promoted post which would mean travelling a long distance each day, undertaking demanding training courses, or putting in extra hours. Their emotional satisfaction derives from their domestic life, not from the pursuit of status. For these reasons, women remain at the lower end of the labour market and also seem reluctant to participate in trade union affairs. Certainly more women are now joining the unions, but the Scottish Trades Union Congress of 1976 was largely typical in that of 510 delegates attending its annual conference, only 35 were women.[36] Throughout the centuries, Scotswomen have been willing to demonstrate in public about economic, ecclesiastical and political issues, but they have done so over matters which affected them directly and personally. Their lack of participation in the Trades Union movement has stemmed not from the allegedly passive feminine nature, but from the fact that they have a differing set of priorities from their masculine colleagues.[37]

Women's own attitudes apart, the outlook by 1980 seemed depressing. In 1977, female gross average hourly earnings in Britain had reached a peak of 75.5% of those of men, but since then there has been a decline and in 1979 the figure was back at 73%. Female employment always suffers in time of economic difficulty, not least because so many women are employed part-time and are the first to go when there are redundancies. The Equal Opportunities Commission observed in their Annual Report in 1980 that working women were experiencing a growing feeling of insecurity. In part, this was because of the general rise in unemployment, combined with the high rate of inflation, in part 'because of the view, increasingly openly expressed, that the place of women is in the home'. Old ideas die hard. The Commission concluded with the warning that these factors have had the effect of encouraging an inclination 'to shelve equal opportunities policies, as a luxury which the nation cannot afford, and to increase the sense of frustration and resentment amongst many women'.[38]

If attitudes are slow to change, perhaps society may look to the women in the professions for a lead in altering the general outlook on female employment. Certainly they remain relatively few in number, but since the passing of the Sex Disqualification Removal Act of 1919, women have been able to enter more and more professions which had hitherto remained exclusively masculine preserves. For example, they soon established themselves in the

[311]

law. Margaret Kidd, daughter of a Linlithgow solicitor, was the first woman to be admitted to the Faculty of Advocates. That was in 1923. Miss Kidd then married and had a daughter, but continued her career and in 1948 was the first woman in Britain to become a King's Counsel. In the course of a distinguished career she was in 1960 appointed as Sheriff Principal of Dumfries and Galloway, then in 1966 became Sheriff Principal of Perth and Angus. Nine years later, she was created Dame Commander of the British Empire. Scotland's second woman advocate, Sheriff Isobel Sinclair, was admitted to the Faculty in 1949 and by 1981 twenty-five women were members, two of them sheriffs and two of them Queen's Counsel. Women are also becoming solicitors in increasing numbers. By 31 October 1980, there were 864 female solicitors in Scotland, forming almost 15% of the total number. Even more significantly, the proportion of women being admitted to that profession is rising every year. In 1979 just over 30% of the new entrants were women, and in 1980 the figure was 33.25%.[39]

In medicine too, women have been making their mark, and by 1979 just over 21% of the doctors employed in hospitals and 17% of the general practitioners were women. There is, of course, a particular pattern to be observed. Women tend to be found in the sphere of community medicine, and indeed 30% of the doctors working in this area were female. Predictably, fewer women occupied senior positions, but nevertheless one consultant in ten was a woman, as were 15% of the senior registrars and 21% of the registrars. Since 1920, women have been admitted as Fellows of the Royal College of Physicians of Edinburgh, and by 1978 twenty-nine were females resident in Scotland. Similarly, in the list of Fellows of the Royal College of Surgeons of Edinburgh published in 1974, no fewer than thirty-one were women domiciled in Scotland, as were twenty-three of the Fellows of the Royal College of Obstetricians and Gynaecologists in 1979. Presumably these totals will rise in the future, for more women than ever before are now being admitted to medical schools.

Doctors apart, the Health Service employs a number of women in other professional posts. Only 7% of their physicists were women in 1979 but almost half the total number of biochemists were female and women clinical psychologists actually outnumbered their male colleagues, albeit by a small margin. Surprisingly few women have taken up dentistry in the past. In 1979, 10% of the general dental practitioners were women, but there was only one female dental hospital consultant compared with seventy men, only three senior registrars out of a total of twenty, but sixteen out of fifty-seven registrars. This increase at the more junior level again suggests possible future development.[40]

Other professions follow this same pattern, with indications of an advance in the 1970s and the promise of future expansion. For instance, engineering has been a field not usually associated with women, although the Institution of Civil Engineers admitted its first female Scottish member in 1939 when Miss Mary Fergusson joined its ranks. By January 1981 there were only thirty-one women members resident in Scotland, out of a total of 62,000 men and women throughout Britain. The distribution of these thirty-one members is, however, significant. Miss Fergusson herself was a Fellow, there were three members, twelve associate members and fifteen student members. Obviously, although the numbers are still very small, there are more women than ever before taking an interest in a hitherto almost exclusively masculine sphere.

Careers requiring mathematical skills are likewise attracting more women. In 1923, the Institute of Chartered Accountants admitted its first lady member and by the summer of 1981 there were 502 among the total 10,368 on the Institute's Roll. At that time there were also sixteen women chartered surveyors, predominantly in the public sector and mainly in the valuation side of the profession. Two at least were taking a prominent part in the affairs of the Scottish Branch of the Royal Institution of Chartered Surveyors and had been among the prizewinners in the Institution's examinations. Women have been admitted to the Scottish Faculty of Actuaries from 1919 onwards, although by the mid 1950s only three had qualified as Fellows of the Faculty. By 1981, seven had become Fellows and the number of female students was increasing noticeably. Women are also beginning to find a place in the upper echelons of banking. The Royal Bank of Scotland appointed its first lady bank manager in 1970, and it now has two employed at that level.[41]

The last decade has similarly seen women being ordained as ministers of the church in small but increasing numbers. To take the established Church of Scotland as an example, six women in May 1967 petitioned the General Assembly to allow women to enter the ministry, and three years later Miss Elizabeth B. F. Kinninburgh was ordained. In 1972, Mrs Euphemia H. C. Irvine became the first female parish minister when she was appointed to

Milton of Campsie Church, Lenzie, near Glasgow. By 1981, thirty-five of the Church of Scotland's ministers were women, as were eight of the licentiates (who are licensed to preach but are not seeking a parish) and thirteen of the probationers.[42]

Only in the field of politics have women seemed to play a diminishing part. By 1980 there had been only 109 female members of parliament in Britain, of whom sixteen were Scottish. From 1974 until 1979 Scotland actually had four women MPs, two of whom achieved cabinet status. One was Florence Horsburgh, the Conservative who became Minister of Education, the other Judith Hart, who was Paymaster General under the Labour government from 1968–9. In 1980, however, there was only one female MP representing Scotland, Judith Hart, although two other women, Janey Buchan and Winifred Ewing, were members of the European Parliament in Strasbourg. Women are also under-represented on the public bodies appointed by the Scottish Office: in 1979, 3556 men were members but only 1245 women.[43]

Taken as a whole, it seems that the development of professional careers for women has been a fluctuating process. In the 1920s and 30s, when these new career opportunities were an exciting novelty, women made rapid progress. From 1930 until 1950 there was a lessening of impetus, and in the 1960s it seemed that women were maintaining but not increasing their share in professional life. The statistics for women entering the professions in the early 1980s would, however, seem to indicate a new period of advance and indeed hardly a week goes by without the newspapers noting some novel feminine achievement, as women become prison governors, submariners and racehorse trainers.[44]

Will this expansion continue, or is it only a brief flurry of activity? It is, of course, impossible to predict the future and much will depend upon the economic condition of the country. However, there is another important factor. In spite of recent legislation, in spite of birth control and maternity leave, day nurseries and child minders, modern women are still having to choose between matrimony and a full professional career. It is extremely difficult to rise to eminence in any profession if a woman devotes the best part of a decade to having and rearing her children, that same decade when her male colleagues are gaining vital qualifications and experience. Of course it is possible for women to decide not to marry: indeed, for the first time since the Middle Ages it is becoming easier to be a single woman. The despised image of the frustrated spinster is gradually being replaced by the more exciting figure of the career woman who enjoys independence and a high salary and is even envied by the young mother at home with her children, momentarily regretting her unused talents and qualifications. It is also possible for married women to decide not to have children, or to return to work when their babies are still no more than infants. Yet the fact remains that most women do wish to bear children and bring them up personally, at least in their earliest years.[45]

Whether this is the result of conditioning or of an innate feminine impulse remains a matter for debate, nor is this debate particularly Scottish. The question is equally relevant in England, in the rest of western Europe and in the United States. There is no denying, however, that Scotswomen have brought to the struggles of the twentieth century that same energy, humour and determination which has characterized their predecessors. The figure of the resolute female has been a familiar one in Scotland for centuries, and the modern women who have joined in the fight for the vote, equal opportunities and an academic education are the natural successors of those who toiled in the fields, ran businesses, defended castles and rescued endangered male relatives.

It seems that throughout Scottish history women have enjoyed an unusual degree of influence despite the constraints of law and convention. Overbearing some of them may have been, outspoken and honest to the point of rudeness, but they earned the respect of those who knew them. Perhaps the last word should be left to Don Pedro de Ayala, the Spanish ambassador who was sent to Scotland in 1498. Writing his report home, he not only extolled the gracefulness, the beauty and the elegance of the Scottish women: 'They are,' he said, 'absolute mistresses of their houses and even of their husbands.'[46]

NOTES

The spelling in all quotations has been modernized.

ABBREVIATIONS

A.P.S.   *The Acts of the Parliaments of Scotland* ed. T. Thomson and C. Innes (Edinburgh 1814–75)

B.O.E.C.   *Book of the Old Edinburgh Club*

D.N.B.   Leslie Stephen and Sidney Lee, *The Dictionary of National Biography* (London 1917)

D.O.S.T.   *A Dictionary of the Older Scottish Tongue* ed. W. A. Craigie (Edinburgh 1933–)

*N.L.S.   National Library of Scotland

P.S.A.S.   *Proceedings of the Society of Antiquaries of Scotland*

S.H.R.   Scottish Historical Review

S.H.S.   Scottish History Society

*S.R.O.   Scottish Record Office

S.R.S.   Scottish Record Society

S.T.S.   Scottish Text Society

*The abbreviations S.R.O. and N.L.S. do not imply ownership by the institution concerned, but serve merely as an indication of the location of the various documents.

Introduction

1. Margaret Bain, 'Scottish Women in Politics' in *Chapman*, xxvii, xxviii (1980).

Chapter 1: FOR BETTER OR WORSE

1. Lucy Mair, *Marriage* (London 1971), 74–8.
2. Louis A. Barbé, *Margaret of Scotland and the Dauphin Louis* (London 1917).
3. *The Scots Peerage* ed. Sir J. Balfour Paul (Edinburgh 1904–14, hereafter cited as *S.P.*), i, 19, 5, 8, 16–18.
4. *ibid.*, v, 587–9; *Calendar of Papal Letters to Scotland of Clement VII of Avignon 1378–1394* ed. Charles Burns (S.H.S. 1976, hereafter cited as *Papal Letters of Clement VII*), 188–9; *Calendar of Scottish Supplications to Rome 1428–1432* ed. A. I. Dunlop and I. B. Cowan (S.H.S. 1970, hereafter cited as *Scottish Supplications*), 246–7; *S.P.*, v, 595.
5. Jennifer M. Brown, 'The Exercise of Power' in *Scottish Society in the Fifteenth Century* ed. Jennifer M. Brown (London 1977), 59.
6. *S.P.*, iii, 228.
7. *ibid.*, i, 5; A. A. M. Duncan, *Scotland: The Making of the Kingdom* (Edinburgh 1975), 245–7; *The Original Chronicle of Andrew of Wyntoun* ed. F. J. Amours

(S.T.S. 1903, hereafter cited as *Chron. Wyntoun*), v, 63.

8. James Campbell, *Balmerino and its Abbey* (Edinburgh 1899), 494–5; *S.P.*, iv, 266; *c.f. S.P.*, i, 115; Sir William Fraser, *The Chiefs of Grant* (Edinburgh 1883, hereafter cited as *Chiefs of Grant*), 85; *Scottish Supplications*, 119; *Calendar of Documents relating to Scotland* ed. J. Bain (Edinburgh 1881–8, hereafter cited as *Cal. Docs. Scot.*), iv, no. 792; *S.P.*, ii, 115, 152–3.

9. *Papal Letters of Clement VII*, 174; *Statutes of the Scottish Church 1225–1559* ed. David Patrick (S.H.S. 1907), 39; John Dowden, *The Medieval Church in Scotland* (Glasgow 1910), 251–6; David Hay Fleming, *The Reformation in Scotland* (London 1910), 478–81.

10. Sample based on volumes i–iii of *S.P.*, taking the daughters of dukes and earls.

11. *S.P.*, iv, 258–9; *Protocol Book of Gavin Ros 1512–32* ed. J. Anderson and F. Grant (S.R.S. 1908), 88–9; *c.f.* Lawrence Stone, *The Crisis of the Aristocracy 1558–1641* (Oxford 1965, hereafter cited as *Crisis of the Aristocracy*), 591–4.

12. *e.g.* cases in *Calendar of Papal Letters to Scotland of Benedict XIII of Avignon* ed. Francis McGurk (S.H.S. 1976); *Hary's Wallace* ed. Matthew P. McDiarmid (S.T.S. 1968), 25–9, 109–10.

13. Helena M. Shire, *Song, Dance and Poetry at the Court of Scotland under James VI* (Cambridge 1969), 11–22; Roger Boase, *The Origin and Meaning of Courtly Love* (Manchester 1977), 1–61.

14. *S.P.*, ii, 426–7; Duncan, *op. cit.*, 400; *c.f. Cal. Docs. Scot.*, ii, nos. 376, 602, 709, 1750; *Documents illustrative of the History of Scotland 1286–1306* ed. J. Stevenson (Edinburgh 1870), i, 317.

15. *S.P.*, i, 156–7.

16. Denis Bethell, 'Two Letters of Pope Paschal II to Scotland' in *S.H.R.*, xlix, i (April 1970), 33–45; David Baird Smith, 'Canon Law' in *An Introductory Survey of the Sources and Literature of Scots Law* ed. H. Mackenzie (Stair Society 1936, hereafter cited as *Sources of Scots Law*), 183–92; *Baron David Hume's Lectures* ed. G. Campbell H. Paton (Stair Society 1939, hereafter cited as *Hume's Lectures*), 1.

17. *Protocol Book of Dominus Thomas Johnsoun 1528–78* (S.R.S. 1920, hereafter cited as *Prot. Bk. Johnsoun*), 8; *Carte Monialium de Northberwic* (Bannatyne Club 1847), 72.

18. *Protocol Book of Mr Gilbert Grote 1552–73* (S.R.S. 1914, hereafter cited as *Prot. Bk. Grote*), 7.

19. A. E. Anton, ' "Handfasting" in Scotland' in *S.H.R.*, xxxvii, ii (1958), 91; *c.f.* Charles Rogers, *Social Life in Scotland from Early to Recent Times* (London 1871), i, 102–4; *Hume's Lectures*, 20–1.

20. Barbara E. Crawford, 'The Pawning of Orkney and Shetland' in *S.H.R.*, xlviii, i (1969), 51n., 52n.; *Prot. Bk. Ros*, 494.

21. *S.P.*, v, 37; *Prot. Bk. Johnsoun*, 144.

22. *Regiam Majestatem and Quoniam Attachiamenta*, ed. Lord Cooper (Stair Society 1947, hereafter cited as *Regiam Maj.*), 167, 169, 126–30; *The Practicks of Sir James Balfour of Pittendreich* ed. P. G. B. McNeill (Stair Society 1962– , hereafter cited as Balfour, *Practicks*), i, 99–100, 105–7.

23. *Selections from the Family Papers preserved at Caldwell* ed. William Muir (Paisley 1883), i, 76.

24. *Prot. Bk. Grote*, 71.

25. *ibid.*, 47.

26. *Prot. Bk. Johnsoun*, 73.

27. Crawford, *op. cit.*
28. *Prot. Bk. Ros*, 23–4.
29. Anton, *op. cit.*, 91.
30. See Chapter 3.
31. John Beveridge, 'Two thirteenth-century songs with the original melodies recently discovered in Sweden' in *P.S.A.S.* (1938–9), 280.
32. *The Exchequer Rolls of Scotland* ed. J. Stuart and others (Edinburgh 1878–1908), i, 119, 218.
33. *Regiam Maj.*, 291, 126–30, 328, 148.
34. *Charters of the Abbey of Inchaffray* ed. W. A. Lindsay, John Dowden and J. Maitland Thomson, (S.H.S. 1908, hereafter cited as *Inchaffray Chrs.*), 222–3.
35. Duncan, *op. cit.*, 563; G. W. S. Barrow, *Robert Bruce and the Community of the Realm of Scotland* (London 1965, hereafter cited as Barrow, *Bruce*), 20–1.
36. *Chron. Wyntoun*, v, 263; *S.P.*, iv, 142–3.
37. *Chron. Wyntoun*, vi, 10–11.
38. *Inchaffray Chrs.*, p. lxvii; *Cal. Docs. Scot.*, iv, 125.
39. *The Scottish Correspondence of Mary of Lorraine* ed. Annie I. Cameron (S.H.S. 1927, hereafter cited as *Mary of Lorraine Corresp.*), 46–7, p.xxii, 21.
40. *S.P.*, i, 185.
41. Derek Baker, ' "A Nursery of Saints": St Margaret of Scotland Reconsidered' in *Medieval Women* ed. Derek Baker (Ecclesiastical History Society 1978), 119–42; Duncan, *op. cit.*, 124.
42. *Papal Letters of Clement VII*, 174, 181; *S.P.*, ii, 262–3.
43. *S.P.*, v, 585; i, 19.
44. Barrow, *Bruce*, 230, 212.
45. Ronald Ireland, 'Husband and Wife: Divorce, Nullity of Marriage and Separation' in *An Introduction to Scottish Legal History* ed. Lord Normand (Stair Society 1958, hereafter cited as *Introduction to Scottish Legal History*), 90–8.
46. Duncan, *op. cit.*, 583; *S.P.*, iv, 297; i, 196; i, 337.

Chapter 2: WOMEN'S WORK

1. Christina Hole, *English Home Life 1500–1800* (London 1947), 15–16; Olive Schreiner, *Women and Labour* (London 1978), 33–41.
2. Harvey Graham, *Eternal Eve* (London 1960, hereafter cited as *Eternal Eve*), 18.
3. *Foreign Correspondence with Marie de Lorraine, Queen of Scotland, from the originals in the Balcarres Papers* ed. Marguerite Wood (S.H.S. 1923–5, hereafter cited as *Balcarres Papers*), i, 78–9; *The New Statistical Account of Scotland* (Edinburgh 1845, hereafter cited as *N.S.A.*), i, 272–3; J. Lesley, *The History of Scotland from the Death of King James I in the Year 1436 to the Year 1561* (Bannatyne Club 1830), ii, 254; Alison Hanham, 'A Medieval Scots Merchant's Handbook' in *S.H.R.*, i (1971), 107–8.
4. A. R. Howell, *A Short Guide to Paisley Abbey* (Paisley n.d.), 3.
5. *Accounts of the Lord High Treasurer of Scotland* ed. T. Dickson and Sir J. Balfour Paul (Edinburgh 1877–1916, hereafter cited as *T.A.*), ii, 41; *Cal. Docs. Scot.*, i, 438 no. 2229.
6. Margaret H. Swain, *Historical Needlework* (London 1970, hereafter cited as *Historical Needlework*), 4, Plate 10.
7. *T.A.*, ii, 401, 463.

8. *ibid.*, i, 305; Margaret Ward Labarge, *A Baronial Household in the Thirteenth Century* (London 1965), 176–7; Rosalind K. Marshall, *Mary of Guise* (London 1977, hereafter cited as *Mary of Guise*), 259.

9. Gordon Donaldson, 'The Cistercian Nunnery of St Mary, Haddington: History (II)' in *Transactions of the East Lothian Antiquarian and Field Naturalists' Society*, v (1952), 15; *T.A.*, ii, 238.

10. *Balcarres Papers*, iv, 45.

11. *T.A.*, ii, 132.

12. Duncan, *op. cit.*, 573; Norman A. T. Macdougall, 'Foreign Relations: England and France' in Brown, *op. cit.*; *Mary of Guise, passim.*

13. John Knox, *The First Blast of the Trumpet against the Monstrous Regiment of Women* printed in *The Works of John Knox* ed. David Laing (Edinburgh 1855, hereafter cited as Knox, *Works*), 351–410.

14. *Cal. Docs. Scot.*, i, no. 2379; *The Hamilton Papers* ed. Joseph Bain (Edinburgh 1890–2), i, no. 189.

15. *S.P.*, ii, 258; *Cal. Docs. Scot.*, iv, no. 392; *Liber Conventus S. Katherine Senensis Prope Edinburgum* (Abbotsford Club 1841, hereafter cited as *Liber Conventus Senensis*), xxii.

16. Percy W. L. Adams, *A History of the Douglas Family* (Bedford 1921), 6.

17. *Chron. Wyntoun*, vi, 19, 60–1; Ranald Nicholson, *Edward III and the Scots* (Oxford 1965), 230; *S.P.*, ii, 435; Ranald Nicholson, *Scotland: The Later Middle Ages* (Edinburgh 1974, hereafter cited as *Scotland: The Later Middle Ages*), 133.

18. *Joannis de Fordun, Scotichronon* (Edinburgh 1759), ii, 325.

19. *Chron. Wyntoun*, v, 263; *Cal. Docs. Scot.*, ii, no. 174; *N.S.A.*, vi, 688.

20. *Chron. Wyntoun*, v, 91; Campbell, *op. cit.*, 110–21; Duncan, *op. cit.*, 413, 586; *Inchaffray Chrs.*, 192; *Liber Conventus Senensis*, xxii.

21. *Cal. Docs. Scot.*, iv, no. 1800.

22. *Extracts from the Records of the Burgh of Edinburgh* (Scottish Burgh Records Society 1869–92, hereafter cited as *Edin. Recs.*), i, 217, 11, 27; ii, 141.

23. *Registrum Secreti Sigilli Regum Scotorum* ed. M. Livingstone and others (Edinburgh 1908– , hereafter cited as *R.S.S.*), i, no. 1423; *T.A.*, i, 13–41, 73, 227, 258.

24. *Extracts from the Records of the Royal Burgh of Lanark* ed. R. Renwick (Glasgow 1893), 1, 2, 6.

25. W. C. Dickinson, *Scotland from the earliest times to 1603* (Edinburgh 1961), 233–51; T. C. Smout, *A History of the Scottish People 1560–1830* (London 1969, hereafter cited as Smout, *Scottish People*), 157–65.

26. *Charters and Documents relating to the Burgh of Peebles 1165–1710* ed. W. Chambers (Edinburgh 1872), 133, 162, 173, 194, 197.

27. *Edin. Recs.*, i, 2; *Roll of Edinburgh Burgesses and Guild-Brethren 1406–1700* ed. Charles B. Boog Watson (Edinburgh 1929), i, 2–3.

28. *T.A.*, i, 52; *R.S.S.*, i, no. 2684; *T.A.*, ii, 297.

29. *The Burgh Court Book of Selkirk 1503–45* ed. J. Imrie, T. I. Rae and W. D. Ritchie (Scottish Record Society 1960), 43.

30. *T.A.*, i, 224, 228; ii, 288, 258, 23, 297.

31. Dundee Seal of Cause, MS copy in possession of the Dundee Incorporation of Bonnet-makers; *Edin. Recs.*, i, 198–201; ii, 22–4. I am grateful to Dr Helen Bennett, for these references and for her valuable comments.

32. *Edin. Recs.*, i, 197, 76; ii, 14.

33. *Scottish Supplications*, 148.

34. *ibid, 31.*
35. *John Edgar, History of Early Scottish Education* (Edinburgh 1893), 120–1.
36. *Cal. Docs. Scot.*, ii, no. 185; *Facsimiles of the National Manuscripts of Scotland* (Edinburgh 1870), ii, p. xlix.
37. John MacQueen, 'The Literature of fifteenth-century Scotland' in Brown, *op. cit.*
38. Grant G. Simpson, *Scottish Handwriting 1150–1650* (Edinburgh 1973), 6–8, 40; Duncan, *op. cit.*, 449.
39. *Collections for a History of the Shires of Aberdeen and Banff* ed. Joseph Robertson (Spalding Club 1843), 524n; *S.P.*, vi, 305–6.
40. D. E. Easson, 'The Cistercian Nunnery of St Mary, Haddington: History (I)' in *Transactions of the East Lothian Antiquarian and Field Naturalists' Society*, v (1952), 11–12.
41. Gordon Donaldson, *The Scottish Reformation* (Cambridge 1960), 8; Anthony Ross, 'Some Notes on the Religious Orders in Pre-Reformation Scotland' in *Essays on the Scottish Reformation 1513–1625* ed. David McRoberts (Glasgow 1962, hereafter cited as *Scottish Reformation Essays*), 234; *Liber Conventus Senensis, passim*; *e.g.* S.R.O., Ailsa Muniments GD25/9/23A, B, D; W. Moir Bryce, 'The Convent of St Katherine of Siena' in *B.O.E.C.*, x (1918), 127.
42. David McRoberts, 'Material Destruction caused by the Scottish Reformation' in *Scottish Reformation Essays*, 424; John Durkan, 'Education in the Century of the Reformation', *ibid.*, 155.
43. S.R.O., Ogilvy of Inverquharity Papers, GD205/22/1a; Ailsa Muniments, GD25/1/214; Boyd Papers, GD8/50; Ailsa Muniments, GD25/9/23A; Ogilvy of Inverquharity Papers, GD205/11/33. I am much indebted to Dr Margaret H. B. Sanderson for drawing my attention to these early examples of ladies' writing; S.R.O., Dalhousie Muniments, GD45/27/108; Ailsa Muniments, GD25/9/23A.
44. *Mary of Lorraine Corresp., passim.*
45. William Boyd, *Education in Ayrshire through seven centuries* (London 1916), 16.
46. *Not in God's Image: Women in History* ed. Julia O'Faolain and Lauro Martines (London 1979, hereafter cited as *Not in God's Image*), 193–5.
47. Duncan, *op. cit.*, 451–3.

Chapter 3: COURTSHIP AND MARRIAGE

1. Louisa G. Graeme, *Or and Sable* (Edinburgh 1903), 532.
2. *Crisis of the Aristocracy*, 624–5.
3. Rosalind K. Marshall, 'The House of Hamilton in its Anglo-Scottish Setting in the Seventeenth Century' (Edinburgh University Ph.D. thesis 1970, hereafter cited as Marshall, 'House of Hamilton'), 44–9.
4. S.R.O., Breadalbane Papers, GD112/40/1; *Chiefs of Grant*, i, 243–4.
5. Hamilton Archives, C1/8464; W. Fraser, *Memorials of the Montgomeries* (Edinburgh 1859, hereafter cited as *Memorials of the Montgomeries*), i, 216–7; S.R.O., Hume of Marchmont Papers, GD158/2697/13/32; *S.P.*, ii, 477.
6. *Crisis of the Aristocracy*, 616, quoting *Archibald, Marquis of Argyll, Instructions to a Son* (1661), 41, 43.
7. *Correspondence of Sir Robert Kerr, 1st Earl of Ancram and William, 3rd Earl of Lothian* ed. D. Laing (Edinburgh 1875, hereafter cited as *Lothian Correspondence*), 17–18.

8. *Caldwell Papers*, i, 27; S.R.O., Breadalbane Papers, GD112/40/1; Hamilton Archives, C1/6972; *S.P.*, viii, 458, quoting *H. M. C. Report*, xiv, Appendix ii, 305.

9. *S.P.*, i, 544; iii, 488; viii, 602.

10. William Wilson, *The House of Airlie* (London 1924, hereafter cited as *House of Airlie*), 88.

11. S.R.O., Lothian Papers GD40 Portfolio VIII, 13; Marshall, 'House of Hamilton', 112.

12. S.R.O., Dalhousie Muniments, GD45/14/243/1.

13. W. Fraser, *Memoirs of the Maxwells of Pollok* (Edinburgh 1863, hereafter cited as *Maxwells of Pollok*), iii, 335–6; *S.P.*, iii, 444; *Lothian Correspondence*, ii, 453–5.

14. *Registrum de Panmure* ed. J. Stuart (Edinburgh 1874, hereafter cited as *Panmure Registrum*), i, pp. xlii-xliii; *S.P.*, v, 5.

15. W. Fraser, *The Red Book of Grandtully* (Edinburgh 1868, hereafter cited as *Red Bk. of Grandtully*), ii, 246–7; Atholl Muniments, 29 I (10) 216.

16. S.R.O., Clerk of Penicuik Papers, GD18/5171/6.

17. *Maxwells of Pollok*, ii, 168; S.R.O., Lothian Papers, GD40, Portfolio, III, 71, 66–7.

18. S.R.O., Airlie Papers, GD16/34/200, printed in *House of Airlie*, 93–101; see p. 65.

19. S.R.O., Leven and Melville Papers, GD26/13/401/38.

20. S.R.O., Lothian Papers, GD40, Portfolio VIII, 13; S.R.O., Leven and Melville Papers, GD26/13/432, GD26/13/401, 38.

21. Atholl Muniments, 29 I (10) 216.

22. W. Fraser, *The Chiefs of Colquhoun* (Edinburgh 1869), i, 282–3.

23. *Chiefs of Grant*, i, 251–7.

24. *The Register of the Privy Council of Scotland* ed. D. Masson and P. Hume Brown (Edinburgh 1877–1933, hereafter cited as *R.P.C.*), 3rd series, iii, 341–3, 365–6.

25. S.R.O., Clerk of Penicuik Papers, GD18/5250/1, 2, 4.

26. S.R.O., Leven and Melville Papers, GD26/13/419/113; S.R.O., Seafield Papers, GD248/559/36.

27. Hamilton Archives, C1/7567, C1/6413, C1/7067, C1/7143.

28. Lawrence Stone, *The Family, Sex and Marriage in England 1500–1800* (London 1977, hereafter cited as Stone, *The Family, Sex and Marriage*), 221–304.

29. *Prot. Bk. Grote*, 47, 71, 82.

30. Balfour, *Practicks*, i, 98, 101–5.

31. *Crisis of the Aristocracy*, 632–7; *D.O.S.T.*, i, 637; *A New English Dictionary* ed. J. A. Murray (Oxford 1901), v, 599.

32. Balfour, *Practicks*, i, 105; H. J. Habakkuk, 'Marriage Settlements in the 18th Century' in *T.R.H.S.*, 4th series, xxxii (1950), 15ff; *Crisis of the Aristocracy*, 643–5; S.R.O., Society of Antiquaries Papers, GD103/2/4/33; S.R.O., Ross Estate Papers, GD47/786; S.R.O., Leven and Melville Papers, GD26/13/401/4; c.f. *Crisis of the Aristocracy*, 645–6.

33. *R.P.C.*, 3rd series, iii, 218.

34. G. T. Omond, *The Arniston Memoirs* (Edinburgh 1887, hereafter cited as *Arniston Memoirs*), 5–6; W. Fraser, *Memorials of the Family of Wemyss* (Edinburgh 1888, hereafter cited as *Wemyss Memorials*), iii, 154.

35. *Prot. Bk. Johnsoun*, 144–5; S.R.O., Register of Deeds, 28 July 1654; S.R.O., Biel Papers, GD6/2195; S.R.O., Dalhousie Muniments, GD45/17/641.

36. S.R.O., Tods, Murray and Jameson W.S., GD237/203/1.

37. *Prot. Bk. Johnsoun*, 167–8; *Prot. Bk. Grote*, 89; *Highland Papers* ed. J. R. N. Macphail (S.H.S. 1934), iv, 44–5.

38. *Prot. Bk. Grote*, 71; Hamilton Archives, RH39/1; S.R.O., Perth Sheriff Court Records, SC49/48/30; Hamilton Archives, C1/5892; *c.f.* Christopher Clay, 'Marriage, Inheritance and the Rise of Large Estates in England 1660–1815' in *Economic History Review*, 2nd series, xxi (3) (December 1968), 503–9.

39. S.R.O., Tods, Murray and Jameson W.S., GD237/200/4; *c.f. Crisis of the Aristocracy*, 636–7.

40. S.R.O.,Register of Deeds, 28 July 1654.

41. *ibid.*; *c.f.* S.R.O., Glencairn Muniments, GD39/1/301.

42. S.R.O., Glencairn Muniments, GD39/1/291; *c.f.* S.R.O., Ross Estate Papers, GD47/786; *Wemyss Memorials*, iii, 154.

43. Hamilton Archives, L1/313/25; C1/10641/2; S.R.O., Ailsa Muniments, GD25/8/759; S.R.O., Dalhousie Muniments, GD45/17/641.

44. S.R.O., Nasmith Writs, GD85/265; S.R.O., Perth Sheriff Court Records, SC49/48/28 f.26.

45. *Wemyss Memorials*, iii, 154.

46. Elizabeth Mure, 'Some Remarks on the Change of Manners in my own time, 1700–90' in *Caldwell Papers*, i, 263–4; S.R.O., Leven and Melville Papers, GD26/13/420.

47. Ronald D. Ireland, 'Husband and Wife: Divorce, Nullity of Marriage and Separation' in *Introduction to Scottish Legal History*, 90–8; Ronald D. Ireland, 'Husband and Wife: (a) Post Reformation Canon Law of Marriage of the Commissaries' Courts and (b) Modern Common and Statute Law' in *ibid.*, 82–9; Hamilton Archives, C1/11798; Atholl Muniments, 29 I (8) 262; Rosalind K. Marshall, *The Days of Duchess Anne* (London 1973, hereafter cited as *Duchess Anne*), 122.

48. S.R.O., RH9/1/7, tailor's account book; I am grateful to Dr Margaret H. B. Sanderson for drawing my attention to this item; Lauderdale Archives, L25/15; S.R.O., Clerk of Penicuik Papers, GD18/5221; Rosalind K. Marshall, 'Three Scottish Brides, 1670–87' (hereafter cited as 'Three Scottish Brides'), in *Costume*, viii (1974), 41–5.

49. *Maxwells of Pollok*, ii, 153–4.

50. Alexander Curle, 'Notes on the Inventories of the House of Rossie, near Montrose, dating from the year 1693 to 1740' in *P.S.A.S.*, xl (1905–6), 57–8.

51. 'Three Scottish Brides', 41–5; *Historical Needlework*, 90; Atholl Muniments, 45 III 94; W. Muir, *Gleanings from the Records of Dysart* (Edinburgh 1862), 74.

52. Knox, *Works*, iv, 193–201; vi, 326–7.

53. *Journals of Sir John Lauder, Lord Fountainhall* ed. Donald Crawford (S.H.S. 1900, hereafter cited as *Fountainhall Journals*), 195; Hamilton Archives, C1/10697, 10691, 6164; National Library of Scotland MS 1031, f.136.

54. *Caldwell Papers*, i, 263–4.

55. *A.P.S.*, viii, 350; *Records of the Baron Court of Stitchill 1655–1807* ed. George Gunn and Clement Gunn (S.H.S. 1905, hereafter cited as *Stitchill Records*), 22, 43.

56. Atholl Muniments, 45 II 227.

57. S.R.O., Dalhousie Muniments, GD45/14/245.

58. *S.P.*, v, 379.

NOTES

Chapter 4: HARMONY AND DISCORD

1. See pp. 33–5; Balfour, *Practicks*, i, 111, 93–6; *c.f. Hope's Major Practicks* ed. Lord Clyde (Stair Society 1937), i, 106–37; G. Campbell H. Paton, 'Husband and Wife: Property Rights and Relationships' in *Introduction to Scottish Legal History*, 99–100.

2. Rosalind K. Marshall, *Women in Scotland 1660–1780* (National Galleries of Scotland 1979), 23; Daniel Wilson, *Memorials of Edinburgh in the Olden Times* (Edinburgh 1891, hereafter cited as *Edinburgh Memorials*), 21, 46; S.R.O., Edinburgh Register of Testaments, CC8/8/16.

3. *ibid.*, *c.f. Memorials of the Montgomeries*, i, 49; Simpson, *Scottish Handwriting*, no. 28; A. and H. Tayler, *The House of Forbes* (Aberdeen 1937), 198–9; the original is in Latin.

4. S.R.O., Lothian Papers, GD40, Portfolio IX, 68.

5. S.R.O., Hume of Marchmont Papers, GD158/2787.

6. W. Fraser, *Memorials of the Earls of Haddington* (Edinburgh 1889, hereafter cited as *Haddington Memorials*), ii, 122–6; *c.f.* S.R.O., Lothian Papers, GD40, Portfolio III, 72; Portfolio VIII, 1–11, 13, 17, 21–3, 26, 29, 46, 52, 72; *S.P.*, v, 475–8.

7. S.R.O., Mar and Kellie Muniments, GD124/15/231/2, 12; *c.f.* S.R.O., Hume of Marchmont Papers, GD158/2720; S.R.O., Leven and Melville Papers, GD26/13/419/101; W. Fraser, *The Earls of Cromartie* (Edinburgh 1876, hereafter cited as *Earls of Cromartie*), i, 207.

8. *ibid.*, i, 288.

9. S.R.O., Mar and Kellie Muniments, GD124/15/6; *Wemyss Memorials*, iii, 169–70; *Memorials of the Montgomeries*, i, 259–60; Alexander Fraser, *The Frasers of Philorth* (Edinburgh 1879), 188; S.R.O., Ailsa Papers, GD25/9/38.

10. S.R.O., Clerk of Penicuik Papers, GD18/2147; *c.f. Memoirs of the Life of Sir John Clerk of Penicuik* ed. J. M. Gray (S.H.S. 1892, hereafter cited as *Clerk Memoirs*), 39–40.

11. *S.P.*, v, 301.

12. S.R.O., Register of Consistorial Decreets, Edinburgh, CC8/5/1, ff.49–94.

13. *ibid.*, ff. 239–48; *Lord Hermand's Consistorial Decisions 1684–1773* ed. F. P. Walton (Stair Society 1940, hereafter cited as *Hermand's Decisions*), 75–7.

14. *ibid.*, ff. 274–80.

15. Ronald Ireland, 'Husband and Wife: Divorce, Nullity of Marriage and Separation' in *Introduction to Scottish Legal History*, 90–8; *Hermand's Decisions*, 45–8, 50–3, 71–3.

16. *S.P.*, ii, 165–6; John Stuart, *A Lost Chapter in the History of Mary, Queen of Scots, Recovered* (Edinburgh 1874).

17. *The Commissariot of Edinburgh: Consistorial Processes and Decreets 1658–1800* ed. F. J. Grant (S.R.S. 1909, hereafter cited as *Consistorial Processes*), 1–11.

18. *St Andrews Kirk Session Register* ed. David Hay Fleming (S.H.S. 1889), i, 18–27.

19. S.R.O., Register of Consistorial Decreets, Edinburgh, CC8/5/1, ff. 261–8, 305–82, 546–54.

20. *R.P.C.*, second series, iii, 212–3, 263–4.

21. *ibid.*, i, 301–2; third series, vii, 455–6.

22. *ibid.*, xv, 359–62; second series, iv, 312, 326.

23. *ibid.*, first series, xiv, 582 (wrongly assigned to *c.* 1618); second series, vi, 318–9; third series, i, 346; second series, iv, 290.

24. *ibid.*, iii, 465–6.
25. *ibid.*, vii, 40–2.
26. W. Fraser, *The Douglas Book* (Edinburgh 1885, hereafter cited as *Douglas Book*), iv, 273–6.
27. *The English and Scottish Popular Ballads* ed. F. J. Child (New York 1965), iv, no. 204, 'Jamie Douglas', 90–105; Francis Watt, *The Book of Edinburgh Anecdote* (Edinburgh 1913, hereafter cited as *Edinburgh Anecdote*), 204–5.
28. G. Campbell H. Paton, 'Husband and Wife: Property Rights and Relationships' in *Introduction to Scottish Legal History*, 110–11; *c.f.* G. Donaldson, 'Inter-Diocesan and Inter-Provincial Communication before and after the Reformation' in *Records of the Church History Society*, xii, part ii (1955), 75.
29. *R.P.C.*, third series, x, 147.
30. S.R.O., Hume of Marchmont Papers, GD158/2697/13/36; GD158/2804.

Chapter 5: MOTHERHOOD

1. Knox, *Works*, vi, 199.
2. S.R.O., Leven and Melville Papers, GD26/13/429/7.
3. S.R.O., Seafield Papers, GD248/556/3; *Seafield Correspondence, 1658–1708* ed. James Grant (S.H.S. 1912, hereafter cited as *Seafield Corresp.*), 244.
4. W. Fraser, *The Book of Caerlaverock* (Edinburgh 1873, hereafter cited as *Caerlaverock Book*), ii, 163; Atholl Muniments, 29 I (10) 115.
5. S.R.O., Leven and Melville Papers, GD26/13/466; S.R.O., Clerk of Penicuik Papers, GD18/5248.
6. *Letters and Papers during the Reign of King James the Sixth* ed. A. Anderson (Abbotsford Club 1838), 290; *Chiefs of Grant*, ii, 53–4.
7. S.R.O., Lothian Papers, GD40, Portfolio VIII, 20, 62.
8. S.R.O., Leven and Melville Papers, GD26/13/420; S.R.O., Mar and Kellie Muniments, GD124/15/231/2.
9. S.R.O., Leven and Melville Papers, GD26/13/419/71.
10. S.R.O., Seafield Papers, GD248/46/3.
11. S.R.O., Dalhousie Muniments, GD45/14/243, GD45/14/246.
12. S.R.O., Lothian Papers, GD40, Portfolio III, 74; S.R.O., Leven and Melville Papers, GD26/13/420.
13. S.R.O., Dalhousie Muniments, GD45/26/149; Hamilton Archives, F1/303, F1/320/19, F2/253/16, F2/305/1, F2/286/3: *Maxwells of Pollok*, ii, 151–2; Atholl Muniments, 45 I 63.
14. *Eternal Eve*, 47, 105.
15. *ibid.*; Nicholas Culpeper, *A Directory for Midwives* (Edinburgh 1668).
16. *Eternal Eve*, 102, 105; *The best of our owne: letters of Archibald Pitcairne 1652–1713* (Edinburgh 1979), 33–4.
17. *Eternal Eve*, 100–24; Rosalind K. Marshall, *Childhood in Seventeenth Century Scotland* (Scottish National Portrait Gallery exhibition catalogue, 1976, hereafter cited as *Childhood in Seventeenth Century Scotland*), 16; S.R.O., Seafield Papers, GD248/556/3; Elisabeth Bennion, *Antique Medical Instruments* (London 1979), 111–4.
18. S.R.O., Leven and Melville Papers, GD26/13/420.
19. *ibid.*
20. *Red Bk. of Grandtully*, ii, 271–3, 148–9; Culpeper, *op. cit.*, 143.

21. Michael Flinn *et al.*, *Scottish Population History* (Cambridge 1977), 284; *Diary of Sir Archibald Johnston of Warriston 1632–9* ed. G. M. Paul (S.H.S. 1911), 251; Gordon Donaldson, *The Making of the Scottish Prayer Book of 1637* (Edinburgh 1954, hereafter cited as *Making of the Scottish Prayer Book*), 77–8.

22. *Red Bk. of Grandtully*, ii, 148–9, 271–3; S.R.O., Seafield Papers, GD248/556/3; *Lothian Correspondence*, i, 54–5; W. Fraser, *The Elphinstone Family Book* (Edinburgh 1897), i, 235.

23. Hamilton Archives, F1/636.

24. *S.N.D.*, ii, 335; *Memorials of the Montgomeries*, i, 215–6; W. Fraser, *Earls of Melville and Earls of Leven* (Edinburgh 1890), ii, 240–1; S.R.O., Leven and Melville Papers, GD26/13/432.

25. Hamilton Archives, F2/21; *Memorials of the Montgomeries*, i, 192; *Fountainhall Journals*, 257.

26. S.R.O., Dalhousie Muniments, GD45/26/149; Hamilton Archives, C1/10687, M10/41; *c.f. Eternal Eve*, 35, citing an almost identical case in the writings of Hippocrates.

27. *Red Bk. of Grandtully*, ii, 227.

28. S.R.O., Lothian Papers, GD40, Portfolio VIII, 95; S.R.O., Leven and Melville Papers, GD26/401/29, GD26/13/420.

29. *c.f. William Hay's Lectures on Marriage* ed. John C. Barry (Stair Society 1967, hereafter cited as *Hay on Marriage*), 153; Atholl Muniments, 45 III 47a; S.R.O., Clerk of Penicuik Papers, GD18/5250/6; *Making of the Scottish Prayer Book*, 70, 240–1.

30. G. F. Still, *The History of Paediatrics* (Oxford 1931), 263–4, quoting Hew Chamberlen's English translation of F. Mauriceau, *Traité des Maladies des Femmes Grosses* (London 1683).

31. S.R.O., Dalhousie Muniments, GD45/18/832; Hamilton Archives, F1/345/1; Still, *op. cit.*, 264.

32. *Breast Feeding* (D.H.S.S. Report 1978), see also Chapter 14; *Memorials of the Montgomeries*, i, 207; S.R.O., Clerk of Penicuik Papers, GD18/5286/14.

33. Stone, *The Family, Sex and Marriage*, 263, 427; S.R.O., Dalhousie Muniments, GD45/26/149; *Hay on Marriage*, 153.

34. S.R.O., Campbell of Barcaldine Papers, GD170/613; S.R.O., Leven and Melville Papers, GD26/13/417/34.

35. Culpeper, *op. cit.*, 136–8; Still, *op. cit.*, 265–6.

36. Hamilton Archives, F2/483/7; *Fountainhall Journals*, 251; *Edinburgh Poll Tax Returns* ed. Marguerite Wood (S.R.S. 1951, hereafter cited as *Edinburgh Poll Tax*), 35, 48, 53, 58; *e.g.* S.R.O., Dalhousie Muniments, GD45/18/832.

37. Still, *op. cit.*, 185–6.

38. Joseph E. Illick, 'Child Rearing in Seventeenth-Century England and America' in *The History of Childhood* ed. Lloyd de Mause (London 1976, hereafter cited as *History of Childhood*), 308–9; Stone, *The Family, Sex and Marriage*, 426–8.

39. Hamilton Archives, F2/268/34; N.L.S., Yester Papers, Acc. 4862/8 f. 1a.

40. Atholl Muniments, 29 I (5) 12.

41. M. J. Tucker, 'The Child as Beginning and End' in *History of Childhood*, 244; Illick, *op. cit.*, 309; S.R.O., Leven and Melville Papers, GD26/13/401/30.

42. R. Monteith, *An Theater of Mortality* (Edinburgh 1704), 17–18, 23–4, 96–7.

43. S.R.O., Seafield Papers, GD248/556/3.

Chapter 6: EDUCATION AND LEISURE

1. Antonia Fraser, *Mary, Queen of Scots* (London 1969), 49–50, 181.

2. *Panmure Registrum*, i, p. xxxvi; *The Maitland Quarto Manuscript* ed. W. A. Craigie (S.T.S. 1920), pp. i-viii; *S.P.*, vi, 92; *The Poems of Alexander Hume* ed. Alexander Lawson (S.T.S. 1902), 4; Elizabeth Melville, Lady Culross, *A Godly Dream, compyled at the request of a friend* (Glasgow 1686).

3. Myra Reynolds, *The Learned Lady in England 1650–1760* (Boston 1920), 9–19.

4. Smout, *Scottish People*, 87–9; Rosalind Mitchison, *Life in Scotland* (London 1978), 44–5; *R.P.C.*, series x, 671–2; *A.P.S.*, v, 21 c. 5; vi, part i, 554 c. 171.

5. H. Vincent Whitelaw, *The House of Whitelaw* (Glasgow 1928), 39. I am grateful to Professor Gordon Donaldson for drawing my attention to this general point.

6. *N.S.A.*, vii, 108.

7. James Grant, *History of the Burgh and Parish Schools of Scotland* (London 1876, hereafter cited as Grant, *Burgh Schools*), i, 527–8; *Stitchill Records*, 103–4.

8. Alexander Law, *Education in Edinburgh in the Eighteenth Century* (London 1965), 32; Boyd, *op. cit.*, 16.

9. Grant, *Burgh Schools*, i, 528.

10. S.R.O., Lothian Papers, GD40, Portfolio III, 75. The psalm book also included the Book of Common Order.

11. Hamilton Archives, F1/78/1.

12. *Fountainhall Journals*, 242; *c.f.*, Hamilton Archives, F1/60/3; Atholl Muniments, 19 I(7) 15; *Douglas Book*, iv, 286.

13. Atholl Muniments, 29 I (8) 95; Hamilton Archives, C1/4180, C1/6791, C1/9776, F1/697/8.

14. *Panmure Registrum*, i, p. lxviii.

15. *The Book of the Thanes of Cawdor 1236–1742* ed. Cosmo Innes (Edinburgh 1859, hereafter cited as *Thanes of Cawdor*), 338, 351.

16. *Lothian Correspondence*, 32.

17. S.R.O., Seafield Papers, GD248/566/85; Hamilton Archives, C1/6609; this quotation given in the original spelling; S.R.O., Leven and Melville Papers, GD26/13/419/64.

18. *Seafield Corresp.*, 42.

19. *Edin. Recs.*, ix, 296.

20. S.R.O., Clerk of Penicuik Papers, GD18/5171/30; Hamilton Archives, F1/400/10, F1/397/26, F1/438/27, F1/504/30, F1/539/17, F1/533.

21. *The Household Book of Lady Grizel Baillie 1692–1733* ed. Robert Scott-Moncrieff (S.H.S. 1911), pp. xlvii–xlviii.

22. S.R.O., Clerk of Penicuik Papers, GD18/2147: playing upon the thorough bass probably meant playing the accompaniment.

23. Antonia Fraser, *op. cit.*, 178–82, 349, 412.

24. Margaret H. Swain, *The Needlework of Mary, Queen of Scots* (New York 1973), *passim. Historical Needlework*, 2–4 plate 10, 17–20, 25–9, plate 16; *c.f. Memorials of the Montgomeries*, ii, 339; *Needlework from Scottish Country Houses* (exhibition catalogue, Edinburgh 1966), no. 8.

25. Hamilton Archives, F1/78/4; S.R.O., Guthrie of Guthrie Papers, GD188/19; National Register of Archives Survey List, Maxwell-Constable of Everingham MSS, 032/57/102.

26. Francis Bamford, 'Some Edinburgh Furniture Makers' in *B.O.E.C.*, xxvii

(1966), 37; S.R.O., Bo'ness Customs Books, E72/5/2, E72/2/4; S.R.O., Leven and Melville Papers, GD26/13/419/5.

27. Thibault *et al.*, *Eighteenth Century Musical Instruments* (London 1973), 82; *An Exhibition of European Musical Instruments* ed. Graham Melville-Mason (Edinburgh 1968), 79; portrait of Margaret, Lady Kerr, formerly attributed to Lely, illustrated in *Women in Scotland*, 62.
28. S.R.O., Leven and Melville Papers, GD26/6/151.
29. Atholl Muniments, 29 I (4) 1; Hamilton Archives, F1/8, F1/342, F1/215.
30. *Chiefs of Grant*, ii, 54.
31. S.R.O., Miscellaneous Papers, RH9/1/27; Hamilton Archives, F1/430/1; S.R.O., Clerk of Penicuik Papers, GD18/1793.
32. *Memorials of the Montgomeries*, ii, 339-40; *Thanes of Cawdor*, 397; *Fountainhall Journals*, 267.
33. S.R.O., Dalhousie Muniments, GD45/14/245.
34. S.R.O., Leven and Melville Papers, GD26/13/419, 35, 43, 72.
35. *Earls of Cromartie*, ii, 91.
36. S.R.O., Dalhousie Muniments, GD45/14/235; the quotation is from John Denham's best-known poem, 'Cooper's Hill', lines 37-8, first published in 1642.

Chapter 7: ACTIVITIES

1. Hamilton Archives, C1/11593.
2. S.R.O., Lothian Papers, GD40, Portfolio III, 74.
3. *Memorials of the Montgomeries*, i, 190-1.
4. S.R.O., Leven and Melville Papers, GD26/13/401/42.
5. *Wemyss Memorials*, iii, 158; S.R.O., Leven and Melville Papers, GD26/13/419/82.
6. S.R.O., Airlie Papers, GD16/34/31; *Red Bk. of Grandtully*, ii, 252-3.
7. Hamilton Archives, L1/201, F2/96/12.
8. *S.P.*, i, 119; i, 234; *Women in Scotland*, 39.
9. *Memorials of the Montgomeries*, i, 182-3.
10. S.R.O., Hume of Marchmont Papers, GD158/2697/13/7; *c.f. Haddington Memorials*, ii, 197-200; S.R.O., Hume of Marchmont Papers, GD158/2693.
11. S.R.O., Airlie Papers, GD16/26/20; Hamilton Archives, F2/365/7.
12. e.g. Atholl Muniments, 45 I 204; D. Wilson, *Memorials of Edinburgh* (Edinburgh 1891, hereafter cited as *Memorials of Edinburgh*), ii, 71; *N.S.A.*, viii, 93.
13. S.R.O., Yule Papers, GD90/2/34; *Lothian Correspondence*, i, p. cviii; ii, 442.
14. *N.S.A.*, iii, 393; S.R.O., Seafield Papers, GD248/46/1; Taylor, *op. cit.*, 330.
15. S.R.O., Breadalbane Papers, GD112/mounted letters/560.
16. Hamilton Archives, C/14019; *Red Bk. of Grandtully*, ii, 247; *Earls of Cromartie*, i, 68; Lauderdale Archives, L16/1.
17. Smout, *Scottish People*, 119; A. Fenton, *Scottish Country Life* (Edinburgh 1976, hereafter cited as *Scottish Country Life*), 160, 54; *Stitchill Records*, 71-2.
18. Smout, *Scottish People*, 180-1; Baron F. Duckham, *A History of the Scottish Coal Industry* (Newton Abbot 1970), i, 95.
19. *Edinburgh Poll Tax*, 12.
20. See pp. 117-20.
21. Hamilton Archives, F2/276/1; *Edinburgh Poll Tax, passim*.

22. Hamilton Archives, F1/818/7; Francis Collinson, *The Traditional and National Music of Scotland* (London 1966), 53.
23. Hamilton Archives, F1/716/7; S.R.O., Yester Papers, GD28/2/54; Lauderdale Archives, L61/59; Hamilton Archives, F2/517/24; *Duchess Anne*, 69; Hamilton Archives, F1/793/1; Lauderdale Archives, L61/60.
24. *R.P.C.*, third series, ix, 499.
25. Hamilton Archives, F2/451/17; S.R.O., Dalhousie Muniments, GD45/18/1004; W. Croft Dickinson, *Scotland from the earliest times to 1603* (Edinburgh 1961), 236.
26. Lauderdale Archives, L61/59; Hamilton Archives, F2/492/6; S.R.O., Dalhousie Muniments, GD45/18/990.
27. *R.P.C.*, third series, ix, 387; *Edinburgh Poll Tax*, 57.
28. Hamilton Archives, F2/492/6.
29. Edinburgh Stent Roll for 1565, Edinburgh City Archives: I am indebted to Dr Michael Lynch for this information, and for his valuable comments; Edinburgh Stent Rolls for 1605, 1614, Edinburgh City Archives: I am grateful to Mr James Brown for these references; *The Commissariot Record of Glasgow, Register of Testaments 1547–1800* ed. Francis J. Grant (S.R.S. 1901, hereafter cited as *Glasgow Register of Testaments*), 67; S.R.O., Airlie Papers, GD16/32/5/16; *The Commissariot Record of Edinburgh, Register of Testaments 1701–1800* ed. Francis J. Grant (S.R.S. 1899, hereafter cited as *Edinburgh Register of Testaments*), iii, 240.
30. S.R.O., Dalhousie Papers, GD45/18/982, 984; N.L.S., MS 5100/102; S.R.O., Dalhousie Muniments, GD45/18/990.
31. S.R.O., Airlie Papers, GD16/33/1/1.
32. *Edinburgh Poll Tax*, 29, 63; Hamilton Archives, F2/401/56; S.R.O., Lothian Papers, GD40/44/2/40; I am grateful to Miss Myrtle Baird of the Scottish Record Office for drawing my attention to the Lothian Reference; *c.f.* John Hill Burton, *The History of Scotland* (Edinburgh 1873), vi, 150, 2n.
33. *Edin. Recs., 1573–89*, 547; Stent Roll for 1583, Edinburgh City Archives; Dr Michael Lynch kindly supplied this information; *R.P.C.*, second series, vi, 621; *c.f.* second series, v, 250; vi, 381–2; Hamilton Archives, F1/175/14; F2/401/62; *R.P.C.*, third series, xiv, 344–5.
34. Hamilton Archives, F2/636, 647; F1/593; S.R.O., Dick-Cunyngham of Prestonfield Papers, GD331/26/23; S.R.O., Bo'ness Customs Books, E72/5/3; S.R.O., Dalhousie Muniments, GD45/8/985; GD45/8/982; GD45/8/983; N.L.S., Newhailes Papers, B2/14; Hamilton Archives, F1/636.
35. S.R.O., Edinburgh Register of Testaments, CC8/8/13, 7 January 1583/4; S.R.O., Dalhousie Muniments, GD45/18/991.
36. *R.P.C.*, third series, x, 207; xiii, 349, 548, 564; xiv, 315; xv, 601–2, 577.
37. *Seafield Correspondence*, 90–1, 95, 96, 150.
38. Hamilton Archives, F2/657/23; F2/451/24; F1/797/117.
39. John A. Fairley, *Agnes Campbell, Lady Roseburn, A Contribution to the History of Printing in Scotland* (Aberdeen 1925), *passim*; *R.P.C.*, third series, viii, 250–1; xii, 22–3; *Women in Scotland*, 53.
40. *Edin. Recs. 1573–89*, 72; *R.P.C.*, third series, i, 181.
41. *Extracts from the Records of the Burgh of Glasgow, 1573–62* ed. J. Marwick and R. Renwick (Glasgow 1876–1909), 138.
42. S.R.O., MS Index to the Books of Adjournal of the High Court of Justiciary; *Scottish Woman's Place*, 47.

43. *R.P.C.*, second series, iii–xiii, *passim*; *Scottish People*, 198–207.
44. *R.P.C.*, second series, iii, 119–20, 109; iv, 230–1.
45. S.R.O., Breadalbane Papers, GD112/mounted letters/768; Harry Graham, *A Group of Scottish Women* (London 1908), 81.
46. *R.P.C.*, third series, x, 483; viii, 366.
47. Mark Napier, *Life and Times of John Graham of Claverhouse*, i, 303; Graham, *op. cit.*, 82–3; *N.S.A.*, iv, 3–4.
48. George B. Burnet, *The Story of Quakerism in Scotland 1650–1850* (London 1952), 137–8.
49. *S.P.*, i, 125; *House of Airlie*, ii, 62–3.
50. *S.P.*, v, 6; James Anderson, *Ladies of the Covenant* (Glasgow 1851), 152; *Memorials of the Montgomeries*, i, 300–1.
51. Simpson, *op. cit.*, 31; David Laing, 'Notes relating to Mrs Esther (Langlois or) Inglis, the celebrated calligraphist' in *P.S.A.S.*, vi, (1868), 284–309; Dorothy J. Jackson, *Esther Inglis, calligrapher, 1571–1624* (privately printed, New York 1937).
52. Collinson, *op. cit.*, 52–3; Ethel Bassin, *The Old Songs of Skye: Frances Tolmie and her Circle* ed. Derek Bowman (London 1977), 2.
53. I am grateful to Dr Helen Bennett for this information and for her valuable comments on the disappearance of the female bonnet-maker burgess.

Chapter 8: THE WOMAN OF THE WORLD

1. S.R.O., Dunglass Muniments, GD206/2/317/4.
2. *R.P.C.*, third series, vi, 292; vii, 37–8; xii, 483–4, 466–7; Henry W. Meikle, *Some Aspects of Later Seventeenth Century Scotland* (Glasgow 1947), 22–3.
3. S.R.O., Dalhousie Muniments, GD45/14/220/145.
4. James H. Jamieson, 'Social Assemblies of the Eighteenth Century' in *B.O.E.C.*, xix (1933), 31–91; Edinburgh Central Library, Minute Book of the Edinburgh Assembly; *Women in Scotland*, 72.
5. *Scots Magazine*, xvi (1755), 268, 293–4; *Boswell in Search of a Wife 1766–69* ed. F. Brady and F. A. Pottle (copyright © 1956 Yale, used with the permission of McGraw-Hill Book Company: this edition London 1957, hereafter cited as *Boswell in Search of a Wife*), 130.
6. *Caldwell Papers*, i, 267.
7. S.R.O., Stair Muniments, GD135/143/3.
8. W. Forbes Grey, 'The Tailors' Hall, Cowgate' in *B.O.E.C.*, xi (1922), 162–70; *Edinburgh Memorials*, ii, 44; Marion Lochhead, *The Scots Household in the Eighteenth Century* (Edinburgh 1948), 282; Hugo Arnot, *The History of Edinburgh* (Edinburgh 1788), 369, 367, 372.
9. *Personal Recollections from Early Life to Old Age of Mary Somerville, with selections from her correspondence* ed. Martha Somerville (Edinburgh 1873, hereafter cited as *Mary Somerville Recollections*), *passim*.
10. S.R.O., Campbell of Barcaldine Papers, GD170/3551/34; *The Caledonian Mercury*, 17 July 1775 and *c.f.* 8 May 1784; *c.f.* S.R.O., Campbell of Barcaldine Papers, GD170/3543; Arnot, *op. cit.*, 366.
11. David Johnson, *Music and Society in Lowland Scotland in the Eighteenth Century* (O.U.P. 1972), 32–3, 11–12.
12. Atholl Muniments, 45 II 227; 45 III 94; *Duchess Anne*, 100; Lauderdale Archives, L61/58.

NOTES

13. *The Anecdotes and Egotisms of Henry Mackenzie* (O.U.P. 1927, hereafter cited as *Anecdotes and Egotisms*), 59–60, 81–3; Johnson, *op. cit.*, 17; *Boswell in Search of a Wife*, 231; *Boswell for the Defence 1769–1774* ed. W. K. Winsatt and F. A. Pottle (copyright © 1959 Yale, used with the permission of McGraw-Hill Book Company, hereafter cited as *Boswell for the Defence*), 272; *Boswell, The Ominous Years 1774–1776* ed. C. Ryskamp and F. A. Pottle (copyright © 1963 Yale, used with the permission of McGraw-Hill Book Company, hereafter cited as Boswell, *The Ominous Years*), 9, 186, 197; *Boswell, Laird of Auchinleck 1778–82* ed. Joseph W. Reed and F. A. Pottle (copyright © 1977 Yale, used with the permission of McGraw-Hill Book Company, hereafter cited as *Boswell, Laird of Auchinleck*), 111, 113, 127, 183, 194, 198, 214, 217, 220, 265, 266, 282, 284; Mrs Atholl Forbes, *Curiosities of a Scots Charta Chest* (Edinburgh 1897, hereafter cited as *Scots Charta Chest*), 256; S.R.O., Seafield Papers, GD248/192/2.
14. *Boswell for the Defence*, 258.
15. Elizabeth Grant of Rothiemurchus, *Memoirs of a Highland Lady 1797–1829* (London 1927, hereafter cited as *Memoirs of a Highland Lady*), 213, 237.
16. S.R.O., Scott of Harden Papers, GD157/2294.
17. S.R.O., Campbell of Barcaldine Papers, GD170/2827/6; Barbara Balfour-Melville, *The Balfours of Pilrig* (Edinburgh 1907, hereafter cited as *Balfours of Pilrig*), 189–95.
18. S.R.O., Campbell of Barcaldine Papers, GD170/2796/2.
19. Alexander Carlyle, *Anecdotes and Characters of the Time* (London 1973, hereafter cited as Carlyle, *Anecdotes*), 39. (Quotations from this book by permission of Oxford University Press.)
20. *N.S.A.*, vi, 210–11; Johnson, *op. cit.*, 42–4; Lochhead, *op. cit.*, 282.
21. From Mr Dugald Bannantyne's scrapbook, quoted in *N.S.A.*, vi, 229–30.
22. *Chron. Atholl*, iv, 202; *Memoirs of a Highland Lady*, 30, 55; S.R.O., Scott of Harden Papers, GD157/2414/5.
23. *Scots Magazine*, xix (1757), 110; xx (1758), 390; xxiv (1762), 221; xxvi (1764), 290; *Boswell's London Journal 1762–1763* (copyright © 1950 Yale, used with the permission of McGraw Hill Book Company), 70; *S.P.*, ii, 74; *Scots Magazine*, xxviii (1766), 55.
24. *Boswell for the Defence*, 34; *Caldwell Papers*, ii, 146.
25. Figures based on details in *The Scots Peerage*; Lord Kames, *Loose Hints upon Education* (Edinburgh 1782, hereafter cited as Kames, *Education*), 12–13.
26. *Mary Somerville Recollections*, 62–4.
27. *Scots Magazine*, ii (1740), 292; iii (1741), 48; i (1739), 592.
28. See pp. 1–31, 63–86.
29. *Caerlaverock Book*, ii, 364.
30. *Red Bk. of Grandtully*, ii, 322; *Caerlaverock Book*, ii, 357–8.
31. *Boswell in Search of a Wife*, 109.
32. *Balfours of Pilrig*, 197; *S.P.*, vi, 22.
33. *Boswell in Search of a Wife*, 117–9; *Correspondence of Thomas and Jane Welsh Carlyle* ed. C. R. Sanders and K. J. Fielding (Edinburgh 1970, hereafter cited Carlyle Correspondence), ii, 309–10, 313.
34. *ibid.*, iii, 250–1, 247, 438; iv, 46–8, 141.
35. Watt, *op. cit.*, 210.
36. *Carlyle Correspondence*, iii, 128–31.
37. Watt, *op. cit.*, 210; *Memoirs of a Highland Lady*, 230; S.R.O., Airlie Papers,

GD16/36/370/1.

38. *Seafield Correspondence*, 437; Hamilton Archives, C1/7991; *Caerlaverock Book*, ii, 361–2; *Scots Magazine*, xxvi (1764), 415–6.

39. James Stark, *Report of the Royal Commission on the Laws of Marriage*, xxxii (1867–8), p. xxi.

40. S.R.O., Clerk of Penicuik Papers, GD18/5299/14; GD18/5254/26, GD18/5299/32; GD18/5256/40, 42.

41. S.R.O., Leven and Melville Papers, GD26/13/557, partially printed in *Wemyss Memorials*, iii, 193–6.

42. Winifred Duke, *Lord George Murray and the Forty-Five* (Aberdeen 1927), 41–2.

43. N.L.S., MS 2956, ff. 177–8.

44. *ibid*., MS 3836, ff. 24–5; *Women in Scotland*, 22–3; *c.f. Memorials of the Montgomeries*, i, 107.

45. *Boswell in Holland 1763–64* ed. F. A. Pottle (copyright © 1928, 1952, Yale, used with the permission of McGraw-Hill Book Company; this edition London 1952, hereafter cited as *Boswell in Holland*), 318.

46. *Boswell: The Ominous Years*, 178, 216.

47. Quoted in *Scots Magazine*, xxiv, 366–7.

48. Thomas Crawford, *Society and the Lyric* (Edinburgh 1979), 25–31.

49. *Calendar of Irregular Marriages in the South Leith Kirk Session Records 1697–1818* ed. J. S. Marshall (S.R.S. 1968), 7–35.

50. S.R.O., Sutherland of Fearquhar Papers, GD347/101.

51. Crawford, *op. cit*., 35–69.

Chapter 9: THE MARITAL BOND

1. *Scots Magazine*, iii (1741), 553.

2. Lady Murray of Stanhope, *Memoirs of the Lives and Characters of the Rt. Hon. George Baillie of Jerviswood and of Lady Grizel Baillie* (Edinburgh 1822), 85; Carlyle, *Anecdotes*, 132.

3. *Memoirs of a Highland Lady*, 82.

4. S.R.O., Clerk of Penicuik Papers, GD18/5254/22/3; *Boswell in Search of a Wife*, 126; *Scots Magazine*, xxvii (1765), 384.

5. Kames, *Education*, 256–8.

6. *Carlyle Correspondence*, iv, 69, 22–32.

7. *Memoirs of a Highland Lady*, 80.

8. *Boswell: The Ominous Years*, 72.

9. S.R.O., Clerk of Penicuik Papers, GD18/5289/4, 8, 9; *Arniston Memoirs*, 94–6; A. and H. Tayler, *The Domestic Papers of the Rose Family* (Aberdeen 1926), 55–6, 60, 65–6.

10. *Memorials of the Montgomeries*, i, 104; *Chiefs of Grant*, ii, 298.

11. *Boswell in Holland*, 354; *Wemyss Memorials*, iii, 242–3.

12. *Scots Magazine*, xlv (1783), 619–20.

13. *Consistorial Processes, passim*.

14. *ibid*., 16, 17, 89, 90.

15. S.R.O., Clerk of Penicuik Papers, GD18/5250/40, 42, 45, 50.

16. *S.P.*, viii, 509; *Consistorial Processes*, 27, 36–7, 82, 21.

17. *ibid*., 18, 69, 19, 37, 42, 121.

18. *ibid*., 49, 61, 77, 95.

19. *Consistorial Processes*, 46; *Chron. Atholl*, iv, 44–6.

20. *Consistorial Processes*, 21, 25, 76, 89.
21. S.R.O., Register of Consistorial Decreets, Edinburgh, CC8/6/21; *Consistorial Processes*, 36.
22. *ibid., passim.*
23. Carlyle, *Anecdotes*, 8, 14; S.R.O., Mar and Kellie Papers, GD124/15/1179, 'Memoirs' of Lord Grange; GD124/15/1374, 1375, 1376, 1377, 1378, 1379, 1380, 1506, 1542; R. W. Seton-Watson, 'The Strange Story of Lady Grange' in *History*, xvi (April 1931), 61, 12ff; David Laing, 'Lady Grange' in *P.S.A.S.*, xi (1874–6), 601; I. F. Grant, *The Macleods: The History of a Clan* (London 1959), 401–4.

Chapter 10: THE LEARNED LADY

1. *Duchess Anne*, 231.
2. *Memorials of the Montgomeries*, i, 346, 349; S.R.O., Seafield Papers, GD248/101/2.
3. S.R.O., Hume of Wedderburn Papers, GD267/7/8.
4. Carlyle, *Anecdotes*, 25; *Scots Magazine*, iii (1741), 279.
5. Carlyle, *Anecdotes*, 39; James Scotland, *The History of Scottish Education* (London 1969), i, 108.
6. *ibid.*, i, 109; Boyd, *op. cit.*, 84.
7. Alexander Law, *Education in Edinburgh in the Eighteenth Century* (London 1965, hereafter cited as *Education in Edinburgh*), 183; Lochhead, *op. cit.*, 243–4.
8. *Scots Magazine*, xxviii (1766), 372.
9. *ibid.*, xxxv (1783), 621.
10. Sir John Sinclair, *Analysis of the Statistical Account of Scotland* (Edinburgh 1826), ii, 127.
11. Jean-Jacques Rousseau, *Emile, ou de l'Education* ed. F. and P. Richard (Paris 1939), 455; *Not in God's Image*, 259.
12. Kames, *Education*, 7–8, 10, 274.
13. Grant, *Burgh Schools*, i, 528–9; Scotland, *op. cit.*, i, 109.
14. M. G. Jones, *The Charity School Movement* (Cambridge 1938), 206–7; Law, *op. cit.*, 47–57.
15. S.R.O., typescript: John Mason, 'Schools on the Forfeited Estates in the Highlands' (1962), 96, 151; e.g. *Boswell's Journal of a Tour to the Hebrides* ed. F. A. Pottle and C. H. Bennett (copyright © 1961 Yale, used with the permission of McGraw-Hill Book Company; this edition London 1963), 108, 138–9.
16. Grant, *Burgh Schools*, i, 530–1.
17. George Chapman, *A Treatise on Education* (London 1784, hereafter cited as Chapman, *Treatise*), 97–101.
18. *Carlyle Correspondence*, iii, 413–4.
19. A. and H. Tayler, *The Domestic Papers of the Rose Family* (Aberdeen 1926), 151.
20. S.R.O., Macpherson of Cluny Papers, GD80/927.
21. *Memoirs of a Highland Lady*, 211.
22. *Scots Magazine*, ii (1740), 73–4.
23. *Mary Somerville Recollections*; Elizabeth C. Patterson, *Mary Somerville 1780–1872* (Oxford 1979); G. J. Tee, 'The Pioneering Woman Mathematicians' in *Mathematical Chronicle* x (1981), 44–7.
24. S.R.O., Scott of Harden Papers, GD157/2831/1, 2.

25. *Carlyle Correspondence*, ii, 304, 196–7, 221; iii, 48, 56; ii, 198; iii, 10.
26. *Caldwell Papers*, i, 208–9, 269.
27. Kames, *Education*, 162.
28. Sinclair, *op. cit.*, ii, 126–9.
29. *The Journal of Sir Walter Scott* ed. W. E. K. Anderson (Oxford 1972, hereafter cited as Scott's *Journal*), 21, 586, 183.
30. *Scots Magazine*, xxvi (1774), 181.
31. *Mary Somerville Recollections*, 156; Henry Cockburn, *Memorials of His Time* (Edinburgh 1909, hereafter cited as Cockburn, *Memorials*), 259–60.

Chapter 11: THE HOME AND BEYOND

1. *Caerlaverock Book*, ii, 374.
2. *Anecdotes and Egotisms*, 132.
3. *Eternal Eve*, 147–52; *Scots Magazine*, xxv (1763), 179; Bennion, *op. cit.*, 116–19.
4. *Eternal Eve*, 167–75.
5. *Scots Magazine*, xxii (1760), 277; xxv (1763), 563; xxvii (1765), 39, 651; xxxii (1770), 457–8; xxxiii (1771), 369; *Eternal Eve*, 146–75.
6. *Mary Somerville Recollections*, 9.
7. *Scots Magazine*, xxix (1767), 26; xv (1753), 516.
8. *ibid.*, xviii (1756), 109; *Caledonian Mercury*, 28 April 1784; *N.S.A.*, i, 731–2.
9. *Eternal Eve*, 193–222; Jack Dewhurst, *Royal Confinements* (London 1980), 1–2.
10. Mortality tables in *Scots Magazine*, i (1739) – xxi (1769): in 1739–40 figures are for Greyfriars only.
11. *ibid.*
12. S.R.O., Clerk of Penicuik Papers, GD18/5250/33; S.R.O., Leven and Melville Papers, GD26/13/792/23.
13. *Boswell: The Ominous Years*, 166, 168, 169.
14. S.R.O., Campbell of Barcaldine Papers, GD170/2034/9.
15. John Kay, *Original Portraits*, ii (Edinburgh 1838).
16. *Scots Magazine*, x (1748), 429–40.
17. *ibid.*, xxvii (1765), 632; Kames, *Education*, 33–4; S.R.O., Moray of Abercairney Muniments, GD24/1/589; *Eternal Eve*, 170; *Scots Magazine*, xxxiii (1771), 670.
18. *Eternal Eve*, 184–5.
19. *Scots Magazine*, x (1748), 431–2; xxiii (1761), 651–2; xxvii (1765), 631–2; Chapman, *Treatise*, 129.
20. *Scots Magazine*, xix (1757), 222; xxiv (1762), 302–5; xxvii (1765), 143–9; xix (1767), 366; xxxi (1769), 486; Smout, *Scottish People*, 272; S.R.O., Campbell of Barcaldine Papers, GD170/1355/11.
21. S.R.O., Mar and Kellie Muniments, GD124/15/771/11; S.R.O., Stair Papers, GD135/143/87; *Red Bk. of Grandtully*, ii, 324; *Scots Charta Chest*, 302; S.R.O., Mar and Kellie Muniments, GD124/15/1777/19.
22. *Scots Magazine*, vii (1745), 400; xix (1767), 430; xxxii (1770), 384; *Memoirs of a Highland Lady*, 126.
23. *e.g.* S.R.O., Seafield Papers, GD248/1154, Lady Findlater's account book, 1724–44; S.R.O., Clerk of Penicuik Papers, GD18/1843, Lady Clerk's household book, 1709–39; S.R.O., Mar and Kellie Muniments, GD124/15/771/11.

24. S.R.O., Stair Papers, GD135/43/43.

25. *Scots Magazine*, xv (1753), 100.

26. S.R.O., Campbell of Barcaldine Papers, GD170/2140/1; GD170/2827/2.

27. Thomas Pennant, *A Tour of Scotland* (London 1776), i, 146; *c.f.* Karin J. Harrington, 'Fisherwomen and Their Place in a Traditional Society' (unpublished University of Stirling dissertation, 1980).

28. S.R.O., Stair Papers, GD135/34; *Scottish Country Life*, 116; *Boswell's Journal of a Tour to the Hebrides*, 85, 152, 219.

29. Smout, *Scottish People*, 241–61, 320–38; W. Ferguson, *Scotland: 1689 to the Present* (Edinburgh 1968), 166–92.

30. Mitchison, *op. cit.*, 97–8; Smout, *Scottish People*, 241–61, 320–438.

31. S.R.O., Seafield Papers, GD248/101/2; S.R.O., Morton Papers, GD150/2473.

32. Edinburgh Register of Testaments, iii; S.R.O., Mar and Kellie Muniments, GD124/15/1179 f. 49; N.L.S., Yester Papers, MS 14658, 14657; *Thanes of Cawdor*, 426; Charles J. Smith, *Historic South Edinburgh* (Edinburgh 1978), i, 63; *Scots Magazine* xxxiv (1772), 276; Hamilton Archives, F1/825/81; *Caledonian Mercury*, 4 June 1774; S.R.O., Morton Papers, GD150/2742; N.L.S., Yester Papers, MS 14658; 14662; *D.N.B.*, xlix, 383; *Women in Scotland*, 52; title page of Ralph Erskine, *Law-Death, Gospel-Life* (Edinburgh 1724); *Anecdotes and Egotisms*, 180.

33. *Edinburgh Post Office Directory 1824–5*; S.R.O., Seafield Papers, GD248/1154; *Boswell in Search of a Wife*, 100; S.R.O., Campbell of Barcaldine Papers, GD170/2852.

34. *Liber Conventus Senensis*, p. xxxvii n.

35. S.R.O., Campbell of Barcaldine Papers, GD170/391/8a.

36. *Edinburgh Register of Testaments*, iii.

37. *Edinburgh Post Office Directory 1824–5*; *Memoirs of a Highland Lady*, 102.

38. S.R.O., Campbell of Barcaldine Papers, GD170/2103/2.

39. *Edinburgh Post Office Directory 1824–5*.

40. *e.g.* David J. Hargreaves, 'Sex Roles and Creativity' in *Sex Role Stereotyping* ed. Oonagh Hartnett, Gill Boden and Mary Fuller (London 1979, hereafter cited as *Sex Role Stereotyping*), 185–99.

41. David and Francina Irwin, *Scottish Painters at Home and Abroad 1700–1900* (London 1975), 76–7; N.L.S., Acc. 3081; *c.f.* Germaine Greer, *The Obstacle Race* (London 1979), 68–87.

42. *c.f.* Virginia Woolf, *A Room of One's Own* (London 1929); *D.N.B.*, i, 86–7; N.L.S., MS 2617, ff. 65–6: I am grateful to Dr Iain G. Brown of the National Library of Scotland for drawing my attention to this reference.

43. *D.N.B.*, ii, 414–7; lix, 97–8.

44. *Anecdotes and Egotisms*, 37; *Edinburgh Anecdotes*, 203; *D.N.B.*, iii, 236–7; xxx, 420, 73–4.

45. *ibid.*, 147–8; Cockburn, *Memorials*, 260.

Chapter 12: THE MARCH OF THE INTELLECT

1. Letter of Elizabeth Brodie, 31 May 1848, in the Brodie Archives: I am grateful to Mr Christopher Hartley of the National Trust for Scotland for drawing my attention to this reference. See also Rosalind K. Marshall, 'The Chatelaine' in *Treasures in Trust* ed. A. A. Tait (Edinburgh 1981), 13–20,

where the date of Elizabeth's marriage is given as 1688 instead of 1838, because of a printer's error.

2. *Carlyle Correspondence*, ii, 317.

3. *ibid.*, vi, 171–2.

4. S.R.O., Hope, Todd and Kirk Papers, GD246/45.

5. Geoffrey Warren, *A Stitch in Time* (London 1976), 28–47; *Historical Needlework*, 41–55, 91–2, 99–113; *Memorials of the Montgomeries* (Edinburgh 1859), i, 368.

6. S.R.O., Campbell of Barcaldine Papers, GD170/2838/1.

7. S.R.O., Murray of Polmaise Muniments, GD189/2/852; GD189/2/923; Warren, *op. cit.*, 23.

8. *Mary Somerville Recollections*, 43; *Memoirs of a Highland Lady*, 8, 38.

9. *The Daily Courant*, 4 January 1860.

10. W. A. Finlay, *Inaugural Address at the opening of Leith Hospital to Women Medical Students* (Edinburgh 1887).

11. *N.S.A.*, i, 299; ii, 16; vii, 490; ii, 145; i, 749; Bassin, *op. cit.*, 20–1.

12. S.R.O., Dunglass Muniments, GD206/4/55.

13. *The House of Airlie*, ii, 243–4; *Scots Magazine*, ii (1844), 20; Frances Balfour, *Lady Victoria Campbell* (London n.d.), 172–3.

14. *N.S.A.*, ii, 353; i, 25; 11, 185; vi, 716; v, 470.

15. *ibid.*, vii, 625 and *passim*.

16. *ibid.*, v, 852; ix, 36; vii, 529–31.

17. *ibid.*, vii, 467; v, 77.

18. *ibid.*, ii, 315; vi, 667; vi, 440; viii, 38; vi, 758.

19. T.C. Smout, 'Aspects of Sexual Behaviour in Nineteenth Century Scotland' in *Social Class in Scotland: Past and Present* ed. A. Allan MacLaren (Edinburgh n.d.), 63–4; Scotland, *op. cit.*, i, 362–7.

20. Boyd, *op. cit.*, 143.

21. *ibid.*, 156; Grant, *Burgh Schools*, i, 537.

22. Scotland, *op. cit.*, i, 362–7; ii, 6.

23. *B.O.E.C.*, xxxix, 195–6.

24. Grant, *Burgh Schools*, i, 526–37.

25. Scotland, *op. cit.*, ii, 80–1.

26. Ellice Miller, *Century of Change* (Glasgow 1975), 5–31.

27. Scotland, *op. cit.*, ii, 63–4.

28. *St Leonards School 1877–1977* ed. J. S. A. Macaulay (privately printed 1977), 2–7.

29. *In Memoriam Sarah Elizabeth Siddons Mair, D.B.E., LL.D.* (Edinburgh 1941), 3–4; Bassin, *op. cit.*, 61–2; *Who Was Who 1941–50*, 752; B. W. Welsh, *After the Dawn* (Edinburgh 1939), 1–6.

30. Welsh, *op. cit.*, 1–6.

31. *Who Was Who 1897–1916*, 480; Gordon Donaldson and Robert S. Morpeth, *Who's Who in Scottish History* (Oxford 1973), 231–2.

32. Welsh, *op. cit.*, 1–9; Bassin, *op. cit.*, 61–2; Scotland, *op. cit.*, i, 353; *Calendar of the Edinburgh Association for the University Education of Women 1889–90*; Memorial of the Edinburgh Association for the University Education of Women to the Scottish University Commissioners, S.R.O., ED9/41.

33. Welsh, *op. cit.*, 11–12.

34. Scotland, *op. cit.*, ii, 158–9; S.R.O., ED9/41.

35. Margaret Todd, *The Life of Sophia Jex-Blake* (London 1918).

36. Scotland, *op. cit.*, ii, 159.

Chapter 13: THE EMANCIPATION OF WOMEN

1. S.R.O., Grant of Monymusk Papers, GD345/1376.
2. See p. 23; S.P., passim.
3. Balfour, op. cit., 87–91.
4. T. C. Smout, 'Aspects of Sexual Behaviour in Nineteenth Century Scotland' in Maclaren, op. cit., 55–85.
5. Kenneth M. Boyd, Scottish Church Attitudes to Sex, Marriage and the Family 1850–1914 (Edinburgh 1980, hereafter cited as Scottish Church Attitudes), 264–84.
6. S.R.O., Campbell of Jura Papers, GD64/1/214.
7. Scottish Church Attitudes, 61–2.
8. ibid., 51; Chron. Atholl, iv, 471; National Museum of Antiquities of Scotland, Country Life Archive, wedding invitation cards.
9. S.R.O., Seaforth Papers, GD46/15/27.
10. N.S.A., passim; I. F. Grant, 'An Old-Time Scots Fisher Wedding' in The Country Heart (July/September 1972), 259–60; J. Moir Porteous, God's Treasure House in Scotland (Edinburgh and Glasgow 1876), 116–17; John Loudon, 'Creeling and Tramping in Lanarkshire' in Scots Magazine (1957), 49.
11. Scottish Church Attitudes, 61–3; Flinn, op. cit., 361; O. Anderson, 'Incidence of Civil Marriage' in Past and Present, lxix (1975), 55; T. C. Smout, 'Scottish Marriage, Regular and Irregular, 1500–1940' in forthcoming publication, The Social History of Marriage ed. Brian Outhwaite.
12. Carlyle Correspondence, v, 316–20, 312–4.
13. Ivy Pinchbeck, Women Workers and the Industrial Revolution 1750–1850 (London 1981 edition), 184; Geoffrey Best, Mid-Victorian Britain 1851–75 (London 1971), 100–9.
14. S.R.O., Dunglass Muniments, GD206/4/59.
15. Patricia Branca, Women in Europe since 1750 (London 1978), 34–9.
16. Pinchbeck, op. cit., 188.
17. N.S.A., iv, 309; vii, 52; v, 233; ix, 76; vii, 23; iii, 80–1.
18. ibid., vi, 329; v, 99, 717, 626–7; Margaret H. Swain, The Flowerers (London 1955).
19. N.S.A., vii, 517; Branca, op. cit., 41–6; James H. Treble, 'The Market for Unskilled Male Labour in Glasgow 1891–1914' in Essays in Scottish Labour History ed. Ian MacDougall (Edinburgh 1978), 123.
20. The Scotsman, 4 September 1874.
21. Branca, op. cit., 53–7.
22. Mary Wollstonecraft, Vindication of the Rights of Women (London 1978).
23. The Law of Husband and Wife in Scotland ed. Eric M. Clive and John G. Wilson (Edinburgh 1974, hereafter cited as Clive, Husband and Wife), 287–9.
24. Eternal Eve, 257–87.
25. Genesis, iii, verse 16; c.f. John, xvi, 21.
26. Eternal Eve, 240–56; Dewhurst, op. cit., 177–8.
27. Eternal Eve, 281–6.
28. J. A. and Olive Banks, Feminism and Family Planning in Victorian England (Liverpool 1964), 85–91; British Medical Journal, 5 October 1867, 283.
29. John Stuart Mill, The Subjection of Women (Oxford 1978), 427, 444 and passim; Susan Moller Okin, Women in Western Political Thought (London 1980), 197–230.
30. Autobiography and Letters of Mrs Margaret Oliphant ed. Mrs Harry Coghill

(Leicester 1974), 15; *Mary Somerville Recollections*, 344–6; Patterson, *op. cit.*, 41.

31. Welsh, *op. cit.*, 1–2; *In Memoriam Sarah Elizabeth Siddons Mair D.B.E., LL.D.*

32. Elspeth King, *The Scottish Women's Suffrage Movement* (Glasgow 1978), 10; Andrew Rosen, *Rise Up, Women!* (London 1974), 7; *The Scotsman*, 7 November 1867.

33. King, *op. cit.*, 10–11; *The Scotsman*, 4 November 1882.

34. Rosen, *op. cit.*, 14–24; Sylvia Pankhurst, *The Suffragette Movement* (London 1977, hereafter cited as *Suffragette Movement*), 3–29, 53–9, 164–70; Emmeline Pankhurst, *My Own Story* (London 1979, hereafter cited as *My Own Story*) 12–13; Sheila Rowbotham, *Hidden from History* (London 1980), 78–9.

35. King, *op. cit.*; *Suffragette Movement*, 191 ff; Rosen, *op. cit.*, 94–5.

36. King, *op. cit.*, 18.

37. *ibid.*, 19–20; *c.f. Boswell: The Ominous Years*, 67.

38. *Who Was Who 1929–40*, 58, 2.

39. King, *op. cit.*, 18–19; *The Suffragette*, 3 January 1913.

40. *The Suffragette*, 31 January 1913, 230, 232–3, 234–5; *Suffragette Movement*, 241–51; Rowbotham, *op. cit.*, 80–9.

41. *The Suffragette*, 18 October 1912; 8 November 1912; 28 January 1913; *passim*.

42. *The Anti-Suffrage Review*, February 1909, 3; March 1909, 6; November 1910, 1; June 1910, 1.

43. Rosen, *op. cit.*, 114–20; *Suffragette Movement*, 301–19; David Morgan, *Suffragists and Liberals* (London 1975), 58–9.

44. *The Suffragette*, 18 October 1912; 8 November 1912.

45. *ibid.*, 27 December 1912; 7 February 1913.

46. *ibid.*, 14 February 1913; 28 February 1913; 14 March 1913.

47. *ibid.*, 21 March 1913; Rosen, *op. cit.*, 188–9; *The Suffragette*, 11 April 1913; 9 May 1913; 30 May 1913; 20 June 1913; King, *op. cit.*, 25; Margaret Bain, 'Scottish Women in Politics' in *Chapman* xxvii, xxviii (1980), 6 ff.

48. *Suffragette Movement*, 260–1; Rosen, *op. cit.*, 222; *My Own Story*, 340–3; King, *op. cit.*, 26.

49. Rosen, *op. cit.*, 255–6; *Suffragette Movement*, 591–5; Rowbotham, *op. cit.*, 99–122.

50. Lady Frances Balfour, *Dr Elsie Inglis* (Edinburgh 1918); Eva Shaw McLaren, *A History of the Scottish Women's Hospitals* (Edinburgh 1919); *D.N.B. 1912–21*, 283.

51. Rosen, *op. cit.*, 260–6; S.R.O., Edinburgh Women Citizens' Association Papers, GD333/3; *The Scotsman*, 19 July 1918; Morgan, *op. cit.*, 134–60.

52. King, *op. cit.*, 28; S.R.O., Edinburgh Women Citizens' Association Papers, GD333/3.

Chapter 14: THE FRUITS OF FREEDOM

1. S.R.O., Edinburgh Women Citizens' Association, GD333/3, 40.

2. Clive, *Husband and Wife*, 11.

3. *ibid.*, 345–6.

4. David Ian Nicholls, *Marriage, Divorce and the Family in Scotland* (Edinburgh 1978, hereafter cited as *Marriage, Divorce and the Family*), 1–2.

5. *ibid.*, 1–2; Clive, *Husband and Wife*, 103.

6. *Marriage, Divorce and the Family*, 2; Clive, *Husband and Wife*, 96–103; *Scottish Woman's Place*, 8, 40.

NOTES

7. *The Succession (Scotland) Act*, 1964; *Marriage, Divorce and the Family*, 4–9.
8. *Dear Dr Stopes: Sex in the 1920s* ed. Ruth Hall (London 1978).
9. Rowbotham, *op. cit.*, 149–58.
10. *Scottish Abstract of Statistics* (H.M.S.O. 1980, hereafter cited as *S.A.S.*), 25, 29, 13; *Scottish Woman's Place*, 4–5; *A Report on an Enquiry into Maternal Death in Scotland 1972–1975* (Scottish Home and Health Department 1978, hereafter cited as *Maternal Deaths*), 17–20.
11. *Fourth Annual Report of the Equal Opportunities Commission* (London 1979, hereafter cited as *E.O.C. Fourth Annual Report*), 57; *Maternal Deaths*, 7–8; Helen Callaway, '"The Most Essentially Female Function of all": Giving Birth' in *Defining Females: The Nature of Women in Society* ed. Shirley Ardener (Oxford 1978), 63–85.
12. *Maternal Deaths, passim*; (*n.b.* the printed table of maternal mortality in this publication is corrected in its erratum slip); M. Flinn, *op. cit.*, 296–7.
13. *Maternal Deaths*, 9–10.
14. *Breast Feeding* (D.H.S.S. Report 1978).
15. Shelley Adams, *Law at Work: Sex Discrimination* (London 1980), 56–68.
16. Clive, *Husband and Wife*, 13, 440–2; *S.A.S.*, 62.
17. *Divorce (Scotland) Act* (H.M.S.O. 1976).
18. Janet Rae, 'Ending on a legal note' in *The Scotsman*, 5 November 1980, 14.
19. Clive, *Husband and Wife*, 289; *Scottish Woman's Place*, 46.
20. M. Holt, 'Co-education in Scotland' in *Women's Employment*, 20 March 1914, 11–12.
21. S.R.O., Report on Separate Advanced Divisions and Secondary Schools for Girls, ED8/17.
22. S.R.O., Board of Education Consultative Committee, Secondary Curricula, Comparative Educability of Boys and Girls: précis of the evidence, by J. C. Smith Esq., H.M. Chief Inspector for the Training of Teachers, Scotland; S.R.O., ED/7/1/26.
23. Andrew McPherson, 'A Longitudinal Study of Scots passing through tertiary education in the 1960s' (hereafter cited as 'Longitudinal Study') in *Scottish Educational Studies*, 5(2), 1973; *S.A.S.*, 75; Joan Taylor, 'Choice: A Male Prerogative' in *Choice, Compulsion and Cost* (S.E.D. 1980), 34–6; Roger J. L. Murphy, 'Sex differences in examination performances: Do these reflect differences in ability or sex-role stereotypes?' in *Sex Role Stereotyping*, 159–66; Alison Kelly, 'Swings and Roundabouts: Trends in S.C.E. Science Presentations 1962' (hereafter cited as 'Swings and Roundabouts') in *Scottish Educational Studies*, 8(1), 1976.
24. *Glasgow University Calendar 1918–20*, 564–83; *St Andrews University Calendar 1920–1*, 368–92, 459–60.
25. *Aberdeen University Calendar 1920*, 501–10, 565–600; *Edinburgh University Calendar 1920–1*, 707–849; U.C.G. full-time students' statistics in *S.A.S.*, 80.
26. Andrew McPherson, 'Nobody wants an ordinary degree' in *The Times Educational Supplement*, 12 January 1973; 'Longitudinal Study'; Dougal Hutchison and Andrew McPherson 'Competing Inequalities: The Sex and Social Class Structure of the First Year Scottish University Student Population 1962–72' in *Sociology*, x, no. 1 (January 1976), 111–16; *Scottish Woman's Place*, 178–9; Alison Kelly, 'Family Background, Subject Specialization and Occupational Recruitment of Scottish University Students: some patterns and trends' in *Higher Education* 5 (1976), 177–88.

27. Freda Newcombe and Graham Ratcliffe, 'The Female Brain: A Neuro-psychological Viewpoint' in Ardener, *op. cit.*, 186–96; Dorothy Griffiths and Esther Savage, 'Sex differences and cognitive abilities: a sterile field of enquiry?' in *Sex Role Stereotyping*, 17–45; Alison Kelly, 'Sex Differences in Science Enrolments' in *Collaborative Research Newsletter of the University of Edinburgh Centre for Educational Sociology* (June 1978), iii, 61–9; 'Swings and Roundabouts', *passim*; Margot Cameron-Jones, 'Sexism in Education' in *Choice, Compulsion and Cost* (S.E.D. 1980), 40–5; Murphy, *op. cit.*; Dougal Hutchison, 'Discouraged Women' in *Higher Education Review*, 4 (3), (summer 1972), 69–70; Helen Weinreich-Haste, 'What Sex is Science?' in *Sex Role Stereotyping*, 168–79; Pauline Marks, 'Femininity in the Classroom: an account of changing attitudes' in *The Rights and Wrongs of Women* ed. Juliet Mitchell and Ann Oakley (London 1976), 176–98; Tessa Blackstone, 'The Education of Girls Today' in *ibid.*, 199–216.

28. *S.A.S.*, 79.

29. *c.f.* Jessie Bernard, *Academic Women* (Pennsylvania 1964), 206–15.

30. *Who Was Who 1961–71*, *passim*.

31. *The Equal Pay Act:* Schedule 1 of *The Sex Discrimination Act* (H.M.S.O. 1975).

32. *The Sex Discrimination Act*; Adams, *op. cit.*

33. *E.O.C. Fourth Annual Report*, 37.

34. *S.A.S.*, 85, 105–11; *E.O.C. Fourth Annual Report*, 73; *c.f.* Kate Purcell, 'Militancy and Acquiescence among Women Workers' in *Fit Work for Women* ed. Sandra Burman (London 1979, hereafter cited as *Fit Work*), 117–18.

35. Taylor, *op. cit.*, 34; *E.O.C. Fourth Annual Report*, 73; Germaine Greer, *The Female Eunuch* (London 1970), 139–61.

36. *Scottish Woman's Place*, 32; Purcell, *op. cit.*, 112–31; Ann Oakley, *Housewife* (London 1974), 73–90; Juliet Mitchell, *Woman's Estate* (London 1971), 123–31.

37. Sheila Rowbotham, *Woman's Consciousness, Man's World* (London 1973), 81–102.

38. *E.O.C. Fourth Annual Report*, 1–2.

39. *Who's Who 1980*, 1409; 'First of the Few' in *The Edinburgh Tatler*, January 1978, 26–7; information from the Law Society of Scotland, The Faculty of Advocates.

40. *Scottish Health Statistics 1979* (H.M.S.O. 1980), 155–9; *Register of Fellows and Members of the Royal College of Obstetricians and Gynaecologists* (London 1979); *The Royal College of Physicians of Edinburgh Directory, 1978*; *The Royal College of Surgeons of Edinburgh: List of Fellows at 31 December 1974*.

41. Information from The Institution of Civil Engineers, The Institute of Chartered Accountants of Scotland, The Scottish Branch of the Royal Institution of Chartered Surveyors, The Faculty of Actuaries, The Institute of Bankers in Scotland.

42. *The Church of Scotland Year Book 1981*; information from the Church of Scotland Press Office.

43. Margaret Bain, 'Scottish Women in Politics' in *Chapman*, xxvii, xxviii (1980); *E.O.C. Fourth Annual Report*, 77.

44. *e.g. The Scotsman*, 8 February 1979; 24 May 1979; 25 September 1979.

45. *c.f.* Simone de Beauvoir, *The Second Sex* (Paris 1949), 690–741.

46. *Early Travellers in Scotland* ed. P. Hume Brown (Edinburgh 1978, reprint of 1891 edition), 47.

INDEX

The occupations indexed are those of women.

abductions 20
Abercairney, Ysende of, wife of Gilbert, 3rd Earl of Strathearn 37, 49
Abercorn, Countess of see Boyd, Marion
Aberdeen 112, 127, 207, 208, 227, 287–9
  Ashley Road School 289
  Central Telephone Office 289
  Musical Society 176
  University 266
Aberdeenshire 100, 160, 254
Aberdeen and Temair, Marchioness of see Marjoribanks, Ishbel
Aberdour 27
abortion 42, 297–8
Abortion Act (1967) 297–8
Aboyne, Lady see Stewart, Lady Margaret
actresses 286, 307
actuaries 313
Adam 44, 83, 103, 281
Adam, Alexander 136
Adam, Jean, poet 242
Addison, Joseph 220
adultery see divorce
advocates 312
Aesop 155
affinity 23
Affleck, Elizabeth 58
Age of Marriage Act (1929) 294
agricultural workers 42, 53, 126, 144, 148, 233, 238
Aikman,William, portrait painter 241
Ainslie, Patrick 101 – see also Kellow, Mary
Airdrie 287
Airlie, Countess of see Drummond, Clementina
Airlie, Countess of see Hamilton, Lady Isobel
Airlie, Countess of see Ogilvy, Helen
Airlie, James, 2nd Earl of 65, 66, 69–70, 161–2 – see also Grant, Mary
Airth 115, 198
Albany, Robert, 1st Duke of 48
Aldowie 188
Alexander III 35, 46
Alexander, Prince 51
Alexander, John, portrait painter 236
Alexander, Lady see Douglas, Lady Margaret

algebra 215–6
Alister, Jean, harvester 233
Allan, Agnes 66
Allardyce, George 105, 111
Allardyce, Mrs George 105
Alloa 231, 234
'Amanda' 190
America 175, 198, 262, 298, 304, 315
anaesthesia 17, 223, 280–3, 298
Ancram, Countess of see D'Arcy, Lady Caroline
Anderson, Andrew 156 – see also Campbell, Agnes
Angus 312
Angus Og, Lord of the Isles 29 – see also O'Cathan, Agnes
Angus, Archibald, 24th Earl of 67, 78–9
Angus, Countess of see Stirling, Katherine
Angus, Countess of see Stuart, Lady Anna
Angus, William, 11th Earl of 67
Annabella, Queen, wife of Robert II 55
Annabella, Princess, wife of (1) Louis, Count of Geneva (2) George, 2nd Earl of Huntly 19, 38
Annand, Rachel 267
Annandale, Countess of see Douglas, Lady Henrietta
Anne, Queen (formerly Princess) 139–40, 168
Anstruther, Christian, widow of Sir William Weir and wife of John Stewart 179
antisepsis 17, 280, 282
anti-suffragettes 287–8
Applegirth see Jardine
Arbroath 210
Arbuthnott, Lady Helen, wife of John Macfarlane of that Ilk 76
Arbuthnott, John, 8th Viscount of 213
archery 45, 134
architecture 305
Ardchattan, The Laird of 237
Argyll 20, 237, 257
Argyll family 64
Argyll, Archibald, 8th Earl of 65
Argyll, Archibald, 1st Marquis of, formerly Lord Lorne 65
Argyll, Countess of see Talmash, Lady Elizabeth

Argyll, George, 8th Duke of   252, 286
Argyll, John, 2nd Duke of   171
Argyll, John, 7th Duke of   270
arithmetic   128, 133, 207, 212, 214–6,
    222, 255
Arniston   135 – see also Dundas
Arnot, Agnes, wife of Lawrence
    Thomson   99–101
Arran   285
Arran, Countess of   see Spencer, Lady
    Anne
Arran, James, Earl of   see Hamilton,
    James, 4th Duke of
arsonists   158
artists   241, 286, 307–8
arts subjects   305 – see also individual
    subjects
Asquith, Herbert H   289–91
assemblies   168, 175, 178
Association for the Higher Education of
    Women   261
Atholl family   85
Atholl, Duchess of   see Hamilton, Lady
    Katherine
Atholl, Duchess of   see Ross, Mary
Atholl, James, 2nd Duke of   183
Atholl, John, 4th Earl of   134
Atholl, John, 1st Duke of   83, 138 – see
    also Hamilton, Lady Katherine;
    Ross, Mary
Atholl, John, 7th Duke of, formerly
    Marquis of Tullibardine   272 – see
    also Moncrieff, Louisa
Atkinson, Henry   50 – see also Atkinson,
    Mrs Henry
Atkinson, Mrs Henry   50
Atkinson, Margaret   52
Auchinleck   277
Auchinleck, Alexander Boswell,
    Lord   195 – see also Erskine,
    Euphemia
Auchinleck, Lady   see Erskine, Euphemia
Auld, Alexander   31
Auld Reekie   see Edinburgh
Austria, Duchess of   see Eleanor, Princess
Avendale   137
Ayala, Don Pedro de   315
Ayr   29, 126, 152, 207, 253, 255, 289
Ayr Racecourse   289
Ayrshire   232, 235, 252, 254, 277, 287,
    290

backgammon (tables)   44, 135
Baillie, Elizabeth, wife of William
    Brodie   248
Baillie, Captain Evan   199
Baillie, Grisel (Girsie)   133
Baillie, Lady Grisel   see Hume, Lady
    Grisel
Baillie, Joanna, dramatist   242–3

Baillie, Miss, wife of Mr Cumming of
    Logie   191–2
Baillie of Jerviswood, Mrs   251
Baillie of Lamington, William   76
bakers   151
Balaclava   249
Balcarres, Colin, 3rd Earl of   172
Balcarres, Lady   see Dalrymple, Anne
Balconie   see Scott
Balcomie House   199
Balfour, David   50 – see also Balfour,
    Elizabeth
Balfour, Elizabeth, wife of David
    Balfour   50
Balfour, Colonel Eustace   286 – see also
    Campbell, Lady Frances
Balfour of Pittendreich, Sir James   28, 34,
    87
Balfour of Burleigh, John, 3rd Lord   66
Balfour, John   66
Balfour of Pilrig, Louisa   179
Balfour, Professor   262
Balfour of Pitcullo, Sir William   66
Balgonie   143
Balgonie, Alexander, Lord   86
Baliol of Barnard Castle, John   36, 48–9
    – see also Galloway, Devorgilla of
Balloch   148
Ballogie   see Forbes
ballooning   175
balls   85, 139, 172–4, 189, 213, 232
Balmerino   49
Balvenie   see Innes
Banff   69, 254
bank clerks   291
bank managers   313
banns, proclamation of   31, 81, 272, 294
baptisms   43, 44, 82, 112, 113
Barcaldine   238, 240 – see also Campbell
Barcaldine, The Laird of   see Campbell
    of Barcaldine, Sir Duncan
Bargany, Lady   see Cunningham, Lady
    Margaret
Bargany, Lady   see Douglas, Lady Jean
Barnard Castle   see Baliol
Barnard, Lady Anne   see Lindsay, Lady
    Anne
Barncluith, The Laird of   113
Barnet   199
Barnton, The Laird of   see Hamilton
Bass, The   see Lauder
Bath   168, 205
Batherston, Mrs   163
Bathgate   78, 280
Bayne, Helen   49
Beaumont of Vescy, Isabella de   48
Beaumont, Mrs   see Montgomerie,
    Elizabeth
Beck, Mr, music teacher   172
beggars   53

Beldam, Valentine 78
Belhaven, Lady see Hamilton, Margaret
Bellenden, Catherine, wife of Oliver
    Sinclair of Pitcairns 37
Bellenden, John, 2nd Lord 177
Bellenden, Mary 177
Bellew, John, 4th Lord 182
Belsches, Mr 183
Bennett, Professor Hughes 263
Bergen 33
Berkshire 243
Berne, University of 266
Berwick 33, 36
Berwick Castle 39
Berwick, Holy Trinity Church 33
Betoun, Elizabeth, wife of (1) John, 4th
    Lord Innermeath (2) James
    Gray 68
betrothals 27–8, 74, 81
bigamy 95
billiards 135
Binning, Lord see Haddington, Thomas,
    1st Earl of
biochemists 312
birth control see contraception
Bisset, Margaret 152
Black, Agnes see Randolph, Lady Agnes
Blackadder, Dr Agnes, wife of Dr Thomas
    D. Savill 308
Blackwood, The Laird of see Lawrie,
    William
Bladenoch, River 161
Blair, Catherine 180
blue-stockings 219–22
Board of Education Consultative
    Committee on Secondary School
    Curricula 303
boarding schools 206–8, 213, 215, 220,
    237, 254, 258–9
Boaz, Mr, conjuror 174
'Bogan of Bogan, Mrs' see Oliphant,
    Caroline
Boghurst, Mary, wife of George
    Preston 99
Bolton, John, harpsichord maker 136
Bombay 182
Bonar, John, merchant 137–8
Bo'ness 149, 154, 214, 236, 251
Bonhard see Cornwall
bonnetmakers 52, 163
Bonnytoun, The Laird of 68
books 54, 59, 93, 123, 128, 133, 137,
    155–6, 193, 215–20, 225, 231, 247,
    250
bookbinders 240
bookkeeping 207
booksellers 155, 157
Borthwick, Isabel, wife of Mr Robert
    Crichton 88
Borthwick, Janet, wife of (1) Sir James

Douglas of Dalkeith (2) George, 1st
    Earl of Caithness 47
Borthwick, Margaret, wife of John
    Thomson 75
Borthwick, Mary 31
Boston 242, 262
Boswell, David 27 – see also Hamilton,
    Lady Janet
Boswell, James 170–1, 173, 177, 179–80,
    185, 192, 195, 228, 233, 235 – see also
    Montgomerie, Margaret
botanists 307
Bothwell, Adam, 2nd Earl of 27 – see
    also Stewart, Agnes
Bothwell, Countess of see Gordon, Lady
    Jane
Bothwell, James, 4th Earl of 97 – see also
    Gordon, Lady Jane; Mary, Queen of
    Scots
Bothwell, Patrick, 4th Earl of 27
bowling 137
Bowman, David 100 – see also Lindsay,
    Bessie
Boyd, Margaret, wife of David, 3rd Earl of
    Cassilis 58
Boyd, Marion, wife of James, 1st Earl of
    Abercorn 159
Braco see Smythe
Brandon, Miss G, governess 237–40
Braxfield, Robert MacQueen, Lord 197
Branxholm 147 – see also Scott
breastfeeding 18, 117–8, 120–1, 229–30,
    299–300
Brechin 210
Brechin Castle 77
brewers 50, 153, 291
bridesmaids 83
bridge-building 48, 147
Britain 309, 311, 314
British Lying-in Hospital 224, 229
Brittany, Duchess of see Isabella,
    Princess
Brodie, Elizabeth see Baillie, Elizabeth
Broomhall, Robert, Lord 66
Brown, Agnes, nun 53–4
Brown, Agnes, postmaster, widow of
    William Seaton 155
Brown, Sara, merchant 152
Bruce, Lady Christian, wife of (1)
    Gratney, 7th Earl of Mar (2) Sir
    Christopher Seton (3) Sir Andrew
    Moray 48
Bruce, George, son of Lord Broomhall 66
    – see also Allan, Agnes
Bruce, of Kinross, Sir John (Mr
    Bruce) 92 – see also Leslie,
    Christian
Bruce, Marjorie, wife of Walter the
    Steward 43
Bruce, Mr see Bruce of Kinross, Sir John

Bruce, Robert   see Carrick, 3rd Earl of
Bruce, Robert   see Robert I
Bruce, Robert   66
Buccleuch, Countess of   see Hay, Mary
Buccleuch, Walter, 1st Earl of   145 – see
    also Hay, Mary
Buchan, Countess of   see -------, Isabella
Buchan, James, 1st Earl of   27
Buchan, Janey   see Kent, Janey
Buchan, John, 2nd Earl of   38–9 – see
    also --------, Isabella
Buchanan, The Laird of   71
Bucknall, Mrs, schoolmistress   237
burgesses   50–1, 152, 163
Burleigh   see Balfour
Burntisland   214–5
Burton, Dr John   225
bus conductors   291
business studies   305
butchers   240
Bute   257
Bute, Countess of   see Campbell, Lady
    Anne
Bute, Countess of   see Dundas, Christian
Butler, Mary, wife of Sir Alexander
    Dick   231
butter saps 113
butter sellers (butter wives)   50, 153–4
butter wives   see butter sellers

cabinet ministers   308, 314
Caithness, Countess of   see Campbell,
    Mary
calligraphers   163
Cambo   see Erskine
Cambuslang   253
Cambusnethan   154
Campbell family   237
Campbell, Agnes, wife of Andrew
    Anderson   156–7, 163
Campbell, Lady Anna   129
Campbell, Lady Anne, wife of James, 2nd
    Earl of Bute   179
Campbell, Caroline   175
Campbell, Lady Catherine, wife of
    Maclean of Duart   40
Campbell of Glenorchy, Sir Colin   44 –
    see also Ruthven, Katherine
Campbell of Glenorchy, Sir Colin   147–8
Campbell of Glenure, Colin   236
Campbell, Colin   20
Campbell, Mrs Colin   118
Campbell, Dr   226
Campbell of Barcaldine, Sir Duncan (The
    Laird of Barcaldine)   175
Campbell, Duncan (Dunkie)   230
Campbell, Lady Eleanor, wife of John,
    2nd Earl of Stair   171, 231–2
Campbell, Lady Emma, wife of Sir John
    McNeill of Colonsay   270

Campbell, Lady Frances, wife of Colonel
    Eustace Balfour   286
Campbell, Mrs Hamilton   252
Campbell, Lady Harriet   177
Campbell, Sir Hugh   130
Campbell, Isabel   236
Campbell, Isabella Hamilton Dundas,
    wife of Lieutenant Lachlan
    Macquarrie   271
[Campbell], James   237
Campbell, Lady Jean, wife of Robert, 4th
    Earl and later 1st Marquis of
    Lothian   70, 106, 129, 142, 144
Campbell of Glenorchy, Sir John   148
Campbell of Glenorchy, Lady   see
    Sinclair, Elizabeth
Campbell, Margaret, wife of Francis, 7th
    Earl of Wemyss   175
Campbell, Margaret   130–1
Campbell, Lady Mary, wife of (1) George,
    6th Earl of Caithness (2) John, 1st
    Earl of Breadalbane   129, 144, 148
Campbell, Mary, wife of Alexander
    Campbell of Barcaldine   228, 237–40
Campbell of Glenure, Mary   230
Campbell, Mary, merchant   153
Campbell of Barcaldine, Miss   232, 238
Campbell, Mor, wife of Hector
    MacLean   20
Campbell, Mr   236
Campbell, Mrs, of Islay   238–9
Campbell, Lady Victoria   252, 286
Campvere   see Wolfort
Campvere, Lady of   see Mary, Princess
Campvere, Lord of   see Wolfort
candlemakers   154
candle sellers   154
Cannes   270
Cape of Good Hope   277
card games   45, 135, 137, 168–9, 173,
    176
Carey, Philadelphia, widow of Sir Thomas
    Wharton and wife of Sir George
    Lockhart of Carnwath   95–6
Carlino, Signor, tightrope walker   172
Carlisle   21
Carlyle, The Reverend
    Alexander   175–6, 190, 202, 206–7
Carlyle, Jean   212–13
Carlyle, Thomas   180–1, 191–3, 212, 219,
    274–5 – see also Welsh, Jane
Carlyle, The Reverend William   202–3
Carnegy, Dr   181–2
Carnwath   see Lockhart
Caroline, Queen, wife of George II   229
Carrick, Marjorie, s.j. Countess of   26, 40
    – see also Carrick, Robert, 3rd Earl of
Carrick, Robert, 3rd Earl of   26 – see also
    Carrick, Marjorie, s.j. Countess of
Carstares, John   67

Carteret, Lady Frances, wife of John, 4th
    Marquis of Tweeddale 177
Cassilis, Countess of see Boyd, Margaret
Cassilis, Countess of see Hamilton, Lady
    Jean
Cassilis, Countess of see Hamilton, Lady
    Susanna
Cassilis, Countess of see Kennedy,
    Margaret
Cassilis, John, 6th Earl of 92–3 – see also
    Hamilton, Lady Jean
Cassilis, John, 7th Earl of 65 – see also
    Hamilton, Lady Susanna
Castle Leod 148
Castle Tioram 203
'Cat and Mouse' Act (Prisoners'
    Temporary Discharge for Ill-Health
    Act) (1913) 290
caterers 151, 309
Cathcart, Alan, 4th Lord 21
Cathcart, Lady see Hamilton, Jean
Catrine 287
Cawdor, Lady see Stewart, Lady
    Henrietta
Chamberlen, Dr Hew 107, 111, 118
Chamberlen, Dr Peter 111
Chambers, Mr, music master 131
Chapman, George 211–12, 230
charitable activities 147, 247–51
chartered accountants 313
chartered surveyors 313
Charteris, Janet, wife of James, 4th Earl of
    Wemyss 183
Charteris, Mrs 183
chastity 26
chemistry 304
chess 44–5, 135
Cheyne, Christian, wife of Sir ALexander
    Seton 36–7
Chiesly, Anna, shopkeeper 153
Chiesly, Rachel, wife of James Erskine,
    Lord Grange 201–4
childbirth 17–18, 42–3, 47, 55, 59, 92–4,
    105–15, 121–2, 177, 223, 231, 250,
    279–83, 297–300, 308, 314–5
child marriages 19, 21, 35–36, 71
child mortality 17, 91, 105, 121–2, 158,
    184, 229, 299
chiropodists 240
Christie, Jean, mantua maker 236
Christison, Professor Robert 263, 265–6
Churchill, Winston 285–6
Church of Scotland 272, 313

churching of women see purification
Cibber, Colley, dramatist 171
circuses 167
Clarendon, Edward, 1st Earl of 156
Clark, Dr William 225
Clarkson, Bessie, merchant 50
cleaners 309
Clelland, Christian, schoolmistress 133
Clelland, Elizabeth, pastry mistress 206
Clelland, Euphan 233
Clephane, Margaret, oyster seller 49
clerical workers 309–10
Clerk, Barbara 82
Clerk, Baron see Clerk, Sir John
Clerk, Christian (Christy) 183
Clerk, Helen 133
Clerk, John 68, 138
Clerk of Penicuik, Sir John 72–3, 82,
    93–4, 115, 133, 197 – see also
    Henderson, Elizabeth; Kirkpatrick,
    Christian
Clerk of Penicuik, Sir John (Baron
    Clerk) 68, 156–7, 182–3, 190, 194
    – see also Stewart, Lady Margaret;
    Inglis, Janet
Clerk, Katherine, wife of William Edgar 75
Clerk, Margaret 106
Clerk, Margaret (Peggy) 183
Clerk, Sophia (Sophie), wife of Gabriel
    Rankin 72–3, 94, 115, 197–8, 227
cloth sellers 50, 152–3, 235
Cluny see MacPherson
Clyde, River 137
coalbearers 148–9, 234
coal sellers 154
Cobham, Robert G 269 – see also Grant,
    Adela
Cockburnspath 47, 253
co-education 126, 254–7, 302–4
Colingtowne, Margaret, Lady 112
Colpi, Mrs, tightrope walker 172
Colquhoun, Lilias, wife of Sir John
    Stirling of Keir 71
Committee on Medical Aspects of Food
    Policy in Britain (1972) 299
Comrie 211
concerts 172, 175–6, 178, 213
Conference on Electoral Reform
    (1917) 291
Conjugal Rights (Scotland) Amendment
    Act (1861) 278
conjunct fee see jointure
consanguinity 22–3, 270
consultants 312–13
contraception 42, 297, 314
cooking 127, 144, 151–2, 206–8, 210,
    212, 247, 253, 255, 257
Cooper, Miss 188
Corelli, Arcangelo, composer 176
Cornwall of Bonhard, Walter 137

corsetmakers 240
Corsfoordbait 80
Corson, Mrs Margaret 83
Cortachy 146
counterfeiters 158
Coupar, James, 1st Lord 66 – see also
Ogilvy, Lady Marion
Coupar, Lady see Ogilvy, Lady Marion
Coupland, Marion, merchant 50
courtly love 26
Craigenputtock 248
Craig Park see Mackenzie
Crail 48
Cramond see Inglis
Crawford, Countess of see Hamilton,
Lady Margaret
Crawford, David, secretary 119
creeling 273
Crichton, Elizabeth 21
Crichton, James, 2nd Lord 56 – see also
Dunbar, Janet
Crichton, Margaret 21
Crichton of Sauchie, Sir Robert 58
Crichton, Robert 58 – see also Erskine,
Dame Christian
Crichton, Robert, lawyer 88 – see also
Borthwick, Isabel
Crichton, William, 5th Lord 21
Crieff 211
Crimean War 249
Cromartie, George, 3rd Earl of 200
Crompton, Elizabeth, wife of Hugh, 3rd
Earl of Marchmont 179–80, 190
Crompton, Mr, linen draper 180
croquet 134–5
Crudelius, Mr 259 – see also Maclean,
Mary
Crusades, The 26
Culpeper, Nicholas 110, 112, 118
Culross 234
Cumin, Charles (sic) Anne, wife of Sir
Thomas Dick Lauder 190
Cumming of Logie, Mr 192 – see also
Baillie, Miss
Cumming of Logie, Mrs see Baillie, Miss
Cunningham, Lady Anna, wife of James,
2nd Marquis of Hamilton 93, 129,
135, 137, 142, 147–8, 160
Cunningham, Lady see Hamilton, Agnes
Cunningham, Lady Margaret, wife of
John, 2nd Lord Bargany 137
Cunningham, Lady Margaret, wife of
John, 5th Earl of Lauderdale 148
Cunningham, Margaret, wife of Sir John
Maxwell of Pollok 109
Cunningham, Lady Marion 79
Cunningham, Susannah, wife of James
Dalrymple of Orangefield 200
Cunningham of Enterkin, William 121
Cupar 50

Dalhousie, Countess of see Moore, Lady
Mary
Dalkeith, Lady see Borthwick, Janet
Dallen, Agnes, fruit wife 153
Dalmahoy of that Ilk, Sir Alexander 196
– see also Paterson, Dame Alice
Dalrymple, Anne, wife of James, 5th Earl
of Balcarres 185
Dalrymple, Anne, wife of Sir James
Steuart of Goodtries 84
Dalrymple, David, wright 154 – see also
Robertson, Janet
Dalrymple, Sir Hew 84 – see also
Dalrymple, Lady
Dalrymple of Northberwick, Hugh, Lord
President of the Court of
Session 168
Dalrymple of Orangefield, James 200
– see also Cunningham, Susannah
Dalrymple, Lady, wife of Sir Hew
Dalrymple 84
Dalserf 253
Dalyell, Agnes 152
Dalzell of that Ilk, Robert 47
Dance, Nathaniel 242
dancing 44, 123, 128, 130, 133, 135,
142, 167–70, 173–4, 178, 206–9, 214,
237
Danzig 30
D'Arcy, Lady Caroline, wife of William,
Earl of Ancram and later 4th
Marquis of Lothian 177
Darnley, Henry, Lord 92, 135
Darroch, Janet 51
Dauphin of France see Louis XI
David II (formerly Prince David) 33
– see also Joanna, Princess
David, Prince see David II
Dawling, John 100 – see also Lyon,
Jean
death mask makers 163
Deceased Brother's Widow's Marriage
Act 271
defence of castles 48, 162
Denham, James, customs official 149
Denmark 298
Dennistoun, Isabella, wife of Gabriel
Hamilton-Dundas 174, 232
Dennistoun, Miss 249
Dennistoun, Mrs 249
dentists 312–3
dentistry 305
Derby, Edward, 12th Lord 177 – see also
Hamilton, Lady Betty
dermatologists 307–8
desertion see divorce
Despard, Charlotte see French,
Charlotte
De Stael, Madam see Necker, Anne
Louise Germaine

INDEX

Dewar, Mrs 174
Dewar, William 29 – see also Marshall, Marion
dice 44
Dick, Sir Alexander 231 – see also Butler, Mary
Dick, Janet 231
Dick, Sir John 145 – see also Paterson, Dame Anna
Dick, Lady – see Butler, Mary
Dick, Lady see Paterson, Dame Anna
Dick Lauder, Sir Thomas 190 – see also Cumin, Charles Anne
dinner parties 173–4
Dirleton, James, 1st Earl of 77
divorce 38–9, 68, 96, 97–9, 102–3, 195–201, 278–9, 300–1
divorce for adultery 68, 96, 98–9, 195, 199, 279, 300–1
divorce for cruelty 300–1
divorce for desertion 96, 99, 279, 300–1
Divorce (Scotland) Act (1938) 300
Divorce (Scotland) Act (1976) 301
doctors 262–6, 286, 291, 297, 304, 307–8, 312
Dolphin, Sara, shopkeeper 197
domestic economy 257, 302
Douglas of Kilspindie, Archibald 37 – see also Hoppar, Isabel
Douglas, Elizabeth, wife of William St Clair 20
Douglas of Parkhead, George 147 – see also Douglas, Marion
Douglas, Lady Helen, wife of Sir James Hall, 4th Baronet of Dunglass 167, 251, 275
Douglas, Lady Henrietta, wife of John, 1st Earl of Annandale 67
Douglas, Lady Isabel, wife of James, 1st Duke of Queensberry 67
Douglas, Lady Isabella, s.j. Countess of Mar 20
Douglas, James, 2nd Marquis of 101–2 – see also Erskine, Lady Barbara
Douglas, Lady Jane, wife of James, 4th Earl of Perth 67, 114
Douglas, Janet, wife of John, 6th Lord Glamis 40
Douglas, Janet 153
Douglas, Lady Jean, wife of John, 1st Lord Bargany 67
Douglas, John 151 – see also Fletcher, Margaret
Douglas, Lady Lucy, wife of Robert, 4th Earl of Nithsdale 67, 135
Douglas, Marchioness of see Erskine, Lady Barbara
Douglas, Lady Margaret, wife of Matthew, 4th Earl of Lennox 92

Douglas, Lady Margaret, wife of Archibald, 8th Earl and 1st Marquis of Argyll 69, 108, 128–9, 142–4
Douglas, Lady Margaret, wife of William, Lord Alexander 67
Douglas, Marion, wife of George Douglas of Parkhead 147
Douglas, Mrs 252
Douglas, Sir William 140
dowry see tochers
dramatists 243
drawing 123, 207, 209, 214, 216, 222, 237, 240–2
drawing teachers 241
dressmakers 235–7
Drum see Somerville
Drumelzier 151
Drummond 179
Drummond, Lady Barbara 179
Drummond, Clementina, wife of David, 6th Earl of Airlie 251
Drummond, Flora see Gibson, Flora
Drummond, Lady Jane 143
Drummond of Logiealmond, Sir John 114 – see also Steuart, Grizel
Drummond, Lady see Steuart, Grizel
Drummond, Lilias, wife of James, 4th Earl of Tullibardine 111–2
dry-nurses 119, 150
Drysdale, Miss, schoolmistress 213
Duart see Maclean
Duke, Jean 100
Dumbarton 19
Dumfries 48, 75, 160, 196, 198, 210, 212, 312
Dumfriesshire 135, 198, 212, 230, 248, 254, 259, 276
Dunbar Castle 48
Dunbar, Anne, wife of James, 4th Earl of Findlater and 1st Earl of Seafield 132, 182
Dunbar, Barbara 100 – see also Sutherland, William
Dunbar, Janet, s.j. Countess of Moray, wife of (1) James, 2nd Lord Crichton (2) James Sutherland 56, 58
Dunbar of Durn, Sir William 132
Dunbar, Mary, wife of Lord Basil Hamilton 106, 182
Dunbar, William, poet 54
Duncan and Flockhart 280–1
Duncan, Miss, schoolmistress 237
Dundas, Christian, wife of James, 1st Earl of Bute 179
Dundas, Elizabeth, wife of Sir Patrick Murray of Langshaw 76
Dundas of that Ilk, George 135 – see also Oliphant, Katherine
Dundas, Sir James 76
Dundas, Mrs, mantua maker 235

[347]

Dundas of Arniston, Robert   194 – see
    also Gordon, Anne
Dundee   52, 121, 200, 285–9
Dundee, Farington Hall   289
Dundee, Musical Society   176
Dundee, Nethergate   287
Dundonald, Archibald, 9th Earl of   234
Dunfermline   37, 211
Dunino, Ellen of   50
Dunipace   253
Dunkeld   80
Dunmore   273
Dunmore, Countess of   see Hamilton,
    Lady Susan
Dunninald   162
Dunoon   252
Dunvegan Castle   150, 163
Durn   see Dunbar
Duscoull, Alison de, guild sister   51
Duscoull, Robert de, merchant   51
Dysart   83

Earnock, The Laird of   113
East Lothian   252
Eccles, William, surgeon   108
economics   305
Eden, Garden of   44
Edgar, Atheling   37
Edgar, William   75 – see also Clerk,
    Katherine
Edgeworth, Maria   222, 244
Edinburgh (Auld Reekie)   30, 43, 49,
    50–3, 57, 72–3, 75, 78, 91, 93–6,
    99–101, 108, 110, 114–15, 119, 126–7,
    130, 133, 135–7, 139, 144, 149–57,
    161, 163, 167–9, 171–6, 178, 184,
    186–7, 193, 196–200, 203–4, 206–9,
    212–13, 216, 218, 221, 225–7, 232,
    235–9, 241, 243, 250–2, 258–9, 261–2,
    266, 284, 287, 289, 291, 303
Edinburgh, Albany Street   237
Edinburgh, Blackford Observatory   289
Edinburgh, Blind Asylum   251
Edinburgh, Calton Hill   175
Edinburgh, Canongate of   45, 151
Edinburgh, Carrubbers Close   172
Edinburgh Castle   35, 154
Edinburgh, City Chambers   293
Edinburgh, Comely Bank   240
Edinburgh, Comely Gardens   170
Edinburgh Commissary Court   196–200
Edinburgh, Cowgate   171–2, 203
Edinburgh, Destitute Sick Society   251
Edinburgh Essay Society   258, 284
Edinburgh Extra-Mural School   264,
    266
Edinburgh, Fettes College   290
Edinburgh, Forrest Road   291
Edinburgh, Forrester's Wynd   173
Edinburgh, George Street   236

Edinburgh, George Watson's Ladies'
    College   258
Edinburgh, Great King Street   175
Edinburgh, Greyfriars parish   227
Edinburgh, Heriot Row   214
Edinburgh High School   195
Edinburgh, High Street   50, 168
Edinburgh, Holyroodhouse   123, 133–4,
    151, 154–5, 161, 168, 170–1
Edinburgh House of Refuge   251
Edinburgh Institute for Young
    Ladies   258
Edinburgh Ladies Educational
    Association   259–60
Edinburgh, Lord Provost of   see
    MacLeod, Sir John Lorne – see also
    Trotter, Mrs William
Edinburgh Lying-in Hospital   226, 251
Edinburgh Merchant Company   256
Edinburgh, Merchant Maiden
    Hospital   258
Edinburgh, Milne's Square   235
Edinburgh, Morelands House   290
Edinburgh Music Festival   175
Edinburgh New Town Dispensary   251
Edinburgh, Oddfellows' Hall   291
Edinburgh, Old Assembly Close   168
Edinburgh, Outlook Tower   293
Edinburgh, Picardy Place   237
Edinburgh, Pleasance of   100, 198
Edinburgh, Princes Street   178, 250,
    285
Edinburgh Royal Infirmary   265–6
Edinburgh, Royal Scottish Museum   289
Edinburgh, Salisbury Crags   175
Edinburgh, Scott Monument   289
Edinburgh, Shandwick Place   260
Edinburgh, St Cecilia's Hall   172
Edinburgh, St Cuthbert's Parish   227
Edinburgh, Surgeons' Hall   265
Edinburgh, Synod Hall   293
Edinburgh, Tailors' Hall   171
Edinburgh University   226, 260–6, 280
Edinburgh, West Bow   168
Edinburgh Women Citizens'
    Association   291, 293
Edmiston, Mrs   see Edmonston, Grisel
Edmonston, Grisel, merchant   154
education   18, 52, 54–60, 123–34,
    205–22, 247–67, 302–8, 312–14
Education Act (1872)   255, 302
Edward I of England   25, 38, 49, 54
Edward III of England   48
Eglinton, Alexander, 6th Earl of   65, 145,
    162 – see also Anna Livingstone;
    Margaret Scott
Eglinton, Alexander, 10th Earl of   177,
    190
Eglinton, Countess of   see Kennedy,
    Lady Susanna

Eglinton, Countess of   see Livingstone, Lady Anna
Eglinton, Countess of   see Montgomerie, Margaret
Eglinton, Countess of   see Scott, Lady Margaret
Elcho, convent at   56–7
Elder, Mrs John   261
Eleanor, Princess, wife of Sigismond, Duke of Austria   19
Elgin   38, 69, 135, 210
Elgin Cathedral 38
Elibank, Lady   181
Elliot, Thomas, factor   203
Elliott, Lady Anna Maria   221
elopements   72–3, 182–5, 187, 198–9
Elouis, Monsieur, harp master   214
Elphinstone, John, 8th Lord   112
Elphinstone, Mary Beatrice Anna Margaret Frances Isabella   112–13
embroiderers   52
engineering   305
engineers   313
England   12, 29, 37–8, 47–9, 56, 72, 78, 118, 121, 124, 127, 130, 132, 136, 155, 189, 205, 213, 223, 227, 259, 262, 272, 297, 299, 304, 315
Enterkin, The Laird of   see Cunningham of Enterkin, William
Epictetus   138
Equal Opportunities Commission   309, 311
Equal Pay Act (1970)   308–9
Erasmus, Desiderius   59
Eric II of Norway   32 – see also Margaret, Princess
Ermengarde, Queen, wife of William I ('the Lion')   48–9
Errol, James, 15th Earl of   199
Erskine   277
Erskine, Lady Barbara, wife of James, 2nd Marquis of Douglas   101–2
Erskine, Sir Charles, of Cambo   153
Erskine, Dame Christian, wife of Robert Crichton   58
Erskine, Euphemia, wife of Alexander Boswell, Lord Auchinleck   195
Erskine, Sir Henry   177 – see also Wedderburn, Janet
Erskine, Colonel John   67 – see also Maule, Lady Mary
Erskine, Lady Mary, wife of (1) William, 6th Earl Marischal (2) Patrick, 1st Earl of Panmure   67–8
Erskine, Sir Robert   20 – see also Menteith, Christian
Erskine, Thomas   92
estate mananagament   47, 93–4, 142, 146, 163
Esther   33

Eton   205
Euclid   216
Europe   136
Europe, Western   42, 118, 123, 209, 226, 229, 315
European Parliament   314
Eve   44, 83, 103
Evelick   see Lindsay
Evota of Stirling   49
Ewing, Winifred   see Woodburn, Winifred
executors   88
Exton, Dr Brudenall   225

Factory Act (1833)   275
factory workers   234, 276
Fairfax, Mary, wife of (1) Samuel Greig (2) Dr William Somerville   171, 178, 214–18, 221, 225, 247, 250, 283
Fairlie, Professor Margaret   308
falconry   45, 137
Falkland   134
Farquhar, Christian, wife of Captain John MacNeill   198
Fawcup, James   31
Fawside, John of   50 – see also Fawside, Mrs John of
Fawside, Mrs John of   50
female suffrage   283–92
Fentonbarns   see Whitelaw
Fergusson family   174
Fergusson, Mary   313
Ferniehirst   see Ker
Fettes, Sir William   240
Fife   37, 48, 50, 183, 200, 252, 276, 289
Fife, Robert, 12th Earl of   23, 38
Findlater, Countess of   see Dunbar, Anne
Findlater, Countess   see Montgomerie, Lady Anna
Findlater, James, 3rd Earl of   73, 132, 155–6 – see also Hamilton, Lady Mary
Findlater, James, 4th Earl of   132 – see also Dunbar, Anne
fine art   260
Finlay, Dr W. A.   250
fireworks   140
Fishar, John   58 – see also Winzet, Isobel
fishwives   153–4, 233, 286
Fleming, Lady Jane, wife of James Grant of Freuchie   64
Fletcher of Saltoun, Andrew   91
Fletcher, Margaret, washerwoman, wife of John Douglas   151–2
Flodden, battle of   27, 47
Flood, Lieutenant Hatton   199
Florence   see Geographical Society of Florence
Fonteine, Edward, dancing master   133, 168

Fonteine, James, dancing master 168
Forbes, Alexander, 11th Lord 88 – see
    also Forbes, Elizabeth
Forbes of Torquhoun, Sir Alexander 100
Forbes of Ballogie, Alexander 117
Forbes of Ballogie, Mrs Alexander 117
Forbes, Anne, portrait painter 241–2
Forbes, Betty, schoolmistress 207
Forbes, Elizabeth, wife of Alexander, 11th
    Lord Forbes 88
Forbes-Robertson, Jean 307
Forbes-Robertson, Sir Johnston 307
Forbes, Lady see Forbes, Elizabeth
forbidden degrees see consanguinity and
    affinity
foreign languages 129–30, 133, 206–9,
    213–14, 217–18, 237, 255–6, 258, 277,
    304
Forfar 176, 211
fornication 84
Forres 38, 210
Forrester, Isobel, wife of Sir John Lundy
    of Lundy 44
Forster Hill, Captain John 199 – see also
    Charlton, Harriet
Forth, Firth of 42, 53, 199
Forth, River 215
Fort William 230
Foulis of Ravelston, George 121
Foulis, Sir John 135
Fountainhall – see Lauder
Fourth Lateran Council 22
France 19, 45, 59, 123, 127, 129,
    132,142, 145, 174, 200, 291
Fraser, Donald, gardener 187–8
Fraser, Luke 195
Fraser, Mrs Luke 195
Fraser, Professor 260
French, Charlotte, wife of Colonel
    Maximilian Despard 285
French, Colonel John 199
French Revolution 278
Freuchie see Grant
Fruitwives 50, 153
Fullarton, John, burgess 29
Fullarton, Mariota, wife of John
    Pettigrew 29
funerals 44, 139
Fyne, Katherine 51

Galloway 312
Galloway, Alan, Lord of 36
Galloway, Devorgilla of, wife of
    John Baliol of Barnard Castle 36,
    48–9
Galloway, John, 7th Earl of 177 – see
    Greville, Lady Charlotte Mary
gambling 45, 135, 137
gardens 45, 147
gardeners 240

Garlies, Lady see Greville, Lady
    Charlotte Mary
Garlies, Lord see Galloway, John, 7th
    Earl of
Gay, John 171
Geddes, Jenny 293
Geddie, Elizabeth, wife of William
    Renton 98
Gellius, Aulus 119
Gendrin, Nicholas 280
General Committee for Woman
    Suffrage 284
Genesis 281
Geneva 83
Geneva, Countess of see Annabella,
    Princess
Geneva, Louis, Count of 19, 38 – see also
    Annabella, Princess
Geographical Society of Florence 217
geography 207, 213
George I 141
George II 229 – see also Caroline,
    Queen
George III 177 – see also Charlotte,
    Queen
George V 290 – see also Mary, Queen
Gerard, Lady Elizabeth, wife of James,
    4th Duke of Hamilton 85, 109–10,
    156
Gibb, Abigail, postmaster 155
Gibb, Alison 288
Gibb, Bessie, merchant 154
Gibb, Elspeth, merchant 154
Gibb, Mrs, taverner 154
Gibson, Agnes, merchant 154
Gibson, Flora, wife of Joseph
    Drummond 285–6, 290
Gilchrist, Dugald 181
Girvan 254
Glamis, John, 6th Lord 40 – see also
    Douglas, Lady Janet
Glamis, Lady see Douglas, Janet
Glanderston, The Laird of see Mure
Glasgow 113, 175–6, 179, 196, 198,
    206–7, 234–5, 238, 242, 249, 252–8,
    261, 277, 284, 289–90, 297, 314
Glasgow, Archibshop of see Paterson,
    John
Glasgow, Bath Street 285
Glasgow, Hutcheson's Girls' School 258
Glasgow, Mr Burrell's Dancing Hall 176
Glasgow, Queen Margaret College 261,
    266
Glasgow School of Cookery 257
Glasgow, St Andrew's Hall 284, 290
Glasgow University 224, 266, 282, 288
glass-blowers 240
Glen, James 146
Glen, Mrs 146
Glenartney 211

Glencarse   see Murray
Glenorchy   see Campbell
Glenure   see Campbell
Gloag, Eliza   174
glovers   240
golf   134
Goodtries   see Steuart
Gordon, Lady Anna, wife of James, 3rd
   Earl of Moray   147
Gordon, Anne, wife of Robert Dundas of
   Arniston   194
Gordon, Dr Alexander   227
Gordon, Duchess of   see Howard, Lady
   Elizabeth
Gordon, Duchess of   see Maxwell, Jane
Gordon, Lady Elizabeth   99
Gordon, Isabel, wife of Alexander
   Milne   99
Gordon, Lady Jane, wife of James, 4th
   Earl of Bothwell   97
Gordon, Lady Janet   40
Gordon of Rothiemay, Lady   127
Gosport   181
Goulden, Emmeline, wife of Dr Richard
   Pankhurst   285, 288–90
Govan   48, 252
governesses   213, 237–40, 277
Grace, Grizel, wife of John Welsh   191,
   219
Graham, Margaret, wife of Thomas, 9th
   Earl of Mar   38
Graham, Margaret   98
Grahame, Elizabeth, wife of James
   Somerville of Drum   72
Grahame, Violet, wife of Douglas, 5th
   Duke of Montrose   288
Grange, James Erskine, Lord   202–204
   – see also Chiesly, Rachel
Granger, Lybra, nurse   150
Grant, Adela, wife of Robert G.
   Cobham   269
Grant, Sir Arthur   269
Grant of Rothiemurchus, Elizabeth   176,
   181, 190–2, 213–14, 231, 237
Grant, Sir James   206
Grant of Freuchie, James   64 – see also
   Fleming, Lady Jane
Grant of Freuchie, James   72 – see also
   Stewart, Lady Mary
Grant of Grant, James (The Laird of
   Grant)   107
Grant, James, educationist   256–7
Grant, The Laird of   see Grant of Grant,
   James
Grant, Lilias, wife of Sir Walter Innes of
   Balvenie   106, 137
Grant, Mary, wife of (1) Lewis, 3rd
   Marquis of Huntly (2) James, 2nd
   Earl of Airlie   65, 69–70
Grant, Miss, schoolmistress   207

Grant, Mrs, of Laggan   see MacVicar,
   Anne
Grant, Mrs   see Ironside, Jane
Grant, Sophia   206
Gray, Agnes, harvester   233
Gray of Dunninald family   162
Gray, Isabel   68, 133
Gray, James   68 – see also Betoun,
   Elizabeth
Gray, Lady   see Ogilvy, Marion
Gray, Margaret, harvester, wife of Mr
   Wills   233
Gray, Patrick, 4th Lord   68 – see also
   Ogilvie, Marion
Greig, Samuel   216–17 – see also Fairfax,
   Mary
Greek   258, 260
Greenlaw   31, 75
Greenock   108, 176, 238–9, 242, 253
Greenock Ladies Association   251
Gregory, Dr John   221–2
Grenville, Hester, wife of William
   Pitt   224
Gretna Green   198
Greville, Lady Charlotte Mary, wife of
   John, Lord Garlies, later 7th Earl of
   Galloway   177
Grierson, Professor Herbert   267
Grierson, John, shopkeeper   95
grocers   240
Gruoch, Queen, wife of Macbeth   17
Gueldres, Mary of   see Mary of Gueldres,
   Queen
guild sisters   51
Guillemeau, Jacques   119
Gunning, Elizabeth, wife of James, 6th
   Duke of Hamilton   177, 232
Guthrie, Lady of   see Lyon, Margaret
Guthrie, Widow   151

Haddington   45, 56, 155, 170, 218–19,
   248, 250–1
Haddington, Countess of   see Ker, Lady
   Juliana
Haddington, Countess of   see Lindsay,
   Lady Christian
Haddington, John, 4th Earl of   77, 79
Haddington, Prioress of   see Hepburn,
   Elizabeth
Haddington, Thomas, 1st Earl of   89–90
   – see also Ker, Dame Juliana
Haddock, Nancy   153
hairdressers   309
Halhill   see Melville, Sir James
Haliburton, Margaret   123
Haliburton, Marion, wife of George, 4th
   Lord Home   58
Hall of Dunglass, Sir James   167 – see
   also Douglas, Lady Helen
Hall, Lady   see Douglas, Lady Helen

Hamilton 110, 151–2, 242
Hamilton family 64, 80, 154
Hamilton Palace 78, 150
Hamilton, Agnes, wife of William
    Cunningham of Caprington 109
Hamilton of Innerwick, Sir Alexander
    (The Laird of Innerwick) 89
Hamilton, Dr Alexander 226
Hamilton, Anne, *s.j.* 3rd Duchess of 68,
    71, 79, 85, 110, 112, 116, 118–21,
    129–31, 137–8, 144–5, 147–8, 150,
    152–3 – see also Hamilton, William,
    3rd Duke of
Hamilton, Lord Archibald 65–6, 68
Hamilton, Lord Basil 106, 113 – see also
    Dunbar, Mary
Hamilton, Lady Basil see Dunbar, Mary
Hamilton, Lady Betty, wife of Edward,
    12th Lord Derby 177
Hamilton, Lord Charles, later Earl of
    Selkirk 120
Hamilton, Lady Christian 93
Hamilton, Eleanor (Nellie), daughter of
    Lord Basil Hamilton 182
Hamilton, Elizabeth, writer 243–4, 247
Hamilton, Elizabeth, spinner 152
Hamilton, Elizabeth, aunt of Gavin
    Hamilton 30
Hamilton, Gavin, Commendator of
    Kilwinning 30
Hamilton of Barnton, George 113
Hamilton, Henrietta, Lady
    Orbiston 168–70
Hamilton, Lady Isobel, wife of James, 1st
    Earl of Airlie 143–4, 146, 161
Hamilton, James, 2nd Marquis of 65,
    113, 129 – see also Cunningham,
    Lady Anna
Hamilton, James, 4th Duke of, formerly
    Earl of Arran 64, 73, 78, 85, 131,
    150–2, 156 – see also Spencer, Lady
    Ann; Gerard, Lady Elizabeth
Hamilton, James, 6th Duke of 232 – see
    Gunning, Elizabeth
Hamilton, James George, 7th Duke
    of 177
Hamilton, Lady Janet, wife of David
    Boswell 27
Hamilton, Jean, wife of Charles, 9th Lord
    Cathcart 177, 229
Hamilton, Lady Jean, wife of John, 6th
    Earl of Cassilis 93
Hamilton, John, chamberlain of
    Kinneil 82
Hamilton, Lady Katherine, wife of John,
    1st Duke of Atholl 68, 120, 138
Hamilton, Marchioness of see
    Cunningham, Lady Anna
Hamilton, Lady Margaret, wife of John,
    17th Earl of Crawford 131

Hamilton, Lady Margaret, wife of James,
    4th Earl of Panmure 76, 80, 82, 85,
    108, 113, 130, 137, 140, 153–4,
    168–70
Hamilton, Margaret, wife of John, 1st
    Lord Belhaven 108
Hamilton, Margaret, wife of Henry
    Johnston 196
Hamilton, Marion 249
Hamilton, Lady Mary see Dunbar,
    Mary
Hamilton, Lady Mary, wife of (1)
    Alexander, 2nd Earl of Callandar (2)
    Sir James Livingstone (3) James, 3rd
    Earl of Findlater 73
Hamilton, Lady Mary, daughter of James,
    Earl of Arran 121, 129–30
Hamilton of Silvertonhill, Robert 77
Hamilton, Lady Susan, wife of (1) John,
    2nd Earl of Dundonald (2) Charles,
    3rd Marquis of Tweeddale 73, 78,
    115, 120–1, 139–40
Hamilton, Lady Susan, wife of George,
    5th Earl of Dunmore 273
Hamilton, Lady Susanna, wife of John,
    7th Earl of Cassilis 129
Hamilton, Widow 151
Hamilton, William, 2nd Duke of 154
Hamilton, William, 3rd Duke of 78, 82,
    133, 144–5 – see also Hamilton,
    Anne, *s.j.* Duchess of
Hamilton-Dundas, Mary 174
Hamilton-Dundas, Mrs see Dennistoun,
    Isabella
Hampton Court 127
Handel, George Frederick 175
handfasting 27–8
Handyside, Dr P. D. 264–5
Harden see Scott
Harper, Janet, fishwife 153
Harris 204
Hart, Dame Judith see Ridehalgh,
    Judith
hatters 240
hawkers 242
Hawthornden 94
Hay, David 22
Hay, George 119
Hay, Helen, wife of Archibald Johnston of
    Warriston 112
Hay, John, 8th Lord, of Yester 65
Hay, Lady Margaret, wife of Robert,
    Lord Ker, later 3rd Earl of
    Roxburghe 136
Hay, Lady Margaret, wife of John, 16th
    Earl of Mar 91–2, 107
Hay, Lady Mary, wife of General John
    Scott of Balcomie 199–200
Hay, Mary, wife of Walter, 1st Earl of
    Buccleuch 145

Hay, Sir William 22
Hay, William 117
headmistresses 307-8
Hebrides, The 233
Heiskir 203
Hempseed, Bessie, fishwife 153
Henderson, Elizabeth, wife of John Clerk
of Penicuik 93-4, 133
Henderson, Widow, coal seller 154
Henrietta Maria, wife of Charles I 129
Henry III of England 21, 35-6, 46
Henry VIII of England 46
Henryson, Robert, poet 55
henwives (poultrywomen) 151
Hepburn, Anna 107-8
Hepburn, Elizabeth, Prioress of
Haddington 45
Hepburn, Lady Jane, wife of Robert
Lauder, younger, of the Bass 27-8
Hepburn, Mrs 238
Hepburne, Christian, wife of George, 4th
Earl of Winton 66
Hepburne, Lady Jane, wife of George, 3rd
Lord Seton 47, 49
Herbert, Lady Winifred, wife of William,
5th Earl of Nithsdale 182
Herbertson, Alexander, looking-glass
maker 198 – see also Stuart, Marion
Heriot, Janet, beggar 53
Hermand, George Fergusson,
Lord 174-5
Herries, John, 6th Lord of Terregles
65
Hewitt, Joseph, cabinet-maker 196 – see
also Lambie, Elspeth
Hill, Colonel 95
history 209, 258
Hog, James, burgess 52
Hog, Mrs James 52
Hogg, Bessie, embroiderer 52
Hoggart, Isabel, harvester 148
Holland 59, 172
Home, Alexander, 3rd Lord 27 – see also
Stewart, Agnes
Home, Alexander, 6th Lord 22
Home, Beatrix 22
Home, George 146
Home, Henry see Kames, Henry Home,
Lord
Home, Lady see Haliburton, Marion
Home, Lilias 22
honeymoons 85
Hooker, Richard, theologian 138
Hope, Margaret, wife of Patrick Scott of
Rossie 82-3
Hoppar, Isabel, wife of Archibald Douglas
of Kilspindie 37
Horsburgh, Dame Florence, M.P. 308,
314
houseparties 232

Howard, Lady Elizabeth, wife of George,
1st Duke of Gordon 106
Hudson, Edith 287
Hume, Alexander 124
Hume, Lady Grisel, wife of George
Baillie 133, 190
Hume, Mr James 89
Hume, Mrs James 89
Hume, Patrick 104
Hunter, Dr William 224-5
Hunter, Mr, history and literature
master 258
hunting 45, 134
Huntly, Countess of see Keith,
Elizabeth
Huntly, George, 2nd Earl of 38 – see
also Annabella, Princess
Huntly, George, 4th Earl of 37 – see also
Keith, Elizabeth
Huntly, Marchioness of see Grant, Mary

impotence 95
Imrie, Catherine, servant 200
incest 158
Inchaffray Abbey 49
Inchcolm, monastery of 53
Inchtuthill 143
India 181
infare 86, 273
infertility 42, 122
Inglis of Cramond family 68-9
Inglis, Dr Elsie 286, 291
Inglis, Esther 163
Inglis, Janet, wife of Baron Clerk 194
Ingram, Sara, taverner 154
Innermeath, Lady see Betoun, Elizabeth
Innerpeffray 33
Innerwick, The Laird of see Hamilton of
Innerwick, Sir Alexander
Innes, Lady see Grant, Lilias
Innes, Sir Walter of Balvenie 107, 137 –
see also Grant, Lilias
innkeepers 154
inoculation 230
International Council of Women 286
Institute of Chartered Accountants
313
Institution of Civil Engineers 313
Inveresk 207, 251
Inverlochy 95
Invernessshire 95, 176
Ireland 272
Ironside, Jane, wife of Sir John Peter
Grant 231, 250
Irvine 254, 277
Irvine Academy 254
Irvine, Euphemia H. C.,
minister 313-14
Isabella of Angouleme, Queen, wife of
John of England 21

Isabella, Princess, wife of Frances, Duke of
    Brittany 19
Isabella, Princess, daughter of William I
    21
Islay 239 – see also Campbell, Mrs
Israelites 132
Italy 136

Jacob 132
James I 19, 38
James II 29, 31, 45, 56
James III 31, 50–1
James IV 27, 31, 43–5, 47, 50, 52
James V 45, 58
James VI 127, 144
James VII and II 168, 171 – see also
    Mary of Modena
Jamieson, Margaret, candlemaker 154
Jardine, Captain William, of
    Applegirth 198 see also Motte,
    Barberie de la
Jeffrey, Francis 222
'Jenny' 214
Jerviswood see Baillie
Jex-Blake, Sophia 262–6, 304
Joan, Princess, daughter of James I 19
Joanna, Princess, of England, wife of
    David II 33
John of England 19, 21–2 – see also
    Isabella of Angouleme
Johnson, Margaret, wife of John Thomson
    of Bathgate 77
Johnson, Dr Samuel 233
Johnston, Archibald, of Warriston 112
    – see also Hay, Helen
Johnston, Henry servant 196 – see also
    Hamilton, Margaret
Johnston, John, mason 119
Johnston, Mrs John, wet-nurse 119
Johnston, William 142
Johnstone family 64
Johnstone, Christian, novelist 243
Johnstone, Mary 33–4
jointures 75–80, 103, 145, 272

Kames, Henry Home, Lord 178, 191–2,
    209, 211, 214, 220, 229, 231
Kauffman, Angelica 241–2
Kay, John, caricaturist 228
Keith, Anna, 'Lady Methven' 160
Keith, Elizabeth, wife of George, 4th Earl
    of Huntly 37, 58
Kellow, Mary, wife of Patrick
    Ainslie 101
Kelly, Deborah, wife of George
    Morrison 198
Kelso 289
Kemble, Charles 171
Kennedy, Grace, author 243

Kennedy, Katherine, wife of Thomas
    Kennedy of Bargany 58
Kennedy, Katherine, merchant 153
Kennedy, Lady Margaret, wife of Bishop
    Gilbert Burnet 138
Kennedy, Margaret, wife of Gilbert, 3rd
    Earl of Cassilis 58
Kennedy, Lady Susanna, wife of
    Alexander, 9th Earl of Eglinton 205
Kennedy, Thomas, of Bargany 58 – see
    also Kennedy, Katherine
Kensington 140
Kent, Janey, wife of Norman
    Buchan 314
Ker, Dame Juliana, wife of (1) Sir Patrick
    Hume of Polwarth (2) Thomas, 1st
    Earl of Haddington 65, 89–90, 104,
    145–6, 167
Ker, Lady see also Scott, Janet
Ker, Sir Thomas of Ferniehirst 88–9
    – see also Scott, Janet
Kerr, Anne, s.j. Countess of Lothian, wife
    of William, 3rd Earl of Lothian 147
Kerr, Bessie, merchant 50
Kerr, Lady Elizabeth, wife of Colonel
    Nathaniel Rich 67
Kerr, John, merchant 94–6 – see also
    Scott, Cecily
Kerr, Lady see Campbell, Lady Jean
Kerr, Lady Margaret 112
Kerr, Margaret, Lady see Hay, Lady
    Margaret
Kerr, Mr 174
Kidd, Dame Margaret DBE, QC, wife of
    Donald S. Macdonald 312
Kilbirnie 277
Kilconquhar, Adam de 26
Kildrummy Castle 20, 48
Kilmarnock 253
Kilpatrick, Christian, wife of Sir John
    Clerk of Penicuik 190
Kilspindie see Douglas
Kilwinning see Hamilton
Kincardine 285
Kincavil 31
Kinnaird 148
Kinneil 82, 137
Kinneil Castle 137
Kinninburgh, Elizabeth B. F.,
    Minister 313
Kinnoull, The Lady of see Erskine,
    Dame Christian
Kinnoull, Thomas, 7th Earl of 91
Kinross see Bruce
Kirkurd see Scott
knitting 210, 212, 249, 252–3
Knox, John 46, 112, 115, 124

Ladies Edinburgh Debating Society 258
Ladies' Highland Association 251

Laggan   see MacVicar, Anne
Lambie, Elspeth, wife of Joseph
    Hewitt   196
Lamington   see Baillie
Lanark   25, 50
Lanarkshire   80, 126, 148, 154, 200, 224,
    253, 303
Lancashire   198
landladies   235
Langshaw   see Murray
Latin   130, 212–13, 215, 217–18, 222,
    255, 258, 260
Lauder, Isabel   113
Lauder, Jane   147
Lauder of Fountainhall, Sir John   113,
    119, 129, 138
Lauder, Sir Robert   147
Lauder of the Bass, Robert   27
Lauderdale family   151
Lauderdale, Countess of   see
    Cunningham, Lady Margaret
Lauderdale, John, 1st Duke of   66, 150–1
Laurie, Professor   256
Lavallet, Monsieur   99
Lawrie, Major Robert   199 – see also
    Ruthven, Elizabeth Maria
Lawrie, William 'The Laird of
    Blackwood'   101
Leah   33
Learmonth, Christian, milliner   236
Legal Aid (Scotland) Act (1949)   301
Legatt, William   119
Leith   52, 99–100, 154, 174–5, 183, 187,
    291, 303
Lennox, Countess of   see Douglas, Lady
    Margaret
Lennox, Duncan, 8th Earl of   23
Lennox, Isabella, s.j. Countess of   23
Lennox, James, 2nd Duke of   67, 79
Lennox, Matthew, 4th Earl of   92 – see
    also Douglas, Lady Margaret
Lenzie   314
Leslie, Christian, wife of (1) James, 2nd
    Marquis of Montrose (2) Sir John
    Bruce of Kinross   92, 113
Leslie, George   121
Leslie-Melville, Lady Jane, wife of Francis
    Pym   228
Leslie, Katherine, wife of George, 1st Earl
    of Melville   118, 136
L'Espinasse, Monsieur, French
    master   214
Lessells, Agnes   98
Letham   118
Lethington   see Maitland, Sir Richard
Leuchars Station   289–90
Leven   289
Leven, David, 3rd Earl of   81, 106–7,
    109, 111, 113, 115 – see also Wemyss,
    Lady Anna

Leven and Melville, Countess of   see
    Thornton, Hariet
Levington, Isabel, wife of William, 1st
    Lord Ruthven   24
Leviticus   22
Liberton   252
Liebig, Justus   280
Lightbody, Mrs Robert, merchant   153
Lillie, Agnes   148
Lindores, John, 3rd Lord   66 – see also
    Ogilvy, Lady Marion
Lindsay, Sir Alexander, of Evelick   184
    – see also Murray, Amelia
Lindsay, Lady Anna, wife of John, Earl
    and later Duke of Rothes   105,
    122
Lindsay, Lady Anne, poet, wife of Andrew
    Barnard   243
Lindsay, Bessie, Mrs David Bowman   100
Lindsay, Lady Christian, wife of John, 4th
    Earl of Haddington   111
Lindsay of Vayne, David   162 – see also
    Mrs David Lindsay
Lindsay of Vayne, Mrs David   162
Lindsay, Fanny   202
Lindsay, Lady Henrietta   79
Lindsay of Evelick. Lady   see Murray,
    Amelia
Lindsay, Margaret, wife of Allan
    Ramsay   184–5
Lindsay, Robert   24
Linlithgow   27, 31, 252, 312
Linlithgow, Countess of   see Hay, Lady
    Helen
Linton, Margaret of, burgess of
    Peebles   51
Lister, Joseph   282
literacy   59–60, 124–9, 131–2, 155, 207,
    210–11, 213–15, 252–4
Little Cumbrae   162
Liverpool   217, 274
Livingstone, Lady Anna, wife of
    Alexander, 6th Earl of
    Eglinton   106, 113, 117, 143, 145
Livingstone, William   154 – see also
    Wilson, Helen
'Lizard, Mary'   214
Lloyd George, David   286, 291
Lochhead, James   207
Lochindorb Castle   48
Lochwinnoch   125
Locke, John   117, 155
Lockhart, Bessie, merchant   50
Lockhart of Carnwath, Sir George   95
    – see also Carey, Philadelphia
Lockhart Wishart, General James   199
    – see also Murray, Mary Ann
logic and metaphysics   260
Logie, Andrew   146
Logiealmond   see Drummond

London   36–7, 47, 63–4, 77, 90, 95, 106,
   110–11, 116, 119, 127–9, 136, 138–41,
   148, 155, 168, 170–2, 176–7, 179,
   184, 189, 194, 199–200, 203, 205–6,
   208, 224, 227, 231, 236, 241–3, 250,
   280, 284–6, 290
London, Bloomsbury Square   198
London, Covent Garden   243
London, Drury Lane   243
London, Fleet Prison   198
London, Haymarket   202
London, Ludgate Hill   198
London, The Meads   139
London, St Martin's Lane   241
London, Serle Street   250
London University   283
London, Vauxhall Gardens   170
London, Westminster School   205
London, Whitehall   79, 127
Lord President, Court of Session   see
   Dalrymple, Hugh
Loretto   see shrines
Lorne, Lord   see Argyll, Archibald, 1st
   Marquis of
Lorraine, Duke of   155
Lossiemouth   290
Lothian, Countess of   see Campbell,
   Lady Jean
Lothian, Countess of   see Kerr, Anne
Lothian, Marchioness of   see Campbell,
   Lady Jean
Lothian, Marchioness of   see Montagu-
   Douglas-Scott, Lady Victoria
Lothian, Robert, 4th Earl and later 1st
   Marquis of   70, 106, 114, 153 – see
   also Campbell, Lady Jean
Lothian, William, 3rd Earl of   112 – see
   also Kerr, Anne
Loudon   252
Louis, Dauphin of France, later Louis
   XI   19
Louk, Henry   27
Lovat, Simon, 12th Baron   195
Low Countries   127, 145
Low, William   80 – see also Morgan,
   Janet
Lundy, Lady   see Forrester, Isobel
lying-in   43, 114–15, 228
Lyon, Jean, wife of John Dawling
   100
Lyon, Margaret, Lady of Guthrie   58

M., Miss, governess   213
Macbeth   17 – see also Gruoch
MacDiarmid, Hugh   11
MacDonald, Flora   11, 293
Macdonald, Lady Margaret   177
Macdonald, Dame Margaret   see Kidd,
   Dame Margaret
Macdougall, Alexander   118

Macfarlane of that Ilk, John   76 – see
   also Arbuthnott, Lady Helen
MacKay, Kathy   188
Mackay, Miss   287
Mackenzie, Lady Augusta, wife of Sir
   William Murray of Ochtertyre   200
Mackenzie, Sir George   159
Mackenzie, Henry   173, 243
Mackenzie, James, of Craig Park   179
Mackenzie, Lady Jean, wife of Sir Thomas
   Steuart of Balcaskie   231
Mackenzie, Mrs Leslie   291
Mackenzie, Mary   200
Mackintosh, Anne   174
Mackintosh, Margaret   174, 175
MacLagan and Rodger, Misses,
   milliners   236
MacLean of Duart   40 – see also
   Campbell, Lady Catherine
MacLean, Hector   20 – see also
   Campbell, Mor
Maclean, Mary, wife of Mr Crudelius
   259–60
Maclean, William, dancing master   133,
   168
Macleod, Alan   150
MacLeod, Sir John Lorne, Lord Provost
   of Edinburgh   293
Macleod, Mary, bard   150, 163
MacMillan, John, distiller   200–1 – see
   also Marshall, Anna
MacNeill, Captain John   198 – see also
   Farquhar, Christian
MacPherson, Mrs, of Cluny   239
Macquarrie, Lieutenant Lachlan   271
   – see also Campbell, Isabella H. D. C.
MacVicar, Anne, wife of James Grant of
   Laggan   221, 243
McAllaster of Tarbet, Charles   78
Mcbean, Angus   95 – see also McIntosh,
   Isabel
Mcbean, Mr   95
McIntosh, Isabel, wife of Angus
   Mcbean   95–6
McLaren, Priscilla   284
McLaughlan, Margaret   161
McNeill of Colonsay, Sir John   270 – see
   also Campbell, Lady Emma
McNish, Sally   196
Mair, Captain John   95
Mair, Dame Sarah Elizabeth
   Siddons   258, 284
Maitland, Anne, wife of Robert, 2nd Earl
   of Winton   94
Maitland, Isobel, wife of John, 8th Lord
   Elphinstone   82
Maitland of Thirlestane, Sir John, Lord
   Chancellor of Scotland   94
Maitland, Lord Chancellor   see Maitland
   of Thirlestane, Sir John

Maitland, Lady Mary, wife of John, 2nd Marquis of Tweeddale 66
Maitland, Mary 123
Maitland of Lethington, Sir Richard 123
Malcolm III 37, 54
Malthus, Thomas 282
Manchester 226, 285
Mann, Mrs Jean, M.P. see Stewart, Jean
Manningham, Sir Richard 225
Mansfield, William, 1st Earl of 199
Mantua makers (mantle makers) 197-8, 235-6, 277
Mar, Countess of see Douglas, Lady Isabella
Mar, Countess of see Graham, Margaret
Mar, Countess of see Hay, Lady Margaret
Mar, Countess of see Stewart, Lady Mary
Mar, Countess of see Stuart-Menteath, Philadelphia
Mar, John, 9th Earl of 101
Mar, John, 16th Earl of 90-2, 107 – see also Hay, Lady Margaret
Mar, Dowager Countess of see Maule, Lady Mary
Mar, Thomas, 9th Earl of 38 – see also Gordon, Margaret
March, Countess of see Randolph, Lady Agnes
March, Countess of see Seton, Christiana
March, Patrick, 4th Earl of 48 – see also Randolph, Lady Agnes
Marchmont, Countess of see Crompton, Elizabeth
Marchmont, Hugh, 3rd Earl of 179-80, 190 – see Crompton, Elizabeth
Margaret, Queen, wife of Alexander III 35-6, 46
Margaret of Denmark, Queen, wife of James III 50
Margaret, Queen, wife of James IV 45, 47, 50
Margaret, Princess, wife of Eric Magnusson, King of Norway 32, 54
Margaret, Princess, daughter of William I 21
Margaret, Princess, daughter of James I 19
Margaret, Princess, daughter of James II 56-7
Marie Antoinette 188
Marie de Coucy, Queen, wife of Alexander II 45
Marischal, William, 6th Earl of 68 – see also Erskine, Lady Mary
Marjoribanks, Ishbel, wife of John, 1st Marquess of Aberdeen and Temair 286

marriage choice 18-27, 63-4, 170, 177-9, 186-8, 268-71, 294, 306, 308
marriage, civil 295
marriage contracts 28-31, 68, 74-81, 271, 294
marriages, irregular 28, 31, 74, 182, 187, 200, 273-4, 295
Marriage Notice (Scotland) Act (1878) 272
Marriage (Scotland) Act (1939) 295
Marriage (Scotland) Act (1977) 294
marriage service 87, 105
marriage tokens 80
Marriage with the Deceased Wife's Sister Act (1907) 270
Married Women's Policies of Assurance (Scotland) Act (1880) 279
Married Women's Property (Scotland) Act (1877) 279
Married Women's Property (Scotland) Act (1881) 279, 294
Married Women's Property (Scotland) Act (1920) 279
Marshall, Anna, wife of John MacMillan 200-1
Marshall, Margaret, washerwoman 151
Marshall, Marion, wife of William Dewar 29
Martin V, Pope 53-4
Mary, Queen of Scots 11, 43, 89, 97, 123-4, 134, 293
Mary I of England 46
Mary of Gueldres, Queen, wife of James II 29, 31, 45
Mary of Guise, Queen, wife of James V of Scotland 37, 43, 45-6, 58
Mary of Modena, Queen, wife of James VII and II 113
Mary, Queen, wife of George V 290
Mary, Princess, wife of Wolfort, Lord of Campvere 19
masquerades 139, 168
Masson, Professor David 259, 262, 264
maternal mortality 17, 223, 226-7, 297-9
mathematics 255, 258, 260, 283, 304
mathematicians 171, 178, 214-18, 221, 225, 247, 250
Mauchline 287
Maule, Lady Mary, wife of (1) Charles, 10th Earl of Mar (2) Colonel John Erskine 67, 231
Mauriceau, Francois 107
Maxwell of Monreith, Sir Alexander 200
Maxwell, Eglantine, dramatist 243
Maxwell, Lady Elizabeth, wife of William, 2nd Duke of Hamilton 77
Maxwell, Elizabeth, widow of the town clerk of Dumfries 159

Maxwell, Jane, wife of Alexander, 4th
    Duke of Gordon   177, 243
Maxwell, of Pollok, Sir John   82, 109
Maxwell, John, of Pollok   65
Maxwell, John   67
Maxwell, Lady   see Cunningham,
    Margaret
Maxwell, Margaret   200
Maxwell, Lady Mary, wife of Charles, 4th
    Earl of Traquair   106
Maxwell, Mary, wife of William 17th Earl
    of Sutherland   177
Maxwell, Robert, 4th Lord   27 – see also
    Stewart, Agnes
Maxwell, Sir William   113
May, Isle of   42
Maybole   254
medicine   41–2, 107–9, 114, 118, 121,
    143–4, 225, 250
Meigle   99
Mellerstain   272
Melrose   49
Melville, Countess of   see Leslie,
    Katherine
Melville, Elizabeth   124
Melville of Halhill, Sir James   123
Melville of Monimail, Robert, 2nd
    Lord   113
members of parliament   307–8, 314
Menteith, Christian, wife of Sir Robert
    Erskine   20
mercantile law   304
merchants   101, 152–4, 235
message girls   277
Methven, Lady   see Keith, Anna
Midlothian   148
midwives   17, 42, 108–110, 112–13,
    223–6, 240, 300
Mill, John Stuart   283
Miller, Margaret   161
milliners   236, 277
Mills, Henry, comedian   200 – see also
    Cunningham, Susannah
Milne, Alexander   99 – see also Gordon,
    Isabel
Milton of Campsie   314
ministers   313–14
miscarriages   107–8, 160
mistresses   43, 53, 66, 202
'Modish, Mrs'   189
Moffat   115, 238
Moidart, Loch   203
Moncrieff, James   153
Moncrieff, Mrs James   153
Moncrieffe House   272
Moncrieffe, Louisa, wife of John, 7th Duke
    of Atholl   272
Monimail   252
Monreith   see Maxwell, Sir Alexander
Montagu-Douglas-Scott, Lady Victoria

Alexandrina, wife of Schomberg, 12th
    Marquis of Lothian   260
Montgomerie, Alexander, Lord, later 9th
    Earl of Eglinton   70–1
Montgomerie, Lady Anna, wife of James,
    3rd Earl of Findlater   105, 122
Montgomerie, Lady Christian
    (Christie)   205
Montgomerie, Lady Eleanor   117
Montgomerie, Lady Eleanor, wife of
    David Dunbar of Baldoon   138
Montgomerie, Elizabeth, wife of John
    Beaumont   185–6
Montgomerie, Lady Jean, wife of Sir
    Alexander Maxwell of
    Monreith   194
Montgomerie, Lady Margaret
    (Peggy)   205
Montgomerie, Margaret, wife of Hugh,
    5th Earl of Eglinton   117, 145
Montgomerie, Margaret, wife of James
    Boswell   185, 192, 228, 235
Montgomery, Jean, seamstress   152
Montrose   285
Montrose, Dowager Marchioness of   see
    Leslie, Christian
Montrose, Duchess of   see Graham,
    Violet
Montrose, James, 7th Marquis of   162
Monzie   211
Moodie, Barbara   200
Moore, Lady Mary, wife of William, 3rd
    Earl of Dalhousie   106
Moray, Bishop of   see Spynie, William de
Moray, Countess of   see Dunbar, Janet
Moray, Countess of   see Gordon, Lady
    Anna
Moray, Countess of   see Seton, Katherine
Moray, James, 3rd Earl of   147 – see also
    Gordon, Lady Anna
Moray, James, 4th Earl of   56 – see also
    Seton, Katherine
Moray, James, 18th Earl of   72
Moray, James, 19th Earl of   72
Morayshire   210
More, Elizabeth, wife of Thomas
    Rocheid   100
More, Sir Thomas   124
Morgan, Agnes   80
Morgan, Janet, wife of William Low   80
Morrison, George   198 – see also Kelly,
    Deborah
Morrison, John, weaver   198
Morrison, Margaret   289
Morton   73
Morton, barony of   47
Morton Castle   47
Morton, John, 5th Earl of   69
Mortonhall   see Trotter
Mossman, Mr   240

Motte, Barberie de la, wife of Captain William Jardine of Applegirth 198
Mowbray, Patrick, lawyer 152
Moy 95
Muir, Adam 80 – see also Muir, Margaret
Muir, Janet, widow 31
Muir, Margaret, wife of Adam Muir at Corsfoordbait 80
munitions workers 291
murderers 158
Mure of Caldwell, Elizabeth 84, 170, 220
Mure of Glanderston, William 67
Murray, Alison 22
Murray, Amelia, wife of Lord George Murray 183–4, 194
Murray, Amelia, wife of Sir Alexander Lindsay of Evelick 184
Murray, Lady Augusta see Mackenzie, Lady Augusta
Murray, Eliza, seamstress 235
Murray, Lady Elizabeth 112
Murray, Lady Elizabeth 176
Murray, Lady George see Murray, Amelia
Murray, Lord George 183–4, 194 – see also Murray, Amelia
Murray, Mrs James, of Glencarse and Strowan 183–4
Murray of Polmaise, John 249
Murray, Mrs John 106
Murray of Polmaise, Margaret 249
Murray, Dame Mary 22
Murray, Mary Ann, wife of General James Lockhart Wishart 199
Murray of Langshaw, Sir Patrick 76 – see also Dundas, Elizabeth
Murray, Lord William 85–6, 140 – see also Nairn, Lady
Murray, Sir William, of Ochtertyre 200 – see also Mackenzie, Lady Augusta
music 44, 127, 130–1, 133–7, 172–3, 188, 206–7, 209, 213–14, 237, 277
Musselburgh 42, 215
Mutter, Barbara, candle seller 154

Nairn 233, 273
Nairn, Margaret, s.j. Lady, wife of Lord William Murray 66, 85–6, 138, 140–1, 247
Nairne, Caroline, Lady see Oliphant, Caroline
Nasmyth, Alexander, landscape painter 216
National Society for Women's Suffrage 284
natural science 260
Necker, Anne Louise Germaine, Madame de Stael 219

Neilson, Miss, schoolmistress 207
Netherliberton 119
Newburgh 276
Newcome, Henry 138
New Earnings Survey (1979) 309–10
Newhaven 153, 286
New Jersey 161
Newliston 233
Nicholson, Dr Alleyne 264
Nicholson, Mr 260
Nightingale, Florence 250
Nisbet, Archibald 198 – see also Provan, Amelia
Nith, River 48
Nithsdale, Countess of see Douglas, Lady Lucy
Nithsdale, Countess of see Herbert, Lady Winifred
Norham, Treaty of 21–2
Norris, John 78
Northesk, Countess of see Wemyss, Lady Margaret
Northesk, David, 4th Earl of 71, 80, 82, 107 – see also Wemyss, Lady Margaret
North Uist 203
Norwell, John 154 – see also Young, Isabel
Nottingham 21
nuns 47, 49, 53, 56–7, 67
nurses 51, 150, 163, 240, 277, 288, 291, 307–8

Oban 253
O'Cathan, Agnes, wife of Angus Og, Lord of the Isles 29
O'Cathan, Guy, of Ulster 29
Ogilvie, Lady Griselda, wife of James Cheape 287–8
Ogilvie, Janet 160
Ogilvie, Marion, wife of Patrick, 4th Lord Gray 58
Ogilvie, Miss 215–6
Ogilvy, Helen, wife of James, 2nd Earl of Airlie 152–3, 161
Ogilvy, James, 5th Lord 145 – see also Forbes, Jean
Ogilvy, Lady Margaret, wife of Patrick Urquhart of Lethintie and Meldrum 161–2
Ogilvy, Lady Marion, wife of (1) James, Lord Coupar and (2) John, 4th Lord Ogilvy 66
Ogston, Alexander, bookseller 155 – see also Stevenson, Martha
Old Cumnock 287
Old Monkland 253
Oliphant, Andrew 98
Oliphant, Caroline, poet, wife of William, 5th Baron Nairne 243

Oliphant, John   24
Oliphant, Katherine, wife of George
    Dundas of that Ilk   135
Oliphant, Mrs Margaret   see Wilson,
    Margaret
opera   140
opera singers   307
Orangefield   see Dalrymple
Orbiston, Lady   see Hamilton,
    Henrietta
Orkney   20
Oswald, Mrs   249
Ould, Sir Feilding   225

pageants   170, 293
Paisley   43, 126, 277
pall-mall   see croquet
Pankhurst family   285, 289-90
Pankhurst, Christabel   287
Pankhurst, Mrs   see Goulden, Emmeline
Panmure   130
Panmure, James, 4th Earl of   76-7, 80,
    113, 151-4, 168 - see also Hamilton,
    Lady Margaret
Panmure, Patrick, 1st Earl of   68 - see
    also Erskine, Lady Mary
Pantin, Monsieur, dancer   173
Paris   236
Parker, Fanny   288
Parker and Jones's Circus   167
Parkhead   see Douglas
Paschal II, Pope   27
Pasteur, Louis   282
Paston Letters   12
pastry schools   206, 208
Paterson, Dame Alice, wife of Sir
    Alexander Dalmahoy of that
    Ilk   196
Paterson, Dame Anna, wife of Sir John
    Dick   145
Paterson, John, Archbishop of
    Glasgow   196
Pechey, Edith   264
Peebles   51
Peebles Tolbooth   51
Pencaitland   252
Penicuik   156 - see also Clerk
Penicuik, Christian, wife of Edmund
    Rutherford   24
Penman, James, Goldsmith   119
Pennant, Thomas   233
Penne, Bessie, butter seller   49
Penny, Janet   78
penny weddings   85, 272
Penson, Mr, pianoforte master   214
perjurers   158
Perth   78, 152, 239, 290, 312
Perth Prison   290
Perth, Duchess of   see Douglas, Lady
    Jane

Perth, James, 4th Earl of   114 - see also
    Douglas, Lady Jane
Perthshire   80, 134, 211, 232
Peterhead   176
Pethick, Emmeline, wife of Frederick
    Lawrence   285
Pethick Lawrence, Mrs   see Pethick,
    Emmeline
Pettigrew, John   29 - see also Fullarton,
    Mariota
Philiphaugh, Battle of   161
physics   304
physicists   312
Pilrig   see Balfour
Pisan, Christine de   59, 125
Pitcairn, Ann   181-2
Pitcullo   see Balfour
Pitt, Mrs William   see Grenville, Hester
Pittendreich   see Balfour
planting   45, 148, 233
plays   44, 128, 139-40, 142, 168, 170-2,
    175-6, 178-9, 189, 193
poets   19, 45, 124, 150, 163, 221,
    242-3
political economy   260
Pollok   see Maxwell
Polmaise   see Murray
Polwarth, East Mains of   146
Polwarth, Alexander, Lord   190
Pope, Alexander, poet   220
postmasters   155
poultrywomen   see henwives
pregnancy   42-3, 47, 91, 93, 105-9,
    113-14, 160, 279, 297, 300
Preston, George, surgeon   99 - see also
    Boghurst, Mary
Prestwick   287
Primrose, Miss, schoolmistress   207, 215
Pringle, Elizabeth   248
printers   156-7
prison governors   314
processions   44, 140
professors   307-8, 310
property, matrimonial law of   28, 35, 87,
    144-6, 274, 278-9, 296
prostitutes   53, 157
Provan, Amelia, wife of Archibald
    Nisbet   198
psychologists   312
puerperal fever   114, 226-7, 299
puppets   135
pure science   305
purification (churching of women)   43,
    115
Pym, Lady Jane   see Leslie-Melville,
    Lady Jane
Pythagoras   156

Quakers   161, 182
Queen, Mr John, writing master   129

Queensberry, Duchess of   see Douglas, Lady Isabel

racehorse trainers 314
Rachel   33, 132
Ramsay, Allan, poet   173
Ramsay, Allan, portrait painter   184–5
 – see also Lindsay, Margaret
Ramsay, Amelia   185
Ramsay, Cuthbert   27 – see also Stewart, Agnes
Randolph, Lady Agnes, 'Black Agnes', wife of Patrick, 4th Earl of Dunbar and 2nd Earl of March   48
Rankin, Gabriel, merchant   72–3, 197–8
 – see also Clerk, Sophia
rape   24
Ravelston   see Foulis, George
Redcastle, tower of   162
Renfrew   257, 276
Renfrewshire   125, 232, 277
Renton, William   98 – see also Geddie, Elizabeth
Representation of the People Act (1918)   291–2
Representation of the People Act (1928)   291
Reynolds, Sir Joshua, artist   242
Rich, Colonel Nathaniel   67 – see also Kerr, Lady Elizabeth
Richard II of England   55
Richard, Prince, son of King John of England   21
Richardson, Samuel, author   242
Richieson, Margaret, harvester, wife of Thomas Vair   148
riddles   44–5
Ridehalgh, Dame Judith, wife of Anthony B. Hart   314
riding   135, 139
Riviera   270
Robert I (Robert Bruce)   26, 33, 38–9, 43, 47–8, 60
Robert II   20, 38 – see also Annabella, Queen
Robertsland House   290
Robertson, Colonel David   199
Robertson, Janet, taverner, wife of David Dalrymple   153–4
Robertson, Margaret, seamstress   235
Robinson, Mary, wife of William Rose   194
Rochester   37
Rocheid, Thomas   100 – see also More, Elizabeth
Rodgerson, Mary, wife of Alexander Stevenson   198
romantic love   25, 71–2, 80, 179–81, 183–7, 219
Rome   54, 110, 184, 241

ropedancers   172
Rose, Anna   213
Rose, William   194 – see also Robinson, Mary
Roseburn   157 – see also Campbell
Roseburn, Lady   see Campbell, Agnes
Roseneath   108
Ross, Alexander, Bishop of   38
Ross, Countess of   see ------, Euphemia
Ross, Lady   see Scott, Margaret
Ross, Mary, wife of John, 1st Duke of Atholl   85
Rossie   see Scott
Rothes, Countess of   see Lindsay, Lady Anna
Rothiemay   see Gordon
Rothiemurchus   see Grant, Elizabeth
Rousseau, Jean-Jacques   186, 191, 209, 214
routs   173–4
Rowe, Nicholas, dramatist   171
Roxburgh   152
Roxburghshire   276
Roxburghe family   64
Royal Bank of Scotland   313
Royal College of Obstetricians and Gynaecologists   312
Royal College of Physicians of Edinburgh   312
Royal College of Surgeons of Edinburgh   312
Royal Commission on Marriage (1865)   272
Royal Geographical Society   217
Royal Institution of Chartered Surveyors   313
Royal Society   217
Ruddiman, Alexander   98
Ruglen, John, 1st Earl of   73
Rutherford, Edmund   24 – see also Penicuik, Christian
Ruthven, Elizabeth Maria, wife of Sir Robert Laurie of Maxwellton   199
Ruthven, James, 5th Lord   199
Ruthven, Katherine, wife of Sir Colin Campbell of Glenorchy   44, 135
Ruthven, Margaret   23–4
Ruthven, William, 1st Lord   23–4 – see also Levington, Isabel
Ruthven, William, 4th Lord   22
Ryle, Janet   77

St Adrian's   see shrines
St Andrews   98, 161, 258, 287, 289
St Andrews, Gatty Marine Laboratory   289
St Andrews, St Leonards School   258
St Andrews University   66, 261, 267
St Bartholomew's Eve, Massacre of   163
St Bothans   53

St Cecilia's Day 172
St Clair, William 20 – see also Douglas, Elizabeth
St Katherine of Siena 49, 57
St Kilda 204
St Margaret, wife of Malcolm III 37, 54, 293
St Paul 135, 192
saleswomen 277
Salmon, Agnes, fruitwife 153
saltbearers 149
Saltoun see Fletcher
Sanger, Margaret 297
Sanquhar 276
Savill, Dr Agnes see Blackadder, Agnes
Schaw, Captain Frederick 173
schoolmistresses 52, 127, 133, 157, 206–7, 210–11, 213, 215, 236–7, 242, 277, 286, 302–3, 307, 310
science 209
Sciennes see St Katherine of Siena
Scone 39
Scotland *passim*
Scott, Cecily, wife of John Kerr 94–5
Scott, Grizel 121
Scott, Harriet 174
Scott, Janet, wife of Sir Thomas Ker of Ferniehirst 89
Scott, Janet, shopkeeper 152
Scott, General John, of Balcomie 199 – see also Hay, Lady Mary
Scott, lady Margaret, wife of Alexander, 6th Earl of Eglinton 162
Scott, Margaret, wife of James, 6th Lord Ross 113
Scott, Margaret 217–18
Scott, Mary, of Harden 217–18
Scott, Mr, baker 173
Scott, Mr, writing master 214
Scott, Patrick, of Rossie 82–3 – see also Hope, Margaret
Scott, Sir Walter, of Branxholm 147
Scott, Walter, of Harden 175–6
Scott, Sir Walter 221, 243
Scott of Kirkurd, Sir William 89
Scottish Certificate of Education 304–5
Scottish Council of the Red Cross 288
Scottish Education Board 302
Scottish Faculty of Actuaries 313
Scottish Office 314
Scottish Trades Union Congress 311
Scottish Women's Hospitals 291, 293
Scottish Women's Suffrage Federation 291
sculptors 307
Seafield, Countess of see Dunbar, Anne
seamstresses 152, 197, 235
Seaton, William, postmaster 155 – see also Brown, Agnes
Selkirk 52

Sellar, Professor William Y. 260
Semple, Andrew 21
separation 102–3, 195, 278
Serbia 291
servants 42, 53, 149, 187–8, 230, 237, 247, 253, 275–7, 296
Seton 134
Seton, Sir Alexander, Captain of Berwick 36–7 – see also Cheyne, Christian
Seton, Christiana, wife of George, 10th Earl of Dunbar and 5th Earl of March 47
Seton, George, 3rd Lord see also Hepburne, Lady Jane
Seton, Jean, merchant 155
Seton, Katherine, wife of James, 4th Earl of Moray 56
Seton, Lady see Cheyne, Christian
Seton, Lady see Hepburne, Lady Jane
Seton, Thomas 36–7
Seton, William 36–7
Sewell, Lucy 262
sewing 41, 43–5, 52, 57, 118, 125–7, 131, 133–5, 139, 206–13, 215, 222, 232, 235, 237, 247–9, 252–3, 255, 277, 288, 302
sewing-school 126, 208, 252
Sex Discrimination Act (1975) 309
Sex Disqualification Removal Act (1919) 311
Shakespeare, William 172, 242
Shallard, S. D. 287
Shepperd, Mrs 236
sheriffs 312
shopkeepers 49, 50, 152–5, 197, 235, 240
shrines
  Our Lady of Loretto, Musselburgh 42
  St Adrian's, Isle of May 42
Shrubhill 175
Siddons, Sarah, actress 171, 243
Silvertonhill see Hamilton
Simpson, Alexander, maltman 98
Simpson, George, burgh assessor, Leith 291
Simpson, Sir James Young 280–3, 298
Sinclair, Anne, wife of George, 1st Viscount Tarbat 148
Sinclair, Elizabeth, wife of Sir Duncan Campbell of Glenorchy 135
Sinclair, Isabel, Q.C. 312
Sinclair, Sir John 209, 220
singing 44, 123, 140, 133–5, 173, 187, 205–6, 211, 234
Skinner, George 153
Skye 204
Slains 233
Smart, John, lawyer 98
Smart, Mr, dancing master 214
Smellie, Dr William 224–5
Smith, James 105
Smythe Braco, Patrick of 63

INDEX

social sciences 305
Society of Antiquaries of Scotland 56
Society for the Progagation of Christian
Knowledge (S.P.C.K) 210–11
solicitors 312
Somerville, Mrs Arthur 287
Somerville, James, of Drum 72 – see also
Grahame, Elizabeth
Somerville, Mary see Fairfax, Mary
Somerville, Dr William 217, 222 – see
also Fairfax, Mary
Soranus 110
Soubeiran, Eugene 280
South Berwick, convent of 53
Southesk, Charles, 4th Earl of 82
Spain 243
Spencer, Lady Anne, wife of James, Earl
of Arran 114
spinning 29, 41, 59, 93, 144, 152–3,
210–12, 231, 234–5, 237, 247
spinsters 26, 308, 315
spirit dealers 240
Spynie Castle 135
Spynie, William de, Bishop of Moray 38
Stair, Countess of see Campbell, Lady
Eleanor
Stair, John, 2nd Earl of 171, 232–3 – see
also Campbell, Lady Eleanor
starchmakers 100
Steuart, Sir George, of Grandtully 179
Steuart, Grizel, wife of Sir John
Drummond of Logiealmond 114
Steuart, Sir James, of Goodtries 84–5
Steuart, John 179
Steuart, Lady see Dalrymple, Anne
Steuart, Margaret 112
Steuart, Mr 200
Steuart, Sir Thomas, of
Grandtully 111–2, 144
Stevenson. Alexander, dancing master
198 see also Rodgerson, Mary
Stevenson, Margaret, fruitwife 153
Stevenson, Martha, bookseller, widow of
Alexander Ogston 155–6
Stevenston 252
Stewart, Agnes, wife of (1) Adam, 2nd
Earl of Bothwell (2) Alexander, 3rd
Lord Home (3) Robert, 4th Lord
Maxwell (4) Cuthbert Ramsay 27
Stewart, Agnes, henwife 151
Stewart, Sir Alexander, 'the Wolf of
Badenoch' 20, 38 – see also ------
Euphemia, Countess of Ross
Stewart, Lady Anna, wife of Archibald,
styled Earl of Angus 79
Stewart, Dr 228
Stewart, Lady Gabriela 67
Stewart, Grace, milliner 236
Stewart, Lady Henrietta, wife of Sir Hugh
Campbell of Cawdor 138

Stewart, Lady Isabella see Lennox,
Isabella, Countess of
Stewart, Janet 24
Stewart, Jean, M.P., wife of William T.
Mann 308
Stewart, John 179
Stewart, Lady Margaret, wife of Charles,
4th Earl of Aboyne 223
Stewart, Margaret, shopkeeper 235
Stewart, Lady Mary, wife of James Grant
of Freuchie 72
Stewart, Mary, wife of John, 2nd Earl of
Mar 131
Stewart, Miss 174
Stewart, Mr 174
Stewart, Sir Murdach, later 13th Earl of
Fife and 2nd Duke of Albany 23
– see also ------- Isabella, Countess of
Lennox
Stirling 51–2, 210, 236, 285
Stirling Castle 49
Stirling, Sir John, of Keir 71, 231
Stirling, Katherine, wife of Archibald, 5th
Earl of Angus 58
Stirling, Lady see Colquhoun, Lilias
Stirlingshire 232, 243, 253
Stitchill 126
Stobhall 112
stokers 291
Stone of Destiny 39
Stonefield see Waddell
Stopes, Dr Marie 297
Strasbourg 314
Strathbogie, David of 48
Strathearn, Countess of see Abercairney,
Ysende of
Strawhatmakers 240
Strowan see Murray, Mrs James
Stuart, Dorothy M., novelist 307
Stuart, Marion, wife of Alexander
Herbertson 198
Stuart-Menteath, Philadelphia, wife of
John, 15th Earl of Mar 231
submariners 314
Succession (Scotland) Act (1964) 296, 301
suffragettes 283–93
Susanna 33
Sutherland, Captain James 199–200
Sutherland, Janet, wife of George, 1st
Lord Banff 99
Sutherland, William 100 – see also
Dunbar, Barbara
swaddling 18, 115–17, 230
Sweetheart Abbey 49
Swift, Jonathan 220
Syme, Professor James 263

tables see backgammon
Tailor, Helen 83
Tait, Miss, dressmaker 235

INDEX

Tait, Professor 260
Talmash, Lady Elizabeth, wife of
    Archibald, 10th Earl of Argyll 67
tapsters 153
Tarbet see McAllaster
Tarbat, George, 1st Viscount of 73, 81,
    92 – see also Wemyss, Margaret *s.j.*
    Countess of
Tasso, Torquato 219
taverners 66, 153–4
Tay, River 49
Taymouth 232
tea drinking 172–3, 176, 219, 248, 287
telegraphists 278
telephonists 278, 285
Temple, Sir William 155
Ten Hours' Bill (1847) 276
Tennant, Isabel, wife of John
    Winning 30, 75
terce 29–30, 32, 34–5
thieves 158
Thomson, John 75 – see also Borthwick,
    Margaret
Thomson, John 77–8 – see also Johnson,
    Margaret
Thomson, Lawrence 99–101 – see also
    Arnot, Agnes
Thomson, Walter 101
Thomson, Mrs Walter 101
Thornton, Harriet, wife of John, 9th Earl
    of Leven and Melville 227
Tibet 277
Timothy 135
tochers 23, 29–31, 64–5, 76–80, 103,
    271–2
Tolquhoun see Forbes
Tours 19
Tranent, Stair Park House 289
transportation 161
Traquair 151
Traquair, Charles, 4th Earl of 179
Traquair, Countess of see Maxwell,
    Lady Mary
travel 43, 54, 139, 176–7, 203, 205,
    232–3, 237–40, 270
Trotter, Mrs, of Mortonhall 252
Trotter, Mrs William, wife of the Lord
    Provost of Edinburgh 174
trousseaux 81–2
Tullibardine, Countess of see Dent,
    Elizabeth
Tullibardine, Countess of see
    Drummond, Lilias
Tullibardine, Dowager Countess of see
    Drummond, Catherine
Tullibardine, Marquis of see Atholl,
    John, 7th Duke of
Turing, Katherine, embroiderer 52
Tweed, River 51
Tweeddale, Charles, 3rd Marquis of 73
    – see also Hamilton, Lady Susan

Tweeddale, John, 1st Marquis of 150
Tweeddale, John, 2nd Marquis of 66
    – see also Maitland, Lady Mary
Tweeddale, Marchioness of see Carteret,
    Lady Frances
Twickenham 91
Twyford, Anne 130
typists 278

Ulster 29
Union, The 182
Universities (Scotland) Act, 1889 266
university education 258–68, 304–6, 308
university lecturers 307
upholsterers 240
upsitting feasts 43

Vair, Thomas 148 – see also Richieson,
    Margaret
Vayne see Lindsay
Venetian Company of Tumblers 172
Victoria, Queen 249, 282, 285
vintners 240
Violante, Signora, ropedancer 172, 206
Virgil 255
Virgin Mary, the cult of 60
Voltaire, Francois Marie Arnouet de 219

Waddell of Stonefield, Mrs 252
Wales 299, 304
Waldrum, Mary, wife of Patrick, 1st Earl
    of Panmure 116
Wallace, Anna 153
Wallace, William 25
Walwood, Kate, burgess 51
Wanlockhead 273
Wars of Independence 25, 48
Warwick, Robert, 26th Earl of 67
washerwomen 150–2
washing 127, 144, 152, 247, 253
Waughton 119
waxmakers 52
weaning 18, 99, 121
Webster, Isabel 118
Wedderburn, Janet, wife of Sir Henry
    Erskine 177
weddings 32, 44, 72, 83–4, 91, 139,
    272–3, 294–5
wedding celebrations 32, 81–2, 84–6,
    272–3
wedding dresses 81, 83–5
wedding presents 82–3
Weir, Christian, butterwife 153
Weir, Widow 179
Weir, Sir William 179 – see also
    Anstruther, Christian
Welch, Widow 250
Welfare Food Scheme (1940) 299
Welsh, Jane, wife of Thomas
    Carlyle 180–1, 191, 212, 218–20,
    248–50, 274–5

Wemyss 136
Wemyss, Countess of see Charteris, Janet
Wemyss, Lady Anna, wife of David, 3rd Earl of Leven 81, 105, 107, 109, 111, 113–5, 118, 121, 136, 143
Wemyss, Lady Betty 181
Wemyss, The Earl of (unidentified) 181
Wemyss, David, 3rd Earl of 140
Wemyss, James, 4th Earl of 183, 198 – see also Charteris, Janet
Wemyss, Sir James 82
Wemyss, Lady see Campbell, Margaret
Wemyss, Lady Margaret 73
Wemyss, Lady Margaret, wife of David, 4th Earl of Northesk 71, 80, 107, 139–40
Wemyss, Margaret, s.j. Countess of, wife of (1) James, Lord Burntisland (2) George, Viscount Tarbat 70–1, 73, 76, 79–81, 92, 114–15, 121, 131, 136, 139, 143, 167
Wemyss Bay, Kelly House 290
Western Isles 252
wet nurses 18, 51, 99, 117–20, 150, 228, 230, 299
Wharton, Dame Philadelphia see Carey, Philadelphia
White, Dr Charles 226
Whitehead, David 50 – see also Whitehead, Mrs David
Whitehead, Mrs David, cloth seller 50
Whitekirk 290
Whitelaw, Isabel 125
Whitelaw, Margaret 125
Whitelaw of Fentonbarns, Robert 125
widows 26, 35, 45, 53, 67, 70, 73, 145, 149, 152, 253, 271, 294, 296, 308
Wightman, Margaret, servant 52
'Wigtown martyrs' see McLaughlan, Margaret; Wilson, Margaret
Wigtown 161
William I (the Lion) 19, 21–2, 48
William of Orange 140
Williamson, Isabel, clothseller, wife of Thomas Williamson 50
Williamson, Thomas 50 – see also Williamson, Isabel
Wills, Margaret see Gray, Margaret
Wilson, Euphan, harvester 233
Wilson, Helen, innkeeper, widow of William Livingstone 154
Wilson, Janet, merchant 154
Wilson, Margaret 161
Wilson, Margaret, wife of Francis Oliphant 283
Wilson, Miss 174
Wilton 276
Winchester 21
Winning, John, merchant 30, 75, 78 – see also Tennant, Isabel

Winton, Countess of see Maitland, Anne
Winton, George, 4th Earl of 66 – see also Hepburne, Christian
Winton, Robert, 2nd Earl of 94 – see also Maitland, Anne
Winzet, Isobel, wife of John Fisher 58
wireworkers 240
witches 151, 158–9
Wolfort, Lord of Campvere 19 – see also Mary, Princess
Wollstonecraft, Mary 278, 283
Women's Educational Union 302
Women's Franchise Association 284
Women's Freedom League 286
Women's National Anti-Suffrage League 287–8
Women's Social and Political Union (W.S.P.U.) 285–7, 290
Woodburn, Winifred, wife of Stewart M. Ewing 314
Woodhall, Meg, burgess of Peebles 51
woodwork 255
wool merchants 51
Woodman, Bessie, burgess 51
Worcester, Battle of 162
World War I 290. 293, 296, 298, 306
World War II 298–9, 305
writers 217, 222, 242–4, 283, 307–8
Women's Royal Naval Service 307–8

Yair 248
Yester, Lord see Hay, John
Yester, Master of see Tweeddale, Charles, 3rd Marquess of
Yester, Susan, Lady see Hamilton, Lady Susan
York, James, Duke of see James VII and II
Young, Isabel, merchant, widow of John Norwell 154
Young, Professor Thomas 226
Young Women's Christian Association (Y.W.C.A.) 252
------, Barbara 104
------, Christiana, wife of Patrick, 8th Earl of Dunbar 37
------, Euphemia, Countess of Ross 38
------, Hannah, maidservant 188
------, Isabella, wife of John, 2nd Earl of Buchan 38–40, 47
------, Isabella (or Elizabeth), wife of William, 5th Earl of Mar 39–40
------, John, servant of the 2nd Marchioness of Hamilton 142
------, Mariota, mistress of Sir Alexander Stewart 38
------, Maria, servant 237
------, Mariota 53
------, Little Nanny, servant 230
------, Master Robert, chamberlain of Dame Juliana Ker 146